THE IMPERIAL IDEA
AND ITS ENEMIES

By the same author

WEST-INDIA POLICY UNDER THE RESTORATION
DOCTRINES OF IMPERIALISM
THE HABIT OF AUTHORITY

THE IMPERIAL IDEA
AND ITS ENEMIES

A Study in British Power

BY

A. P. THORNTON

PROFESSOR OF HISTORY IN THE UNIVERSITY OF TORONTO

*Such a thing as the government of one
people by another does not and cannot
exist.*

JOHN STUART MILL

MACMILLAN
London · Melbourne · Toronto

ST MARTIN'S PRESS
New York
1966

MACMILLAN AND COMPANY LIMITED
Little Essex Street London WC 2
also Bombay Calcutta Madras Melbourne

THE MACMILLAN COMPANY OF CANADA LIMITED
70 Bond Street Toronto 2

ST MARTIN'S PRESS INC
175 Fifth Avenue New York NY 10010

PRINTED IN GREAT BRITAIN BY
LOWE AND BRYDONE (PRINTERS) LTD., LONDON

PREFACE

MANY books have been written that describe the expansion of the British Empire, and trace the development of the British Commonwealth of Nations. This book is not intended to add to their number.

What it tries to do is to set out and to account for those changes in attitude towards the British Empire which have been adopted by men in power, by men out of it, and by public opinion in general during the past hundred years; and to assess the impact these various attitudes have made at different times on the role played by Great Britain in world affairs. The great question, What became of the British Empire? is one which, in 1957–58, it seems proper and timely to ask. The answers that men give to this question will always vary according to their particular training and temperament. Why this should be so is itself one of the subjects that is examined in the pages that follow.

The sources for such a study as this are so numerous and of so varied a kind that I have felt it pointless to draw up a bibliography which could prove only of doubtful utility to anyone else. Practically any book or article, written between 1860 and 1957 and concerned in any way with British domestic or international development, expresses attitudes and views which have been pressed into service here. For my purpose school history texts current, say, in 1890 or in 1920 are as valuable as the most scholarly historical treatise. In *Hansard* and in the *Round Table* of course are to be found the richest seams of gold; but plays, poems, and novels have all contributed to the store, even if by no means all that they contain. (The assumptions of Sir Henry Newbolt are plainer than those, say, of George Meredith, but there is a great deal of work to be done on this branch of the imperial theme.)

People have been as great a help to me as books. Anyone who takes a serious interest in public affairs at all has an opinion on this subject which in every case has its own historical context. To all these people who have so roundly spoken out — friends, acquaintances, and strangers, and in particular those of my father's generation who clearly recall what imperial emotions stirred them both in youth and in maturity, I owe warm thanks. To my colleague Mr. J. D. Hargreaves of the University of Aberdeen, who read and most helpfully criticised the first two chapters, and who verified a number of references which I was unable to check myself, I owe an especial debt.

Throughout I refer to public personages by their surnames, whether these gentlemen are alive or dead — whether Pitt or Churchill, Palmerston or Nehru. Titles are given once only, and statesmen who have more than one name during their careers are called by that under which history knows them — Disraeli, not Beaconsfield; Cromer, not Evelyn Baring. Where the text deals with affairs in the nineteenth century, when statesmen are consistently found referring to 'England' and 'English policy' where they mean 'the United Kingdom' or 'the policy of Great Britain', I too refer to England and English policy, without at all wishing to offend my Scottish fellow-countrymen. (It is doubtful whether the name of Britain ever crossed Disraeli's lips.)

This book of course makes no pretension to have set down the last word on its theme. Indeed the chief fascination of the theme lies in just this: that no last words on it are possible. All that is set out here is a commentary. That there are other things to say than those that are said here I know very well, and these I shall look forward to reading, from the pens of others, in due course.

A. P. T.

THE UNIVERSITY OF ABERDEEN
14 *August* 1957

CONTENTS

NOTE

The following abbreviations are used in the footnotes:

DBFP, I, iv   *Documents on British Foreign Policy 1919–1939,* ed. Sir Llewellyn Woodward and Rohan Butler, First Series, Volume IV (London, H.M.S.O., 1956).

RT   The *Round Table:* a quarterly on British Commonwealth Affairs.

Mansergh, *Documents*   Nicholas Mansergh, *Documents and Speeches on British Commonwealth Affairs, 1931–1952,* 2 vols., (Royal Institute of International Affairs, London, 1953.)

Hansard's Parliamentary Debates are referred to as follows:

(1) 4 H 53, 45:   Fourth series, volume 53, column 45

(2) 5 H 233, 1953:   Fifth series, volume 233, column 1953

(3) 5 H of L 40, 240:   Fifth series, House of Lords, volume 40, column 240

The map of the Sykes-Picot agreement, on p. 166, is adapted from that appearing in David Lloyd George, *The Truth About the Peace Treaties,* (Gollancz, London, 1938), II, p. 1024.

INTRODUCTION

A DEFINITION OF TERMS

IDEAS in politics, as elsewhere, are forced to fight a grinding battle with circumstance. Sometimes, when the struggle is short, first their surface and then their core get worn to nothing. But, if their strategy is guided by a genuinely creative and receptive imagination, political ideas may emerge from their inevitable campaigns with renewed strength, able to make a challenge to a second generation in greater confidence than they faced the first. So directed, a political idea, necessarily flexible in form, may indeed come to terms with circumstance, but it never does so entirely on the enemy's conditions.

It has also to equip itself very variously. In it must glow the reflection of those hopes and plans for society, and for their own place in that society, that men indulge in only in moments of respite from their everyday affairs. The idea must be one that can catch and fire the imagination of the young. The young are not members of society: they live on its frontiers. They are still uncommitted, sceptical of all the accepted principles and quick to condemn this acceptance as a kind of cowardice. But they do not doubt as yet that better principles exist. The principle, the cause, the idea that gains them must therefore hold out both a challenge and a promise. Although it may make much of reason, it is not reason that acts as its dynamo. Finally, it must have an obvious quality — summarising in itself something that men have hitherto felt, but have not known how to express.

An idea fulfilling these conditions will be strong enough to force circumstance itself to obey its dictation.

In the last generation of the Victorian era, many men thought they had found just such an idea. It became their faith, that it was the role of the British Empire to lead the world in the arts of civilisation, to bring light to the dark places, to teach the true political method, to nourish and to protect the liberal tradition. It was to act as trustee for the weak, and bring arrogance low. It was to represent in itself the highest aims of human society. It was to command, and deserve, a status and prestige shared by no other. It was to captivate the imagination and hold fast the allegiance of the million by the propagation of peculiar myths — one among which was the figure of Queen Victoria herself, who became depersonalised, as an idea: the idea of the Great White Queen. While encouraging and making profit from the spirit of adventure, it was nevertheless to promote the interests of peace and commerce. While it was to gain its greatest trophies in war, it was to find its main task in serving the ends of justice, law and order. It was an idea that moved, an idea that expanded, an idea that had to continue to move and to expand in order to retain its vitality and its virtue.

Those who believed it was their duty to see to it that all these things came to pass, who identified themselves with this cause, called themselves Imperialists, and the cause, the idea itself, Imperialism: 'that greater pride in Empire,' as Rosebery defined it in 1899, 'which is called Imperialism and is a larger patriotism.' It is in the sense of this definition that the terms 'imperialist' and 'imperialism' will be used in this book.

Imperialism, Sir Keith Hancock has reminded us, is no word for scholars.[1] It has been analysed too often, given too many shades of meaning. In our time it has become a football, a war-cry, a labelled card in a sociological laboratory. Originally a term borrowed from France, and in low repute accordingly, those in Great Britain who adopted it — Curzon, Rosebery, Milner in their day, Churchill and Amery the day after — gave it all the English virtues, and saw no shame in describing themselves as Imperialists, with the capital letter. Imperialism belongs to its own time in British history, is of its own period; and the historian is not justified in ignoring it or in casting about for a better description because strange winds have blown upon and through it since.

Yet it should be emphasised that the attack on the imperial idea, whose course this book attempts to describe, was a failure on one sector of the long front. The purely intellectual argument against it made no headway, for imperialism was a faith and an emotion before it became a political programme; and even when its enemies had successfully overturned the political programme the faith and the emotion survived. What was contemptuously called 'jingoism'

[1] W. K. Hancock, *Wealth of Colonies*, (Cambridge, 1950), p. 17.

was able to win and hold the favour of the mass of the people for less than twenty years, but the imperial principle, animating an imperial code, remained the dynamic in the thought and action of the governing classes of England until after the close of the twentieth century's second would war. They did not lose their faith in the idea, nor their own self-confidence, just because the times had changed and the great days of Empire had gone. Despite heavy propaganda and the rewriting of the textbooks, no emotional capital was invested by imperialists in the idea of the Common-wealth, that pale usurper of the true principle of imperial unity; to Winston Churchill the much-vaunted Statute of Westminster of 1931 was a piece of 'repellent legalism'.[1] Those of their own number who trimmed to the new, hostile ideas were right in thinking that in so doing they played a necessary political part — but it was not one that they took pride in. It was a Cabinet dominated by the Unionists which in 1921 conceded to Irish revolutionaries that Home Rule whose very possibility of existence was denied in the Unionist party name. 'Our own policy,' said Austen Chamberlain in the House of Commons,

> the Unionist policy, died . . . not because it was inherently wrong. I believe it was the best we could do for Ireland, for England, and for the Empire. It died because, if that policy were to be successful, it needed continuity, patience, perseverance — and our people would not pursue it connectedly through the changes of party warfare.
>
> Is there any wisdom, any statesmanship, in being blind to facts? Is there any consistency or honour in refusing to recognise the judgment of the people, or their inability to mean the same thing for long enough to carry it to a successful conclusion?[2]

It was a profound analysis. It was not quarrelled with: it was let pass, in a grim silence.

Latter-day imperialists were to complain that they had no effect-ive leader, who could command the attention of the people — but the same thing could have been said of the socialists, their principal foe. How and where the democracy was to be led at all, was the problem facing both Right and Left in Britain in the years between 1919 and 1939; and the only solution agreed to by both sides was that the matter had better be shelved for the present. In this

[1] 5 H 297, 11 February 1935, 1645.
[2] 5 H 150, 17 February 1922, 1461–2.

vacuum of thought and idea, the imperialist myth — that these things had once been better ordered by the Victorian giants who had held a map of the route, now wantonly thrown away — was one that had much influence with the Left itself, which could not but recall that Gladstone had become the people's William in the heyday of imperialism itself, thus ending his career, in the words of his own disciple, James Bryce, distrusted and detested by four-fifths of the upper classes of England. Nor was it Gladstone's principle of non-intervention in foreign affairs, or his belief in the virtues of the Concert of Europe — two nostrums inherited by the Labour party — that had won him his position as a leader of democracy. He had achieved this because the magnetism of his personality was such as to put men who heard him discourse on policy in touch with the great human principles of justice and truth and fair dealing among men — principles whose existence his listeners dearly wanted to be made manifest to them. Gladstone was convinced that there was a moral order in the world, of which politics was part; and men were very willing to be converted to an idea that promised them an unfamiliar dignity and a welcome self-respect.

Yet it was a curious relationship. Gladstone could never understand why it was he could rouse the people of England and Scotland to such passionate fury on the wrongs of Bulgaria or Armenia, but never raise any response from them on the wrongs of Ireland. Disraeli, interested in none of these issues, could have told him. Generous, genuine emotions were easily summoned up to confront a case of great and obvious injustice like Turkish oppression in the Balkans: but to assume that Ireland had wrongs at all was to be led inevitably to the view that Englishmen and Scotsmen were her oppressors — and this was a standpoint which the Victorian public could not take and still retain its self-respect. In this one instance, Gladstone seemed to be taking away with the one hand what he was holding out in the other.

In fact Gladstone had little *political* imagination, and, in consequence, little foresight. Had he not been a consummate master of parliamentary techniques, indeed, he would never have been fitted to cross swords with Disraeli at all. Disraeli was an artist in politics, whose principal achievement was his own career. But he had an imaginative appreciation of the nature of political power which no one in his generation could match. (Only Arthur Balfour, among

his successors, was to equal him in this.) Himself a product of the
Romantic movement, he retained the high-flown attitudes of an
earlier era, and could speak to a prosaic House of Commons of the
necessity to hold the East in fee without having to pretend it was a
joke. He joked indeed when he wrote those celebrated letters to the
Queen in language that might have suited some Grand Vizier's
communications to an awful Empress-who-must-be-obeyed. But it
was not a joke based on ridicule, for in his own mind these roles did
approximate to his own kind of reality.

The majesty of power Disraeli saw as a genuine element in the
world. Thus, to approach it with some show of pomp and circumstance was not to indulge in theatrical nonsense — even if admitting
that it was a show. When he spoke of jewels in the imperial diadem,
Conservative members would say that this was just Dizzy's way,
but he was putting into words for them romantically patriotic convictions that they themselves would never express — words that
were far beyond the powers of expression possessed, for example,
by that 'average chuckleheaded Indian officer' to whom Sir Garnet
Wolseley, W. S. Gilbert's 'modern major general' and a staunch
imperialist, was so often heard to refer. Sir Henry Lawrence, one
of the best men who ever served in India, had once written that it
was 'the due admixture of Romance and Reality that best carries a
man through life'. Disraeli seemed to know what that precise admixture should be. It was this inner sureness of touch and grasp,
this mastery of occasion, that had carried him against all odds into
the command of the political ideas of so many dukes, squires,
soldiers, lawyers, brewers, and private gentlemen. Disraeli, his
party felt, dumbly but truly, knew what politics were *about*.

What were they about?

They were, simply, about power. The extent and magnitude of
the British Empire provided visible expression of the power of
England in the affairs of the world. In Disraeli's view, England's
position in the world depended very largely on what England herself *thought* to be her position in the world. It was therefore essential for her to give full publicity to her own assessment, and to do
that so successfully that other nations would come to take it as the
only possible assessment, including it always in their own international calculations as a constant factor. All imperialists were to
follow Disraeli in this diagnosis. It was their certainty that it contained the fundamental truth that armoured them against so many

attacks, and that gave them resilience to survive the blows of their enemies' most damaging weapon — ridicule. Indeed they turned the same weapon against their attackers. For what nonsense it was, for the Left to talk of the imperialist view of international politics as unsound, out-of-date, old-fashioned! Power never went out of fashion. The day that England permitted her power to go out of fashion, that day her great history would end. Holding this conviction, the imperialist was assured that it was he alone who, in an age of shifting opinion and sentimentality, saw the world straight. Men must eat before they moralise: and it is hard for a Briton to eat at all regularly if he is not prepared to keep guard on the sea-lanes through which the food comes to his table. This was the centre-board of the imperialist's platform, and on it he remained unshaken.

Power is neither used nor witnessed without emotion. Power and emotion are thus the themes of this story. How the battle went against the imperial idea, how severely the ranks of those who enlisted under that banner were thinned, how the forces of war, of nationalism, and of democracy mounted at first a separate and ultimately a combined assault against the imperialist position, it is the object of these pages to show.

I

THE EMERGENCE OF EMPIRE

ONE hundred years ago, 'Empire' was a word that had a history to live down. It denoted a type of domestic and international power organised along lines divergent from all the accepted British traditions of home and foreign policy. It would be hard to say which in their day received more vilification from the British press: Nicholas I, Emperor of all the Russias, the self-appointed policeman of Europe and the destroyer of Hungarian liberty, or Napoleon III, Emperor of France, whose romantic brand of fascism bewildered the hardiest observer — causing Lord Palmerston in 1860 to draw up a £12-million estimate for a system of fortification for the southern English coast that would have needed 100,000 troops to man it. In the view of all Englishmen of substance, whose own idols were progress, Free Trade, and the *pax Britannica*, 'Empire' was a foreign joss, whose worshippers, where they were not simply benighted, were assumed to be the sinister agents of the forces of wrong. Secure in that mid-Victorian power which was based jointly on the buoyancy of her economy and her navy, Great Britain had no need to pursue policies of national self-aggrandisement. Having no need, she had accordingly no business to seek to do so.

It was because Palmerston believed that this British power should be put to use rather than passively enjoyed that editors, publicists, and his political opponents took such strong exception to what they called his hectoring interference in the affairs of foreign nations. They argued always that it was not and never could be to our interest to meddle in other people's concerns, to read lessons in constitutional behaviour to autocrats one day and to encourage insurgent factions the next, to support the dangerous doctrine of 'nationality' in one case and to ignore its aspirations in others. Certainly, let the nations of Europe follow the example of liberal England, if they chose: but let them do it, now as in Pitt's day, by

I

their own exertions. England, just because she was England, was a free agent, above the ideological battles of Europe. If she went down into that arena she risked both her dignity and her security.

This was the central theme of the nineteenth century's most celebrated debate on British foreign policy: the 'Don Pacifico' inquest of June 1850.[1] Every argument used cast its shadow far.

To Richard Cobden the Radical leader, the representative of Manchester and the textile north, the doctrine of self-assertion and interference was pointless because it was wasteful, and dangerous because it was both. Did we not recall that we had spent over £800 millions interfering with revolutionary France sixty years back — for no very clear reason, and with no very tangible result? Did not Whigs, of whom Palmerston was one, respect any longer the dictum of their great hero, Grey of the Reform Bill, who in 1830 had so strongly objected to trafficking with an unsettled Europe in any shape or form? What principle was it we were now acting upon, in this specific case of this dubious Pacifico — this Levantine who had called in the British Government to help him collect what was probably a fictitious debt incurred when his alleged property was allegedly destroyed by some Athenian rowdies? If there was a principle here at all, it was a startling one: for if we were in future to send fifteen ships-of-war — more than Nelson had had under command at the battle of the Nile — to collect debts of £6,400, then not only could we not reduce our burdensome warlike establishments, but plainly we had not establishments enough. If such policies were pursued they would set all Europe by the ears, and the Powers would band together against us in righteous self-defence.

This point was taken up by Sir Robert Peel, sometime Conservative Prime Minister but for the last four years the leader only of a small band of Free Trade Conservatives. He had hitherto approved the Whigs' domestic policy, he said, as this had been liberal and conservative policy'. (This generation had not yet learned to put these two adjectives into separate mental compartments.) But in foreign policy the Whigs had perverted the use of that great engine of diplomacy which should always be employed by civilised society to maintain peace. Let Palmerston take care how his panacea of self-government was adapted by the foreign Powers he was so pleased to prescribe for. 'Self-government! Who shall

[1] 3 H 111, 24–28 June 1850, 228 ff.

construe what is the basis of self-government?' How, Peel wondered, would we like it if these other Powers one day thought it their mission, too, to introduce the idea into India? He warned the Government in words that were the better remembered, as he uttered them less than a week before he died:

> You are departing from the established policy of England: you are involving yourselves in difficulties the extent of which you can hardly conceive.

Gladstone, at this time a member of Peel's group, took the stand he was always hereafter to maintain when in Opposition, although when in office circumstances were often to combine to move him from it. He too held by the principle of non-intervention. Intervention was a self-isolating policy. Palmerston might indeed defend it on the grounds that here and there it had been successful, but the success of anything was no evidence of its worth. From whom had we taken a commission to become universal schoolmasters, the censors of vice and folly abroad? What kind of attitude of mind was it that presumed to describe the combined opinion of civilised Europe as emanating from 'a knot of foreign conspirators'? Gladstone rebutted the views of J. A. Roebuck, who had introduced the motion defending Palmerston's policies, that the law of nations was, accurately speaking, no law at all. On the contrary, it was for him a great and noble monument of human wisdom, founded on the combined dictates of reason and experience. Gladstone would not face Roebuck's direct implication, that the law of nations had no power to enforce these dictates. What he complained of was that England should take it on herself to act as the lawgiver. Foreigners, he declared, were anyway unwilling to be guided by Englishmen, for they were too often sensible of something that galled them in an Englishman's presence,

> and I apprehend it is because he has too great a tendency to self-esteem — too little disposition to regard the feelings, the habits, and the ideas of others.

More, much more, was to be heard in the world of this galling presence, and of this 'peculiar weakness of the English mind.'

But Roebuck maintained that moral influence was the ruling principle of Palmerstonian policy. It was because the people of

England were careless about the course of foreign affairs, and insulated in all their habits, that their Foreign Minister was all the more responsible. This opinion Palmerston himself, in his masterly defence that lasted for four hours, made the centrepiece of his argument. England by her traditions and institutions was the natural guardian of liberty. But because liberty was indivisible, it was not for England to congratulate herself on being an outpost in a sea of autocracy. She must see to it that her ideas were asserted, her influence felt, and her anger feared. There were always two kinds of revolutionary abroad in the world. There was the man who clambered on to barricades; and there was the 'blind-minded' reactionary who would stop if he could the movement of time itself. The actions of both menaced the Liberal tradition, and it was for the Liberal to neutralise them, to hold the balance between them. This he could do only if he had the power. This he could do only if he were prepared to use his power. The Pacifico case was perhaps, as his critics agreed, a trifle, but trifles as much as affairs of moment could be covered by the one great principle. A British subject in a foreign land must be able to feel and proud to say that he was a citizen of a Power whose fame and influence spanned the world, and whose reputation was his sufficient shield — as Paul had been able to say to those who would have taken him, *civis Romanus sum.*

This is the first, and still the most famous, enunciation of a doctrine which two generations later was accepted as part of the *mystique* of the fully-developed imperial idea.

Palmerston won his vote, and a popular triumph. But it was still too early, in 1850, to convince either his own party or Opposition groups that his was the infallible method. Neither side were agreed that British power was a necessary dynamic in the ordering of the world's affairs. If, as Roebuck suggested, the British public was indifferent to and ignorant about foreign affairs, that was because their rulers and employers had made Great Britain an industrial workshop, and as a result were for ever insisting that it was necessary to be on good terms with foreigners, whom we either wished to keep or to make customers. This we could not expect to do if we were constantly interfering in their internal politics.

Of all speakers who examined the issues exposed by the investigation of Palmerston's conduct, only Disraeli applied the test of efficiency to it. Had it in fact gained the ends for which it had been put in train? (Disraeli was then leader of the Conservative party in the Commons, but not greatly trusted by it, and still stamped in the public mind as the political slayer of his own chief, Robert Peel.) What was England's interest, he asked, in Europe? It was now, as it had ever been, to maintain the balance of power on that continent. Had Palmerston's activities served that interest? On the contrary. It was a great English interest that the north of Italy should continue to belong to Austria, which, as a first-class military Power, was able to keep France, whose ambitions in Italy were notorious, at a safe distance. It was an English interest that Sicily should continue to belong to Naples, a weak kingdom, and not to a major Power in the Mediterranean. It was an English interest that the provinces of Schleswig and Holstein should continue to belong to Denmark, a weak Power on the Baltic, and not to Prussia, whose militarism had plainly not yet reached the objectives it had set for itself. But all these interests, Disraeli declared, had been given up — because Palmerston loved to play patron to incipient nationalism. The Foreign Secretary was not even consistent in applying his principles. Had he read to the Tsar a sharp Palmerstonian lecture in 1849, when Russian forces crushed the Hungarian nationalist rebellion? He had not. In that case Palmerston had bethought himself (and quite rightly) that it was England's interest not to pick a quarrel with Russia, however much true-thinking Englishmen disliked that country's internal régime and external policies.

Thus, whereas Gladstone had complained that it was no part of a Foreign Secretary's duties to go pricking into the lists like a crusader of old, Disraeli pointed out that the armour the crusader wore was under proof. Now as later, he concentrated on what seemed to him the essential thing. It was one thing to strike attitudes, another to be ready to take action, and to be confident of taking it successfully. For success, the essential thing was power.

That the power of Great Britain, whose use was here being so minutely debated, was economic and industrial, everyone knew. Very few thought it worth emphasising. Fewer still forecast a time when it might no longer be true. The contemporary evidence was so comforting. In 1850 England was already on her plane of ascendancy. Between 1842 and 1872 British exports rose in value from £60 million to £312 million, a rate of increase that had never before existed and which was not to be repeated. In these same 30 years, the volume of foreign trade rose in value from £130 million to £669 million. The principal British export to Europe was the technique of industrialism itself, a process made the easier by the progressive lowering of European tariffs. British trade thrived in places where no British flag flew. The investor who put his money to work in the United States as Americans moved westward saw a better return from it than any he could ever expect to get from a Canadian or an Indian railway. It was not 'Empire', but the wide world itself that was the oyster, ready to be prised open by the force of British capitalist enterprise. To lock up any part of the world as an enclave of Empire was to narrow the natural channel of British commerce and to diminish the volume of its returns. The figures proved this: between 1855 and 1859 the average value of British trade to foreign countries was £209 million, as compared with £76 million for the trade to the Empire. To think 'imperially' was to think restrictedly, defensively. It was to follow those same rigid principles of Protection as a national good which had been under sap and siege ever since Adam Smith had first loosed his volleys against them.

Smith, the Glasgow professor, had left no message to posterity as to the nature of an imperial idea. In his own time he had observed none at work — only a clumsy process of colonisation instituted for the sole purpose of raising up communities of customers. England, after a century of practising commercial restriction and monopoly, had been left in his judgment with what could not properly be described as an Empire at all. Rather was it a Project, which had cost, which in his own time continued to cost, and which he was assured would go on costing the country immense expenditure without ever balancing this with any profit. Smith's *Wealth of Nations*, an anatomy of human progress, was published in the same year (1776) as thirteen British colonies in America combined to break out of the imperial ring. When it was afterwards found that the new United States of America, created as a result of this rebellion, was a better customer by far for British goods than ever the thirteen colonies had been, his book began to take on the aspect of a sacred text. Disciples arose to promote the science of political economy, disciples far more radical in outlook than the conservative Smith. Among them were men who set out to attack not merely these outmoded theories of imperial control, but the political authority of England itself. This, though not ultimately an unrewarding task, was nevertheless a slow one.

For the men who governed England were never intellectuals,

studying economic trends and taking a chance on theories of the market. Pitt might declare that everyone was now a pupil of Adam Smith, just as a century later Harcourt was to declare that we were all Socialists now. Neither of them meant it. The rulers were determined not to be infected with the principles either of American Democrats, or of French Jacobins, or of any English disciples of these septs. Property was still property, the bedrock of the English constitution and indeed the basis of every civilised society. After the American disaster, what was left to us of our property oversea must still be firmly governed, its affairs strictly regulated. The official view was, and remained, that it was because the American colonists had been carelessly granted too much liberty, which they had converted into licence, that the disaster had come about. Not more but less liberty, was the cure for obstreperous colonists, who must learn that obedience to the Crown was a subject's first duty, wherever under the sun he might find himself. The Crown Colony system was based on this premise — and how much better it was, Sir Frank Swettenham was to declare in 1905 out of the depths of his Malayan experiences, than any system of party politics![1]

Accordingly, Pitt's Government, in passing an India Act in 1784, a Canada Act in 1791, and the Act for the Union with Ireland in 1800, set out to assert this principle of imperial control in these three highly-contrasted properties. They were all Acts 'for the better government of' our possessions, and succeeding British Governments were resolved to maintain them. Nearly sixty years divide the surrender at Saratoga from the issue of Lord Durham's report on the causes of the unrest in Canada: in that long time no self-governing constitution was granted to any British dependency. Political reform in England itself, thought quite practicable in 1790, was delayed some forty years while England first fought and then digested the doctrines of the French Revolution. Even when, in 1832, a measure of reform was granted, the dreaded 'democracy' was still kept at arm's length by a middle class that distrusted it even more than did the aristocracy.

Men who own property are not often able to see it as a problem in political science. Mid-Victorian proprietors were no exception. They felt, moreover, that those who maintained that it was such a problem might be discounted, as their views were always so contradictory. But here they were mistaken, as it was the very fact of

[1] In C. S. Goldman (ed.), *The Empire and the Century*, (London, 1905), p. 887.

disagreement that kept such problems alive from one generation to the next. It was in this context that Radicals did the cause of Empire a service. They disagreed about it, as about other things. They made it a controversial question. They made men think about it who had not thought about it, and come to some new conclusions.

The Radical movement contained two different schools of thought about the British Empire. One insisted that the Empire would disintegrate if it were not better tended, if radical overhaul of the political ideas that governed it was delayed much longer. The other school averred that it was pointless to plan for the future of an Empire that did not have any future, that was bound in the nature of things to disintegrate anyway. It was this school, led by political economists and dubbed with Manchester's name, that made the deeper impress on its own time. The Manchester school was later accused of 'separatism' — but this was a term invented by those who wanted to make it appear that the opposition to ideas of imperial consolidation was more choate than it actually was. Separatism was not a movement, but an assumption. People had been assuming that the British Empire would vanish for close on fifty years, and they were by no means all Radicals. Once the Cobdenist Free Traders had triumphed, abolishing the Corn Laws in 1846 and the Navigation Acts in 1849, it was clear that the white colonial Empire had had its economic foundations dynamited beneath it. It was assumed that these oversea outposts had no other foundations. It was assumed that they continued in being mainly because no politician of any party saw any advantage in breaking what legal ties were left. It was assumed for a generation after the abandonment of Protection — not in Manchester only, but in governing circles too — that the colonies would use their powers of responsible government to set themselves up, in no long time, as independent democratic republics on the model of the United States of America. When one of the first things the colonies did with their fiscal freedom was to clap duties on British as well as on foreign imports, it was an assumption that was doubly confirmed.

All the arguments seemed to lie on this side. It was surely easy to deduce correctly from the famous precedents of the American Revolution, and the Latin American Revolution. White colonists must already have made their deductions. Such an opinion ruled the thinking of the permanent officials who ordered the day-to-day business of the Colonial Office between 1835 and 1868: such men as James Stephen the younger, Herman Merivale, Henry Taylor, and Frederic Rogers (Lord Blachford). But, although Taylor might consider that our remaining North American possessions, the colonies that had inexplicably failed to rebel, were a *damnosa hereditas*, they were all agreed that it was their duty to prevent any colony from breaking with the mother country in bitterness and anger, as the thirteen had done. Theirs was an attitude of resigned expectation, coupled with a devotion to routine: it was not one likely to foster either in them or in those they influenced any marked feeling of self-satisfaction at the existence of a far-flung Empire. Nor did it. Indeed, such a sentiment would have been thought unworthy by such men as Cobden, Anthony Trollope, Robert Lowe, and Goldwin Smith — all of whom stressed that dependency itself was a humiliating condition, from which both the superior and the subordinate suffered. Colonial 'loyalty' they considered as adoption of easy virtue. We were told indeed, was Cobden's comment, of the 'loyalty' of the Canadians — but this was surely an ironical term to apply to people who neither paid our taxes nor obeyed our laws nor held themselves liable to fight our battles; who repudiated our right to the sovereignty over an acre of their territory, and who claimed the right of imposing their own customs duties even to the exclusion of our manufactures. It was because he held this opinion that Cobden welcomed the local movement for confederating the British North American colonies. This was a step in the right direction. It would lead to separation, and the end of the imperial link.

The officials however necessarily used a warier language than this. The cutting of the cable, to take James Stephen's phrase, was distinctly held to be a matter that must be left to the timing and the inclination of the colonists themselves. It was in accordance with this notion that the Colonial Office gave its wards the constitutional freedoms they all felt they had a right to — as freeborn Englishmen — the better to equip them for the day of independence. Colonists were awarded, for example, the right to alienate the unoccupied lands in their own territory, lands which had been regarded by British Governments for a century past as the particular patrimony of the Crown itself, whose duty it was to hold such lands in trust for the colonists' own posterity. This was done by a Conservative Government: and, in his celebrated Crystal Palace speech in 1872, Disraeli was to make much of the point that this should not have been done *gratis*. Conditions should have been made. An imperial control over these lands should have been retained, an imperial tariff imposed, and a representative council set up in the metropolis — in the cause of centralisation, in the cause of Empire. It was a reflection that had dawned on him some twenty years too late, and, like many of Disraeli's on the actual facts of a colonial question, it had in it more plausibility than sense. He had clearly borrowed it from the doctrines of that other school of Radicals, those who wished to overhaul and strengthen the imperial organisation — that band of 'Colonial Reformers' who were the sworn enemies of the Colonial Office's day-to-day unimaginative practice.

This small Radical group, whose members believed that reform in methods of colonial governance was a natural corollary to political reform at home, has won more attention from historians than their contemporaries ever found time to allot to them. They have been elected to fill the position of that 'creative minority' that is assumed to lurk within every generation. Something too much has been made of this. The Colonial Reformers indeed made an impress on a generation not their own, but so did the Manchester Radicals with whom they so profoundly disagreed. Both schools in fact share the same significance, already noted: they kept the Empire in the public sight as a public issue. Empire needed its propagandists, for its connexion with foreign policy was not obvious in a time when no challenger to the British Navy rode the seas.

The cause of colonial reform could however boast a quite respectable Radical pedigree. The 'father of Reform' in England, Major John Cartwright himself, had in 1771 propagated an idea of Empire as 'a firm and brotherly league', which he hoped might be called the Grand British League and Confederacy. Such a league would of course when constituted dispense with Colonial Office — or 'Downing Street' — government. The Empire would then become a group of free, equal states, with a co-ordinate legislation and a common Crown, the Imperial Parliament acting as its protector against foreign encroachment. Cartwright's contemporaries — Radicals whose main energies were directed down other courses, such as Granville Sharp, Joseph Priestley, and Richard Price — had also believed that in free association lay the best bond of kinship. During the American rebellion Price insisted, as did both Edmund Burke on his right and Tom Paine on his left, that it was for English liberties that the Americans were fighting. Such ideas could not have been conceived at all, and certainly could not have been propagated against virulent opposition, had the men who held them not been animated by a great amount of intellectual passion. Radicals *cared* about the organisation and principles of political and economic life, and because they did so they forced their opponents — who on principle wanted to be able to rebut conclusively any Radical notion — to examine their own preconceptions, with a new and particular scrutiny. It was of course easier to be passionate about politics than about economics, as promoters of the 'dismal science' very soon found out. The arrival of the redoubtable Jeremy Bentham in the Radical camp, feeling strongly and arguing brilliantly about order and method, and bearing his banner of utility as a standard by which all things must henceforth be judged, was thus of the utmost assistance both to the political and to the economic Radicals. Benthamite argument was used thenceforward as a quarry where materials could be mined for the building of the two separate Radical schools of thought.

What Bentham said about colonies in the 1820's, latter-day Radicals like Henry Labouchere in the 1890's, or Josiah Wedgwood in the 1920's, dearly loved to reiterate. Bentham's picture of the colonial scene was derived from Adam Smith, but touched in with his own colours, all of which were sombre. Colonies throttled our expanding commerce and created artificial markets. Their possession endangered peace, as they made this country a much easier prey to an enemy. They also cost a great deal of money, none of which was repaid — and no one should forget that society was injured by every particle of unnecessary expense. Lastly, they gave administrative employment to a particular class, the ruling class, which therefore had a vested interest in their retention — an interest it was apt to disguise beneath all sorts of high-minded argument.

Yet, despite all these disadvantages, Bentham came to the conclusion — as, years away, did Labouchere and Wedgwood — that we could not 'emancipate' the colonies. Why not? Because, after all, there was the future to consider. These colonies and their problems set a challenge to statesmanship. Might they not be so guided as to serve greater interests than those of Peninsular veterans and financial speculators? Was it not a national duty to see to it that they were so guided? Assuredly, if they were abandoned, the colonies would founder. The metaphor indeed could be strengthened: we would be scuttling the ships we had ourselves launched.

No sincere Radical, then or later, failed to appreciate that the colonies provided him with a field for social and political experiment, with a proving-ground for his theories, which could be put into practice in an atmosphere unpoisoned by such baleful and reactionary traditions as hampered all reform in England itself. For this reason if for no other colonies deserved their chance in life. They should not be looked on as so many conveniently distant Fleet hulks, dumps for human refuse, places to which paupers might be shovelled. Emigration thither ought to be controlled by the State, and instituted on a sound moral and social basis. A deliberate effort should be made to rebuild and reanimate these new societies by exporting to them, not our misfits and our unemployables and our criminals, but a fair cross-section of English life. It was to win a public for these ideas that Gibbon Wakefield and Charles Buller and William Molesworth, Radicals who first called themselves Colonial Reformers, drew up schemes of 'systematic colonisation' for the guidance of the Colonial Office — whose support they failed to win mainly because they simultaneously conducted a campaign of ridicule against its officials.

Lord Durham, the Byron of the Radical Reformers, struck the full imperialist note, and in consequence holds an honoured place still in the imperial pantheon. The colonist of Great Britain, he declared, was linked to a mighty Empire. It would be neither prudent nor honourable to abandon our countrymen just because our foolish theories of 'Downing Street government' had plunged them, as in the two Canadian Provinces in the 1830's, into disorder and confusion. The experiment of keeping the colonies, and of governing them properly, ought to have a trial — before we abandoned for ever the vast dominion, the 'ample appanage' which God and Nature had combined to give us in the New World, so that we might at once supply the wants and fire the hopes of our surplus population. Durham's remedy for the condition of the two Canadian Provinces, set out in a Report of 1839 which a later generation was to make famous (his own did not think much of it) consisted of the institution of a type of municipal self-government. He did not use the words 'responsible government'. These words had no clear meaning in his own time, and he had certainly no intention of making the Canadian colonists responsible for their own government entirely. To Great Britain must be left the overriding responsibility for defence, for the proper regulation of imperial trade, and for the disposal of the unalienated lands. But this line of segregation — between what was one day to be known in India as 'reserved' and 'transferred' subjects — was never either clearly marked or enforced by statute, and it was easy for colonists to pour through the gap in this constitutional frontier. Before a dozen years had passed they had won the control they wanted over their own trade, their own tariffs, and what they regarded as their own public lands. In so doing they drove a coach-and-horses through the Reformers' programme of systematic colonisation; for the latter's scheme of State-aided emigration had always been interlocked to State control of colonial lands, since it was the proceeds from the sale of these lands that built up the fund that financed the emigrant in the first place. When colonists were granted in 1865 the right to amend their own constitutions, this seemed to the Colonial Reformers the coping-stone on that 'edifice of separation' which their fellow-Radicals had been so busily building.

But neither Radical group could truthfully say that it ever established entire command over public opinion, whether in colonial or in any other affairs of state. The greatest of Radical victories, the repeal of the Corn Laws, was only made possible by Sir Robert Peel, who brought up enormous Conservative reinforcements behind Cobden's vanguard. The public hero of the fifties was no Radical, but Lord Palmerston: and the great popular movement was not a passion for political science, but a simple and honest Russophobia. Moreover, mid-century Radicals concentrated their energies on particular issues, and some of these grew stale: not until a later generation did Radicalism leave its architechtonic theories aside and become as emotional as the forces it attacked. (It was then, of course, that it really began to make its converts.) In the fifties it was still complacent, still too apt to think that all right-thinking men must come, at the last, into its camp. This was a deduction not borne out even by the facts of the fifties themselves. One great battle had indeed been won, but there were still other fields to gain.

In a large part of the world Adam Smith's much abused 'commercial system' was still in being. Indeed it was thriving remarkably, as a glance at the ledgers in Leadenhall Street, where the

Court of Directors of the East India Company sat in state, was enough to show. The commercial system had not in fact, whatever was thought to be the case, begun to die of natural causes just because some colonists in America had chosen to make so public an objection to it. The practice of monopoly, and the enforced consignment or 'enumeration' of all produce to a defined market was still the commonplace in that Empire in the East which had India at its centre, and which knew nothing of advanced political theory or self-government. In this world England had no competitor, her trade needed no Protection. The dominant sea-power, England was the immediate neighbour of any country that had a coastline. The East, washed by oceans, could look to the one supplier, although indeed it was allowed its other customers, since these were few and none of them were rich. Singapore was certainly a 'free port' from its opening in 1819, but its harbour-master was always British, and it was British capital that built the wharves and insured the commerce that passed through them. The policy later known as that of the 'Open Door' in China was one that had for long been pursued in the eastern seas by private persons who had every intention of ensuring that it was they themselves who would act as custodian of the door once they got it open. (Whose door it was in the first place, they did not consider a matter of importance; and their discovery that the United States saw some moral obligation in the policy to keep the door open for whomsoever might wish to pass peaceably through it, gave these eastern traders a shock from which they were slow to recover.) Similarly, when the British 'opened' the Karun River in Southern Persia in 1889, in the hope that it would become a highway of regional commerce, Salisbury the Foreign Secretary took pains to assure his opposite number at St. Petersburg that England sought no especial advantage, that the commerce of the area in question would be open to all the world. The answer he got was sharp enough. 'C'était là,' said Giers, 'une manière de parler.'[1]

It was a manner of speaking that, as Europe expanded, carried less and less conviction. Adam Smith's world had been static. He had not taken into account what might happen if it were to be added to, if continents opened and new markets were revealed after the mists had been parted by the explorer. Would the doc-

[1] Giers to Staal (Russian ambassador, London), 16 November 1888; A. Meyendorff, *Correspondance Diplomatique du Baron de Staal*, (Paris, 1929), I, 443-4.

trines of Free Trade apply here? Could they? Was the commercial principle of the first comer to such a scene likely to be one of international altruism? In these new worlds, such as the world of 'Darkest Africa' on which the explorers of many nations were busily shedding light throughout the 1850's and 1860's, circumstances might be such as to force a revision of judgment concerning the proper relation of men, money, and markets. David Livingstone's own principle was the introduction into Central Africa of a pattern already accepted on the West Coast of that continent: the pattern of commerce and Christianity. He did not advocate white settlement, but it was not clear how commerce was to thrive in a savage land without it, or without at least the imposition of both a white police force to protect it and a white managerial class to organise it. Commerce connoted competition — in these circumstances another complication. The first comer on a scene whose commercial future was literally incalculable therefore tended more and more to make a fresh appreciation of the virtues of monopoly. He put straight questions. Why go to work at all, why break your hands and risk your life on the blunt tasks of pioneering in heathendom, if you, your countrymen, and your posterity are not to reap the fruits of your labour entire? To be sure, such a man was naturally an independent, and preferred not to be meddled with or constricted by his own Government. But when competitors from other nations came, as he was early assured they must, it was only to his own Government, cheese-paring and schoolmarmish though that might be, that he could look for protection. So great a magnate as Cecil Rhodes fought what he called 'the imperial factor' in South Africa for most of his public life; but he had to come to terms with it, as a client, at the last, in defence of himself and his huge interests.

What was true of Africa would be true of China — and perhaps of the Ottoman Empire when its long-awaited day of dissolution came. These were all lands of opportunity. Opportunity is never a commodity that men are eager to share. It was therefore likely that, when once the other European nations had graduated after their period of industrial and technological instruction at British hands, the mercantile middle class that set the pace for Britain's commercial policy overseas would be forced to support protection, commercial and other, once again. They would have to accept that State policy that was later to be known as Imperialism.

But much more evidence had to be collected, before any broad appeal based on such a line of thought could expect to succeed. There were two very distinct 'interests' which events had to convert, and the men involved were stubbornly conservative.

Hardest to convert to ideas of Empire as opportunity was the majority of middle-class capitalists themselves. To them, while profits continued high and domestic wages low, foreigners were still customers, not competitors. For them, Cobden had already spoken: *civis Romanus sum*, he informed Palmerston, was not a very attractive motto to put over the doors of our counting-houses abroad. Speculative investment in unknown territories might indeed suit the dubious book of such adventurous *chevaliers d'industrie* as Baron Julius de Reuter — a British subject who in 1872 got a concession out of the Shah of Persia that promised to put that country's entire economic future into his hands. But sensible traders asked, was such a country likely to have a viable economic future at all? This was a question they went on asking of every other venture of a similar character, often getting no answer but a prospectus, right through the greatest days of imperialism itself. What the 'City' was prepared to risk, and what the Liverpool Cotton Exchange was convinced was safe, were always two different things.

Question and doubt were similarly expressed by the second class of people whom these new ideas had still to attract, namely the governing class of England. This, of course, was not bred to mercantile ways at all, and although it made a necessary political alliance with the great commercial interests of the country, it still respected the frontier that divided the man of rank from the man of trade. The aristocracy and the gentry who ordered the social conventions of England, and imposed them on the middle classes, knew well enough that the electorate — by 1885 consisting of five million males — contained very few members who had loose capital to invest in unauthorised economic enterprises overseas. Rich men who wanted to be richer, who commanded neither public nor parliamentary support, must not be allowed to involve the country in that kind of political commitment which was the inevitable consequence of economic patronage. Were oriental potentates, planters in Fiji, opium-traders in China, to be given the 'right' so successfully exploited by Don Pacifico — to summon up the might of England if their financial deals went awry? It was in this spirit that Granville the Liberal Foreign Secretary refused to give any official countenance to Reuter's Persian project, which at once dissolved. Another fifteen years were to pass before the Baron's schemes for commercial exploitation in Persia, admittedly revised a little and cut down in scale, found ready support in high Conservative Government circles.

A great deal of spadework had therefore still to be done before imperial expansion in any of its forms could be said to command any intellectual support at all. All who worked in this field had to be prepared to put up with a heavy barrage of scepticism. Two examples illustrate this. The Conservative Ministry that in 1858 took over the governance of India from the Company and made it a dominion of the Crown, did so in the conviction that it was loading the country with an unwelcome burden. No one spoke of marching towards a glorious destiny. Sixteen years later, while the argument was going on whether or not Fiji should be annexed, Kimberley, a former Colonial Secretary exclaimed how intolerable it would be if it were to become a recognised principle that British subjects, landing on territory unoccupied by other Europeans in any part of the globe, could pledge England to the extension of an Empire 'which was certainly not too small at the present time'.[1]

Yet, intolerable or not, this was a principle that faced a sunlit future. For even as Kimberley spoke, new facts were beginning to demand the adaptation, if not yet the renovation, of all the existing principles. Since Trafalgar England had had the oversea world to herself, but this era was passing. 1870–71 was a year full of incident, that ushered in an age of incident, of hasty telegrams, frontier clashes, and naval scares: an age that was to end, fittingly, with a typical incident — the murder of an imperial prince in a colonial town in Europe. Russia now opened the wicket-gate to the Mediterranean on the Bosphorus, closed to her since 1856 by the combined prohibition of the Concert of Europe. The Concert was now inoperative, for the future of Western Europe was at the same moment being locked up, and the key held, by the new German Empire that was proclaimed in Versailles while Paris struggled in the grip of a strange new revolutionary idea. On this new stage it seemed there was room only for the active: there was assuredly neither room nor time for people who wished to stand still and make calm assumptions that they were free agents, above all this noise and ambition. In France, in Germany, in the United States,

[1] 3 H 221, 17 July 1874, 192.

the tariff barriers mounted. Commerce and peace, which the mid-Victorian Free Trader had taken to be aspects of a selfsame condition of society, now began to look like natural enemies: as in the eighteenth century, war and trade were being welded by acquisitive nations into a double-headed instrument of policy. Trade was beginning to be thought of less as an international service than as a nationalised industry.

Once Germany's industrial revolution was complete, and her technicians began to raise their own buildings on the borrowed foundations, the Prussian Army made a gainful alliance with the steelyards of the Ruhr. By subsidising shipping, the new German Empire introduced the German freighter into the seven seas, where its success — for it was both roomier and faster than its average British counterpart — early began to foster in certain minds in the *Wilhelmstrasse* the idea that it would be necessary to have a German navy to protect this new development of the national energy. It was not a pressing necessity; but what was implied in the idea was clear enough. A great Power could not permit its seaborne commerce to be protected by a foreign navy. Great Britain would assuredly do the work of protection with full competence: but to permit her to do it at all was to become a political satellite, something not to be thought of in the first full flush of nationalist pride. This was a point whose political reality and future implication Disraeli had grasped long before Tirpitz began to hammer it home into the hearts of the German public.

As yet, however, the consumers of the world, including the German public, continued to make welcome the British free trader. They wanted to. They also had to. Britain still commanded the sources of raw materials and had the pick of the profitable markets, markets to which her preponderant mercantile marine ensured all goods a swift and safe passage. This was a hard fact of power. It was their careful assessment of its significance that stimulated the rival producers of Europe to enter the overseas world, the world of tropical raw resources, themselves. 'Of all rivals,' Professor Eric Walker has noted,

> France was the most persistent and exclusive, since some of her Republican leaders were persuaded that she could not remain a first-class Power unless she drew from her dependencies all that she required to that end.[1]

[1] E. A. Walker, *The British Empire*, (Oxford, 1943), p. 83.

So begins what its enemies were always to call the imperialist illusion: that power increases and status is enhanced in proportion to the extent of territory that a nation exclusively commands.

Assessing the range and depth of illusion, and calculating the capital that may be made from it, is a vital part of the politician's business. In this task no one was better skilled than Disraeli, who as the 1870's opened thought the time ripe to insert an ideology of Empire into the comfortably domestic atmosphere of the English political scene, and to instruct Conservatives that their ordained tasks of conservatism extended beyond their own shores. The charge immediately brought against him, and still heard, that he invented British Imperialism in order to dish the Whigs once more, of course contains some truth in it: for Disraeli was the leader of the Conservative party in Opposition, whose duty it therefore became to exploit any errors of commission or omission made by the Liberal party in power. The Liberals had made indeed more than the permissible number. But this is not all that can be said, or should be said. What Disraeli did was to fashion, out of materials that lay ready to hand, a new dress for the argument that he had been consistently propounding for a great part of his political life: that England, if she were to remain a Great Power, must *function* as such.

Certainly the political and economic conditions favoured a restatement of this kind. By 1870 it seemed that the expansion of British trade was coming to a stop: in three years the export trade had dropped by £11 millions. In this time of industrial stress, men were asking questions which they would not have needed nor known how to frame twenty years back. Was the country's industrial future secure? It was because there were doubts of a favourable answer that so much currency was given to the bold assertion that trade followed the flag — or that it assuredly would do so if the flag gave it any encouragement, if the flag itself ventured out. It was argued that the colonies that already enjoyed the protection of the flag had grown greatly in population and prosperity in the last two decades, and that there seemed no reason why this process, at least, should come to a stop. As the argument proceeded, other questions emerged. Was the separatist assumption anyway valid? Was it even proper? Was it not a dereliction of duty towards our own people to hold it? Were Free Traders now and evermore bound to be right about everything? Cobdenist Radicals were

c

themselves struck with astonishment when it became plain that most of their firm opinions on the virtues of a *laisser-faire* economy were rejected by an enfranchised people. Seen from below, Cobdenism was not moral worth enthroned: it was only an employers' movement, and all heads need not bow in reverence as the banner of Free Trade passed.

Was it, after all, Free Trade alone that had kept the sun high in the sky for so long? Would reliance on it, now that the future was clouded, carry the country through, and provide the people — growing in numbers at the rate of some 200,000 a year — with both work and food? Was there not a case for saying that even in the mid-century period, the Free Traders' heyday, other factors had been at work, and that to those other factors much was owed: to the incidence of war, to the influence of International Exhibitions, to the discovery of gold both in California and in Australia? Figures showed that British exports to France and to Russia were double in the late fifties what they had been before the Crimean War. They showed, too, that in the gold-rush years between 1846 and 1850 our exports to the United States had also doubled in value. During the Australian gold-rush years between 1850 and 1853, our Australian trade had increased sevenfold, from £2 million to £14 million. Moreover, it was during this same period that the development of the European railway system, largely financed by British capital, had made such strides, causing new ports to be opened, and leading to the reduction of foreign import duties on British manufactures.

Now, as the seventies opened, foreign competition was increasing, and at home the introduction of new machinery and techniques was throwing more and more men out of work. It was estimated there were more than a million paupers in the country. By employment at home we could reckon to feed only half the population at most. But we still had properties oversea, unexploited, underdeveloped; an Empire, to which the British working man could emigrate, and where he might better himself. Why then should we not try to build up the Empire rather than rest content to see it disintegrate? It was not difficult to label separatism itself as an employers' movement. Middle-class employers saw no objection to an increase in the labour-pool in this country, as they could bring wages down lower still. An Empire that drew that pool into other channels was something they might be expected to object to. They forgot that they let the 'condition of England question' fester at their own peril, and still looked on all State-aided emigration schemes as economic error, the thin end of a wedge which might prise open the floodgates of what *The Times* called 'communistic doctrines'. Officials of the State and Liberal politicians apparently shared this opinion. The working men who in the spring of 1870 presented a petition to the Queen, which urged that emigration should be encouraged and the colonial tie thus strengthened, met the answer from the Home Secretary that emigration, like other things, obeyed natural and not man-made laws, and that it was into the United States that the surplus must continue to flow. (Of 167,000 artisans who quit the United Kingdom in 1869–70, 133,000 went to the democracy in the West.) When this matter was pressed in the House of Commons, Goschen denied that any action by the State was necessary, and seemed content to take the increased consumption of gin and beer as his index to the continuing prosperity of the working classes of the country.

While the working classes revived their interest in emigration, the educated classes were reading such books as Charles Dilke's *Greater Britain* (1868), which drew a glowing map of the future that awaited what he called the Anglo-Saxon race if it would only develop its various homes oversea. Ideas of unity and centralisation were gaining ground, drawing sustenance from the unification movements that had just reached their culmination both in Italy and in Germany. The federal form of government, which had been preserved at desperate cost in the United States, and instituted in desperate optimism in the new Dominion of Canada (1867), was attracting to itself that intellectual following it was never entirely to lose. The Liberal W. E. Forster, writing a series of articles on this subject in *The Times* during 1870, won a fine victory, for he converted *The Times* itself — whose leader columns stopped hailing in advance the day when Canada would decide to cut the imperial tie. James Anthony Froude feared that an England oblivious of Empire might sink into becoming a community of harmless traders; while John Ruskin complained that even this would have its dangers, as Manchester was properly equated with Mammon. Froude and Dilke both pointed to the unpleasant cesspit civilisation that was fast developing in an industrial *laisser-faire* Britain, and emphasised the fresh air and the better circumstances of life for the mass of the people that the colonies were so well able to supply.

It was Froude who laid a particular emphasis on the inter-relation between the colonial question and the condition-of-England question, and railed at those supposed statesmen who had not the wit to see this.[1] How sad it was, that Gladstone and other genuine Liberals had allowed their consciences to be locked up either in Ireland or in Manchester! France at that moment was under assault by the Prussians, but could one doubt that France, whatever her immediate fate, would ultimately recover? And why? Because there were five million landed proprietors in France, men who had a stake in their country's destiny. How many such were there in England? Thirty thousand at the most. Could England, once the spell of her insular security was broken — as well it might be in this new, militarist age — say as confidently as France that she could weather any storm? What was the use of enormous wealth if we could not defend it? And how could we defend it, un-less we saw to it that the whole nation had an interest, a stake in the stability of the country? Where political economy was the sole rule of statesmanship, we must not expect patriotism in the people. Who was there, these degenerate days, who cared for the English commonwealth? The modern House of Commons was a House of rich men. Each successive House of Commons would be a House of richer men. Its members would always object to any great scheme for imperial settlement because wages in this country would at once rise, and the profits of those other rich men whom they so well represented would at once fall.

This view, so long propagated, so nearly accepted — that the colonies were a burden on us — was inevitably an interested view. The interests were those of the landowning and employing classes. The view was a distorted one. What was the truth? Without colonies the natural growth of our population must continue to overflow into foreign countries, be lost to us for ever, and take with it no doubt a great deal of that bitterness which had so signally stamped the thought and action of the Irish in America. It was nothing less than treason, Froude exclaimed, to abandon them.

Radicals themselves went some — though of course not all — of the way with this argument. They were never as devoid of human sentiment, or so much in love with money, as Froude declared, and even as early as 1849, when Roebuck published his *Colonies of England*, there was general agreement among them that the stand-

[1] J. A. Froude, 'The Colonies once more', *Fraser's Magazine*, September 1870

ard of utility was an intellectual concept too remote from the sentiment of the mass of the people, whose kin it was who had founded
and who were still building society in these oversea lands. When
times were fair in England the people had never acquiesced in the
opinion that colonies were useless: now that times were bad they
were even less likely to agree. It might then be possible to concili-
ate both this popular feeling and the views of the more rock-ribbed
economists. The colonies already in being, instead of being encouraged to go out and fend for themselves, might be maintained
to mutual and lasting benefit without the old waste and extravagance, thus making possible the existence of a free-trade, self-
governing empire of settlement colonies in affection and harmony,
with emphasis on the common tie of kinship. It was an idea that attracted the Manchester school even when Roebuck wrote his book,
for its members, like the philosophic Radicals, had no objection to
seeing the area in which their doctrines should hold sway being
further extended.

Moreover, the general feeling agreed with what both Bentham
and Froude insisted upon: that colonies, whether one saw a glorious future awaiting them either as part of a world-wide Empire or
as free and democratic republics, could not be dumped down in the
meantime by the wayside by the imperial Government. Even extreme economists like Joseph Hume, who was forever railing at the
expense we were put to in providing for colonial defence, bowed to
a call of duty in this matter. Our overeager forebears, bemused by
economic doctrines that were now fortunately exploded, had be-
queathed these embarrassing properties to us as a legacy and a trust.
As such they had to be maintained so long as maintenance was
asked for.

Indeed, they were Liberals like Gladstone and Cardwell — who
did not like to be called Radical, thinking the term inapplicable —
who went further against the tide of this opinion than the Radicals
themselves, by adopting an attitude on the issue of defence that
orthodox political and public opinion took strong exception to.
Mid-Victorian sentiment laid much stress on the responsibilities of
place and position: and it seemed an odd way of shouldering responsibility for a British Government to proceed to strip weak
colonies of their garrisons of imperial troops, on the grounds of
economy alone. But Gladstone went a very long way down Cobden's road before he perceived his tactical blunder, and indeed he

was never able fully to retrieve it. It was one thing for a Commons' Select Committee to suggest, in 1865, pulling out of our pestilential West African settlements — sending an official to any one of which, in Blachford's opinion, was tantamount to murder[1] — but it was another, and looked on as another, to leave a colony of British settlers to the mercy of native savagery, as seemed a likely outcome in the case of New Zealand.

The Treasury, however, had always made little of such emotional distinctions. Gladstone had been Chancellor of the Exchequer in Palmerston's Government in 1860, when the matter of colonial defence was grappled with in earnest. In that year, when the total expenditure on colonial defence amounted to some £3¼ millions, the Government divided British dependencies into two classes, 'colonies proper' and 'stations' such as Hong Kong and Gibraltar. No one, obviously, could defend the latter class of establishment save ourselves, but the Commons committee examining the matter agreed that in respect to the first class, the 'responsibility and cost of the military defence . . . ought mainly to devolve upon themselves'. Thereafter the Australian colonies and some others even of the second class (Ceylon, Mauritius, the Straits Settlements) were required to pay £40 per head per British soldier towards the upkeep of the garrison, and imperial forces everywhere were gradually reduced.

When Gladstone became Premier in 1868 he applied this principle with his customary unimaginative thoroughness. Yet his standpoint was logical. Freedom had its burdens as well as its privileges: no one was free who relied on another for his own defence. This was true — but it was a diagnosis that colonists in his own day, and citizens of the Dominions in a later day, preferred to ignore. His Secretary for War, Cardwell, when proposing to reduce the garrison in Canada by 10,000 soldiers, also hit on an exact but unpopular truth when he remarked that the true defence of British colonies was the fact that they lived under 'the aegis of the name of England, and that war with them is war with England'. Colonists were more conscious of the obverse of this, that war with England was war with them, and that it was therefore England's business to see to it that they were properly protected. Cardwell's policy was certainly looked upon by the Canadians as amounting to an unfriendly act.

[1] 3 H 227, 17 February 1876, 390.

It was this lack of imaginative understanding that Disraeli, and imperialists after him, exploited politically. The colonies did not wish to break the bonds with Britain, and they had always expressed resentment at the more ebullient Radical assumptions. Britain supplied them with their best, and in the Australasian case their only market. Canada, with good reason, feared absorption by the imperialist United States (and to this day Canadians express impatience with the myth of the 'undefended border' invented by both British and American historians); Australasians living in a vast land surrounded by vaster seas did not want to cut themselves off spiritually from all other human companionship. To them, England was, and was to remain, an idea rather than a place: the idea of 'home'. Self-government having removed the Downing Street irritant, the natural loyalism of kinship found nothing to grate its teeth on, and so could sentimentalise about the imperial bond without feeling irked by it. Moreover, the determined inclination observable in high quarters in England that the colonies had better go was an added encouragement to colonists (who had little else to be recalcitrant about) that it would be an assertion of their natural rights as Englishmen if they insisted on staying. And they did insist on staying, and developed an imperial idea of their own a dozen years before Disraeli's spade-work had yielded any concrete results in England. Leading Canadian politicians like Sir John A. Macdonald and Sir Alexander Campbell referred to themselves as 'Englishmen' — a transference of loyalty no contemporary Scot would have been capable of. The colonial connexion thus continued to hold, disproving the prophecies of the Radical economists and upholding the prescience of the Radical Colonial Reformers.

Its existence therefore became a political factor, which was much debated in the early seventies. How could it best be utilised? Derby, afterwards Disraeli's Foreign Secretary, thought it best not to try, but to continue to rely on the sentiments of colonial loyalty and affection. Disraeli himself, although he had been quick to note how seriously the Liberals had misunderstood these sentiments, made no pronouncement on this matter. For him, colonies were part of the British realm, and as such possessed intrinsic value. But what a colonist was, as a political animal, he would have been put to it to say. Certainly the ownership of colonies involved England in responsibility, but it was one that Conservatives were proud to shoulder, because acceptance of responsibility befitted a great

Power. It was a British interest to maintain the Empire. When we talked of British interests, we meant — or we should mean, in Disraeli's opinion — material British interests, 'of that character which are the sources of the wealth or securities for the strength of the country.'[1] Centralisation of control was necessary, so that these interests might be preserved and conserved the more efficiently. But Disraeli when in office after 1874 turned the active qualities of his mind to the Eastern Question, and what he had in view, if he had anything in view, when he spoke mysteriously on this subject, we do not know.

But while the Liberals were still in power, open to charges of neglect both of the condition of England and of the rights of property, of interference in private enterprise, of meddling in Irish matters best left alone, of riding roughshod over colonial sentiment, and of being asleep while great movements which they did not understand sped on to some remarkable goal or other, Disraeli could exercise his gifts of political invective and at the same time seriously restate his theme, to audiences now far more receptive than any he had ever had, how the greatness of England was a duty laid upon her.

In speeches in the country in 1872 he emphasised again how it was England's part to play a moderating and mediatorial role in the world's affairs.[2] Since the Danish fiasco in 1864 — when after much Palmerstonian warning that Denmark would be supported by England against the demands of Prussia in regard to the duchies of Schleswig and Holstein, Prussia had done precisely as she pleased — that part had not been played. As a direct consequence, at Prussia's instigation in 1866 and in 1870–71, two wars had shaken the foundations of the European state-system without England's having had a word to say either as to the cause or to the course of them. In 1864 Palmerston had sought to excuse his inaction over the duchies on the ground that, since England had no allies, she could not act alone. This doctrine Disraeli had then hotly repudiated: 'If England is resolved upon a particular policy, war is not probable.' He had not changed his view. England had no right to abdicate from the affairs of Europe: it was a dereliction of duty, a fall of honour. The Gladstonian Liberalism that had succeeded the

[1] 3 H 237, 17 January 1878, 3415 ff.
[2] See T. E. Kebbel, *Selected Speeches of the Earl of Beaconsfield*, (London, 1882), II, 3–133.

Palmerstonian Whiggery had proceeded to mount an attack on many British institutions, in the name, forsooth, of progress and reform. Not the least of these institutions was a foreign policy explicitly stated, based on defined British interests, and respected by the nations of Europe. But, so successful had been this Liberal campaign that, as Disraeli told a Manchester audience, his very statement that he was about to discuss 'foreign affairs' must cause in his hearers the now customary reaction — everyone would be sure that he was going to deal with matters in which they, as Englishmen, had no concern.

This, he insisted, was a dangerous illusion. A major shift of power had taken place abroad. There were 'vast and novel' elements in the situation, among which must be included the rapid development of the United States, assertive and triumphant after its victory in maintaining the Union itself. These elements would one day, if not at once, have to be reckoned in our national account. The balance of power which it was England's eternal interest to guard had been tipped; indeed, by 1875 Disraeli was writing privately that he thought it had vanished. Such a situation could not be coped with merely by sitting down to watch all these interesting events take place. England must return to that international arena which she should never have left, and help to plan the pattern which the future should take. Large issues might well be decided by what might seem at the time to be small points of dispute.

It was not a question — as he declared in 1878 when under hot Liberal fire for his 'forward policy' in Afghanistan — of the Khyber Pass: it was a question that concerned the character and influence of England in Europe. The world was governed by conciliation, compromise, varied interests, and the recognition of the rights of others — but with this recognition was coupled the assertion of our own.[1] It was not an ideal world, not the world idealists would have us aim for, but it was one we must live in, and, what was more, work and act in. The cry that an active England would be an isolated England he disposed of in much the same terms as Palmerston in the Pacifico debate had shrugged off the same charge. There were, after all, two kinds of isolation. There was the isolation that came from decay. That was a sign of impending insignificance. But there was also the isolation that came from self-confidence, from extreme energy, from abounding resources, and above

[1] 3 H 227, 8 February 1876, 98.

all from the inspiration of a great cause.[1] Disraeli did not call this isolation splendid — but he would not have quarrelled with the term.

Here lay the hard core of Disraeli's case, and it was never chipped away by his opponents. His actual ignorance of conditions in India and the colonies could not affect it. He knew what he wanted their possession to represent. As recently as September 1866, when Chancellor of the Exchequer, he had written that

> Power and influence we should exercise in Asia; consequently in Eastern Europe, consequently also in Western Europe

and had gone on to object to the existence of colonies which we did not actually govern.[2] To Disraeli (as to the majority of his generation) a self-governing colony was a contradiction in terms. Nevertheless he felt that, as British possessions, they were demeaned if they were referred to as merely a collection of counting-houses overseas. The Empire too was a British institution — and because the Liberals had mishandled it, it required a defender.

The Liberals themselves were aware of this, and endeavoured to change tactics before it was too late. A loan to New Zealand, from which colony for reasons of economy the Liberal Government had insisted on withdrawing the imperial garrison even while the Maori trouble still smouldered, had been brusquely refused in March 1869 — but fourteen months later it was effusively granted. Indeed, Granville, then Colonial Secretary, was distinctly heard to refer to the place as 'a great possession of the Crown'.[3] These were terms quite unprecedented, which startled New Zealanders who had grown accustomed, after thirty years, to the official view that colonisation in their islands had been made in error — an error which could not be recouped, but which time would probably correct when New Zealand joined its neighbour to form an Australasian Republic.

Simple kindness to New Zealanders, however, could neither affect the strength of the case that Disraeli presented, nor simplify its complexities. For anyone who seriously set out to make an inventory of British property and assets was bound to ask himself some difficult questions as he went on with it. The first thing to do

[1] 3 H 237, 17 January 1878, 3415 ff.
[2] Disraeli to Derby, 30 September 1866; G. E. Buckle, *Life of Disraeli*, (London, 1921), IV, 476.
[3] J. E. Tyler, *The Struggle for Imperial Unity*, (London, 1938), pp. 2-3.

was to sort out the assets from the liabilities, and this was by no means easy. For, if it was a matter of equating possessions with power, just what had England to assert, in the scales of the new militarism that had emerged in Europe? She had certainly nothing to match the new Army of the new German Empire. She would indeed hardly have had an Army at all, worth calling such, had not the Duke of Wellington when peace broke out in 1815 managed to salt away some 70,000 troops in the colonial garrisons, and had not Palmerston been able to exploit Englishmen's inborn suspicions of Frenchmen by getting Parliament to put through in the fifties both a Militia and a Volunteers Act. Even so, in 1854 — two years after Wellington died — when the muster of the British Army stood at 141,000 men, of that number 40% was still tucked away in the 14 colonial stations. Gladstonian economies had since whittled down the strength of those stations, which now appeared to be painfully unprotected in an era wherein a new French Republic was beginning to build up a new military organisation whose leaders, monarchists and imperialists in disguise, intended to use it both to erase the stains of Sedan and Metz and to create oversea another France unhampered by republican notions of democracy.

To be sure, there was the British Navy. But in the 1870's its ships were sadly antiquated — although the British public knew neither this nor the fact that technical expertise in matters of speed and armament had also passed to France. The Navy did indeed guard the sea-routes and the commerce of the world, but that kind of duty by its very nature had to be carried out far from public sight. Moreover, belief in and support for the Navy could be made an issue of divergence in party politics only with considerable effort, as the Radicals themselves agreed that ships-of-the-line were policemen essential to the protection of their Free Trade emporium, and indeed constituted a 'Blue Water School' long before the Admirals themselves found out that political lobbying was a good thing both for the Service and their own careers. Even Cobden felt that the existence of Admirals, as a class, was an unfortunate political necessity — although there were, it went without saying, far too many of them, who never went to sea at all but lounged about in 'holes' like Malta and Naples.[1]

[1] See *Speeches of Richard Cobden*, ed. John Bright and J. E. Thorold Rogers, 2 vols., (London, 1878).

There was, then, no sword to brandish. The game had otherwise to be played. The only counter, it seemed, that England had ready to play, at a table where the rules of the game were composed in Berlin, was the circumstance that she had inherited from a more turbulent past a great deal of property in various parts of the globe — some of it valuable, but most of it not — and that over these places her flag flew. How was this fact to be made at once exciting at home and impressive abroad?

Here was a political task involving great difficulty. It was a challenge both to Disraeli's own *flair* for the practicable, and to the self-satisfied conventional opinions of an England which had a tradesman's knowledge of his customers, but no insight into the forces at work in Europe, nor any realisation that for England a 'spirited foreign policy' was a necessity at all.

On many this realisation never dawned. Solid and unexpected opposition, for example, attended the passage through Parliament of the Royal Titles Bill — which was to make Queen Victoria an Empress in India from 1 January 1877. Much was heard of the allusive dangers that lay behind this alien and exotic title, dangers which would menace the traditions of English constitutional usage and practice — traditions which were of course, then as in 1689, safe only in the hands of Whigs. Disraeli's argument that Parliament's sanction to this new title would signify to the world at large in an unmistakeable manner, that the Parliament of England was resolved to uphold for ever the Empire of India, was construed as impertinence not by Liberals only but by *The Times*: who, pray, had suggested the contrary? And what had the world at large to do with the title of the Queen of England? To many there was something genuinely distasteful in the innovation, even to those who did not suspect any lurking intention to rule England after the fashion of Henry VIII. The word 'imperialism' itself, in these days of Disraeli's Premiership (1874–80) always appeared in self-conscious quotation-marks, even in Conservative newspapers and quarterlies — in this distinction keeping a proper company with the equally exotic *prestige*, another French import that took twenty years to lose its italics. Imperialism was still equated with Caesarism, arbitrary power. In Disraeli's hands it was a mantle — spuriously attractive, perhaps, to weaker minds — thrown over policies whose essence and purpose were mysterious, and whose consequences were generally hidden from the watchful eye of Parliament until it was too late to prevent the presentation of a *fait accompli*. A die, somewhere, had been cast, and all our fortunes wagered on it.

Indeed, had not Russian policy emerged once more as a menace to the Ottoman Empire, and consequently to England's line of communication to the East, it is doubtful whether Disraeli's efforts to convert his party and the country to activity in international affairs would have survived his first two years of office. He was now an old man, and the Royal Titles issue was the last he argued in the Commons, retiring as Beaconsfield to the Lords in October 1876. 'Things which would have fired him twenty years ago fail to move him now,' wrote a distinguished 'Anglo-Indian', Sir Bartle Frere, who wanted the Government to underwrite his plan for a sensible modification of India's north-western frontier. But Frere's judgment was premature, both as to the local issue with which he was concerned and as to policy in general. A Russian invader on the Eastern stage, the only political arena to which both Disraeli's heart and imagination were thoroughly attuned, stirred and revived all his capacities. Marshalling his personal forces with those of the public's Russophobia was in fact a simpler task than bringing to any concrete point the humanitarian sense of outrage inflamed by Turkish atrocity in Bulgaria, fervently and skilfully though Gladstone led this latter campaign. Disraeli set out to manipulate Europe and to neutralise Russian action as no English statesman had managed to do since Palmerston. In 1840 Palmerston, to protect Turkey from onslaught, had summoned up the Concert of Europe, including Russia, to bring France to order and make her drop her support for the ambitious Mehemet Ali of Egypt, who thought himself better qualified (as indeed he was) to sit as Sultan in Constantinople. Now, in 1878, though the characters had changed roles, the play was the same. Disraeli was determined that one Russian Governor-General should not reach Constantinople while another dismembered Anatolia. And neither of these things occurred.

But Disraeli and his Foreign Secretary, Salisbury, returning in triumph under a Conservative banner of 'peace with honour' from the Congress of Berlin in the summer of 1878, were assumed in fevered articles written by Liberals to have committed the country without its consent to the pursuit of strange new courses whose accomplishment could act only to the nation's detriment. This opinion was thoroughly confirmed when in November, while Parliament was in recess, the Indian Army was sent across the frontier of Afghanistan by the Viceroy, Lytton, as a counter-move to the despatch by Russia of a military and diplomatic mission to Kabul. The Liberals and Radicals resented being called on to vote supply for policies they objected to: but, as the troops were already in the field, consuming food and shooting off ammunition that must certainly be replaced, their hands were tied to imperialism's chariot wheel. (The same predicament befell Liberals in October 1899, when, again during the Parliamentary recess, the South African War began.) High-handedness of this sort no doubt appealed to the feelings of vainglory easily enough stirred in the mass of the people — but surely this sentiment of jingoism was one which it was a duty of the true statesman to curb rather than to encourage? Our possession of India, and the mobilised Army always on call there — two facts never assimilable anyway by the Radical *pur sang* — was now, it seemed, to be made the excuse of adventuring into Balkan, Armenian, Cypriot, Egyptian, and Afghan affairs. We were now to take out definite stock in the futures of these dubious Levantine territories, where previously we had been content to play the part of the honest broker amid the contending claimants.

To say this was to gloss over certain aspects of the British record in the 'Eastern Question', but still it was no bad point to make. Palmerston's anti-Russian and pro-Turkish policy had assuredly been reared on an Indian base; for the continued possession of India in British hands was a British interest, and, although Disraeli had quarrelled with his interpretation, it was to the maintenance of British interests that Palmerston had devoted his long life. But Palmerston had believed, too, in the *status quo*, and had only made serious intervention in European politics — although he would frequently interfere with European politicians — when he felt it was in danger. Indeed, he had twice by positive action risked war in the 'Eastern Question', and had once actually waged it (in the Crimea), just to preserve things as they were. He had lost his battle to prevent the creation, under French auspices, of a canal at Suez — not because he was a foolish obscurantist, but because he knew that, while a canal at Suez would certainly benefit the commerce of mankind, it would also cause a major realignment of power in the Mediterranean and in the Levant, and this above all things he wished to avoid. For the same reasons Palmerston objected in principle to the granting of loans to foreign governments, and to practical application of the notion — which he was prepared to concede was true — that there were many parts of the world which would be better governed by England than by their own nationals. Here his standpoint was no distance from Cobden's own, who always insisted that we were a nation with limited powers and duties, urging that we must confine ourselves 'to guarding the just interests of this Empire'. (Cobden had known, too, that behind Palmerston's doctrine that the Ottoman Empire's security from outside attack was just such an interest, lay the support of the British public as a whole. He had deplored this on the public's behalf: 'it is through your national pride that cunning people manage to extract taxes from you' — but he accepted it, as a fact.)

Disraeli, in contrast, appeared by his action not to be greatly interested in the *status quo*, a humdrum state of affairs at best. He was going to tangle with Russia in the Balkans — and so immobilise the Indian Army on its present frontiers, beyond which loomed the immensity of Russian Central Asia, wherein ambitious officers were assumed to lay nightly plans for the reduction of Hindostan. He was going to involve us further in the fiscal maze in Egypt — and so tangle with France, who thought our presence there both needless and baleful. And, by thus tangling with France, he was going to present Bismarck with a fine opportunity for stirring up the muddied waters, and for neutralising when he pleased the policies of England, of France, or of both Powers at once. As to the destiny of the Ottoman Empire, core of both Palmerston's and Disraeli's thought, the two men strongly differed. Palmerston had been content to hold the ring. To Disraeli the only hope of strengthening that disastrous imperial structure lay in improving the condition of its inhabitants: not, he hastened to add, out of reasons of vague philanthropy, or because of some wild sentimentality such as possessed Gladstonian Liberals, but because it was in England's interest that the Ottoman Empire should be a strong state, secure within as well as without. His Foreign Secretary, Salisbury, indeed at one time during the Berlin negotiations thought of imposing a 'Resident', in the Indian style, on the Sultan, to keep him and his government on the right lines.

The principle, in sum, was one of interference — and not one of interference now and abstention hereafter. It was a policy of continued interference that was adumbrated. Read through the eyes of his critics, Disraeli's spirited foreign policy of imperialism was one long tissue of onerous commitment. For surely, it was the interest of England to limit herself to the minimum of international engagement indispensable to assure the maintenance of peace. But this — this was a blank cheque drawn on the future, on which other nations might write their terms! Imperialist tactics were bound to reflect the tactics of the horsetrade: for it was not long before it became clear that Salisbury, in arranging to take over Cyprus from the Turks to counteract the Russian occupation of Kars and Batum, had been compelled to grant France a *quid pro quo*. He had tacitly agreed that she might, in her own time, proceed to the invasion and reduction of Tunisia. In Tunisia lay Bizerta, the best harbour on the North African coast, and only nine hours' sail from the British base at Malta. Was not this risking rather than safeguarding the security of that so-much-heard-of route to India?

No one however ventured to say that the question of the ownership and tenancy of Constantinople was not a British interest. It was because he centred his attention on this 'key to India' that Disraeli was not distracted by the storm that arose over his handling of the Russo-Turkish crisis. In July 1877 it had seemed likely that the Russian forces would capture the city. By August Disraeli's mind was examining possibilities of sending a British corps into Armenia, or perhaps to Tiflis in Georgia. But the Turkish stand at Plevna delayed, and finally made impracticable, a Russian advance on the capital. The peace imposed by Russia on Turkey at San Stefano created a 'big Bulgaria' that was designed to be a satellite of Russia in the Balkans, thus alarming both the German and the Mediterranean Powers. Before the Congress was called at Berlin juxtapositions of aim and interest were made: Bulgaria was reduced in size, and Russia, having made a strong gain, had no wish to set on foot a league of all Europe against her. The Congress, with Bismarck in the chair, disposed of the San Stefano treaty and pledged itself to see to it that in future the Turks treated its subject races more in accordance with Christian principles. It was against this background that Disraeli, committed to a spirited foreign policy in advance, took up the part of an embattled crusader for the national honour. He continued to defy lightning whose electromotive force had in fact already evaporated, playing his drama out in the European spotlight, with Bismarck, who admired a fellow-showman, applauding gently. It was their quite correct suspicion that this was all a performance, that matters had already been arranged with the Russians, and that the Prime Minister was determined to make it appear that it was he alone who had so arranged them, that so infuriated English Liberals.

Disraeli's gesture in bringing 7,000 troops from India to Malta in the spring of 1878 was hailed as a fitting symbol of this new, and essentially meretricious, policy. The Premier's own role in settling the destiny of the Eastern Question—so stormed the Liberal statesman, Sir William Harcourt — had been to combine the principles of Lord Bolingbroke with the practice of Lord Bute: two figures for ever absent from the roll of English worthies. Disraeli's guide in foreign policy appeared to be his own works of fiction, and in particular the pages of his *Tancred*. This was the unlamented Napoleon III all over again — one mountebank aping another. 'The policy of the Government was an Imperial policy? Yes, sir, it was an Imperial policy — it was a servile imitation of the imperialism of the Second Empire!'[1]

The Way We Live Now, the remarkable novel written by Trollope in 1873, describes the backcloth against which this new policy was to be played out. He dislikes it. He sees that international money is beginning to attract to itself that social power in English political life which had hitherto been reserved as the exclusive privilege of the aristocracy. Now moneyed men, selecting their fatherland as other men selected their banks, were using the Stock Exchange as their base, whence they made forays into high politics. The dealings of Trollope's money-baron Melmotte with the Emperor of China provide a straight reflection of Baron Reuter's short-lived transaction with the Shah of Persia to exploit the commercial future of that country. The age of the *concessionaire* — the man who could buy his way into a country, or into a country-house — was upon us. Success became status; and according to such principles was the way we lived now.

This seamy side of money-imperialism was thus the one that first came uppermost, that made most display whether its speculations succeeded or failed; and this exposure, coming so early in the day, made for the imperialist movement as a whole more enemies than it was ever able to get rid of.

For Radicals always made it their especial business to keep this aspect of imperialism — what Leonard Courtney called Emporial-

[1] 3 H 263, 13 December 1878, 767.

D

ism and a later generation of nationalists Colonialism — in full and embarrassing view. As a consequence of this, the men on the other side, the devotees of the cause of commercial empire, sought to convince people that they, too, were men who followed a star — that they did not seek to live by bread, stocks and cotton, or gold-mine dividends alone, but wished to use whatever profits their skill brought them to fulfil a beneficent, a civilising mission in the world. When such a declaration of purpose was made by Cecil Rhodes, the public was inclined to accept it; but when it came from his court of South African millionaires, from Park Lane, it was found harder to swallow. Plainly, these were all men who worshipped Mammon, who cared more for the five per cent than for the philanthropy that they threw in as a sop to sentiments which they not only did not share but which they actively detested. This Radical charge was however somewhat over-emphatic. As it turned out, simple plutocracy made very few political friends of any significance, and what social gifts its members could boast they were left to exercise in the circles that surrounded Albert Edward as Prince of Wales. Their political allegiance was naturally given to the imperialist party, to that Conservatism which ruled the shires and dictated the conventions of the London season. But the Conservative leaders—inmates of the establishment jocularly known in back-bench circles as the 'Hotel Cecil' — did their best to keep at arm's length this first generation of over-successful financiers. (The latter's sons, however, once they had been processed in the normal way through the public schools, were made very welcome.) Thus, Rhodes' gift of £10,000 to the Irish Home Rulers' funds, while it neither embarrassed the Liberals nor gratified the Irish for more than five minutes, genuinely scandalised the Conservative and Unionist party—because such conduct, committed by the most notorious red-map-maker of the day, seemed to cast ridicule on all those other, and higher, imperial aspirations to which they, as Conservatives, were now bound.

It was ironical, indeed, that these new men, the late-Victorian equivalent of the eighteenth-century 'nabob', should so often have won and held the fascinated attention from the Liberal left wing despite itself; for those who approved the principle that a man should rise from nothing by means of his own efforts were sometimes hard put to it to withhold their admiration from the personalities of those capitalist Empire-builders whose methods and character, coarsened by too much money, they so sincerely deplored. It was

Chamberlain, himself a Radical capitalist, who best understood the 'Africans' Goldie and Rhodes, and Salisbury, observing this, wisely left it to his colleague to do what business had to be done with them. And it was because Chamberlain had just this touch and understanding that his erstwhile Radical colleagues bayed on his track with such venomous gusto.

It is not of course money, but the love of money, that is the root of all evil. That capital might be employed for beneficent ends, might fulfil a genuinely missionary task, had never been denied. It was a principle that stood on dangerously quaking ground: still, with care and conscience, it was possible to pick a path towards it. Trollope had remarked in an account of *The West Indies and the Spanish Main* (1859) — an area where all things physical and spiritual struck him as being in a state of peeling decay, and this despite some centuries of European contact and imperial rule — that 'mission' was a word 'foully misused'.[1] But he never said that mission itself was a misconceived idea. Burke's doctrine of trusteeship, that power exercised over a native race ought to be employed ultimately for the welfare of that race, had been part of the English intellectual climate of opinion since the trial of Warren Hastings. It had been given a vehement restatement in the Report of the 'Aborigines Committee' of the House of Commons which was published in 1835. This Report had used some comminatory language about that type of colonisation, that kind of settler, which wilfully contravened Burke's principle: language which had since boomed annually from the missionary and humanitarian sects whose headquarters in London was Exeter Hall.

The 1835 Report had pronounced against the enterprise of colonial pioneers in general, against the cupidity and criminal greed they invariably displayed when penetrating the territories of uncivilised peoples. It was the duty of Government, plainly, to curb such oppression at all times; for it to assist in schemes of colonisation, whether systematic or not, in such areas was only to connive at crime. Providence had signally blessed the British Empire. It was surely self-evident that its advantages had been given it 'for some higher purpose than commercial prosperity and military renown'.[2] A higher Power would one day enquire of us,

[1] pp. 83–5.
[2] Quoted in A. P. Newton, *A Hundred Years of the British Empire*, (London, 1940), p. 111.

taking evidence from our own record, how we had dealt with the 'untutored, defenceless' savage whom circumstance had placed in our charge — and if it could be said that we had neither tutored nor defended him, it would assuredly go hard with us.

To all these views the Victorian conscience still adhered, and neither Trollope nor anyone else who commanded and wished to retain the public ear, disputed the point that mission was a duty laid upon us. Those who insisted that this was all a lot of hypocritical nonsense caused genuine anger, that was not diminished by the fact that the critics could produce more chapter and verse concerning colonists' misdemeanours than their defenders could summon up evidence of colonial virtue. Mission was an imperial idea before the politicians adapted it, and it was to have a longer history than political imperialism itself. Thus, many Radicals offended more bitterly than they ever knew when they sought to reduce everything to a flat level of self-interest, and to assume that all men all the time were guided by nothing else, and that the principle of utility was as noble a dogma as any that ever issued from a church. The most influential Radical thinkers realised this themselves, and did their best to break away from the pure bread-and-butter doctrines of the political economists, which held out no appeal to mankind's best hopes. A succeeding generation of Socialists rebelled entirely against their political thinking. Ramsay MacDonald was to write in 1907 that 'the base money-making Manchester school, devoid of national pride and subordinating everything to trading profits, never existed — but it very nearly did';[1] and Robert Blatchford added in his angry book, *Merrie England*, that the Manchester school would have had us believe that our people were too base and foolish to lead wise and honest lives.

The English public however has always been better equipped than most in the ability to ignore opinions it dislikes. For example, when Lord Blachford commented in 1885 that, to suppose that the Anglo-Saxons, 'the great exterminators of aborigines in the temperate zone', would when confederated set a new and exceptional example of justice and humanity, seemed to him 'a somewhat transcendental expectation',[2] he was regarded as an eccentric. To be sure, his views had been warped by his eleven years as Permanent Under-Secretary in the Colonial Office, whose collective memory

[1] Ramsay MacDonald, *Labour and the Empire*, (London, 1907), p. 12.
[2] *Pall Mall Gazette*, 19 January 1888.

was still seared by the battles waged in the 1820's and 1830's between the missionary societies, the Aborigines Protection Society, and Exeter Hall on the one side, and colonial settlers anywhere in the world on the other. They had been genuine motives of humanitarian mission that had caused the British Government to extend its legal rule over New Zealand, Sarawak, the New Hebrides, and other Pacific islands, in order to stop the ruthless European buccaneering that was going on against the native populations. Even Goldwin Smith, who while Regius Professor of Modern History at Oxford wrote books encouraging the opinion that a dissolution of the imperial tie with the colonies was not only inevitable but proper, and who insisted that *prestige* was always illusion and imposture, conceded that we had a mission to stay in India, in order to prevent the return of anarchy to that country. Adult 'colonies' contradicted common sense, but India, and other 'native territories', were not adult.

Charles Dilke, held by his racialist theme of a *Greater* Britain, in which by 1970 there would be some 370 million 'Anglo-Saxons', saw no future for the race in its possession of alien dependencies, which were surely an obstruction to its true development. Mission he tended to discount, seeing India in particular from an idiosyncratic angle. For he argued that if we really wanted to please the Hindus we should spend £10,000 a year in support of native literature, and another £10,000 a year on fireworks to amuse the masses. But he did not expect to make many converts to that policy. John Bright on this took the orthodox line: he saw our task in India — though he doubted our ability as much as our will to perform it — as one of bringing enlightenment to a dark place on the earth.

English Whigs like Lord John Russell and the third Earl Grey, who stood well to the right of their Radical supporters and knew a great deal more about actual problems of colonial governance than any of them, considered the maintenance of the colonial connexion a bounden duty on us. English courage and capital, often more of the first than the second, had been heavily invested in oversea territories. Some we had reclaimed from barbarism, others we had relieved of some other European influence. In neither case could we leave, and allow barbarism and anarchy to return. In this view, mission was a charge and a responsibility: and it agrees with Kipling's thirty years ahead. It was not a joy or a source of strength.

Any *passion de gigantesque* was alien to mid-Victorian thinking. Agreed, it was not right for a nation always to be thinking exclusively in terms of exports and imports, as Cobden conceded. But we had no need to do this, for we had other interests. The phrase that 'British interests were eternal' was a perfectly proper one, if British interests were equated with the propagation of peace and the rule of law.

Most certainly it was not right, not right at all, that a nation should put its head into the clouds and there dream imperial dreams. Many feared that India in particular was too much beset with tinsel trappings. 'I do not know at this moment, and I have never known,' said Bright when the Crown was taking India over from the Company in 1858, 'a man competent to govern India.'[1] Twenty years later the eighth Duke of Argyll, a leading Whig who had held the India Office for six years, remarked how great an effect the possession of the Indian Empire had had on the national temper. It was regarded with a passionate pride and jealousy — feelings which were 'but slightly founded on any deliberate estimate of the good we may be doing there'.[2] Pride of possession and instinct of dominion, like other primary passions of the mind, were liable to irrational excess and abuse. Argyll conceded that there was, maybe, no natural connexion between Conservatism and a low morality in politics: but his implication was that there might very well be an artificial connexion, and that India and all the array of dominant Empire might supply it.

The blank ignorance of British people about India indeed made this outcome more likely. Indian policies were matters for experts, for the few. Public opinion was not brought to bear on them at all. In the old days before 1858 the Court of Directors of the East India Company had disposed of office in India by means of simple patronage, and, accordingly, almost solely to Europeans. Since the Mutiny and the takeover, the Crown had extended the patronage, but it was still the monopoly of Europeans simply because they were Europeans: if one had a white skin one was *ipso facto* a loyalist. These 'Anglo-Indians', a closed set, indeed took great pains to convince that part of the public that was at all interested, that every European in India was working in a noble cause and that his work would be ten times more efficient if he were not

[1] Speech at Birmingham, 24 June 1858.
[2] Duke of Argyll, *The Eastern Question*, (London, 1879), I, xii, xiv; II, 215, 217.

jostled while he was about it, or upset by ill-founded comment by members of Parliament and journalists who had never been in India. In rebuttal, a *mot* of Palmerston's was often resuscitated. 'When I wish to be misinformed about a country,' the great man had said, 'I ask the man who has lived there thirty years.'

This Liberal contention — which was never abandoned — that the possession of Empire hampered rather than helped England's position in the world, had a hard core to it. An imperialist policy that involved expansion of territory must necessarily bring about entanglement with whatever State lay beyond the immediate imperial pale. England was a commercial sea-power, and Sir William Harcourt, leader of the 'Little Englanders' in the 1890's, was again only echoing Cobden when he declared himself as great an advocate of British maritime supremacy as any jingo. Affairs at sea we could do our best to control; at least, Cobden's sour question — shall two drunken captains of frigates at the Antipodes cause war? — had not, so far, been given affirmative answer. But this new sort of Empire, whose greatest pride was apparently the Indian Army, would give to England land-frontiers which, in the long run, she would not be able to defend. Where there were 'obligations of honour', 'imperial necessities', 'scientific frontiers', and the like, there would be complication and commitment from which the country would never get free. England would no longer be able to hold the balance of power: she would become a weight in its scales.

No charge made against imperialism was more deeply felt than this — that it committed not just a Government of the day, or a particular political party, but posterity as well. Posterity would have to take a path it might very well dislike, but the choice would no longer be its own. British foreign policy had long been based on non-commitment, on the principle that the country was a free agent, a member of no *bloc* or power-group, with no pre-ordained enemies or allies. It was a British interest that this state of affairs should continue. But British 'imperial policy' seemed to be based on the absolutely opposite principle. Imperialists were taking risks they had no right to take.

It was not as if this kind of country was entirely unmapped. The mid-Victorian generation was itself the posterity of an imperialist age, and it had seen its own policies hampered by that simple fact. The existence of the long open frontier of the Canadian Provinces had compelled England to keep on good terms, often in the face of truculent provocation, with the United States of America. In 1863–1864, amid the complexities of the Schleswig question, Palmerston had had to play a hand without a trump in it, because the bulk of the effective British Army was at that moment in Ontario and Quebec, on guard lest the Northern Union Armies should swing their campaign into Canadian as well as Confederate territory. Again, in Southern Africa in 1852 and 1854, a Conservative Government in this country had 'let the frontier go' altogether, had thrown over responsibilities for the area north of the Orange River and had allowed the Boers to make good their claim to have trekked out of the sphere of British influence and control, simply because it refused to face any longer the commitment that retention of control over these frontiersmen involved: the constant troubles with the savages of the unknown hinterland, which brought no benefit of any sort to anybody and which cost the British taxpayer great sums of money into the bargain.

Moreover, the whole record of the expansion of British rule in India itself was but a comment on the theme, later to be popularised by the Americans, of the 'manifest destiny' that draws on those who stand by a moving frontier — in the Indian case a frontier not of settlement but of government, of the *Raj*, extending in ever-widening circles the zone of law and order, the sway of the commissioned officer and the covenanted civil servant. This was a process whose results were too striking to be ignored even by those who most disliked it. Wilfrid Scawen Blunt, a Conservative who refused to extend his conservatism to Empire, seeing in it only a usurpation of other people's rights, felt compelled to agree that in Asia our hands were tied, and that we had 'to submit to the conditions of Empire' so long as we held India. (Yet who could foresee that on a distant day a British Foreign Secretary, Sir Edward Grey, would concede to Russia Constantinople, Disraeli's key to India, with a somewhat similar expression on his lips? It was done, he said, because of 'the logic of our imperial position'.)[1] India already held British foreign policy a captive. Fear of a Russian drive through Central Asia towards that expanding Indian frontier had conditioned British policy towards Russia in Europe for close on fifty years, and during that period it was well known that the fires of popular Russophobia were kept tended by influential Anglo-Indians who urged the home Government constantly to bestir it-

[1] E. Kedourie, *England and the Middle East*, (Cambridge, 1956), p. 35.

self, to 'do something' to take the measure of this menace. Lytton, Disraeli's personal choice of a suitably spirited Viceroy, always stressed how the Indian frontier was become an imperial frontier.

His Liberal detractors could not but concede he was right, although they did not share his pride in the discovery. If Russia once succeeded in gaining influence in Afghanistan, the buffer state that divided Russian Central Asia from British India, there at once was an end put to the promotion of any separate British policy in the affairs of the Balkans and the Ottoman Empire. Indeed, the mere distant presence of Russia in Asia was later a sufficient deterrent to both British political parties from doing anything to rescue the Armenians from Turkish rapacity and atrocity, despite pledges given at Berlin in 1878 that the Armenian question was one of particular interest to the British public conscience. That there was a British phobia about a Russian initiative in the East became a European commonplace, and in 1899 Tsar Nicholas II mentioned it as such in a letter to his sister: to paralyse British policy, not just in the Near East, but in the Far East and in South Africa, he had only to order by telegraph the mobilisation of the forces in Russian Turkestan. Here Nicholas went too far, and was mistaken. But nobody thought he was.

Thus, to those who wished England to live a life of limited powers and limited duties — and Salisbury's subsequent gibe that Gladstone was 'the apostle of absolute negation in foreign affairs'[1] had considerable point — imperial frontiers were national liabilities, burdens irrevocably imposed. This was the theme that Gladstone developed in his Scottish, or 'Midlothian' campaign, in 1879–80, which gives the best summary of the Liberal doctrine on world policy.[2] It is noteworthy that his argument was based on the assumption that England was, despite all Disraeli's aberrations, still a free agent, able to recoup and to retract. That imperialism was not only a policy but a public state of mind in Europe, which could hardly be affected by any results of a general election in Great Britain, it took Gladstone long to comprehend.

The strength of Great Britain and Ireland, he insisted, lay within the United Kingdom itself. This had been forgotten. Since Disraeli's Government took office in 1874, Fiji, the Transvaal, and

[1] 3 H 294, 26 February 1885, 1317.
[2] See W. E. Gladstone, *Political Speeches in Scotland, 1879–80*, (2 vols., Edinburgh, 1880).

Cyprus had been added to our responsibilities. We had debouched from the Straits Settlements into the interior of the Malayan peninsula, with what results for good or ill no one yet could tell. There had been an Afghan and a Zulu war, both attended with spectacular disaster. We had since 1875 involved ourselves so deeply in the financial affairs of Egypt, a Turkish dependency, that it seemed unlikely we could ever get free, and if we once took control of Egypt it would make us a territorial Power in the Mediterranean, which our present ownership of Gibraltar and Malta did not. Moreover, we might find Egypt prove to be the embryo of an African Empire, in the same way as the Indian Empire had developed from Bengal. By the Treaty of Berlin and the Cyprus Convention attached to it we had guaranteed the Armenian frontier of Turkey — wherever that might be — and Turkey herself against any future Russian assault. Surely, our hands were full?

Our strength was insufficient to meet such calls on it. It had always been a fundamental tenet of Gladstonian foreign policy that we should set up no claim ourselves which we did not allow to others in the ordering of international relations; and it followed from this that anyone who departed from that principle committed treason against public law and the peace and order of the world. But now, 'inflamed and flattered by high-sounding discourses about the great position of England', we were being asked to approve that England should become the teacher and instructor of every nation in the world. If we expected these nations to be grateful we were much in error. Doubtless we would set about to improve conditions in Cyprus, for example: but we should not look for gratitude or any lasting attachment from the people there because we gave them (for our own purposes as much as for theirs) some better roads.

Certainly, we must maintain our hold on India. We owed a duty to the peoples of that land. The origins of our Empire there might, perhaps, 'ill bear examination', but we who had inherited it must try to redeem it from past error, and elevate it into honour. But did our possession of India necessitate our grasping at every avenue of approach to it? (Because I have a house in York and a house in London, Palmerston had once said, must I own all the inns on the way?) Yet what else was the claim of the imperialists who had rallied beneath Disraeli's banner of a spirited foreign policy? It seemed to be this: that a small island at one end of the world, having got hold of a vast territory at the other, was entitled to say with respect to every land and sea lying between its own shores and any part of that great possession, that it had a preferential right to the control of that intermediate territory, in order to safeguard (so the term went) the road to India. Gladstone's glare, bent on his Glasgow audience as he concluded, may be imagined 'That, gentlemen, is a monstrous claim!'

In the course of these assaults on the Conservative position Gladstone was careful to disclaim the charge so frequently heard on Conservative hustings, that he and his party were separatist in sentiment. Gladstone declared that he believed now, always had believed, in the British Empire. How could he do otherwise? Was it not a fact of life? Did not these great colonies exist overseas, peopled by men and women of British blood? Yet surely there was a difference in being justly proud of, and anxious to maintain, this colonial connexion, and in being intoxicated by the thought that we also controlled great dependencies whose races, alien from our own in blood, custom, and religion, had and could have no say in their own destinies. The British Empire which we had a right to praise was that which had been created by the labour of our own kinsmen. It had passed through the stage of dependency, and no one would wish to bring that status back.

But the existence of British despotisms in the world, however benevolent, raised a moral question. Were not the Boers of the Transvaal, so recently swept within the imperial fold (1877) after they had enjoyed a generation of independence, a people like the Bulgarian subjects of Turkey, rightly struggling to be free? It was the dependent state of Ireland that had so bedevilled the whole history of Anglo-Irish relations since the Union of 1800; and in this case, too — though Gladstone had not become aware of this himself in 1880 — he was reaching the conclusion that nothing in that relationship could be mended until the state of dependence was abolished. Home Rule had solved the impasse in the Canadian colonies in the 1830's, and had given a great blessing to the Australasian colonies in the 1850's. Let not the Tories pretend that this nostrum of colonial self-government had been any prescription of theirs. The only striking fact in the history of the relations of the Tory party with the colonies was the loss of the United States. Lord Durham and his school of Radical Colonial Reformers who had handed down the doctrine had never been *persona grata* at the Carlton Club. How little, indeed, Tories still knew of actual colonial conditions might well be illustrated from the remarks of Disraeli himself in the House of Commons as recently as 1876, when he had expressed the opinion that white colonists were transients, men who went out to the far ends of the world 'to fleece a flock or find a nugget', and who, if successful in such ventures, returned at once to the haunts of civilisation here at home.[1] On that occasion it had been the Liberal, W. E. Forster — who was later, in 1884, to become the stalwart founding member of the Imperial Federation League — who had delivered the proper rebuke to this levity.

Colonists, he had said, were founders of a Commonwealth.[2] This was some eight years before Lord Rosebery, who conceived his imperial ideas on his Australian tour of 1883–84, set out the phrase again.

But although Gladstone might parry the charge of separatism effectively enough on the hustings, and won this 1880 election despite the fervour with which it was made, he was never able to dispose of it completely. When after five years of Liberal rule it was made plain that the electoral triumph of 1880 had given only the very slightest setback to the force of the imperial idea itself — for did not the anti-imperialist Liberals pursue as spirited a foreign policy as any that Disraeli ever devised? — the imperialist was able to put an extra polish on the accusation. He did not really believe that the Liberals were going to break up the Empire; but he knew that they would put no fervour into the work of either extending or maintaining it. They would not share his patriotic enthusiasms, and for this he would not forgive them. Because they carried out imperialist actions against their own grain, they wore an air of guilt which was particularly infuriating. For the true imperialist took more pride in the possession of India, in the pace of the British march in Africa, in the dexterity with which his own country forestalled the wicked intent of rivals, in the thought that we now 'counted' in world affairs, than ever he could summon up in respect of the rather humdrum glories of colonial self-government. (Moreover, self-governing colonies often pursued radical and socialist policies which he never clearly understood.) Thus, the chain linking the earlier charge of disinterest in the Empire with the later accusation that Liberals and Radicals were prepared to see parts of

[1] 3 H 227, 9 March 1876, 1726.
[2] 3 H 228, 16 March 1876, 146–7.

the Empire handed over to its enemies, to the Queen's own enemies
— the charge of 'pro-Boerdom', or spiritual treason — is a short
one. Men who did not 'believe in' the British Empire, all of it, were
to be pilloried as men who believed only in the parish pump, little
Englanders oblivious of their country's true role and duty in the
world. They were people, accordingly, in whose hands the destiny
and honour of the country would never be safe: people whom,
even though by some mischance they got office again, it would be
a patriotic duty to obstruct and confound. Men who did not believe in the superiority of England over what the sardonic Liberal
W. S. Gilbert called 'French, or Turk, or Proosian' were
plain fools.

This length of chain, coiled up, indeed put a weapon in the
hands of the imperialists too powerful for them ever willingly to
relinquish it. The 'khaki election' of 1900, held at what was hailed
to be the successful conclusion of the Boer War, saw it inflict its
severest casualties on the ranks of the foe. All who, for one reason
or another, leagued together in detestation of Gladstone and all
his works, made use of this weapon whenever there was a favourable
occasion. The twenty years that spanned between the Midlothian
and the khaki elections were to provide many such.

Both sides to this bitter dispute continued to accuse the other
of ignorance of the nature of the world in which we all had to live.
It was pleasant to be liberal, but could we afford Liberalism?
Could we afford the sort of political Liberalism that had no means
of asserting itself in international affairs? What use were good
intentions in the world that Bismarck surveyed? Would goodwill
expressed at St. Petersburg stop the Russians in Central Asia,
where in the space of twenty years, since 1864, they had enveloped
a territory as great as Asia Minor in extent? That it was not amiable
sentiment, but power, that must supply the basis of British policy
lay at the root of the imperialists' conviction. Joseph Chamberlain
in particular, whose Radical past taught him that political power
could be, if correctly used, a dynamo in social and economic fields,
was convinced that it could be so used imperially and internation-
ally. Amid all his distractions he sought a solution to the problems
that beset strong executive government in a democratic system, and
he left to a diminishing band of disciples the task of carrying out
the schemes he propounded. Power might tend to corrupt, as
Gladstone's friend Lord Acton had liked to observe — but that

was a risk that a great nation must run, and the lesser risk of two: for a nation that did not have confidence in its power, and make it manifest, would assuredly sink. Great Britain would become, warned Tennyson darkly in his *Idylls of the King*, 'a third-rate isle', unless she took steps now and always to see to it that she did not. So it was, that the imperialists came to rely on the State and on State policies as much as did their sworn enemies, the Socialists — and this despite the influence of the long and attractive tradition of *laisser-faire*. Liberals and Radicals who continued to hold to that tradition declared that the imperialists would in time reach their logical conclusion — they would impose a State tariff and they would raise a State Army. And so they did.

At the time and for long after imperialists shrugged this off as abuse. They insisted that to rely on principles of *laisser-faire* alone, in face of a militarist Europe, was not only foolish but dangerous; and there were already a few publicists, still speaking softly but prepared to risk the remark that in the domestic field too the dogma had its disadvantages — as exemplified in the shipping of wheat from the opened American prairies to the eager British consumer throughout the 1870's, a process which was going far to wreck the basis of the British agricultural economy. But in Europe in particular it was surely obvious that nationalism, having gained its local objectives, was ready to export itself. Europe, having built up its own tariff walls, was ready and eager similarly to fortify the distant places of the globe.

In such circumstances the continuance of British commercial predominance was not a law of nature: and even if it were, it was man's business to get control of laws of nature and to usurp their powers, not to succumb to their apparent authority in a spirit of weak and fatalistic resignation. Biology when applied to politics takes on a peculiar aspect: as the doctrines of Malthus had once been used by the timorous to block measures of social progress, so what was understood to be the opinions of Darwin were now ransacked by the self-confident, in order to bolster their own opinion that those who survived in the world were those who took most pains to see to it that others did not. Assuredly Darwinism set its face against gutlessness. The weak would go to the wall: and in this case the weak were those who stood still, those who let the world move past them. Let us not find ourselves among that number.

Indeed it had been true, a generation ago, to say that Britain's oyster was the wide world itself, that in every market she could sell the cheapest and make the most profit. But the times had changed, and were changing now. Now she must consolidate and centralise the control of what markets she was entrenched in, to keep them to herself. Now she must take care lest competitors reached new potential markets before she did. Now she must establish 'spheres of influence' over vast areas where only a handful of her citizens had ever set foot. Empire, if correctly organised, was power, wealth, fame, influence.

All the ideas and formulae current in the last twenty years of the century, for constructing an Imperial Federation, for renovating the system of Imperial Defence, for building a customs-union on the model of the German Imperial *Zollverein*, were natural deductions from this premise. Those who devoted themselves to these schemes, laid these plans, were imperialists who did not consider that their imperialism was, as they were told, a great and dangerous commitment, which would constantly involve us in quarrel. It promised instead a form of family solidarity and insurance, so strong that no one would risk provoking quarrel with it. It did not necessitate a 'spirited foreign policy', designed mainly to capture castles in Spain. It was a policy of forethought and good sense, for which posterity — so often descried pointing the accusing finger — would be properly grateful. Men who sincerely believed this always hotly denied that they were still dressed in what Wilfrid Blunt called 'Dizzy's suit of imperial spangles'.[1]

As they saw it, the establishment of a firm foreign — or, to give it its right name, an imperial — policy, based on the protection and maintenance of the British Empire, with a watch always kept for gainful opportunity of extending it, was the necessity that faced the country and its Government both of this day and of the days that should follow.

[1] Wilfrid Scawen Blunt, *My Diaries*, (London, 1919), II, 74.

II

THE IMPERIAL IDEA AT ITS
ZENITH

THE legacy of Disraeli's policy of commitment could not be so
easily got rid of as Gladstone had made it appear to the
burghers of Dalkeith. Indeed it could not be got rid of at all.
The imperialist insistence that England was and must remain a
positive factor in the ordering of world affairs was not one that
could be passed over as if it had never been made. 'British interests'
was a concept that held meaning for both political parties; but
Liberals who were content to equate those interests with the interests of humanity in general, with good government, common
action, equal rights, freedom, and peace, found they were fast being
left behind by the march of events. The years of Liberal rule,
1880–85, saw the creation of the Triple Alliance in Europe and the
beginnings of the European scramble for colonies. Disraeli's world,
which the Liberals had thought illusory, his own catchpenny invention, was in fact the real world — one of jealous nations, competing for favourable positions in the sun.

More, therefore, was required than the issue of statements concerning British interests. One had now to go down into the dusty
arena of international politics in order to promote and to assert
these interests, and to give them as permanent a form as could be
devised by spreading knowledge of and arousing enthusiasm for
them among one's own countrymen. People who did not believe
this was necessary nevertheless found themselves forced down into
the arena too — to proselytise for their own cause of non-intervention. In the opening confusion they often found themselves fighting on the other side. Many of those who objected vehemently to
spirited policies of oversea expansion were strong humanitarians,
and how humanitarianism or Christianity itself — both of them
nothing if not spirited policies — could be exported to savage lands
save in military baggage-cars, and maintained there safely save by

imperial garrisons, was as yet far from plain. In the noise of this
political battle it was often difficult even for high-minded men to
evolve clear trains of thought as to the principles that should guide
our policy. The moral obligations pertaining to a civilised status
might be appealed to more often than they were accurately assessed, but such things did in fact exist; and it was a genuine public
instinct as to the 'honour of England' — a term always more easily
capable of distortion than definition — that found honest expression in 1885 in the national outcry that succeeded the death of
Gordon in Khartoum.

Ideas still inchoate as the decade opened were given much first
class intellectual material to work on. At Cambridge Professor
Seeley delivered a famous series of lectures in the spring of 1881,
which he afterwards published as a book, under the title of *The
Expansion of England*. This book was addressed to the general
reader, and that it is still alive may be proved both by the fact that
it continued to sell remarkably for the next fifty years,[1] not going
out of print until 1956; and also that no two interpretations of
what Seeley was talking about appear to agree. 'These historical
lectures dealt in the main', wrote Professor A. P. Newton on page
240 of his book *A Hundred Years of the British Empire*,

> with the great wars of the eighteenth century, and this gave the false
> impression that the British Empire had largely been founded by war
> and conquest — an idea that was unfortunately planted firmly in the
> public mind, not only in Great Britain, but also in foreign countries.

Newton wrote that in 1938, when to admit any capacity for ruth-
lessness in the British past might well have embarrassed the
National Government in its dealings with two of those foreign
countries who had already received so unfortunate an impression.
For it would indeed be hard to prove that large areas of the British
Empire in the nineteenth as well as in the eighteenth century were
not won by war and conquest, while conceding that in other areas
again moral pressure was found sufficient.

Seeley's book summarised a decade of argument for the cause of
imperial unity. He looked for clues in history as Disraeli had looked
for them in politics and as Dilke had sought them in his brilliant
crystal bowl. These clues, rightly interpreted, must lead us to the

[1] *e.g.* it sold 11,000 copies in 1919, 3,000 in 1931. (Information from Messrs.
Macmillan.)

E

conclusion that it was Britain's destiny to become a world-state, so that she might meet and test the future in company with those other great states whose full day of power had not yet dawned — Russia and the United States of America. To teach the correct interpretation was the great thing. When we had accustomed ourselves to contemplate the whole Empire together and to call it all England, Seeley argued, we should see that here too was a United States. He did not concern himself at all with what colonial attitudes either were or were likely to be to this purely English argument, but in this he was fully representative of the school at whose head he now found himself, for no imperialist ever seriously examined colonial ideas lest he should find they led him back along the path of different identity to that separation which he was determined to go on thinking was unthinkable.

Much the best part of Seeley's book contains his thought on the future of India. He remarked, what few had ventured to say since Macaulay had issued his blast of contempt against Hindu philosophy and religion, that we were not able to astonish the Hindu as we could astonish the barbarian, by putting before him ideas that he had never dreamed of. So we would have to put before him something else. It was true, he conceded, that our possession of India vastly increased our dangers and responsibilities. Nevertheless withdrawal would be 'the most inexcusable of all conceivable crimes'. For the essence of British dominion in India was a moral one: it was that of the modern over the medieval world. He laid great stress on the power of ideas to move men, and on the point that the British Empire must find for itself an idea which might appeal to all the races within it, an idea to act as a dynamo for the world-state that it was so necessary to bring into being. Did not the weakness of all the Empires of which history had record lie in this alone, that they had been nothing 'but a mere mechanical union of alien nationalities'?

The Radical John Morley, reviewing this work by the Regius Professor of Modern History at the University of Cambridge, commented with some acidity how greatly its tone differed from that published by a Regius Professor of Modern History at the University of Oxford twenty years since: Goldwin Smith's *The Empire*.[1] After taking some mild exception to Seeley's assertion that no previous English historian had collected the right clues concerning

[1] John Morley, *Macmillan's Magazine*, February 1884, 241 ff.

the history of England, Morley pointed out that the territorial expansion of England was strictly secondary and a corollary to the industrial expansion of England within its own shores. To direct us along a path towards a world-state, into a Greater Britain, a grand Imperial Union, was a gesture no doubt with its attractions, but what happened at the far end of the road? Where was the constitutional wizard who would draft for us the bill that should settle the respective powers of the colonial legislatures, the British legislature, and the Universal Greater British legislature? An Imperial Federal Union, Morley insisted with remarkable prescience, would always break down on two questions: tariffs and natives. Colonial representatives at Westminster would doubtless be glad to vote our money, but would always refuse to allow us to vote theirs. And how could a Federal Union obtain any more power than the Colonial Office now had to prevent, say, a Parliament in Cape Colony from passing a Vagrant Act (which it had just done) whose principal object was to place the blacks under the necessity of working for whites at low wages? And where in such a scheme could be fitted in the *propugnacula* of Empire, stations such as Hong Kong, Gibraltar, and Malta? It was not just the difficulties Morley emphasised: he objected to the whole route mapped out by Seeley and the Imperial Federation League. If our ideal was a great Roman Empire, which should be capable by means of fleets and armies of imposing its will upon the world, then it was satisfactory to think that the ideal itself was an unattainable one.

But Morley's tone was more regretful than pugnacious, for he was aware the tide was running the imperial way. The great thing, as Seeley's book suggested, was to recognise that the world was in movement, that old assumptions required inspection, and if they were found to be outmoded, must be discarded. The Liberals, by their tradition, ought themselves to have been the first to recognise this, and to apply their skill to the new problem, how to live in a world that thought force a solution to political issues. Some of them indeed did so, for the Liberal intellectuals like Morley were always excellent diagnosticians of the public ill. But too many of them were inclined to turn their faces to the wall at the sight. Frederic Harrison, writing only two months after the great Liberal triumph in 1880, warned that nothing would or could be greatly changed.[1] Too much had happened. What race, what hemisphere,

[1] F. Harrison, 'Empire and Humanity', *Fortnightly Review*, June 1880.

what latitude, had not seen the unsheathed sword of Britain? These crimes, he insisted, were not the special work of Lord Beaconsfield and the party he led: they were the work of the military and commercial aristocracy of England. Imperialism was the creed of all who found in the military Empire the glory and the strength of England — and they formed the bulk of the official and governing classes, under whichever political chief they were sworn to serve. Statesmen, journalists, and preachers came to every question of policy or morality bound by the silent influence of a half-uttered thought: 'Come what may, the Empire must be saved.'

Yet this bondage could be broken, though not indeed in a day, if only Empire were regarded as a passing responsibility, and not as a permanent greatness of our country. This was surely commonsense, as was the argument that had been raised for forty years or more: an aggregate of dependencies which was for ever disturbed or menaced, for ever awaiting or forestalling attack, which contributed nothing to the home government in money or men or resources of any kind, was not a strength but an increasing weakness. It must pull down 'the strongest race that ever trod the earth'; and as it pulled them down, it would hurry them from one crime to another.

Already it was true that in the British Empire subject races got as little free national life as was given in the Ottoman Empire. How this ground the consciences of all true Liberals! Yet this kind of thing was done from 'no innate spirit of mischief', only because we were guided by a vicious tradition and set in a false situation.

In 1870 Liberal thinkers had objected that Gladstone was bound too closely to Manchester policies. Now in 1880 they objected again that his mind was not free to roam as it should over these new and vital questions: it was locked to Ireland. This in itself would not have been so injurious to the national interest had he ever conceded that there was anything to the Conservatives' point, that the pacification of Ireland must be made subordinate to the interests of the United Kingdom and the Empire as a whole. Impervious to this, Gladstone was to lose not only the Whig grandees like Hartington but the Radical leader, Joseph Chamberlain, who could have been won: and by losing Chamberlain, presented as a hostage to imperialism the best Radical mind in politics.

Yet the Liberal leader incurred more suspicion both from his own party and from the imperialists than he ever really deserved. The feeling that he was wild and unpredictable he did a great deal to encourage, but his record of action between 1880 and 1885, whatever may be said about his Home Rule activities in 1886, is not one that gives much support to that view. He was beleaguered by circumstances whose significance he did not leave himself enough time to assess. Sensible men on both sides of the House knew that some degree of what is now called 'bipartisanship' in foreign and domestic policy was essential if the party system of government was to work at all. In particular, it was clear that all relations with other countries would become impossible if an incoming party reversed, on what it called principle, everything that its opponent had been doing. But this was precisely the policy with which Gladstone was returned to power in 1880, voted in by an electorate apparently animated by no sentiment that a Conservative could understand other than that it was time for a change. Accordingly Midlothian damned Gladstone for ever in the drawing-rooms of England, and nowhere more irretrievably than in those of Windsor, Osborne, and Balmoral.

Nevertheless this policy was never carried to its logical conclusions. The Treaty of Berlin was an international engagement, and Granville on his arrival in the Foreign Office told the Turkish Ambassador 'that to dissent from the expediency of an international arrangement was a very different thing from reversing it after it had been concluded'.[1] The Cyprus Convention was harder for Liberals to stand by, as this had been arranged in the dark, outside the deliberations of that Concert which the Treaty of Paris of 1856 had established to guard the interests of the Ottoman Empire. Nevertheless Cyprus remained under the British flag. Because it did so, Liberals were constrained to honour Salisbury's pledge, and to allow the French flag to be hoisted over Tunisia in 1881. But Gladstone in Midlothian had made two specific pledges to reverse Conservative action, in Afghanistan and in the Transvaal. What was to happen about them? Again no clear application of principle could be observed. The city and province of Kandahar in Afghanistan were evacuated by British troops in the spring of 1881, but at least Roberts had had time to avenge the bad defeat inflicted on them the previous summer at Maiwand: but the evacuation of the Transvaal, in August 1881, followed hard upon a bad defeat of British troops at Majuba, no steps whatever being taken to rectify

[1] H. W. V. Temperley and L. M. Penson, *Foundations of British Foreign Policy*, (Cambridge, 1938), p. 401.

the military situation. The Kandahar evacuation was condemned as foolish: the Transvaal evacuation as cowardly. In both cases charges of dereliction of duty were levelled against the Liberal Government.

For the question that had been put by Hartington, the Secretary of State for India, to a delegation of embattled Anglo-Indians pressing him to retain Kandahar: 'Gentlemen, what right have we to be there?' — was now countered with the demand, What right had we to leave? Evacuation left clients — whom a few years more would make loyalists — in the lurch: Kandaharis who feared the vengeance that would come down from the hills, Britons who awaited Boer reprisal in the Transvaal, and African natives who were now to be left to the mercy of the frontier rifleman. And could it be said that British interests were served by these actions? The Afghan Amir, a man who had spent twelve years in Russian Turkestan, was pledged to be guided in his external relations by the Viceroy of India: in other words he would have no truck with Russia. But who could trust the bond of an Afghan Amir, in whose country we had debarred ourselves from having British agents to watch and report? The Transvaal Boers were pledged to retain the 'suzerainty' of the Queen of England, but no one was clear what that word meant, and it was certain the Boers would not debate the matter with any enthusiasm. Apparently the Liberals hoped all would turn out for the best — but that was not a policy.

This charge of dereliction of duty was to become familiar. It was a dereliction of our duty to guard the Pacific to allow the Germans to colonise New Guinea, having debarred our own Queensland colonists from doing so. It was a dereliction of our duty to keep strangers out of the Indian Ocean to allow the French to penetrate Madagascar. It was a dereliction of our duty to the Irish people to do any kind of business at all with Parnell's Nationalists; and (when in his 1886 Government Gladstone came out for Home Rule itself) it was a dereliction of our duty to preserve the United Kingdom to give the Irish an Irish government. It would certainly be a shocking betrayal of Ulster loyalism if it were handed over to the mercies of a parliament on College Green. (This handy weapon, to be used by his imperialist posterity with great effect, was forged in a flash by Lord Randolph Churchill.) It was, finally, a dereliction of our duty to the European bondholders of Egyptian loans to allow conditions of anarchy to prevail in Cairo — and it was in this odd case that the Liberal Government accepted the charge and endeavoured to pacify its critics.

The British intervention to quell Arabi's attempt at a nationalist *coup* in Egypt, the bombardment by a British naval squadron of Alexandria in July 1882, and the subsequent occupation of both Cairo and the Suez Canal by imperial troops commanded by Sir Garnet Wolseley, marked — depending on the point of view from which these matters were judged — either the Liberals' coming-of-age as imperialists, or, the betrayal of every principle for which the party professed to stand. The Gladstone Government, deserted at an hour of crisis by their French colleagues in Egypt, and rebuffed by a Concert of Europe from which Bismarck had already removed the essence, went ahead with a spirited foreign policy indeed. 'A bombardment is a horrible thing,' was Granville's private comment, 'but it will clear the air and accelerate a solution of some sort or other.'[1]

What was the problem that required an accelerated solution? It was the problem that Palmerston had done his best not to have set: the problem of a weak state with a priceless asset, beset by people only too anxious to lend it money. The only British interest in Egypt, as Palmerston had never tired of pointing out, was the existence there of a thoroughfare, free and unmolested, for the passage of our mails and men to India and the East. In the days before the Suez Canal was opened we had had no problem. The Turks had been glad to oblige us, and, in 1858, 5,000 British soldiers had travelled on the Suez railway *en route* to India to deal with the Mutiny. Anglo-Indians had long pressed, and the Foreign Office had long toyed with, the idea of laying a railway from the Mediterranean down the Euphrates Valley; but Palmerston had withheld his support from this admirable strategical concept because its construction would involve us too deeply in the internal administration of the Ottoman Empire, and would inevitably provoke Russia. But the French, inevitably provoking England and not greatly caring, went ahead to back de Lesseps' project, and in 1869 the canal at Suez was opened to international traffic. The commercial advantages to England were at once as obvious as Palmerston's critics on this subject had always pointed out: but the political disadvantages were equally as acute as he had always pointed out to his critics.

[1] 12 July 1882, ibid., p. 420.

The Suez Canal was more than a highway. It was an adventure in finance-capital, and it brought to Egypt vagrant *chevaliers d'industrie* as well as honest merchants. It introduced the Khedive Ismail to the delights of the European system of credit, to such effect that the public debt of Egypt rose in sixteen years (1863–76) from £3 million to £91 million. Interest on loans he contracted reached 9%, and a loan of £32 million to Egypt in 1873 yielded only £20 million. Ismail was a spendthrift of a high order, but he never met anyone to point out the error of his ways. While his credit was good the going was good, and so the guardian of the British lifeline to the East fell more and more into the hands of French and Levantine capitalists who would not greatly concern themselves with strategical issues. In this state of affairs, where the Canal was an international corporation subject to a Turco-Egyptian charter, to French maritime law, and to the operation of British diplomacy, a complicated 'Egyptian Question', as part of the general Eastern Question, came into being.

That it was a political question of the first importance for England Disraeli had no doubt. His action in buying up Egypt's share (44%) in the Canal Company, which the Khedive in his financial plight would have sold to the French, together with his entitlement to 15% of the profits, was an effort to strike a balance. It was not more than that: popular opinion thought at first that he had bought the Canal, or control of the Company — in the public mind, then and later, there was no meaningful distinction between the two — but this was not possible. What Disraeli did was to give England a distinctive and important financial footing in a country where everything was geared to the power of the franc. To the charge that the interest we now had in the Canal, and in the Khedive's financial ventures, was such that we would be forced to make Egypt some kind of fiscal protectorate, he had no straight answer to make. The thing was clear on the face of it: 'but it was not I,' he commented to a friend with some feeling, 'who built the Suez Canal.'

Derby explained to the House of Lords that what we wanted in Egypt was an uninterrupted passage and the absence of any foreign control.[1] He explained it more simply to the French Ambassador: England did not want any exclusive right in Egypt, but only to stop anyone else from getting one. When Gladstone attacked Disraeli's *coup* in buying the shares as a dangerous financial adventure,

[1] 3 H 227, 8 February 1876, 43.

Disraeli answered him that it was a political transaction. The Canal was the road to India, and Egypt was an inn by the way. No more than Palmerston did Disraeli wish to own the inn: but we must have some say on what sort of tenants it contained. It was now that the sea-route to India began to take on a certain romantic glow that had never attached itself to the painstaking scheme for building a line down the valley of the Euphrates.

The French were the men in possession in, though not of, Egypt, and plainly we should have to work with them. This was a nuisance, but it was a fact that had to be faced. When in 1877 it became a possibility that Russia would bring down the Ottoman Empire, there was a general assumption in Europe that England would take her chance to make off with Egypt; but Salisbury assured the French that England was turning and would continue to turn a deaf ear to all suggestions of that kind. It was the Government's intention to keep as far clear of Egypt's internal finances as was possible: Evelyn Baring, the British member on the public *Caisse* or Commission of the Public Debt, was appointed to his post not by the Government but by the British bondholders. But Anglo-French relations continued distant. French opinion as much as that of English Liberals was startled by the British acquisition of Cyprus in 1878. Against whom in the Levant did the British require a *place d'armes*? The explanation, that they wished to have a vantage-point for guarding the affairs of Armenia, and for keeping an eye on what the Russians were doing somewhere near Mount Ararat, seemed to the French a little thin. They were of course mistaken: Salisbury was wondering whether not only Cyprus but Alexandretta might be taken over, for from there a railway down into Mesopotamia might be started after all — this would rescue us at least from all the Egyptian complications with the French. The French construed this British desire to be rid of them to be positive rather than negative: and when Egyptian finances crashed in 1879, and the powers of Europe thought it better for the future security of their investments that Ismail should be deposed, the joint Anglo-French 'Dual Control' suffered much from mutual irritation and suspicion.

The French had to be endured. What was unendurable was that a third irritant should enter in the person of Arabi Bey and his zealous young band of reformers. Egypt was a lay figure, to both the British and the French: signs of life in it were startling in their implications. A nationalist movement, in the opinion of the British Agent, Colvin, had some admirable features, but it must learn beyond what limits it could not go, and there were disturbing signs of xenophobia to be perceived in this one. Nor was the new Khedive, Tewfik, to be trusted: the idea of an Egyptian Army — though not one commanded by Arabi — seemed to appeal to him. Matters came to a head in riots and disorder: Europeans feared for their lives and property, events took a lurch into that limbo where the expected becomes the unusual and the remarkable the commonplace — and the English Liberal Government occupied Egypt.

Here was a forward policy indeed. Or was it? The Liberal reluctance to admit it caused more uproar among Conservatives than the policy itself. The Government refused to recognise that in the international sphere a watershed of policy had been reached. Gladstone still wished to pursue non-intervention in Egypt — still wished to walk, as Granville put it privately, on the edge of the razor. The Liberal refusal to face facts brought another series of charges of dereliction of duty down in thunder upon the Government Front Bench.

We ought not to leave the frontier of our new Egyptian *protégé* open to incursion by the fanatical dervishes of the Sudan. We ought not to close the frontier, for that cut off legitimate and traditional Egyptian influence from the Sudan. We ought to avenge the defeat of Hicks, a British officer in the Khedive's employ who tried in 1883 to take an Egyptian force to Khartoum, then being besieged by the Mahdi's levies. So we ought not to send Gordon — not on the retired list, but a serving British Army officer — to evacuate all remaining Egyptian detachments from the Sudan. Having sent him, we ought not to prevent him from using whatever men and methods he thought best fitted to help him in his task. We ought to have sent a relief expedition to his aid, months before he asked for one. We ought not to have deserted him — while he was taking no step to carry out his orders — so that he fell victim to the dervishes at Khartoum a few days before Wolseley's relief columns could reach him (26 January 1885). This was the last and conclusive charge: for Gordon's death aroused the Government's opponents and many of its supporters to a sense of shock and rage which did not pass. Hartington, who at the India Office had loyally swallowed misgivings about the propriety of evacuating Kandahar, parted spiritual company with the Liberal tradition henceforward. Wolseley himself, whose intellectual leanings were towards Liberalism, now threw in his lot with the imperialists.

Gordon's end was construed as a symbol that British interests, and the traditions of mission and of courage, were held cheap by the Liberals, and as a sign that in their hands the honour and security of the country was not safe.

Gladstone himself did not understand this charge. Gordon's death had been a misfortune, as the death of a brave man must always be, but the resultant howl of anger alarmed him less for his own political prospects than for the sanity of those who uttered it. What kind of British interest, definable to commonsense, was an interest in the Sudan? We had gone into Egypt because there was a risk the country might pass to hostile hands, its administration be subverted, and its debts repudiated. To Gladstone a debt was a debt, and it was part of the public law of Europe that it should remain enforceable. (That the debt itself might be usurious was beside the point of principle.) The good government of Egypt was a British interest — so far was he forced to concur with the imperialists — but a *British* government of Egypt was no such thing. It would be an unwarrantable burden. It was therefore our intention, as soon as we had restored the position in Egypt and made life and property there secure, to take our forces away. He would not concur that Egypt was an anteroom to India whose keys we must keep, for where did that argument lead? Why, it led straight into the barbarities of the Sudan, as an anteroom to Egypt — and ten years later Gladstone was to observe that it led straight down the Nile Valley into Uganda, as an anteroom to the Sudan. This sort of thing was not policy but lunacy. Our interests in North-Eastern Africa must be kept to a minimum: Egypt was to be accepted as a task in hand, but as a task with an appointed end. It was false to say we had a duty to Egypt to guide her in the arts of civilisation, a duty which cancelled the pledge we had made to retire. We had no mission in that area, and could not invent one. It was a greater mission to see to it that the British Isles themselves were governed in harmony and peace.

The Liberal Prime Minister was permitted to repudiate the Sudan — as Salisbury jeered, to go to Khartoum to please the Whigs and to leave it to please the Radicals of his party.[1] But in 1886 he was not permitted to repudiate responsibility for the proper

[1] 3 H 294, 23 February 1885, 1317.

government of Ireland by giving it Home Rule — an imperial issue
if ever there was one. The Conservative nostrum of 'twenty years of
resolute government' was thereafter to find areas of application
further afield than Ireland with the full approval of the majority of
the electorate, which used its new enfranchisement — given it by
the Liberals in 1884 — to vote into and maintain in power the Conservatives from 1886 to 1905, with only a three-year Liberal inter-
val (1892–95), during which an unfortunate Liberal Cabinet
appeared to observers 'like Polar explorers marooned on a melting
ice-floe'.[1] So unexpected a development was this, that it could not
fail to make a deep impress on Liberals themselves: even Wilfrid
Lawson on the Radical wing could not say, as Gladstone himself
had said when the Tories won in 1874, that they had been drowned
in a torrent of gin and beer. (The 'Liquor Power' was formidable,
but not that formidable.) It could only mean that Liberalism was
out of touch with the people, that its ideas of progress were no
longer related to the kind of progress that the democracy wanted.
It was noteworthy that Gladstone's last genuinely popular act, one
that drew approval even from Balmoral, was the attitude he adopted to the Russians' displacement of some Afghans from the
frontier village of Penjdeh in 1885; for, in calling on Parliament for
a vote of credit of £11 million to enable the Government to pursue
a warlike policy if necessary, he proved that to the Indian frontier
at least, thus early, bipartisanship had come.

Just prior to this a conference had been convened at Berlin,
under Bismarck's chairmanship, to decide what modes and methods
should govern the action of the Powers that were preparing to partition Africa. Although very few of the concrete decisions adopted
on this occasion were ever adhered to by these Powers, this was still
an important affair. It made it clear that imperialism was abroad in
the world, was the recognised *Zeitgeist* and an approved European
policy; and that not to be an imperialist was not to be present, was
to be an absentee from great transactions. It was private enterprise
that had opened Africa, and both the British and the Germans
hoped that private enterprise would have the lion's share in exploiting it while Government was content to hold the ring. Four
Chartered Companies each were launched in the 1880's by both
Britain and Germany, with this intention in mind. Of the British
companies, two of whose charters were granted by Liberal and two

[1] J. A. Spender and C. Asquith, *Life of Asquith*, (London, 1932), I, 91.

by Conservative Governments, three operated in Africa. The fourth concerned North Borneo, and as this unexpected foray into eastern waters represents the first positive action of the anti-imperialist Liberals in the imperial arena, it deserves some atten-tion. It came up for discussion in 1882,[1]

Granville, introducing the Bill to legalise the charter, went out of his way to deny that this granting of a charter to the trading enterprise already established in Borneo constituted an imperial policy. But, if an advantageous case arose which gave political and commercial favours to the nation, while involving it in no extra duties, would it not be 'an act of doctrinaires' not to take the matter up? (But what else were Liberals, their opponents must have wondered, but doctrinaires?) The Government had been advised by their law officers that the new charter did not pledge them to afford any greater degree of support and protection to the Borneo Company than would be extended if it were simply incorporated under the Companies Act. The charter did not vest any sovereignty in the Government; the latter's power was limited to a power of objection and dissent in any matters conducted by the Company which might affect foreign Powers, or were concerned with native questions. Any disregard of the Government's views on these matters might entail cancellation of the charter.

Now, this was not much of a case, and its inadequacies would have been rubbed in further by the Conservatives had they not as a whole approved of the policy, if not of this explanation put forward on its behalf. But some criticisms could not be resisted. Borneo did not exist in a vacuum: other foreign Powers had something to say. As recently as January 1880 the Conservative Government had assured both the Spaniards and the Dutch that we were not con-templating the establishment of any kind of dominion in North Borneo. The protests now made by Spain and Holland against the Liberal Government's action were, however, treated with con-siderable brusqueness. It would have been interesting to note the Government's attitude had Germany made any comment on the business. Moreover, the possession of a great area like North Borneo was surely excessive enjoyment for a commercial company run on limited liability principles. Did it not say in the charter that the Company was authorised and empowered by the Queen to acquire the sovereign powers? Did that not imply that sovereign

[1] 3 H 267, 13 March 1882, 708-24.

powers in North Borneo were within the Queen's gift? Did it not say that every director was to be a British subject? And, while observing the existing customs of the natives, as the charter instructed, were these British directors cheerfully to acquiesce in slavery and head-hunting, which were among these existing customs? (It was because of a similar obligation that Gladstone in 1873 had set his face, unsuccessfully as it had turned out, against any annexation of Fiji.) Did it not all come to this: that the Government was creating a British political Company, to use as a puppet? The Government was in fact 'filibustering by proxy' because it lacked the nerve to do the thing in the open.

To all this Gladstone could not find anything very effective to say. (Alfred Dent, the Borneo trader, was not the first or the last entrepreneur to say to a British government, give me two good reasons why not.) British enterprise, Gladstone noted, had always had a tendency to expand, and sometimes to expand in undesirable ways: it was not forty years since the days of Rajah James Brooke in this same North Borneo, who had summoned up Her Majesty's ships from the China station to fight his private battles among the Dyak head-hunters. It could not be made a penal law for Englishmen to go and settle beyond the existing limits of the Empire, but it was necessary to obtain what control one could over such tendencies — both for the sake of the Englishmen themselves, and for that of the (sometimes unfortunate) peoples amid whom they settled. It was on this principle that during these same past forty years we had been compelled to accept hegemony over vast areas of the Pacific. This Borneo case, then, was not an annexation.

In law Gladstone was right. If it was anything, it was a 'permission to view'. Later critics were to object to this entire principle of chartering companies of men who often confused the desire to make money with the desire to govern men, and whose officials indulged in gasconading in the name of the English people. But anything that diminished direct reponsibility was hailed in the 1880's as a genuine contribution to the relief of our overburdened governmental system, which not only had too great a volume of business to digest but the burden of Irish obstruction also on its back. Moreover, Gladstone and other statesmen may genuinely have thought that commerce and politics were looked on as entirely separate things beneath the tropical sun. The wording of the Borneo charter was used as a *pro forma* when the Royal Niger Company was permitted to begin an official career in 1886: but George Goldie found too much that was vague in it, and wrote down what he wanted the politicians to give him. It was his Niger charter that the Conservatives copied when in 1888 they allowed William Mackinnon to establish the Imperial British East Africa Company. These Companies all operated within a particular 'sphere of influence' — a phrase much in favour at the Berlin African Conference — whose frontiers were never ascertainable. Not surprisingly their agents indulged in a great deal of filibustering by proxy, staging many a frontier incident where no frontier was. Frontiers that have status in law must have received the *imprimatur* of Government, and thus Government action in Africa could not long be delayed. European Governments indeed concerted seven international agreements on African frontiers between 1890 and 1894.

For they had found out that it was one thing for a lone explorer to open a country — another to keep the country opened. It was felt that railways were the best means of doing this; but here again no Chartered Company — save Cecil Rhodes' own empire, the British South Africa Company chartered in 1889 — had the wherewithal to build railways. Moreover, what capitalist would consent to lay a railway, a tangible property, along the ground of an intangible fiction like a sphere of influence? No two views agreed as to what this concept meant, except that the area in question was staked out for its protector's use in his own good time. The British had some experience of the concept at work in India: there, there had been such a thing as the 'country power', in whose sphere all chieftains paid tribute for their protection. Englishmen like Lugard, Thomson, Johnston, Rudd, Sharp; Frenchmen like de Brazza, Monteil, Marchand; Germans like Nachtigal and Peters — all walked up and down Africa with packets of 'treaty forms' in their kit. These treaties, when marked with the X of the local potentate, were worth only what the European Chancelleries said they were worth. A potentate who had struck a bargain with a Portuguese might find his territory within the sphere of an Englishman or a German instead, without his own opinion being asked. In three months of 1884 Germany staked out all her colonial claims, both in Africa and in the Pacific. France between 1880 and 1886 consolidated positions already held, or found new ones to consolidate, in Tahiti, Tonkin, Tunis, Madagascar, and the New Hebrides, and established agreement with Germany about spheres in Africa.

But all these colonial 'spheres of influence' were only dice in an international game controlled from Europe. Bismarck, when asked what would prevent the French in Africa from entrenching on the less well-manned German territories there, answered briefly, 'A sortie from Metz.'[1] (He may not have meant this — but it was a disagreeably Bismarckian thing to say.) Baring in Egypt, now Viscount Cromer, kept in mind what he felt was too often lost sight of, that Berlin and not Cairo was the true centre of gravity in Egyptian affairs. But Salisbury at least looked at matters from the same angle. 'The threat of making us uneasy in Egypt through the actions of France,' he wrote in November 1887, 'is the only weapon Bismarck has against us, and we are free of him in proportion as we can blunt it.'[2] Control and centralisation were therefore the essential things: too much colonial buccaneering in Africa was dangerous, and might upset the balance carefully poised in Europe.

No European Power ignored this possibility, and it is because each took pains to insure against it that the scramble for favourable position in Africa did not become lethal. But the boundaries soon hardened, and the sphere of influence, the useful invention of one decade, was obsolescent in the next. Salisbury warned the Liberal Government in June 1894 that it was not safe these days to establish your title to a large territory and then to leave it there without making any effort to assert it in a practical and effective way: 'the whole doctrine of paper annexation is in a very fluid and uncertain condition.' His colleague Chamberlain, the Liberal-Unionist leader, had made the same discovery in regard to developments in the hinterland of the old settlements in West Africa. He declared that we must not allow the history of the Gambia and Sierra Leone colonies — two enclaves locked within French territory — to be repeated in the case of the Gold Coast.[3] He and the agents of the commercial interest in West Africa therefore set to work to see to it that history took another turn.

The stakes of this game were not African territories alone. Asia contributed. The Anglo-Indians, who had long wished it possible

---

[1] A. J. Marder, *Fear God and Dread Nought*, (London, 1952), i, 191.

[2] 2 November 1887; Temperley and Penson, *Foundations of British Foreign Policy*, p. 460.

[3] 4 H 53, 24 February 1898, 1622.

to enunciate some equivalent of the Monroe Doctrine which would seal off the immediate perimeter of India from any other foreign intervention, were now expressing the traditional anxiety not only about the north-western frontier but about the security of the eastern flank as well. The French could already be found — so George Curzon informed readers of the *Nineteenth Century* — at a place called Dien Bien Phu, a place quite valueless save as an outpost on a line of advance which if followed would take the French deep into Siam and so to Burma's eastern gate; for Lord Randolph Churchill's spirited annexation of Upper Burma in 1886 had not surprisingly stirred the French, at their base on the Mekong in Indo-China, into equivalent action in the same theatre of operations. Where else the French would go was still a matter for conjecture. The skirts of the Chinese Empire were thus being rent, and the Manchus were being pressed into the European loan-market, a sure sign — as the Khedives of Egypt could have told them — that their end was beginning.

It was already anyone's guess whether the Chinese or the Ottoman Empire would fall first, and a matter for hard calculation in the Chancelleries to whom should be allocated valuable portions of the débris; and although firm arrangements as to the destiny of the Turkish Levant were not made until the twentieth century's first world war was under way, Salisbury had some interesting conversations with St. Petersburg as to the possible disposal of the Turkish heritage in 1898. Keeping thus one if not three steps ahead of events, the Governments of Europe experienced considerable exhilaration as they set to work to expand the frontiers of Europe, and with them the area of the civilised life.

What kind of exhilaration this was in England, is hard now to discover — looking back from an age that does not know what exhilaration is. It can be argued that it was produced by some kind of moral morphia, injected into the body politic in order to dull the pain caused by the loss of the mid-Victorian supremacy. The fall of foreign investment in the 1870's, the intermittent depression of the 1880's, the passing of industrial leadership to the United States and Germany, had made Englishmen conscious — as Macaulay's generation had not been conscious — that their lead was after all not secure, that a glorious destiny must be worked for, not simply awaited. Chamberlain's hunt for a policy, foreign, domestic, imperial — any policy — that would bring his country and himself

F

some spectacular success bordered at times on the feverish. Certainly a constant activity, an inability to remain still, the use of a shrill tone, may all be signs of nervous disorder; and the emanations of jingoism at its worst indeed provide proper study for those who wish to understand group neurosis. What, for example, can be made of the incident of the Mahdi's head? To desecrate the tomb of a religious leader, to use his skull as a football, to strew his bones in the Nile: these are symbols of a state of mind easier to imagine than to describe, and no explanation could be returned to the indignant questions put by Winston Churchill on the matter in the House of Commons, for there was none that was rational. It was therefore in vain that John Morley urged the House not to forget that, although native and oriental governments might be and indeed generally were cruel, fierce, and violent, yet nevertheless the peoples who lived as subjects to them were often contented enough, and in their own manner experienced a satisfaction that 'they could never derive from boons conferred upon them by the cast-iron benevolence of foreigners and aliens.'[1] Nor was the wry comment of the Sherif of Mecca likely to command applause in the west. Speaking of the doings of the British imperialists in Asia, he had observed that '*ses victimes sont condamnés à vivre*'. Imperialism, now with the official stamp of European culture upon it, appearing in print without deprecatory quotation-marks, was not to be put out of countenance by such asides from the Radical member for the Montrose Burghs or from some impertinent potentate of Islam.

For to all educated Englishmen, the term 'oriental government' was merely a synonym for malevolent despotism. The Ottoman Empire continued to exist as a sovereign state because it was a European necessity, and a particular British interest, that it should do so; but a series of Whig, Tory, and Liberal Governments in England had pressed on a succession of Sultans the urgent need that they should set about reforming their entire governmental structure. Such a reform must entail the establishment of an efficient and honest administration under the rule of law. But the plain fact, one plainly realised by the Sultans themselves, was that no such policy could be applied to the administration of an oriental State without wrecking it and strewing its very foundations broadcast. By its intrinsic nature, an oriental State was incapable, even

[1] 3 H 294, 23 February 1885, 1077.

had it had the will, of transforming itself into a simulacrum of Victorian England.

Englishmen had already discovered the truth of this in their dealings in India: the English Resident at the court of the native prince, who, at first anxious only to guide and to suggest, ended by usurping all the governing powers of that prince, was a stock figure in the history of the expansion of the British *Raj*. In India, moreover, in this same cause of imposing reform from above, the English had gone further than they would ever have dreamed of doing at home. They had deliberately reduced the feudal classes, the one genuinely conservative element in the subcontinent, to political impotence. They had thus 'democratised' the Indians, while maintaining their own exclusive autocratic form of government. In so doing they made it inevitable that the eventual aspirants for national leadership in India would not be scions of the old dynasties, which had at least the tradition of sovereign power, but the English-educated clerks who had no such tradition — men who were anyway resentful at being compelled to occupy the lowly posts they held because no others were open to them. The English put not their trust in princes or in the proletariat: only the aliens in India, the English themselves, could be relied upon to pursue policies of progress, and to ensure a good and incorrupt government.

Seen in this light, imperialism was a rescue-service. Men so different as Rhodes and Cromer, Livingstone and Milner, Curzon and Chamberlain, shared the missionary impulse. The ambition Cromer set for himself so early as 1882 sets the keynote of all his later policies in Egypt, and of all similar policies elsewhere. He wanted to lead the Egyptians from bankruptcy to solvency, and so on to affluence; to lead them from the tyrannies of their Khedive to the principles of British justice. But if these things were to be done, it was first necessary to use one's power to sweep away the many obstacles that lay in the path.

Plainly, then, the task of teaching the processes of the West to the inhabitants of the East, of disseminating civilised principles among backward races, would be a long one; but that consideration should not be allowed to deter us. It was this that made the Liberal Government's quick promise to evacuate Egypt, to take the troops away within six months, impossible to fulfil. Having destroyed the only government the Egyptians had, the Liberals could not get up and go, leaving the ground cumbered behind them, and without

having installed a better government in its place. Better government could not be set up overnight: to excavate the foundations took
time. In January 1883 Granville, explaining the action England
had taken, informed the Powers of Europe that we would stay in
Egypt in the meantime to give advice; but twelve months later he
was pressing Cromer to see to it that when advice was given to the
Khedive, the Khedive followed it. 'Surely,' Cromer protested
that same year,

> it is a cruel fate that drives me, with all my strong opinions against the
> extension of territory and the assumption of fresh responsibilities, and
> with strong anti-Jingo convictions that deepen each year I live, to be
> constantly making proposals which, at all events at first sight, have a
> strong Jingo flavour.[1]

Indeed it was a cruel fate, as his Liberal masters who had already
suffered it could have told him — and Cromer's later proposals
even at a second or third reading seemed to have the same tang. By
1887 he had reached the firm conviction that to give power in
Egypt to any of Wilfrid Blunt's nationalist friends in Cairo was
'only a little less absurd than the nomination of some savage Red
Indian chief to be Governor-General of Canada'.[2] By 1892 he was
lecturing the new Khedive, the young Abbas II, in such round
terms that he expected to have 'no further trouble' with him[3] —
but in fact he made Abbas an enemy of the British for life. Power
cannot corrupt the incorruptible, but it certainly grows on people:
and although anything written by Blunt about Cromer must always
be read with caution, there is much point to his remark that the
latter's annual reports on Egypt, presented to Parliament, were
written 'as usual, in his first-chapter-of-Genesis style'.[4]

Good government was better than self-government, although
orientals, particularly Egyptians, could not be expected to understand this. Chamberlain, at the time of the British invasion still a
Radical, and therefore an opponent of fighting for the interests of
bondholders, approved our plans to introduce reforms for the sake
of the fellaheen. His friend Dilke was not so stirred by this cause.

---

[1] Baring (Cromer) to Northbrook, 4 April 1884; Lord Zetland, *Cromer*,
(London, 1932), p. 92.
[2] Baring (Cromer) to Salisbury, 1 May 1887, ibid., pp. 164–5.
[3] Baring (Cromer) to Rosebery, 12 November 1892; Rennell Rodd, *Social and
Diplomatic Memories*, (London, 1922–25), I, 196.
[4] Blunt, *My Diaries*, II, 98.

In all Egypt, he observed in a recapitulatory debate in 1893, there was nobody of weight who wanted us except our own officials. We could not allow a National Assembly to meet, because we knew what it would say.[1] Evacuation of Egypt, like the execution of Scheherezade, would thus always be postponed for some good reason. But imperialists who saw there was a paradox here defended it as a necessary element in the situation, odd though it might appear to uncomprehending outsiders. Lord Randolph Churchill insisted that 'Egypt for the Egyptians' could only, paradox or no paradox, be attained by a prolonged British occupation, acquiesced in by Europe at large, and provided for by a firm and unquestioned British administration. The Egyptian case was part of a great whole. The maintenance of the British Empire depended upon the determination of the British people to pursue a just and a righteous policy — upon their continuing to fulfil, as the years went by, 'their great, their proud, their peculiar mission' of diffusing among the peoples who were now, or who might later become, subject to their rule, the blessings of civilisation, freedom, and peace.[2]

Alfred Milner, who published his book *England in Egypt* in 1892, declared that paradox was rooted in the soil of Egypt — and such was the success of the book that this phrase was quoted about as if it contained some major truth which must govern all policy henceforward. In Milner's view it was useless to import European skills into a backward country without also bringing in European authority to control their employment; and it was in the sense of this conviction that he considered himself, quite without irony, as 'an Egyptian'. Even the Radicals found themselves taking up positions of this kind. When they urged that we ought not to meddle in the Sudan because it would mar the progress that had been made in Egypt, it was of course pointed out to them by imperialists that if they had had their way in the past, there would have been no progress to mar.

These then were the tasks that together made up 'The White Man's Burden'—so defined by Rudyard Kipling in 1899, in an exhortation to the United States' government. He stressed that the reward the white man got for carrying it would assuredly be

> The blame of those ye better,
> The hate of those ye guard

[1] 4 H 11, 1 May 1893, 1646.
[2] W. S. Churchill, *Lord Randolph Churchill*, (London, 1906), I, 156.

and that he must also be prepared to

> Watch sloth and heathen folly,
> Bring all your hopes to nought.

In this enterprise, the imperial mission, there were no gaudy trophies to win, nothing save the satisfaction of knowing that one had done one's duty. The duty passed from one generation to another. In India Jawaharlal Nehru's attention was caught and held by the attitudes of mind that passed with it. In 1936 he wrote how the British approach to Indian problems fascinated even while it irritated — 'the calm assurance of always being in the right', faith in their racial destiny and contempt and anger at the un-believers and sinners who challenged the foundations of the true faith — 'there was something of the religious temper about this attitude.'[1]

This, then, was the temper that expressed the current sentiments of Service and upperclass England as a whole. Imperialism in its best days, of its best type, was always equated with service. Prestige, like all respect, depended on one's conduct and character. 'In Empire,' Curzon wrote, 'we have found not merely the key to glory and wealth, but the call to duty, and the means of service to mankind.'[2]

Critics called this cant — and a type of cant 'more corrupting than the unblushing denial of right'.[3] For even in the high-minded Curzon no one could fail to perceive disturbing signs of self-exaltation, of a kind that could provoke even his professedly imperturbable colleague Arthur Balfour to acute exasperation. Conceit is more contagious than missionary zeal, and there were plenty of people with no particle of Curzon's devotion to the principles of duty and honour who used and cheapened his language. Jingoism, L. T. Hobhouse pointed out, was a kind of moral slang. Imperialism itself was a process of intellectual dry-rot. The notion, said Leonard Courtney, that we must go anywhere to prevent anarchy must be fought against, for when we went to prevent anarchy we created it.[4] Calls to duty were all very well if they were properly answered: there had been such a call in Armenia at the time of the

---

[1] Jawaharlal Nehru, *Autobiography*, (London, 1936), p. 428.
[2] G. N. Curzon, 'The True Imperialism', *Nineteenth Century*, January 1908, 157 ff.
[3] L. T. Hobhouse, *Democracy and Reaction*, (London, 1904), p. 29.
[4] G. P. Gooch, *Lord Courtney*, (London, 1920), p. 176.

Turkish massacres in 1896, but England had preferred not to hear
because, forsooth, of our 'imperial commitments' (an argument
with a future). Service to civilisation and to mankind was not, it
seemed, so readily provided where no question of self-interest was
also involved.

But J. A. Hobson, who wrote in 1902 what was to become the
most famous analysis of contemporary *Imperialism*, was well aware
that honesty in this matter was not all on the one side. He accused
imperialists of 'phrase-mongering', of using what Ruskin had
called 'masked words'. But they did this to conceal their paucity of
thought. Hobson made no charge of hypocrisy. Hypocrisy, after all,
is a product of the reason, an assessment of means. There is never
any enthusiasm in it, and even barefaced greed furnishes no adequate stimulus to a long policy. The real trouble as Hobson saw it
was that the imperialists — well organised in small but interlock-
ing groups, wielding influence not in political theory only but in
social life, in sport, in the public schools, in the cadet forces, in the
scouting movement, in the Press, in the pulpit — believed in what
they said and in what they were doing, and he knew he could not
convince them by any words or by any pages of closely-reasoned
argument that 'every enlargement of Great Britain in the tropics is
a distinct enfeeblement'. Imperialists on the whole knew nothing of
the tropics, and could not be impressed by facts relating to them.
The main point to them was that, if there were tropics in the world,
it was right that a large share of them, at the least, should belong to
England. Presentation of statistics thus could only add fuel to the
camp-fires on each side. How many Englishmen who proclaimed
their outrage at the presence of the French at Fashoda knew where
Fashoda was?

What caused Hobson his greatest depression was his conviction
that modern imperialism, far from being ended after its setback
in South Africa, was only just begun. The lesson that the British
imperialists were drawing from their South African experience
was not that their policy there had been a mistaken policy, but that
their equipment in carrying it out had not been up to the proper
mark, and that therefore a task of repair and renovation of the
available forces was now the first essential.

That imperialism required a moral justification had long been
admitted. Hobson agreed here with Chamberlain, for both men insisted that its only justification could be its contribution to the

civilisation of the world. Where they disagreed, was in that Hobson denied that imperialism made any such contribution, while Chamberlain argued that it was a self-evident fact. A doctrine of trusteeship over backward races had existed as part of English intellectual currency since the days of Burke, but Hobson took for his self-evident fact the historical record as he saw it — that every trustee abused his powers, and thus the whole doctrine of trust was an ideal fiction, a target never consciously aimed at. When the Great Powers did concert together on colonial matters, it was not to lay down a standard of civilised values, but to make business deals, as the present condition of China and Africa testified. In such deals not much was heard of the welfare of Chinese and Africans themselves, who no doubt held opinions on such numerous compulsory labour ordinances as were now the commonplace in all tropical colonies which would not accord with the views of the protectors of those colonies. At best, it was impossible to claim more than this: that some consideration was taken of justice in the exercise of the authority assumed, and that — incidentally — the welfare of the 'lower race' was subserved by the play of economic and political forces not primarily designed to secure that end. It could not be pretended, for example, that Persians had greatly benefited from the return of Baron Reuter to the favour of the Shah, from his Imperial Bank, from his friends' Mining Rights Corporation (on whose board Curzon sat), or from the granting of a monopoly of the purchase, sale, and manufacture of the entire tobacco crop of the country to a new Imperial Tobacco Corporation of Persia. The riots that had resulted in 1891–92 from this last foreign imposition had ushered in a period of internal confusion and disorder which, as Hobson wrote, had not yet come to its end.

The philosopher Herbert Spencer added his support to the anti-imperialists. In imperialism there would always be the relationship of the captive and the free: yet these terms too were misleading, for the relationship itself was one of capture — the guardian was not free to detach himself from the man he led by a chain.[1] Imperialism must therefore always depend on the successful assertion of power. It was in this that Spencer and thoughtful Liberals saw the principal menace to the liberal tradition of England. Imperialism bound itself to spread this tradition, but it had to employ methods while doing so that directly rebutted what this tradition had taught.

[1] Herbert Spencer, *Facts and Comments*, (London, 1902), p. 113.

These methods, the methods of militarism, had penetrated our social life. Note how it was a Salvation *Army*, they were Boys' *Brigades*. See how an undistinguished book like Creasy's *Decisive Battles of the Western World* had gone into thirty-two editions. On what logical ground was the Great Peace Exhibition of 1851 celebrated in its jubilee year by a great naval and military exhibition? To Spencer, militarism was just another aspect of the rebarbarisation of the nation. Intellectual virtues were being relegated to a low place. Where, he asked, in a touch of inspired high comedy, could one find a photograph of all the Senior Wranglers of the year?

Thus passion roused passion to meet it, and the temperature of English politics at the height of the imperialist movement — between 1890 and 1900 — is feverish. Beatrice Webb's assertion that imperialism was only

an impossible combination in British policy of Gladstonian sentimental Christianity with the blackguardism of Rhodes and Jameson[1]

certainly came as direct from her heart as any of Curzon's *dicta* from his.

Imperialism as a policy was the easier to attack in that its adherents themselves belonged to differing groups and promoted differing ideals, thus presenting no firm front of *argument* to rebut their argumentative enemies. Many of the most extreme, the jingos, were incapable anyway of reasoned argument, and it was certainly one of their number who first discovered that the niggers began at Calais. Patriotism may not necessarily be the last refuge of scoundrels, but very often it is the first platform of fools. So much nonsense about racial pride and *kultur* was emitted that it is not surprising that the foes of imperial policy believed it had no firm foundation at all. Here they were wrong, for there was a foundation, built of some such stones as these:

Imperialism is a policy forced upon a civilised nation by the very fact of its civilisation. What had the doctrines of *laisser-faire* led to in England itself but the breeding of domestic barbarism in factories and slums and sweat-shops? What did it lead to overseas but the exploitation by wiseacres of the ignorant? The horrors that resulted — in the Congo, at Putumayo, or in the New Hebrides — were not the results of any 'imperial policy'. Rather were they

[1] Beatrice Webb, *Our Partnership*, (London, n.d.), p. 190.

the consequences of its absence. These things were bound to spring from a lack of control, a lack of imperial governance. Where there was no such governance, civilised vice rather than virtue was the first lesson learned by native races. From this they must be protected. Such races were unable, not having the knowledge, to maintain a civilised rule themselves. Such a rule it was the duty of a civilised nation to provide, and therefore the government of dependencies was a necessity in the modern world. This was surely self-evident: why would anti-imperialists not see it? None of them were callous men, indifferent to suffering: but still they continued to object to any step taken by the State to put an end to such suffering. They seemed content to diagnose evil; they shrank from the cure because the cure involved the use of force. They talked of the sacred principles of liberty and independence as if these principles could be torn from their social context — for what were liberty and independence but products of a civilised law, and what was the independence and liberty of an African savage but a bondage to tyranny and superstition? Under the protection of the British civilised law one quarter of the peoples of the earth had been released from these bonds. Was this not a genuine achievement, of which men might righteously be proud? If imperialism could bring such a thing about, was it not something for all men of goodwill to encourage — to purify, certainly, if such purification was necessary, but to encourage, to assist, to develop? Bernard Shaw, in his *Fabianism and the Empire* (1900), was so impressed by the strength of this argument that he took up a stance at no great distance from that of Chamberlain himself. If the Chinese, he argued, could not establish conditions in their own country which could promote peaceful commerce and the civilised life, then it was the duty of the Powers to establish these conditions for them.

The great *fait accompli* of India under British rule continued to stare both the imperialists and their enemies in the face. Debates on Indian policies usually witnessed one Front Bench hurling *tu quoques* at the other: if something had gone wrong now in India, that was because the other Party had done something inexcusable ten years ago. It would have been gratifying if the frontier had always been in alarm when imperialists held the Government, and always quiescent when Liberals were in office: but Afghans, Pathans, Afridi, and Waziri seemed to count all Englishmen as one, imperialists to a man, and thus kept both sides of the English party-system in a state of agitation. What else did the claims of England to India rest upon, the mild Tory Stafford Northcote had once enquired, but the divine right of good government? How large was this assumption! A divine right? Were Englishmen, then, a race of Mahdis, men with messages from heaven? Good government? — when in Asia the bulk of the troops and the police must always be Asians themselves?

Lytton, Disraeli's Viceroy, whose intellect could always be relied upon to perceive the core of an argument, had turned this particular attack, early in the battle, in a direction that was hard to parry. He agreed that it was just to ask, concerning any policy that involved annexation, what was going to be the limit of it. He realised that war and conquest were thought by many men quite sincerely to be utterly detestable, and he joined them in condemning wars that were anywhere undertaken to gratify personal ambition, to indulge national vanity, or to provide active service for an army. But once that had been said, there was more to say. War and conquest were still potent agents of civilisation. Conquest by the Romans had made possible at length the diffusion of Christianity and the development of public law. It was from savages that Englishmen and Spaniards had wrested control of the Americas. The Russian Empire had been formed after a series of wars with barbarous tribes of which Europe knew nothing. The whole history of British rule in India supplied a further example of the same theme. Where did the critics of conquest *per se* draw the line? They objected to his own Afghan policy because it involved conquest; but, on that ground, had we any right to Peshawar, to Lahore? To Delhi and to Calcutta? To India itself? 'My Lords,' Lytton said,

I believe that the most consistent and candid of my critics would answer these questions plainly and directly enough. They would say, and indeed some of them have said, we have no business in India at all. It was by crime that we acquired our power in India. The only justification for its maintenance is that its downfall would be injurious to the natives; and the only attitude that befits us in that country is one of penitence for the sins of our forefathers, with an anxious desire to expiate, if possible, their fault.

But just because critics held that view, it disqualified them from forming any trustworthy opinion on the policy best calculated to

maintain and uphold the Indian Empire. No one should try to administer an institution of which he entirely disapproves. (Here
Lytton showed his ignorance of English party tradition.) He declared further that he would not himself attempt to refute these
views, as they were held so passionately that no argument could
convince to the contrary. But he did not believe, nor did he suppose
that the English people believed, that an Empire could have been
founded on robbery and fraud, when we were told in the same
breath by those who made that assertion that the Empire so founded
must nevertheless be maintained because, if it were not, 200 millions of people would be relegated to the anarchy and bloodshed
from which they were slowly emerging:

> 'Grapes do not grow on thorns, nor figs on thistles': and it is surely not
> under the protection of thieves and robbers that men sit beneath their
> own vines and figtrees in undisturbed enjoyment of the peaceful
> fruits of honest labour.[1]

Lytton's patent sincerity could not but impress. Even more impressive, twenty years later, was that of Milner. The young men
who heard Lytton's argument, who looked about them in the early
eighties and considered these matters, were men who came to look
askance on the rigid views of their seniors, who still spoke of Cobden in tones that an Israelite might have used who had accompanied Moses. Milner in his youth, like Cromer all his life, was a
Liberal. His sense of mission expressed itself at home in his interest
in the policies and ideas of Socialism. The true imperialist, in his
view, could not help being a zealot for social improvement, and
must feel that the existence in Great Britain of so vast an unskilled
population, at the mercy of every adverse economic wind, was a
national disgrace. Socialism was never a nightmare to Milner,
something which could be countered only by cowering under the
bedclothes. There was, he felt, a nobler Socialism, born of genuine
sympathy and a lofty and wise conception of what was meant by
national life. The true antidote to revolutionary and anarchical
Socialism was practical social reform.[2] Opinions like these kept him

[1] Lady Betty Balfour, *Lord Lytton's Indian Administration*, (London, 1899),
pp. 445-47.
[2] Speech, 29 October 1907. For Milner's views in general see the collection of
speeches and papers published in 1913 as *The Nation and the Empire;* and Edward
Crankshaw's searching analysis, *The Forsaken Idea*, (London, 1951).

out of the Conservative party even when he had thrown over his
allegiance to Free Trade — unlike Cromer, who always kept his —
while his views on imperial questions were to sunder him entirely
from the Liberal party. Milner thus became what he called himself,
a civilian soldier of the Empire.

They were Indian civilians who first founded the proconsular
tradition: the Lawrence brothers in the conquered Punjab, Bartle
Frere in peaceful Bombay, whose ideal of Empire was more a per-
vading influence than a system of administration. But it is in
Milner that the tradition has its greatest exponent. Above all else,
the role of proconsul called for a remarkable singleness of mind. It
was this quality that led Courtney to call Milner's 'a lost mind'. It
was the same quality whose lack in Henry Lawrence had finally
divided him from his brother John. Milner like John Lawrence saw
straight, but narrowly. For example, in 1897 he declared that South
Africa was the weakest link in the imperial chain, and accordingly
set out to strengthen it. But here he set himself an impossible task,
as the Boers of the Transvaal and the Orange Free State had conceived their destiny in quite other terms. When they made their
views plain in action, Milner saw no need to change his course.
When after a prolonged war, which they lost, they had convinced
everyone else that they were a nation, they never changed Milner's
mind. In 1906 he was still declaring that he could not understand
how anyone who was not a pro-Boer could regard with equanimity
the prospect that the very hand that had drafted the Boer ultimatum
of October 1899 might within a year or so be drafting Minister's
Minutes for submission to a British Governor-General who would
virtually have no option but to obey them. In 1908 Milner saw the
then Government in South Africa as 'government by the com-
mandos', and in 1909 expressed his impatience with the vaunted
'triumph' of the Liberal Government's settlement of the Union.
Was there something wonderfully original or ingenious about just
throwing up the cards?

It was for a Government to govern, for an Imperial Government
to govern imperially. To Milner, both the British Constitution and
the party system — the twin delights of Sir William Harcourt's
heart — were 'antiquated and bad'. They made it simpler for
people to do nothing than to have a positive policy. Together they
composed a system that would never be able to cope with the firm
running of the Empire. In this diagnosis he was quite right — but

his prescription for the trouble, to change the Constitution and to reconstruct the party-system, was entirely impracticable. Milner indeed never clearly understood just how massive were the walls at which he elected to beat his brilliant head. There was more in the opposition to his plans than ever met his eye. There were some things, more firmly based than oriental governments, which could not be so easily swept away in the strong and confident tide of an overriding imperial idea. Where, he asked, were the masons to build the structure of a unified Empire? That was the prime necessity. A unified Empire would be the strongest Power in the world: but a power for good, and a power for peace. It was not domination by Great Britain that Milner sought, but the creation of a fraternity of a group of nations which would be British in spirit even if it could not be all British in race: 'a co-operative Commonwealth'. This sentiment could be heartily applauded by Canadians and Australians, but Milner was not primarily interested in sentiment. An imperial sentiment indeed existed, but that alone did not and could not constitute a practical and effective union. It only made one possible. Loyalty to the Empire, however inspiring it might be as a motive of action, was becoming more and more difficult to practise. This would always be so, while the conception of the Empire as a single State was not embodied in any institution other than the Crown.

There was not even such a thing as an 'Imperial Service' that a man could enter. New machinery was necessary, new ideas, new ideals. Let a Federal Council be constituted, and it need not sit in London at all: let it meet at Sydney, at Ottawa, at Johannesburg even. Let the British Empire become an institution. Let Imperialists serve it anywhere in the world. 'When we, who call ourselves Imperialists,' Milner insisted,

> talk of the British Empire, we think of a group of states, independent of one another in their local affairs, but bound together for the defence of their common interests and the development of a common civilisation; and so bound, not in an alliance — for alliances can be made and unmade, and are never more than nominally lasting — but in a permanent organic union.[1]

As for the dependent Empire in the tropics, that must be brought to the same degree of maturity and prosperity as the great white

[1] Speech at Johannesburg, 31 March 1905, *Nation and the Empire*, p. 90-1.

Dominions — but there history had decreed that Britain's alone was the task.

The whole task was one for Titans. And the Titans were never to be found. The men that Milner himself trained in South Africa — men like Leopold Amery and John Buchan, Geoffrey Dawson and Lionel Curtis, who carried the impress of Milner's ideology on their thinking to the end of their days — were to spend many of those days trying to add the necessary cubits to the stature of their political contemporaries: if never quite failing to influence, never quite succeeding in guiding, and themselves remaining (although often in high position) on the fringes of the country's political life, eccentrics and seers, whose prestige was never commensurate with their powers.

Yet in Milner's ideology there was a ringing appeal, an appeal that awoke echoes that even the iron clamour of the twentieth century never wholly obliterated. In his own time it made a deep mark on the Liberal Party itself, and the wrath which Liberals wreaked on Milner when his South African policy went so far astray is itself witness to the influence and force of his ideas. For Milner said nothing illiberal. Liberals had long been men who promoted missions, were devoted to duty, who subordinated selfish interests to that of a concert of nations. The march of the times had made Liberals search their consciences in a way that had not been necessary in the calm days before Disraeli. The existence of legacies, the existence of trusts, posed new moral responsibilities which could not be ignored. We had, for example, by arduous work and the use of the power of the British Navy extirpated slave-trading at sea: was it not a natural corollary to this policy that we should go into Eastern Africa, into the hinterland there, to put an end to the Arab emporium based on the overland slave-trade? Was the torch lit by Livingstone to be allowed to sputter out?

It was Lord Rosebery, once Gladstone's delighted host during the Midlothian campaign, who caught the public attention as the Liberal who had squared to this and to similar problems, the man with a mission, the man of the future. Rosebery as distinctly as Joseph Chamberlain after him saw Empire as a necessity of international power. It was for this reason that the one-time ringmaster of Midlothian took great pride in his establishment of the principle of continuity in foreign policy when he succeeded Salisbury in 1892 as the Liberal Foreign Secretary. Rosebery held that foreign policy

had become more of a colonial policy, and that it was every day becoming more embodied with colonial interests than ever before.
Formerly, he agreed, our foreign policy had been mainly an Indian
policy, and this had indeed brought us into complications which we
might otherwise have avoided, 'but which we felt were rightly
undertaken to save so splendid a possession.'[1] He conceded that
there were two views on this, but insisted that the other view was
more than a little myopic. The moving finger had writ, and facts
were facts. Since the seventies we had been laying our hands 'with
almost frantic eagerness' on every tract of territory adjacent to our
own, or desirable from any point of view that we thought it desirable to take. That had had two results. Firstly, we had excited to an
almost intolerable degree the envy of other colonising nations, so
that we might reckon, in any future international complication, on
their active malevolence. Secondly, in the process we had acquired
so enormous a mass of territory that years must pass before we
could settle it, or control it, or make it capable of defence, whether
the attack came from within or without. All this had marked out a
policy 'from which you cannot depart, if you would'.[2] The clock
could not be turned back.

But of course Rosebery was not one of those Liberals who only
wished it could. These were stirring times, full of challenge, testing
the mettle of a nation. It was the mission of England, he declared,
'to make it part of our responsibility and heritage to take care that
the world as far as it can be moulded shall receive the Anglo-
Saxon, and not another character.'[3] Indeed it seemed, as he spoke
from this new and attractive 'Liberal-Imperialist' platform, that
the world could be so moulded, and even that so unlikely a spot as
Uganda — where, if Salisbury was to be believed, four if not five
European Powers were advancing towards the headwaters of the
Nile — should receive this Anglo-Saxon impress.

Uganda became the touchstone between the expansionists, on
both sides of the Houses, and their foes (on Government back-
benches during the 1892–95 administration). Harcourt led the
lamentations with force and skill. Uganda was a horrible quagmire,
another Khartoum in the making, and with a peripatetic Lugard

---

[1] Speech at Leeds, 11 October 1888; 'The Foreign Policy of Lord Rosebery',
reprinted from the *Contemporary Review*, July-August 1901.
[2] Speech at Edinburgh, 9 October 1896, ibid.
[3] Speech at Royal Colonial Institute, 1 March 1893, ibid.

more culpable even than a stationary Gordon; for after all, Gordon
had been the accredited agent of a British Government, while
Lugard was only the servant of something called the Imperial
British East Africa Company. And what precisely was that? What
were its purposes and ideas? Had a body of men interested in commerce the right to pledge the authority of the British nation to a
host of bloodthirsty savages, groups of whom wore their Catholic
and Protestant beliefs as they did their leopard-skins? Were the
days of the East India Company come again? Were we going to set
up, by dubious proxy, another Indian Empire in Africa? Was Sir
Percy Anderson at the Foreign Office going to be allowed to draw
his Central African frontiers as far north as the Mediterranean?
Did we really expect that running a railway into Uganda — supposing the thing were feasible — would disconcert the slave
traders? — as if we were going to run them off the route like a rival
omnibus company?[1] For the axe that missionaries were grinding
Harcourt had little respect; but the missions found in Rosebery a
valuable friend. He told a deputation from the Anti-Slavery Society
in October 1892 that in Central Africa the Government had set its
hand to the plough, and that the continuity of moral policy,
exemplified in this matter of extirpating the slave-trade, was a moral
force by which England had to be judged. This was language no
distance at all from Chamberlain's, who exclaimed that he could
not understand this measuring of duty and honour by the money it
cost, and that it was Britain's 'manifest destiny' to be a great
colonising and civilising power.

The Uganda case had one merit, in Harcourt's eyes. Unlike
Nyasaland — which Cecil Rhodes had been privately financing, at
a cost of £10,000 a year, since 1889 — it had to be fought out in
Parliament. A great deal of Harcourt's anger at these colonial transactions sprang from this point, that they were so seldom done in
the open. In these faraway territories there were troops, missionaries, commercial travellers, and Foreign Office agents all hard at
work, all with their own plans, and none of whom bothered to
consult either the opinion of Parliament or of the nation as to
their validity. A few men were left to partition a continent. It was
too much to expect of human nature, however high-minded and
honourable one assumed everyone involved to be, that they were

[1] 4 H 2, 4 March 1892. 71; A. G. Gardiner, *Harcourt*, (London, 1923), II,
193-5.

G

not making some blunders as they went along — blunders for which we should all be held responsible. Imperialists might like to think they had a strong centralised government. Harcourt only wished they were right — for then at least they would have been able to keep their enthusiastic agents under distant skies in better control.

Although in fact devoted Empire-builders like Lugard were kept under closer rein than Harcourt knew, here he was touching on a point where Government was particularly sensitive. Since the early 1870's all Governments had found it increasingly difficult to transact all the business of Parliament in the way they would have wished. Both Disraeli and Gladstone at various times had complained about the accumulation of public affairs and the overloading of the administrative system. Chamberlain, always ready to put in train radical overhaul of whatever system he came into contact with for the first time, was quick to suggest that some kind of devolution of local affairs in both Ireland and Scotland might relieve the pressure at the centre, but his political break with Gladstone in 1886 on the question of giving Ireland the outright Home Rule the Irish wanted put out of court for him any further possibility of experimentation in this direction. The procedure of Parliament and the progress of the legislative programme had indeed totally collapsed under the deliberate pressure of the Irish members' obstructive tactics between 1877 and 1882. The procedural revolution in Parliamentary manners and business that these tactics produced had greatly curtailed the time at the disposal both of Front Bench and private members. Business always pressed, and the end of every session saw a race to clear off a mass of arrears in a very short-tempered atmosphere. Thus the known predilection of Disraeli and Salisbury for what was quickly called 'secret diplomacy' did not (and does not) need to be construed as indicative only of their natural guile — as the Radicals always construed it — but might also be attributed to their natural wish to ensure that one vital branch of the national business was organised so as to operate with maximum efficiency.

But Radicals had heard Ministers saying just this for so long that they had some reason to suppose that Ministers had more to hide over and above what might properly be allowed them in the way of diplomatic secrets. It had been as a result of a motion by the Radical Labouchere, carried by a majority of four notwithstanding opposition from both Front Benches, that the estimates for the diplomatic and consular services had in 1868 been separately itemised for the first time on the supply Estimates as a whole, thus giving Members an opportunity to cross-examine the Foreign Office on what it had been doing. It was a motion that had long been annually presented, and which Palmerston had always opposed on the ground that, if it were adopted, there would be brought about several 'most serious and injurious consequences to the public interest'. In 1886 the Radicals, Labouchere again in their van, put forward a motion that it was neither just nor expedient to contract engagements involving great national responsibilities, or to add territories to the Empire, without Parliamentary knowledge and consent. This immensely significant motion was lost by only four votes (108–112); had it been carried the history of the next thirty years might well have been absolutely otherwise. Gladstone as Prime Minister intervened in the debate to say that if the motion were approved the legislature would be given a power over the executive branch which, in his view of the constitution, was quite improper, but he allowed his sympathy with the motives of the movers of the motion to appear none the less. You cannot avoid, he told them, giving great confidence or discretion to the Executive — but he conceded that it was a risk.[1]

Conservative Premiers and Foreign Secretaries admitted no risk. In their steady endeavour to keep Members of Parliament from meddling in what did not (at least at the moment) concern them, they were always able to count on the warm co-operation of the Queen. The Queen held strongly to the old monarchical view that the conduct of foreign affairs was a part of the royal prerogative; and not all the lessons that Palmerston had tried to read to her when she was more malleable, or at any rate younger, had ever convinced her to the contrary — she knew the dynastic structure of Europe so much more thoroughly than any Minister who was in office one day and out of it the next. She always saw England as a European Power, and had warned a Whig Foreign Secretary (Clarendon) in 1869, before any imperialist fever broke out, that the argument that England's only duty was to lend moral support alone to great causes was one that, if we held to it, would lose us our position in Europe.

Only an inner ring of Ministers, sometimes only the Premier and

[1] 3 H 303, 19 March 1886, 1408.

the Foreign Secretary, saw the 'boxes' of foreign despatches in Tory Cabinets. Rosebery carried on this practice in his Liberal administration of 1894–95 — although not, of course, without militant and protracted opposition from his Chancellor of the Exchequer, Harcourt, who objected to having the Treasury committed to policies of which it knew nothing in language as vehement as that used by back-bench members in regard to their ignorance of what the Cabinet was doing or intended to do about foreign affairs. By the 1890's foreign and colonial policies had merged to become imperial policy, controlled by the Foreign Office.

A case in point is provided by the Dongola campaign in the Sudan in March 1896. Since Gordon's death we had held only the port of Suakin on the Red Sea, and this incursion into the Dongola province was an overnight change of frontier policy. It was handled entirely by the Foreign Office and by its Agent and Consul-General in Egypt, Cromer. Although British forces were engaged, the War Office had nothing at all to do with it, and, because the bulk of the expense of it was charged to Egypt, the British taxpayer had no cause to ask awkward questions. Policies so controlled and operated were therefore hardly even ascertainable until some plain *fait accompli* had been presented to the public gaze. The long inquest conducted during the 1920's on the causes of the 1914–18 war was to throw some light on the importance of the permanent officials, particularly on that of Eyre Crowe; but the name of Percy Anderson, who was Salisbury's head of the Africa Department of the Foreign Office — which drew the boundaries of British Africa, most of which still (1957) exist — is still unknown to the public.

Accordingly, Cabinet Ministers who regarded their own colleagues as men who were likely to be more hindrance than help when negotiation on some foreign affair had reached a delicate stage, were loath to encourage Parliamentary interest in the intricacies of foreign policy. Indeed, in 1901 Balfour went so far as to instruct the Under-Secretary for Foreign Affairs not to answer supplementary questions in the House, giving as a reason his view that it was impossible to carry on the difficult and delicate negotiations in which 'an Empire of this magnitude' was so often involved if the Foreign Office was exposed to embarrassing crossfire in public.[1] It was language that Palmerston would have applauded. But latter-day Ministers could never allow their natural irritation

[1] 4 H 66, 7 February 1899, 114; debate on this, 4 H 89, 18 February 1901, 325 ff.

to become marked. Only Salisbury, who became an Elder Statesman while still in office, could afford to lash out sometimes at the
ignorance of the democracy and its representatives. 'When the
great oracle speaks', he rumbled, 'we are never quite certain what
the great oracle said.'[1]

Nevertheless, the fact that the leaders of the two great parties
were, until 1910, members of the same social club — Harcourt, for
example, had more friends on the Tory benches than he had on his
own — made the task of keeping confidential matters confidential
somewhat easier. The conventions were shared. There were things
that were done and things that were not done, and it was to take the
South African War — a major moral issue like no other that confronted the imperialist doctrine — to loosen these invisible chains.
But they were loosened only, not broken. Both Liberal and Conservative statesmen sat as members of the parliamentary committee
that inquired into the Jameson raid of 1895, and, although Radicals
made a great cry about the 'lying-in-state-at-Westminster' which
resulted, the only orthodox Liberal who ventured to rise in his place
to call the conduct and report of this committee a disgrace and a
scandal to the House was the lawyer Sir Robert Reid[2] — who was
at once assumed to have forfeited both his chances of political
preferment and his own position as a highly-respected member.
Only the Irish members, and the lone-wolf Radicals whose ideas
had not changed at all with the times — who had become, so their
opponents twitted them, complete reactionaries eager to apply
policies that would have been immensely effective forty years back
— were apt to ask the really awkward questions. But it was both
easy and convenient to dismiss the Irish as ineradicably seditious
fellows, and Radical wits like Wilfrid Lawson and Henry Labouchere as buffoons whose remarks no sensible man could take
seriously, as they were not themselves serious. Indeed, it was more
than easy, or convenient: it was essential.

Lawson, for example, would remind the House that Dizzy had
always said that expenditure depended on policy. So he hoped
Harcourt would tell Rosebery that. And see Hartington yonder,
that Whig grandee who had been wont to say that if we went in for
intervention in foreign affairs we'd need a conscript army — see
him now, with Chamberlain supporting the Unionists; sitting on
one side of the House, voting on the other, conclaved of a morning

[1] 4 H 36, 15 August 1895, 51.   [2] 4 H 78, 30 January 1900, 211-12.

with Salisbury and sitting in the evening next to Gladstone. There was nothing new (Labouchere would take up the story) in the alliance of the Whigs with the Tories: Palmerston himself had been a Tory in an easily penetrable disguise. To the Whigs, politics had always been a game between two rival aristocratic bands, with office as the stakes. They were always ready, indeed eager, to ally with the Tories when they thought the democratic coach was going too fast for their own comfort. Tories, he added, never could believe that people could govern themselves: they always thought it was necessary for some superior class to step in and govern them. It was pointless therefore to charge Tories with being imperialists. Naturally they were imperialists: they couldn't help it.[1]

What could a self-respecting, orthodox party-member do, in the face of this sort of thing, but laugh? Labouchere in particular, whose philippics against any form of extravagance, fiscal or mental, are remarkable for their cogency and prescience, was never able to scotch the conviction on both Front Benches that he was a 'character', and too clever by half: this, of course, was precisely the attitude whose prolongation had caused Disraeli himself to spend so many years working below his own powers.

For Lawson and Labouchere were underlining a vital point — that a sense of humour ill accords with a sense of self-appointed mission. A man who has a keen sense of humour will never set out to be a proconsul. Difference of opinion as to the nature of England's destiny, therefore, may often be more accurately attributed to individual psychology than to party principle. No one was better balanced and more good humoured than Campbell-Bannerman, and, in the imperialist heyday, no one so underestimated. The Uganda debates had revealed the depth of the cleavage between the young serious-minded Liberal-Imperialists, Rosebery's followers, and the older men: between Edward Grey, Haldane and Asquith on the one side and 'C.-B.', Harcourt, Morley, and Bryce on the other. There was a like rift, though never so deep, on the Conservative side. The older Tories led by Salisbury and his Chancellor, Hicks-Beach, were prepared to play politics and advance British interests against foreign interests in Africa as anywhere else — but they looked askance at moralising over what they did, held aloof from the rosier imperialist language, and were never at home with notions of mission. They looked at life from much the

[1] 3 H 308, 23 August 1885, 280, 355.

same angle as Disraeli had done. (Both the older Tories and the older Radicals were well aware of this, and gave themselves much pleasure trying to calculate what Dizzy would have said had he learned of the young Tories' desire to found a Primrose League in his memory.) The younger Tory set, whose leaders were the 'Souls' — George Curzon, Alfred Lyttelton, the brothers Arthur and Gerald Balfour, St. John Brodrick, George Wyndham — were all exceedingly serious-minded on the subject of the duties of Empire, and might well have called themselves Liberal-Imperialists had this title not already been in use on the other side of the House. To such men the Radicals' wit was not wit at all, but only an ill-bred jeering at matters they could not understand. Non-political radicals like Blunt they could better cope with, and it says as much for George Wyndham as for Blunt, that the two men were lifelong friends.

Here, then, rising to positions of leadership in both the great parties, was the younger generation of politician, believing in Empire as in a common good, and believing in the firm use of power to attain a desirable end.

Nothing in their public school education had led these men to think twice about such a view. The majority of the English public schools were mid-century creations, and from the first they were geared to a code of service to, as expressed in responsibility for, others. They were naturally conservative institutions: a father who, recalling his school with affection, wished to send his son to it, would hardly do so if he believed that everything in the place had been changed just because another forty years had passed. Since the 1870's some science and modern languages had been edging into the curricula, but a boy who wanted to get enough practical knowledge to get into Sandhurst or Woolwich still had to go to a 'crammer' once he had finished his formal education. Liberalism, the creed of adaptation to change, drew little support from those who by the 1890's were enjoying a public school education: these were, said the Liberal *Westminster Review*, the sons of the plutocrats who intended to outdo the aristocrats themselves in their devotion to good form and the things that were done — the things whose cognizance and observance made a boy a member of the team and not an outsider. The games mania, much discussed in the quarterlies, was also a product of the imperialist age, and the destruction of individuality and the regimentation that it was assumed to bring in its train caused alarm in those who recalled the idly attractive unorganised leisure of, say, Eton in the 1840's. These in particular noted that it was Warre of Eton, 'the first great schoolmaster who was neither a good scholar nor a great spiritual adviser',[1] who first suggested compulsory military training in schools.

By degrees 'the public school spirit' became one of the most potent of the imperial elixirs. St. John Brodrick (Lord Midleton), a 'Soul' who held many high posts in his public career, among them the Secretaryship of State for War and the Lord-Lieutenancy of Ireland, could declare in his autobiography — written in 1939 — that no responsibility could ever compare with that of being a member of 'Pop' at Eton. (To be high up at Eton, came an answering comment from Harrovian Winston Churchill, was enough to ruin any boy.) Brodrick of course may not have meant this: but that he felt he meant it is of sufficient importance. At Eton, and schools that endeavoured to, but did not quite, match it, a boy's steps were set on the first part of that steady and inevitable progress towards positions of command over the majority. The government of the country, notes Anthony Powell, again of Eton, was somehow made almost a personal matter.[2] As democracy gained ground this assumption was attacked because of the truth it contained. The public school, wrote Sidney Olivier, was a product of an aristocratic, propertied class, designed to produce a certain type of character for the military, administrative, and professional classes.[3] The definition seemed difficult to shake.

The 'type of character', however, had always come under fire. The characters produced, said the critics, watching youths emerging from public schools during the 1890's, were on the whole healthy, well-mannered, honest philistines, Amiable Bargees who clung to juvenile conventions as the sheet-anchors of their adult lives. By such was the oversea Empire built, by such must it be maintained. But how could it be maintained, in the hands of such people? — men with the public schoolboy's 'unlit imagination', in H. G. Wells' phrase. It was after all (said this school of thought) a combination of Third Form stupidity and Sixth Form arrogance

---

[1] E. C. Mack, *Public Schools and British Opinion since 1860*, (New York, 1941), p. 128.
[2] In *The Old School*, edited by Graham Greene, (London, 1931).
[3] Mack, op. cit., p. 128.

that landed us in the Boer War. (Yet neither Chamberlain, nor Milner, nor Kruger were public school products.) Kipling, railing in 1904 at 'flannelled fools at the wicket and muddied oafs at the goal' was objecting however not to the character of the players but to the nature of their play. What they ought to have been doing was learning to shoot and ride, so that they could have put up a better show fighting the Boers, men who could shoot and ride and who had put them to shame. This was the real 'game' to which youth should be entered. It was a piece of practical advice, and one which was adopted: public schoolboys in Flanders in 1914 shot much better. But few other practical suggestions met as ready a response from the public school world. Science was still no part of an education for a gentleman: chemistry was still 'stinks', as funny in its way as French, and biologists, like H. G. Wells, were inevitably lower-class radicals whose world and outlook did not impinge on one's own.

A gentleman might indeed, though at some risk to his social position, acquire a taste for culture and the arts. Many boys whose tastes were inclined that way had the sense to see to it that their character and status became impregnable by cultivating as assiduous a devotion to cricket, a game that only gentlemen could play, and that only great gentlemen could play really well: one of the few things, indeed, that a gentleman was permitted to do really well. A. C. Benson, an Eton master with sincere devotion to his school and its spirit, came to confess in his *Upton Letters* (1904) that it saddened him sometimes to see those

> well-groomed, well-mannered, rational, manly boys all taking the same view of things, all doing the same things, smiling politely at the eccentricity of anyone who finds matter for serious interest in books, art, or music[1]

— but it was inevitable that this should be so. The great things were the team, the code, the honour of the side, and playing the game. The game could not be played by individualists. The Empire had indeed been built by individuals, but their loyalties had come from the same source. No idealist, no logician, no humorist could govern a dependency for long without becoming aware of certain carking difficulties which might undermine his intellectual position. Accordingly the authorities saw to it, quite properly, that

[1] ibid., p. 164.

idealists and logicians at least got into Government service as infrequently as could be managed — or, if such were already in employment, that they were shunted off on to some administrative siding.

The emotional attachment to the ideas inculcated at such schools lasted a man all his life. It was a clan loyalty, like that which was devoted to Balliol under Jowett, to Garnet Wolseley's staff 'ring', to Milner's South African 'kindergarten', and to the Middle East 'club'. Like all these, too, it was a loyalty devoted to the idea, rather than to any particular practice, of Empire. From such septs have always come the most fervent loyalists, who are loyal not so much to a cause as to themselves, because they are the products and the representatives of a system and a tradition in whose context alone their lives have meaning and purpose. Men stamped in any of these moulds thought it the most obvious and natural thing in the world to pass on their view of the world and its ways entire to the coming generation. Since however there are always three generations alive at any one time, it is hardly possible for the outlook of the grandfather to be other than entirely alien to that of the grandson: it is usually only the sense of 'good form' once more, that prevents the good grandson from pointing this out. But the ideals and the idols may still throw their shadows far: and so too, very often, do the books which embalm for ever the atmosphere that so kindled the imaginations of the age that has gone. Certainly the works of John Buchan and G. A. Henty were to stand in an honoured place on the shelves of all three generations.

Buchan, the Scottish 'outsider' with his idealised admiration for the closed circle of English power, where everyone knew everyone else, where everyone knew where everything was — 'the pass on your right as you go over into Ladakh' — and where everything and everyone not so known was not worth knowing, painted a better romantic picture of Empire than Disraeli, for all his coruscations, ever managed to convey of the world of political power. His books set the standard to which imperialists should conform: a straight and simple standard, but one which only genuine white men were able to follow. Henty, writing for a younger age-group, produced some ninety volumes which are no part of English literature, but are certainly part of the historical evolution of the sentiment of self-confident imperialism. The young reader was enabled to identify himself with a hero who might accompany *Moore to*

Corunna, Wolfe to Canada, might go *With Roberts to Pretoria* or *With Kitchener to the Soudan,* and win his imperial spurs with them all. In one's presence, indeed with one's active assistance, fortresses were stormed and arrogance brought low, dramatic rescues effected and the country's honour redeemed. All this was done in the fresh air, to a code that was always implicit in the character of the hero. Yorke Harberton, for example (*With Roberts to Pretoria*) was a typical public school boy,

> a good specimen of the class by which Britain has been built up, her colonies formed, and her battlefields won — a class in point of energy, fearlessness, the spirit of adventure, and a readiness to face and overcome all difficulties, unmatched in the world.

He is the stamp of all the Henty heroes, and very willing to read about his exploits was an audience composed not only of the young idea at home, but of the Services and the settlers as well, people who were often baffled by the more obscure of Kipling's imperial incantations. Kipling interested himself in the discipline of the imperial idea and its effect upon varying sorts and conditions of men; but Henty delineated only one type of character, and it was comforting for his readers to assume that there was really no other.[1] Henty's British Empire was the gentleman's patrimony overseas: his imperialists were never jingoes, politicians, or promoters. He never took a lad *With Barnato to the Diamond Diggings* or celebrated *A Venture in Argentine Rails.*

The influence of this kind of writing is of course impossible to assess accurately, but that it had influence cannot be denied. The 'Greyfriars' and 'St. Jim's' stories of Frank Richards were still, in the 1930's, reflecting the attitudes and ideals of the 1880's and 1890's. Their illustrations still showed a hero, wrongfully accused, standing in an approved Henty pose: serious, foursquare, right hand clenched across the chest as one who despises the knife thrust of the Pathan — he is, perhaps, being charged with stealing a postal order. (This is, of course, the predicament of Terence Rattigan's *Boy,* whose *Winslow* father (1947) is pure Henty.) It became fashionable to burlesque the Henty hero, but that it was thought necessary to do so proves how tenaciously his image of the English-

---

[1] And cf. Rider Haggard's *King Solomon's Mines,* which sold 5,000 copies in two months of 1885.

man, whom Santayana called the schoolboy master of the world, has survived. For it is the *rightness* of the careers Henty describes that makes them so impressive. It is right to have a strong sense of duty, to rescue the benighted, to help the weak, and to impose stern but just government. And the reward is plain, for Henty's books have as happy an ending as books can well have. His hero earns the respect of whatever great man he has attached himself to. He is conscious of having played some useful part in a great scheme of progress. Even if personally unfortunate, he has borne witness to the strength of a great tradition: a man may not always be success- ful in a quest *For Name and Fame*, but he will hold himself the straighter for having been *Through the Afghan Passes*.

Here was a point of view thoroughly in harmony with that of the Services themselves. The Service class that governed India, con- trolled Egypt, conquered the Sudan, and intended to make an an- nexe of Eastern Africa once the Government had bought out the company promoters, did not make use of slogans, or patriotic songs, or appeals to the flag. They held themselves commissioned to the Queen and to the country, and believed that they took a wider view of that duty than did transitory Governments at West- minster. They propagated this idea with remarkable success, not only among the public but in Cabinet circles as well; for Milner's rapturous reception by the Conservatives in 1900, when the whole Cabinet turned up at Victoria Station to greet him on his mid-term return from South Africa, differs hardly at all from that given to Cromer by the Liberals, on his final retirement from Egypt in 1907. The Services always insisted that the business of India, of the colonies, and of the Services themselves, should never become party matters. There was only one opinion concerning the good govern- ance of these three matters, and that was their own. (What Con- servatives want, said Lloyd George in Limehouse in memorable words, is for the good of the nation: what anyone else wants is party politics.) In the Service view, political parties might be necessary evils at home, where there was a mass opinion whose weight had to be assessed, though it must never be allowed to obstruct paths of duty: but party interference abroad in matters that politicians did not understand, or wilfully preferred to misunderstand, was to be tolerated as little as possible. For was it not the soldier, ultimately, on whom the burden of Empire fell — the soldier who lost his life for its cause? Did this not give him rights not shared by others?

It followed from this, that the notion that imperial frontiers were national burdens was one that soldiers were unlikely to share. Officers had a vested interest in expansion: fighting the enemy, and then garrisoning his territory, kept them employed and brought them renown. An officer might genuinely believe himself and his profession to be above 'politics', but nevertheless his allegiance was automatically given to the expansionist party — and he did not hesitate to make this plain, as may be gathered from a glance at the pages of the quarterlies and weeklies of the imperial day. The rich man could get more easily into heaven, was Wilfrid Lawson's sarcastic comment, than a Liberal could reach a high post in the Army. Certainly, if an officer subscribed to a policy of inactivity, however masterly, he was binding himself to a self-denying ordinance which must hamper his military career. Had he known of them, he would have agreed with the terms of Salisbury's instructions to Lytton in India, to pursue a 'forward policy' in Afghanistan: 'Territories ultimately dependent upon British power for their defence must not be closed to those of the Queen's officers or subjects who may be duly authorised to enter them.' There were many such territories, and it was not for nothing that skirmishes in Burma were called 'subalterns' wars'.

A view of the record of additions to the Empire in the last twenty years of the nineteenth century shows that the subaltern had had ample occasion for the exercise of his skills. In Africa, he assisted in the transference from local to imperial control of 'Nigeria' and Ashanti in the west; and in the east, of British East Africa (Kenya), Uganda, Nyasaland, Rhodesia, Bechuanaland, and (by 1902) of the Transvaal and the Orange Free State. From the Arab world the Sudan, Somaliland, and Zanzibar were abstracted. In the Far East, North Borneo, Sarawak, Pahang, Kowloon, Wei-hai-wei, and Burma all became marked red on the map. By the end of the century the British had extraterritorial rights in thirty-five towns in China. The soldier was not active in all of these places: but the fact of his presence, whether in foreground or background, made their cession to British control a foregone conclusion. In none of these territories, by 1900, was there self-government. The overriding principle, one from the soldier's field pocket-book, was one of 'paramountcy'.

With this record of concrete achievement to refer to, it is no wonder that the Services were highly respected, and that their leaders constituted a political lobby, stronger in clubland than at Westminster, but noted everywhere as a vital factor.

Differing types of civilian came, now and hereafter, to much the same verdict as to the nature of this factor. Derby remarked in 1881 how the Services united almost to a man where there was a question of extending the area of British possessions — adding as an aside that fresh provinces to administer had their attractions for civilians too. This was not, he thought, a selfish feeling. It was partly a natural *esprit de corps*, 'partly an equally natural tendency to overrate the advantages of civilian administration.'[1] Cromer, England's satrap in Egypt, whose views on the virtues of civilian administration were naturally less ironical, nevertheless commented in 1896, as further complication loomed out of the Sudan, that he hoped he might be able to stop the Army in Egypt from marching into the centre of Africa — thus echoing Harcourt, who as already noted feared that British forces would shortly be marching from the centre of Africa to Cairo.[2] John Morley, in the days of his elevation (1906–10) as the Liberals' Secretary of State for India, agreed also in this view, and found it necessary to chide his Viceroy, Minto, to the effect that the Government of India, because of its inescapable military colouration, had always been, and would always be, *Jingo*.

The word made Minto wince, as it was intended to. Yet it was Morley's turn to bridle when Minto wrote him complaining of Parliament's ignorance, and its interference in affairs that it did not, and did not try to, understand. Language of that sort, said Morley sharply, offended him as greatly as Minto himself would be offended if someone were to speak disrespectfully in his presence of the King.[3] No two men tried harder than did Morley and Minto to throw bridges of goodwill across the gulf that divided their views, but the activity made both of them restive, both of them aware that too firm a devotion to the doctrine of compromise — on which subject Morley had once written a book — was, in the upshot, compromising. In fact the Anglo-Indians strongly disapproved of the vulgar jingoism of the music-hall, of the *Pall Mall Gazette* and of the *Daily Mail*, but it was also true that they dis-

[1] 3 H 259, 3 March 1881, 227 ff.
[2] Cromer to Morley, 11 April 1896; Zetland, *Cromer*, p. 225.
[3] Morley to Minto, 17 June 1908; Morley, *Recollections*, (London, 1917),II, 241, 262.

approved even more strongly of Radicals. Jingoism was at least an abuse of a high principle, but Radical Little Englandism was simple disaster. To have a Radical in the India Office as Secretary of State, no matter how mellow people all said he was in his old age, was a circumstance outwith the limits of imagination.

If the views of a man like Morley were not to be trusted, still less so were Radicals who had no experience of office but any amount of confidence in their own omniscience. After 1906 there were far more people in an important position to say the foolish things about India that had long been said in the Victorian Parliaments. In those Parliaments the achievements of Anglo-Indian officials, military or civilian, had seldom won plaudits. When Indian matters arose, expert was left to debate with expert, and the majority of Members went to dine. This should have contented those in India who objected to foolish interventions by men who knew nothing of the subject, but it did not in fact have this effect. Equally irritating were the occasions when Indian matters did arouse considerable degree of Parliamentary comment. When Indian troops were being used outside the borders of India, for what were designated as 'imperial purposes' — as in the cases of the Crimea 1854–56, Persia in 1856–57, China in 1859, New Zealand in 1860–61, Abyssinia in 1867, Perak in Malaya in 1875, Malta in 1878, Afghanistan from 1878 to 1881, Egypt in 1882, the Sudan in 1885 and the Suakin garrison till 1895, Mombasa in East Africa in 1896, and the Sudan again from 1896 to 1899 — a Radical outcry was always raised against Empire on the cheap.[1] The point here was that under section 55 of the Government of India Act of 1858, the revenues of India could not be used without the consent of Parliament to defray the expenses of any military operation beyond the frontiers of that country. This clause had been inserted so that India, in a phrase used by Salisbury in his political youth, which was often to be hurled back at him in later times, should not be used as an 'Eastern barrack in the oriental seas from which we may draw any number of troops without paying for them'[2]. Nor was it Radicals alone who objected to this practice, for Members who had themselves served in India as officials had also their misgivings about increasing the taxation on the Indian peasant in order to pay for policies that no one would ever be able to explain to him.

Again, the continuance of the Government monopoly of the

[1] 4 H 42, 6 July 1896, 801–98. [2] 3 H 190, 28 November 1867, 406.

opium trade from India to China suffered periodic Radical attack
based on both its moral and commercial principle; while the Irish
members could always be relied upon to equate some example of
British misrule in a far province with that in Ireland. Otherwise the
rest was silence. To have one's life-work ignored is the final insult,
and General Gordon, when writing to Esher in 1882, expressed the
resentment of two if not three generations of imperialists. He declared his conviction that the country would come to grief through
laziness and ignorance. 'Six united men,' he urged, 'with honest intentions, would carry enormous weight. There is no doubt that in
the recess you must not go to Scotland and shoot, but must go to
the Colonies.'[1] Esher sympathised, up to a point. For it was a fact
that the English party system was not geared to carry such a burden
as six united men with honest intentions.

What the Services were always looking for, in Parliament and in
the party-system, were clear-cut principles and discipline. As they
could never find either of these things, they assumed that the whole
organisation was as Milner found it, inept and hypocritical.

Service detestation of the Radicals was naturally bitterly recipro-
cated. Imperialists were militarists: and the genuine Little Eng-
lander saw the soldier, the whole 'Service set' as an absolute
menace. Lawson jeered in 1898 that the House of Commons had
degenerated into an Army and Navy Stores, meeting with the main
purpose of voting whatever supplies might be asked for, and to
ratify and register the results of mysterious campaigns. Imperial
governance was a closed circle of influence and power, operated by
the same aristocratic ring that had for so long ruled the destinies of
this country. It had been Bright's theory, and one still warmly
cherished, that the aristocrats had got hold of power in 1689, and
by devolving some of the prestige on to the classes beneath them,
had contrived to retain it. All their highly-publicised regard for the
liberties of Europe, all their excessive love for the balance, of
power, made up 'neither more nor less than a gigantic system of
outdoor relief for the aristocracy'. And what then was Empire, if
not an even greater outdoors, run by and for the same kind of
people? (For on the settler of that day we may take Henty's word:
'The ordinary public school and varsity man', comments one of his
knowledgeable Old Hands, 'if he has no interest [that is, powerful

---

[1] Gordon to Brett (Esher), 1882; Esher, 'General Gordon', *Nineteenth Century and after*, June 1908, p. 933.

family connection] and is not bent on entering the Army, even as a private, emigrates if he hasn't sufficient income to live upon.')

Radicals who believed this tradition was still in full force insisted that the people who were so devoted to it were not now and never had been interested so much in good government as in good government posts. Empire was much too large for the highest statesmanship to which any man had yet attained, and if we were seriously interested in its good government, we would take immediate steps to reduce its size. Cobden had never seen any *point* in our possession of India. Our connection with that country was all a perilous adventure, quite unconnected with Free Trade, and one which put a challenge to our virtue that inevitably could never be met, as no men, anywhere, were that virtuous.[1] But others had seen the point plain enough: Disraeli had caught the imagination of the middle classes with his picture of an imperial world in which their sons, if they rose, would rise to positions of great power.[2] The *Edinburgh Review* was to note in 1903, as a matter of course, and with approval, how the possession of India had afforded to generations of the British upper and middle classes a field for profitable employment.[3]

If the House of Commons could be called a stores, Joseph Chamberlain, Colonial Secretary, was its storekeeper. Had he not told admiring constituents in Birmingham that it was the business of the Foreign Office and the Colonial Office to find new markets and to defend old markets, while it was the task of the War Office and the Admiralty to ensure the protection of both land and sea commerce?[4] Practically anything Chamberlain said, of course, could rouse his enemies to fury, particularly as he went out of his way to say it in language that would provoke fury the sooner. His refusal to be daunted by economic facts was a further irritant. He had stated his belief that England benefited from, and indeed 'almost lived upon' her colonial Empire: yet figures could be shown him proving how enormous a field was covered by the 'almost'. In 1900, the imperialists' high peak, the trade of the United Kingdom with foreign nations stood at £711 million, as

[1] This was Cobden's last speech, 23 November 1864.
[2] Buckle, *Disraeli*, V, 194–6.
[3] *Edinburgh Review* (of Hobson's *Imperialism*), April 1903, p. 356.
[4] Speech at Birmingham, 13 November 1896; A. J. Marder, *British Naval Policy, 1880–1905*, (London, 1940), p. 238.

H

against the figure of £237 million for her trade with the Empire.
But this made no matter: confronted with this, Chamberlain would
as swiftly turn to propagate the doctrine of England as the trustee
of civilisation, a role to which she had every right to appoint herself. Colonial policy he summed up under three heads. We were to
keep what belonged to us. We were to peg out claims for posterity.
If anyone tried to rush these claims, we were to stop them.

To stop them would of course entail the use of armed force. Here
indeed was the crux of the anti-imperialist case, conceded contemptuously to the Radicals without argument. Doctrines of imperialism and paramountcy required a national Army at their backs.
The 'sepoy-Generals', Roberts at their head, were already urging
the introduction of conscription. But it was on Chamberlain that the
wrath always fell.

For three generations the Colonial Office had been a Parliamentary cockshy. It had lacked the dignity of the Foreign Office,
and accordingly had on the whole been occupied by men who, although many of them were able and devoted public servants, stood
in the second grade of public life. It had no tradition even of a
reluctantly-permitted 'secret diplomacy': the Foreign Office's
transactions with European Powers in Eastern Africa, though in
essence they differed little from the Colonial Office's preoccupation
with Western Africa and the French zone there, were accorded a
tolerance at least by the Opposition that was never allowed to
Chamberlain. Standing thus in a political position exposed to the
four winds, Chamberlain created further distrust by the way he
kept using the personal pronoun: a part of speech that no good
Foreign Office man would ever allow to appear in an official document. His constant bombardment of the House with fat colonial
Blue Books — 'telegrams coming forth like hot rolls' — was regarded as emanating more from a desire to promote a personal
publicity campaign than from any genuine zeal to impart information about important topics. The work that Chamberlain did that
was of its nature unspectacular — the investigation he began into
the social conditions of the West Indies, his handling of the confederation movement in Australia, of the minority problems in
Malta — few of his critics ever bothered to examine, or give him
credit for. For Chamberlain, though cut off from his domestic
Radical past, saw in Empire another great slum-ridden Birmingham, a field in which he could work with the Tories and yet not

lose the sympathy of the newer generation of Liberals. He was devoted to the idea of government action as the best engine of social reform. But his very candour was always assumed to conceal guile, and as anti-imperialism was as emotional as its converse, as it depended as much on what men thought to be true as on what was in fact the case, it was the unknown rather than the explained — what was *not* in the Blue Book, however bulky, what was contained in the telegram that did not come forth like a hot roll — that excited the passions of the Opposition benches.

Very few who sat there believed, for example, in the Boer 'conspiracy' to obtain paramountcy in Southern Africa, which Chamberlain, His High Commissioner Milner, and those who had fallen in behind them claimed to have detected, nay exposed, in the Transvaal. Kruger the Liberals cast as a simple embattled farmer, Milner as a simple plotter, Chamberlain as a devious egomaniac. These charges were not ridiculous: but they were not adequate either. Since anti-imperialism over South Africa was as irrational as jingoism itself, it is likely enough that it was Sir Edward Clarke — who had been the Conservatives' own solicitor-general — in his open cross-examination of Chamberlain in the Commons on the details of the negotiations preceding the outbreak of the war, who got further under the Colonial Secretary's skin and made more havoc of his case than did all the philippics of Labouchere and Lloyd George.[1] The Radicals, however, unable to penetrate their enemy's armour, built up a most effective political legend: of the implacable, terrible Joe, steeled in wrath, flouting the pacific leanings of his Premier, Salisbury, and hounding a panic-stricken Cabinet before him.

The middle-of-the-road Liberals in contrast found it genuinely difficult to strike a balance on the South African question. Robert Reid left them to denounce the whole business as a crime, but Campbell-Bannerman and Bryce did their best to give the Government, and Chamberlain in particular, the benefit of the doubt. It was often a painful, and therefore a distinctly infuriating, best. But then, there were so very many doubts: about the auspices of that baleful Raid, about the validity of the Uitlanders' grievances, about the actual influence and extent of Krugerism, about the plans of the magnates and their agents and the extent of their much-vaunted British imperial patriotism, about what Chamberlain would want to do with South Africa if he got his paramountcy

[1] 4 H 77, 19 October 1899, 300 ff.

there, and what he would do with Great Britain if as a result he got control, as he might well do, of the foreign policy of the country as well as its colonial affairs. The Liberals on the right, the Liberal-Imperialists who were staunch for British paramountcy, were left exposed to be the object of the Radicals' venom and the centre's doubts. They were accused by their colleagues of being the possessors of thickened consciences, of being insincere in their Liberalism, Tories in disguise, and of having nailed their colours to the fence. Charges and countercharges were made within the Liberal party ranks that were to be forgiven, but never forgotten: a decade and more later the Liberal Government, come to power with Reid on the Woolsack as Lord Loreburn, were still to distinguish among themselves between those who had kept the pass and those who had sold it, between those who on public platforms had swayed patriotic audiences to enormous applause and those who had been compelled to duck out the back door of halls under police protection in order to escape the consequences of the righteous fury of the people, and their baying cry of 'pro-Boer'.

The emotional fervours of the past are hard to sympathise with just because their essence is so hard to capture. One illustration must suffice to show the inroads they made on reason. Professor J. A. Cramb, a historian at King's College London, lectured to his students in the spring and summer of 1900, when the news from the South African veld was very encouraging, at long last, to British arms. These lectures were later published under the title of *The Origins and Destiny of Imperial Britain*. Patriotism, he told his audiences, was transfigured by a light from the aspirations of universal humanity. The universal hatred with which England was at that moment regarded by the outside world could be attributed to *phthonos*, Immortal Envy. A nation must take its chance to leap on to the back of the white steed of destiny, when that creature approached. Conscription was, after all, but National Service, and war itself had its glories — for the aim of war, when seen in the correct perspective, was not the destruction, but the intensification of life. He likened the battlefield to an altar, in a phrase that a fascist successor, Mussolini, would have avoided. Universal peace was equated with the picture of a world 'all sunk in bovine content'. Speaking of the causes of the South African war, he exclaims, 'It is for the gold, it is for the diamonds of the mines!' — but it is only a quotation from the Radicals, introduced only to be at once refuted:

'No man can believe that — no man, save him whose soul faction has sealed in impenetrable night!'

The lucubrations of a professor may not be important in themselves (though what a man says to the young must leave its impress if he says it well enough), but these were symptomatic of the jingo fever, now no longer the monopoly of music-halls, which so frightened the enemies of aggressive imperialism. The Prime Minister himself spoke out strongly against it. Salisbury noted in 1898, even before the tide reached its height, that there was a danger that public opinion in the country was undergoing too strong a reaction from what he called the Cobdenist doctrines of the 1850's and 1860's. It seemed to believe that it was the duty of England to take everything, to fight everybody, and to make a quarrel out of every difference of opinion. That seemed to him a very dangerous doctrine:

— However strong you may be, whether you are a man or a nation, there is a point beyond which your strength will not go. It is madness: it ends in ruin if you allow yourselves to pass beyond it.[1]

And this of course was just what Tim Healy and the Irish had been saying for years, that Englishmen seemed to think that the Almighty had given them a lease for ever of the universe.

But Cobdenist doctrines, it seemed, had gone for ever, and with them something of value. To these doctrines there had always been a moral as well as an economic basis. Cobden had argued that a Protectionist system, since it was the product of national exclusiveness, would inevitably lead in the future as it had in the past to international rivalries, to wars, to the increase of armaments and of taxation, to ideas of racial superiority, and, in the domestic field, to class legislation. Such burdens placed on the community must inevitably bring about a fatal severance between the forces of capital and labour, would lead to what he dreaded so greatly, the spread of the Socialist creed in England. It would be, he had warned, the Socialists who would seize the state-machine that had been created by the Protectionist party for its own ends. The Protectionists would thus dig the grave not only of their commerce but of their entire society. Free Trade, in contrast, would remove the predisposing causes of Socialism, and at the same time remove all the

[1] 4 H 53, 8 February 1898, 43–4.

dangers to the body politic which were always brought about by the misapplication of its resources.

The Free Traders could point to the record since Cobden had won his battle: fifty years of a doubled prosperity for the working classes, fifty years in which wages had more than doubled, while the price of commodities had fallen by a half or more. Fifty years in which England — save in one inexcusable instance — had lived at peace with the nations of Europe, as it was her interest to do: for the Free Trade statesmen, by emphasising and encouraging the dependence of the country on external food supplies, had made impossible a policy of force and aggression in international affairs. Imperialism, in contrast, was bound to lead back to Protectionism, for the one was the natural corollary of the other: it was no surprise to Radicals, then, that it should be Chamberlain who eventually sought to put back the clock in this as in other spheres of the public life.

For clearly Protectionism had no good economic argument to support it. Did not Britain's home market consume four-fifths of her manufactures? Was not the corresponding figure in the United States' home market as high as 96%? How, in face of this evidence, could anyone say that great countries needed Protection in order to be able to compete? To Salisbury, who saw the world from the Foreign Office angle, Protection was sheer economic error, while to Hartington — now Duke of Devonshire and the most respected of the Liberal-Unionists — it seemed that Chamberlain was dealing in the economics of a world that did not in fact exist. Free Trade was still a liberal tradition that all respected. Great Britain was a Great Power, and could afford it. Not till this condition was changed was the tradition to be discarded. Any application of the imperial idea that encroached on the freedom either of the mother country or of the colonies, as the institution of an imperial tariff assuredly would, was rejected as one that was bound to diminish and not to enhance the imperial power.

Imperialists thus disliked to be told and refused to believe that Protection was an inevitable consequence of their policies. They protested that they did not have a commercial conception of Empire at all: what they had, rather, was an imperial conception of trade. Chamberlain, in seeking to instruct them to see more clearly, and not to be afraid of what they saw, was (and not for the first time) using a logic too keen-edged to appeal to the blunter intelligences of imperialism's more emotional adherents. The essence of imperialism, as Chamberlain accurately saw it, was control; and political and economic factors cannot be so divided and compartmented that the one can be controlled while the other can be left free in its sphere of operation. This was the error the Cobdenists themselves had made, and made too long: they had gone far to convert us into a nation of shopkeepers, and had lost sight of the vital connexion between industry and defence. Economic unity, to Chamberlain and to Amery and their school, was only a first essential step towards unity of defence.

Moral factors were as hard to pare off from the political as were economic factors. Imperialism had already seized control of another element of the liberal tradition — the humanitarian impulse — as a glance at the battlefield of Omdurman, littered with its thousands, could prove. Humanitarianism in England had originally been based on an insistence on the rights of the individual man, and it had made no distinction between white men and other men — such as was now, it seemed, being made every day. Palmerston had been no sentimentalist, but it was he who had put on record, when looking back over his life's work, the comment that nothing in that record had given him greater pleasure than his action in forcing the Brazilians to abolish the slave-trade. Thirty years after his death colonial despatches from colonial Governors in East Africa were referring with irritation to the difficulties that were being caused to their governments by the troublesome activities of what they chose to term 'an anti-slavery faction'. Ah, had not all England once been classifiable as an anti-slavery faction? Was this how imperialism raised high the banner of progress? Was this how the boasted might of civilisation replaced the barbarisms of African savagery?

Orchestration on these themes could at times reach a remarkable pitch. The gentle *littérateur* Augustine Birrell, finding himself President of the National Liberal Federation in 1904, warmed to this part of his duty with great *élan*. What was the future that faced the country under a Tory Government? Why, it was a future

in which no true Liberal could breathe, a future of Imperialism, of Caesarism, of Empire, of expansion abroad in places where no white man can live, of military conscription at home, of false ideals of national greatness and of national honour.

This false Imperialism was a new kind of religion of a most bastard order, vulgar in its conception, dangerous in its growth, destructive of the love of liberty, scornful of the just claims of other races, indifferent to bloodshed. It was fatal to real manhood and to virtue, and could only end in financial ruin, political corruption, decay and death. Strong words, made the stronger because the Liberals in 1904 could see the tide beginning to turn in their favour. Events were going their way. They considered, and publicised the view, that the course that had been taken by the war in South Africa had been a blessing to England, for it had proved that we could not pursue *à l'outrance* the ill-omened policy of paramountcy. It proved that in future we would have to moderate our language, our claims, and our sense of self-esteem. For, had the war been 'over by Christmas', as was so confidently expected in October 1899, that military state which both France and Germany were convinced we intended to set up in South Africa might well have been established. But — Chamberlain, declaring in July 1904 that *our* colonies 'are not ours in any sense whatever of possession', and that there was 'nothing to prevent their separating from us tomorrow' (which was not true) was a very long way in thought, yet only five years in time, from the doctrine of paramountcy.

On the veld the British Army learned a bitter lesson, and its prestige thereafter was low. It cost the country £250 million to subdue a Boer male population which did not outnumber that of Brighton, and to deal with them conclusively we were forced to employ 400,000 troops. Examining these facts, men were forced to ask themselves the question, as they looked out, for once, to that outside world which so suffered from Professor Cramb's *phthonos*: how would we fare against a European enemy? It seemed clear that imperialism and the imperial idea which animated it must either find for itself a better military instrument — the diagnosis that so troubled J. A. Hobson — or it must change the content of its idea, and therefore its tactics, altogether. Campbell-Bannerman spoke for this opinion in his usual commonsensible way:

> The truth is, we cannot provide for a fighting Empire, and nothing will give us the power.

And he added, 'A peaceful Empire of the old type we are quite fit for.'[1] But the point was, could we get the old Empire back?

[1] Campbell-Bannerman to Bryce, 26 January 1903: J. A. Spender, *Life of Campbell-Bannerman*, (London, 1923), II, 88.

A mind very different from Campbell-Bannerman's had also been reflecting on these matters. In 1901 the German Emperor came to England to attend the funeral of his grandmother, Queen Victoria. He came from an Imperial Germany whose population at that moment, at 54 million, was 2 million in excess of that of the entire white population of the British Empire, and whose amount of steel production was half as much again as that of the United Kingdom. Kaiser William remarked to Brodrick, then Secretary of State for War, how unreal he found the ideas of Salisbury, and those of English educated opinion in general, on the question of the balance of power:

'There is no balance of power,' he observed, 'except me, and my thirty Army Corps. England,' he added, 'is shortsighted. Ultimately she will be pressed out between Russia and the United States, as she has no allies.' To Brodrick's cheerful question when this horror might be expected, William II said,

It may be fifty years — but it will come.[1]

[1] Lord Midleton, *Records and Reactions*, (London, 1939), p. 176. Brodrick's artless account deserves to be better known, as, unlike most books of its kind, it throws a lot of light down the 'Corridors of Power'.

III

THE IMPACT OF WAR: (i) THE BOER WAR

THE bill presented when the South African account was due for settlement was not financial only. £250 million were more easily found in the Great Britain of that day than a thoroughly easy conscience. It was now that the promises of imperialism could be measured against what imperialism had performed.

Two reasons for fighting the Boers had been especially emphasised in England: it was absolutely necessary that the Uitlanders in the Transvaal should be given the franchise, and that the Transvaal Government's monopoly of the supply of dynamite to the mines should be broken. When peace came, no one anywhere in South Africa had a franchise to exercise, and the monopoly was still there. The costs of administration were higher than anything previously known. Trade was stagnant, and the Rand magnates had no intention of paying out of their own pockets to help it. Chamberlain had more than once asserted while the war was under way that work in the mines of South Africa would offer a golden future to the British workman who emigrated there, and that this inevitable flood of emigration would prove his critics false who continually claimed that the Dutch would always be in the majority in the country. Now, however, it was clear that the Rand magnates were going to exclude all white labour, because they did not want the domestic history of the Victorian goldfields of Australia to be repeated on the Rand: for British labour would assuredly bring with it the machinery of British Trade Unionism, high wages, and no doubt other democratic claims. Coolie labour imported from China was greatly to be preferred as an instrument to set the mines working again, and Milner as High Commissioner allowed himself to be talked into sanctioning this scheme, thus committing a blunder that was to cast a shadow on his career and blunt the edge of many of his ideas. Indeed, the political significance of this issue of 'Chinese labour' was not, as some Tories professed to think it to their dying day, the mischievous exploitation it suffered from the hands of the Liberals in their election campaign of January 1906, but its impact on the stature and influence of Milner himself, who thereafter carried out his self-appointed mission as propagandist for an organic Empire in an attitude of defensiveness and in a tone not free from gall. As late as 1920 he was still considered by many in the Dominions, and particularly in Australia, as the instigator of a 'Downing Street conspiracy' to constrain the fulfilment of their national status.

Certainly when the issue of Chinese labour first arose it seared the conscience of the public at home, already uneasy about the implications of farm-burning and scorched earth as a military policy, and about the record of the concentration camps set up by the soldiers for Boer women and children; in October 1901 the death-rate of children in these camps had been 344 per 1,000, four times higher than in the worst slums of Glasgow. War in South Africa, undertaken to establish adherence to modern British ideals, as contrasted with those of backward Boers, had brought in some strange results. Was it true, what Campbell-Bannerman and his group had been saying all along, that the whole South African policy had been conspicuous throughout for its undeviating miscalculation, ignorance, and levity?

Even those who hotly denied these charges knew, at least, that they could no longer be shrugged away as mere impertinence. Rosebery, the Liberal-Imperialist leader, had become aware of this and stressed its significance in a letter to *The Times*. The severance between imperialists and their opponents, he wrote, 'is not simply on the war, but is a sincere, fundamental, and incurable antagonism of principle with regard to the Empire.'[1] Sincere, fundamental: these were adjectives of respect that had not heretofore been granted to mere 'pro-Boers'.

The imperial idea had thus suffered a contraction, a loss of moral content, from which it never completely recovered. When the war had begun in 1899, Wilfrid Blunt had noted in his diary his hope that it would prove to be the first nail in the coffin of the British Empire. The British Empire survived, indeed was augmented by, the South African War; but its dynamic of self-confident expansion

[1] 17 July 1901.

was dead. No further emotional capital was invested by the British public in imperial policies, which were soon, once more, to be enclosed in questioning quotation marks. Chamberlain's metaphor of the 'weary Titan' was turned against him: the Titan had now let his weariness overcome him, had ceased to struggle for mighty purposes, had become a Falstaff, gorged beyond digestion.[1] Although the Transvaal and the Orange Free State were certainly not the last territories added to the Empire in the twentieth century, they were the last that were consciously fought for by a majority of the nation.

This majority was never in fact so great as the volume of imperialist publicity had led its members to suppose. The Conservatives had returned to power in triumph at the election held in September 1900, having claimed during the campaign that to vote for the Liberals was to vote for the Boers; but even so, although the Liberals held only 186 seats in the new House of Commons, 2,105,000 people had voted 'for the Boers' as against the 2,428,000 others who had voted for Empire and the doctrine of paramountcy. But, as the war dragged on for two years more, Balfour's Government found itself confronted with an Opposition that was slowly reassuring itself that the country's opinion was changing, that the Liberals' time would come if they could manage to close the serious fissures, themselves caused by the war, in their own ranks. The Government was amazed to find, for example, its announced policy of establishing Crown Colony government in the annexed South African republics — a policy it considered genuinely liberal, as indeed in many ways it was — rejected out of hand in advance by Bryce as futile and unacceptable. Again, when the Chinese labour ordinance was first discussed in the House of Commons, Alfred Lyttelton the Colonial Secretary was the only Minister present on the Front Bench, and the resultant uproar took him and his absent colleagues completely by surprise.

In the House of Lords the Liberals' leader, Ripon, had already put forward his objections to what he called a system of 'semi-slavery', while Stanmore had trounced the analogy hopefully, or carelessly, made by his own Conservative party that the Chinese system on the Rand had much in common with the coolie-indenture system that had long been prevalent in Mauritius and the West Indies. In the Commons Labouchere now roundly denounced it as slavery without qualification, and John Burns declared

[1] Gooch, *Courtney*, p. 337.

that this debate, so ill-attended by the Tories, was the most momentous he had ever heard.[1] That Labour, which now had its own representatives in Parliament, should still be thought of as a commodity which could be imported like parcels was more than an insult: it was a direct threat to every Labour principle. And that Conservatives never appeared to comprehend what the fuss was about was a menace even more startling in its implications than sinister motive itself. How far out of touch with public sentiment, with plain common sense, could imperialists get? Sheer bewilderment — well expressed by Lloyd George — had greeted Lyttelton's statement that he found the idea of education for the children in the Rand concentration camps 'romantic'. And what, Burns asked, was the excuse of the Colonial Secretary for the introduction of this new, alien element into the South African *mêlée*? 'He had only one plea, and that was necessity, which knows no law . . . the plea with which the thief is confronted every day of his life.' Imperialists were always inveighing about the unity of imperial sentiment — but had they made themselves aware of what the Australians and New Zealanders thought of Chinese labour as a cure for economic ill?

Imperialists, long accustomed to shrugging off their opponents' attacks in Chamberlain's own imperious style, now became wrathful, anxious and unsure. Chamberlain himself, although he never retracted in public anything he had said or excused anything he had done, seemed to have lost heart, and when he intervened in debate spoke in mildly argumentative tones of reasonableness such as had not been heard from him for years. With this dubiety came caution in. Naturally it made some pause sooner than others. Ramsay MacDonald's view that the 'man on the spot' conception of imperial responsibility was a negation of the imperial idea was not one that men on the spot could be expected to share.[2] Thus the Cabinet was gravely embarrassed when Curzon, their Viceroy in India, approved a filibustering expedition into Tibet in 1904, talking the language of high paramountcy that in 1898 would have awakened all the expected echoes at home, but which now seemed sadly off-key. No annexation was permitted to take place. Minimised, too, were Curzon's efforts to strengthen the British sphere of influence in the Persian Gulf by touring that area in resplendent

[1] 4 H 130, 17 February 1904, 93–102.
[2] MacDonald, *Labour and the Empire*, p. 41.

state, as Sir John Malcolm had done a hundred years before him: to Lansdowne, Foreign Secretary, all this could be discounted as 'George Curzon's prancings in the Persian puddle'.[1] And when Curzon finally involved himself in an intricate row with his Commander-in-Chief in India, Kitchener, of the two resignations that were bandied about, it was the Viceroy's that his old friend and one-time soul-mate St. John Brodrick, as Secretary of State for India, preferred to accept. This was reckoned to be no time for beating on the imperial drum.

The main preoccupation became, once again, party in-fighting, the bitterness of which expressed the frustration of talents and emotions that had previously been expended on the broad acres of imperial policy. Balfour himself excelled at this kind of thing, and enjoyed many a fierce battle over Education and Licensing Bills; but such measures necessarily provided but flat wine for imperialists. Their leader, Chamberlain, after a visit to South Africa in 1903 — where he assured audiences that the British Empire did not mean braggart declarations, but was based upon a community of sacrifice — fell into retreat, from which he emerged with a new unauthorised programme, that of Tariff Reform, the end of Free Trade, and the institution of imperial Protection. To many Conservatives this seemed a cause more likely to lead to destruction than to popular favour, and many stayed on the fence with Balfour to see whether the electorate would be beguiled by Chamberlain's vision of an imperial emporium or bemused by the Liberals' countercry of dear food all round and a farthing on the loaf.

When Chamberlain left the Cabinet to promote this new venture, no one of his calibre and influence succeeded him at the Colonial Office, his base for eight years: nor has anyone yet done so. The pressure of the Colonial Office was now removed, to the relief of all the foes of imperialism, from the conduct of Britain's foreign policy. British East Africa and its destiny was handed over to the Colonial Office by the Foreign Office in 1905, but G. P. Gooch commented with feeling how fortunate it was that Port Arthur and all the complication attending that Far Eastern harbour were safely retained in proper hands.[2] The Foreign Office itself, suddenly drawing free breath, now celebrated its liberty from Joe and his notions by seeking to put an end to friction in two areas where im-

[1] Lord Newton, *Lord Lansdowne*, (London, 1929), p. 287.
[2] Gooch, op. cit., p. 354.

perialisms clashed, and in doing so put in train two foreign policies which were mutually exclusive.

Plainly diplomacy had much to do in a world grown dangerously hostile, and some experimentation was called for.

For the lesson of the South African war most clearly taken to heart in Europe was that Great Britain was not only a bully, but a remarkably inefficient one at that. Readers of English newspapers were never allowed to learn just how widespread and how deeply felt this opinion was, and how severe the detestation expressed both in France and in Germany, who agreed on little else, in regard to our late doings in South Africa. England had hitherto been able to make her stand in European politics on the ground that the rights and interests of small nations were her particular concern: but after 1899 this attitude appeared to educated European opinion as not merely hypocritical — an adjective applied to it often enough in the past — but as flatly ridiculous. Europe adopted the verdict given its most vivid expression in the House of Commons by the Irish members, that the whole business had been 'got up by the Park Lane South African millionaires for the purpose of grabbing the land and doubling the dividends on the gold-mines', and to this day European (and American) historians of those times have not found themselves able to rescind this judgment. Imperialising Europe had never had much conscience or care how it dealt with 'savage races', as events in the Congo and the Cameroons were shortly to underline, but for a Great Power to deal with Europeans as the British had been dealing with the Boers was seen as something ominous indeed: if England felt it necessary to adopt Prussianism as an international tactic, everyone else sooner or later must presumably follow suit. Once, emphasising the eternal interests of England, Palmerston had declared that so long as England sympathised with right and justice, she would never find herself altogether alone. But now she did find herself altogether alone: precisely because, as the enemies of the imperial idea had long been saying, she had opted to dispense with right and justice, thinking it better, or at any rate more profitable, 'to go about in Bismarck's old clothes'. In an aggressive pursuit of power, status, and prestige — those old, nefarious, Disraelian goals — England had deliberately sacrificed that moral status that had made her so respected a Power, and whose support had made Gladstone in his prime the one factor in Europe that Bismarck himself had never been able to comprehend.

But for better or worse England and her Empire were now còmmitted to promenading in Bismarck's old clothes, and before the Conservatives left office Lansdowne took out two typically Bismarckian 'insurance policies'. In 1902 he made a Convention with Japan, which was directed against Russia in the Far East. This was of a kind that should have shocked his Prime Minister, Salisbury, had the latter retained his old touch and sagacity — for by it each party undertook to go to war on behalf of the other if either were attacked by a combination of two Powers. The Convention was converted to a formal Treaty in 1905, under which Japanese support for our continuing presence in India was exchanged for ours in regard to her control of Korea. In the meantime Lansdowne, after abortive attempts to placate the German Empire without going so far as an alliance with it, had fashioned an *entente* with France in 1904 — with France, the ally of Russia. It was left to his Liberial-Imperialist successor at the Foreign Office, Sir Edward Grey, to carry these odd policies to some kind of conclusion by patching up another Convention, this time with Russia in 1907, in regard to the affairs of Central Asia and Persia. In this instrument was finally slain the Anglo-Indians' dream of establishing a Monroe Doctrine for Asia: and they, at least, were not much surprised when this deal with Russia led ultimately, in 1915, to the consignment of Constantinople itself, one of Disraeli's many keys to India, to the mercies of the Russian Empire.

Grey's policies — or what could be discerned of them from the floor of the House of Commons — were constantly riddled by the smallshot of the Radicals who sat on his left and behind him; they received, too, many heavy blows from C. P. Scott and Sidebotham in the *Manchester Guardian*, F. W. Hirst in *The Economist*, A. G. Gardiner in *The Daily News*, and from Massingham and Brailsford in *The Nation*. To Brailsford and his friends the deal with Tsarist Russia was 'an understanding with a staggering chaos',[1] and in complete contradistinction to the policy openly adumbrated by Grey's own chief, Campbell-Bannerman, who preferred the Duma to the Tsar. As to Asian affairs, Grey was so ignorant — or so declared the Orientalist Professor E. G. 'Persian' Browne of Cambridge — that he hardly knew the Red Sea from the Persian Gulf.[2] The upshot of the 1907 Convention was that, to protect Tibet and

---

[1] C. E. Playne, *The Pre-War Mind in Britain*, (London, 1928), pp. 261, 345.
[2] Blunt, *Diaries*, II, 98.

Afghanistan (and so India) from Russian influence, we helped
Russia destroy Persia's independence. Sin and folly and the constant use of too short a spoon — this was what came of truckling
to imperialism!

When Campbell-Bannerman had taken office in December 1905
before an election was held, he had felt it wise to put the Liberal-
Imperialist brotherhood into his Cabinet. (He sent one of them,
Haldane, to the War Office, that graveyard of political reputation,
with the cheerful comment: 'Serve him right.')[1] But the result of the
subsequent election — a landslide for the Liberals and the return
of 377 members to the Commons, plus another 29 representatives
of the Labour Party — proved that he need not have gone out of his
way to appease an opinion in the country that had lost its electoral
force. But there, entrenched in the highest political offices, now sat
these Liberal-Imperialists, Asquith, Grey, Haldane, in charge of
the country's foreign policy for the next decade, and viewed with
much misgiving by some 150 of their Liberal brethren who styled
themselves 'The League of Liberals against aggression and militarism'. Among these latter 'Lambs', as they were at once called,
were enrolled such staunch pacifists as Lloyd George and Winston
Churchill.

Grey had announced before the election that as Liberal Foreign
Secretary he would continue on the previous lines — a point not
lost on, and at once taken up by, Cambon the French Ambassador.
However, he makes the curious confession in his book, *Twenty-five
Years*, that he never found time to look up the Foreign Office files
to see what his predecessors had been doing between 1895 and
1905.[2] Presumably he carried on as heir to the policy of putting out
boathooks, as Salisbury had done. Yet Grey's view on Britain's
role as a moderating and ameliorating Power was much the same as
Disraeli's. Britain had to be *present* while great events took place.
Believing this, he warned the Radicals behind him that their 'other
foreign policy' of isolation, of what he called the maximum of interference and the minimum of friendship, was simply disastrous.[3]
To this the Radicals were to riposte, after 1914, that there were
degrees even in disaster.

[1] Almeric Fitzroy, *Memoirs*, (London, n.d.), I, 290 ff.; Spender and Asquith,
Asquith, I, 174.
[2] I, 35.
[3] 5 H 31, 27 November 1911, 60.

I

Radicals in general felt as their political forebears had done after Midlothian a generation back — that they had been returned to power with a mandate to reverse what the wicked Tories had been doing, and not with one to go on doing it in the sacred name of continuity of policy. 'It all depends,' said Ramsay MacDonald from the Labour enclave, 'on what you are continuing.'[1] For too long there had been agreement between the two Front Benches to withdraw foreign policy from the sphere not merely of party politics, but of open Parliamentary discussion itself. From this fact, it was charged, all our troubles had sprung. How often, Keir Hardie demanded, had members of the House been told that it was inconsistent with the stage which negotiations had reached that any public statement should be made regarding them?'[2] Was democracy to remain the pawn of the diplomatists? It was a great disaster, the Radical Josiah Wedgwood averred, to have a Liberal Government — because then there was no one to criticise the policy of the Front Bench from a Liberal point of view.[3] It was well known, notorious indeed, that the Foreign Office itself was an illiberal organisation: the fact that Grey had been compelled by political exigency to go outside the Diplomatic Service to provide a suitable ambassador for Washington in the person of Bryce was surely proof that he knew the Foreign Office's own inability to cope with democrats.

Those Radicals who did understand that there could in fact be no such thing any more as a distinctively Liberal foreign policy only blamed the ruinous doings of the imperialists the more severely for having landed all men of goodwill in so infuriating and compromising a plight. English Liberals had in happier times been able (it was said) to choose their foreign friends, and among these the Tsar and the Ottoman Sultan had never been numbered. Constitutionally-inclined and liberal-minded Russians, Persians and Turks got short shrift from the Liberal Government of England. They were Moors who lived in Morocco, but this could never have been guessed from a study of our Liberal diplomatic record. The old argument, that imperialism committed posterity despite itself, had gained in force. Brailsford, bitterly complaining that we were tied to French imperialist ambition, noted the inevitability of that tie none the less. 'We are all paying still', he wrote, 'and for years to come may go on paying, because Lord Lansdowne gave away a piece of Africa that was not his to give.'

[1] Ibid., 78.   [2] Ibid., 134.   [3] Ibid., 2620.

For the deal about Morocco, it was argued, was just another horse-trade of the Cyprus-Tunisia type. In this case French recognition of British paramountcy in Egypt had been exchanged for British recognition of French paramountcy in Morocco. The practical, apart from the moral, worth of this arrangement deserved more investigation than it got. British paramountcy in Egypt was established, and recognised by Europe: the French were yet to assert theirs in Morocco, and in the process of doing so were bound to encounter the Germans. The moral questions were, however, the louder. What rights had Britain in Turkish Egypt, or the French in the Sheriffian Empire? The Germans joined with the English Radicals in asking this question. Deeply chagrined at seeing the end of Franco-British friction over Egypt, and thus losing their own lever of pressure on British policy, the Germans now stood forth as the representatives of the slighted Concert of Europe in Moroccan questions thereafter.

Radical views seemed incomprehensible, naturally, to the majority of English people who took the official view of the *entente* of 1904 — that it was, in fact, a *détente* in the long history of imperial quarrels between Britain and France. Only Rosebery, among major political figures, recognised it for what it actually was, a major realignment of the forces in Europe. Asquith thought that we were 'still free', uncommitted, after 1904, and Eyre Crowe gives evidence that the Foreign Office had no intention of settling down as an inmate of one of the two European camps.[1] As late as 1911 Grey expressed to C. P. Scott his own surprise at finding himself in one. In this case the Germans knew better than Crowe. To get security in Cairo we would end up by supporting French security on the Rhine. So we did. The dangers of war with Germany over Moroccan questions were considerable in 1905, 1906 and 1911. How such a war could have been explained to the British people must have set the Liberal Government a pretty problem, for they were hardly able, like their Conservative opponents, to draw attention to the necessities of the Balance of Power, a concept they had long vilified. Grey's later efforts to placate Germany — by proposing to divide with her the Portuguese colonies in Africa, by giving her by the Baghdad Convention of 1914 all Mesopotamia north of Basra — further compromised the Liberal position with-

[1] Gooch and Temperley, *British Documents on the Origins of the War*, (London, 1928), III, 398–405, 420.

out releasing England from her other commitments. Grey has been often accused of not telling the German people where Great Britain stood in the European line-up; but it must often have occurred to Grey, who was neither the simpleton nor the rascal his various foes took him for, that if he had told the British people where Great Britain stood the British electorate might well have replied by turning him and his Government out of office. In August 1914 the German invasion of Belgium rescued the Liberals from a dilemma the Conservatives did not share, for even prior to that invasion the leading Tories had pledged their support to the Government, which was in their view in honour bound to stand at the side of France and Russia: but the Government was able, safely, to make Belgium the plank on which to walk with credit into the European struggle, and thus the defence of the rights of small nations became once again a part of the English tradition in foreign policy. The Independent Labour Party, when it tried to controvert this view, lost half of its members as a result. In 1922, even, Tories and Radicals had not changed their views why they had gone into war. Austen Chamberlain still declared that the honour of the country had been pledged to France by the policies pursued, or at least sanctioned by Grey, since 1904: while the Liberals and the Labour Party still assured themselves it had all been for Belgium.

While these external dangers gathered, more guessed at than seen, there were more pressing problems, obvious to all, demanding domestic attention. 'Only an extraordinary combination of fortunate circumstances,' so stated the powerful and authoritative Report of the Royal Commission on the South African War, had saved the Empire from the intervention of European Powers. The realisation that this combination of circumstance was unlikely to recur was widespread. The militarist spirit that had upheld us in dealing with the unforeseen difficulties met on the veld had long since cooled, and the conviction that one Englishman was the military equivalent of any half dozen foreigners was no longer firmly held — not, at any rate, by English soldiers. No one now exhorted his audience to corral the white steed of destiny as it approached; perhaps, indeed, it would be better to keep out of its way. Hard reality was beginning to loom through the mist generated by a decade of rhetoric. The truth was, Winston Churchill stated in the Commons in words not themselves free from rhetoric, that war was not a light and easy thing. War with a Great Power, whatever its issue, would end in broken hearts and straitened purses; 'hunger would be in our streets, and ruin in our market-places'; and when it was all over, we would find our most formidable commercial rivals entrenched in all our old vantage grounds.[1] In fact war was not a royal route to riches and success: the great game of expansion which had been played without major mishap since the seventies was now become a potentially lethal activity. War was now the last resource of policy, not one of its best weapons. But however looked upon, war ineffectively waged spelled ruin.

It had been our traditional policy, when engaged with a European foe, to use our sea-power to reduce and occupy, and frequently to retain, his colonies. Other Powers now extending overseas would certainly have noted this tradition, and might decide to adopt it. Lord Roberts, who when commanding in South Africa had found it necessary to send home eleven out of seventeen cavalry colonels, and a large proportion of brigade and corps staffs, had no illusions as to the efficiency of the British war-machine in these dangerous times. In South Africa we had in fact gone far to repeat the experiences of the Indian Mutiny forty years since — which Roberts also remembered — when everyone in a high place had failed in his task. Time to recoup error was not a gift we had a right to from the gods. Roberts urged that there could be no militarism or jingoism in bending our national energies to repair this situation, and he spent the last fourteen years of his long and vigorous life concentrating on that task, campaigning for military conscription in a series of uphill charges against prepared hostile positions. He knew this private war was one of attrition, a process that demanded just that time which he was convinced the country did not have: for, if he could not get even a Tory imperialist War Minister like Brodrick to comprehend his argument that it was a Cabinet Minister's duty to teach the House of Commons its military business and not to suffer it to teach him his,[2] Roberts felt that he was unlikely to make any better headway with the pacific Liberal Government and its cohorts. Haldane at the War Office has found more friends among his intellectual posterity than he could ever muster in high military circles in his own time.

It was not that Roberts and his propagandists spoke obscurely,

[1] 4 H 118, 24 February 1903, 699.
[2] David James, *Lord Roberts*, (London, 1954), p. 395.

or had a case easily demolished. The case was, simply, that since our success as a Power depended on our strength, our foreign policy had to be related to a policy of general imperial strategy. The main lines of this strategy must take no account of present international relations. Imperialism possessed neither natural friends nor natural enemies: the same people could change roles overnight. This was true even of our relations with the Americans, true in a sense that no amount of talk about our 'cousins' was going to change. The unity of the Empire was thus the essential target to aim at. In the long run, failing some complete reconstruction of our present system, both of our imperial constitution and of the economic basis of our policy, no efforts or sacrifices on the part of the mother country would be able to avert either the dissolution of the Empire from within, or, alternatively — or perhaps simultaneously — its forcible disruption from without. We now possessed an Empire whose territory amounted to eleven and a half millions of square miles, eight millions of which lay in the continents of Asia, Africa and America. 'We cannot,' said *Fallacies and Facts*, a handbook of this school of thought, edited by Roberts in 1911 and largely written by Amery and a more subdued Professor Cramb, 'stand in everybody's way without expecting to be jostled.' The Navy was a shield indeed, but a shield was not a weapon. By victory at sea, admittedly, Germany stood to gain the first position in the world — but by defeat at sea she stood to lose nothing beyond the ships themselves and a few colonies of comparatively little value. Great naval victories were often more glamorous than positive, anyway. We won Trafalgar in 1805: but another decade elapsed before the military power of the French Empire was brought low.

But a case presented to the public that demanded of it knowledge both of foreign policy and of military strategy was bound to be greeted with an ignorant stare. In foreign policy the Liberal Government kept its own counsel, and accepted the French *entente* without perceiving it was a signpost to a predetermined future. In matters of military strategy it had more reason to grope in the dark, for every one of its predecessors had done precisely the same thing. Successive British Governments, and the British public following this absence of leadership, belonged to the school of what Charles Dilke, in the masterly survey he made in 1887 of *The Present Position of European Politics*, called 'Luck and pluck'.

What, anyway — Garnet Wolseley when Adjutant-General in

1888 had asked — was the British Army *for*? No clear definition of its duties appeared in its files. A brief glance at these files was sufficient to reveal how far the public assumption, that Great Britain could never again have a war except with savages, would never have to fight *for* the British Empire itself, had penetrated into our military thinking. To glance from the files to a map ought to have been enough to dispose of this lunacy. All our coaling-stations and unfortified ports overseas, whose safety in the day of danger would depend absolutely on a British fleet which, in time of war with a European enemy, could not afford to be there, constituted a standing temptation to predatory Powers. When Russia and France, the most obvious potential enemies to the British Empire, became military allies in 1894 our situation became even more dire. French domination in the Mediterranean made it impossible for us to hope to hold Egypt and the Suez Canal in time of war: we would have to 'cut and run', as Chamberlain risked some measure of popularity in pointing out. The increasing Russian pressure on the Indian borders made our Army there — of 70,000 European and 130,000 native troops — look even more inadequate to its task than previously. Roberts, when Commander-in-Chief in India, had always reckoned that half the native army would be untrustworthy if ordered to take the field against a European foe. Furthermore, although the Indian princes could among them boast a military establishment costing £12 million and amounting to some 390,000 men, it was pointless to reckon this as an asset on our side. Anglo-Indian soldiers were agreed that the friendship and 'loyalty' of a prince was no defence against the hostility of his people towards us — a hostility whose continuance was tacitly assumed.

Nor could the British garrisons in India be reckoned as normal military dispositions of available force. They were troops which would have to be left behind the front line to look after the fidelity of the princes, of their 'partly useless and partly mischievous' levies, and of a portion of our own native soldiery. In fact, our only security in India lay in being able to command confidence among Indian troops and Indian peasants that we were able not only to meet attack, but to counter-attack, and do that successfully. It was all a question of confidence, of that much vilified prestige. Asians would fight on the winning side: this was the watchword of all European nations in Asia. It did not answer, therefore, to salt native regiments with white officers. The bulk of the regiments that had mutinied in 1857 had had their full complement of over 20 white officers. The native regiments must feel, must know, that the British could attack and win.

Could they?

Judging from the money that was expended on military services, this question ought to have produced an encouraging answer. In 1888 the cost of the Army amounted to some £38 million. £18 million were expended on the home Army, and £20 million on the Indian Army. For this expenditure we were rewarded with two Army Corps ready for the field. Germany that same year spent £19 million on her home Army and could produce nineteen Army Corps, with sufficient men in Reserve to make that total up to thirty-five. In a sense we could consider ourselves fortunate to have an establishment at all. Disraeli's Government had introduced in 1875 an establishment of eight Army Corps, and this in itself had caused much alarmed Liberal headshaking. Yet Liberals need not have worried, for this force never actually existed, although it continued to appear on the Army List as the official plan of mobilisation up till 1881. The Penjdeh crisis of 1885 had revealed both that we did not have a plan of mobilisation at all, and that it was absolutely vital to us to pull 5,000 troops out of the Sudan. Even in the Egyptian campaign of 1882, it had taken us a month to mobilise a single expeditionary Army Corps, and to do that we had had to strip the cavalry and artillery at home of their horses. (Yet twelve years before, in 1870, it had taken the Germans precisely fourteen days to put fifteen Army Corps on the French frontier, and they were able to meet the necessity of mounting their cavalry three times over.) On paper, indeed, we had always had plenty of men. If to the Regular Army the strengths of the Militia and the Volunteers were added the total rose to something near 600,000. Even so, from out of this horde, for the Queen's Jubilee in 1887 we were just able to manage to get one not quite fully-equipped Army Corps on to the parade ground at Aldershot. If a general mobilisation were ordered we would be able to put in the field a force equal to that possessed by Bulgaria but less than that of Switzerland. Even for the 'little wars' in the Sudan, we had been compelled to call out the Reserves — Reserves which in the view of any European professional soldier were not Reserves at all, as they consisted of untrained men.

So how could we counter-attack? How could we attack Russia, say, in Manchuria while she was infiltrating into Northern Persia and Afghanistan? Yet what were we, without the means of counter-attack? Only a couple of islands in the Atlantic Ocean, instead of what we fondly believed ourselves to be — an Imperial nation wielding a world-wide power. Ten years before South Africa threw such a glaring spotlight on to the shortcomings of our military administration it was already an accepted opinion among French soldiers that the British Army was an Army to which peace was necessary; and there were not a few who proceeded to point the parallel by recalling that Carthage, too, had been renowned for its incalculable wealth and its unrivalled fleet.

Indeed, Salisbury's discovery in the 1890's that we had backed the wrong horse in supporting Turkey might well have carried him further, to the discovery that in actual fact we had not backed any horse at all. We were physically unable to implement the famous Convention of 1878, to guard the Turks in Asia Minor from Russian encroachment. In Europe we were physically unable to protect Belgium, a commitment dating (though somewhat dubiously) from 1839. These commitments were in a sense luxuries: the British Empire would not fall if the Russians debouched from Erzerum, or Antwerp (like Cherbourg) lay in the hands of a potential enemy. But were we better able to protect the United Kingdom and India, the two lynchpins of the imperial system? (Dilke for one had no doubt that we could certainly not protect the Channel Islands, an opinion that was proved correct sixty-four years later.) On the question of the possibility of a successful invasion of this country, Army and Navy wrangled together and the public watched with great interest, as this was one aspect of the imperial strategy — 'the Englishman's home' — which it could well grasp. But the main point about the wrangle, to the imperialist, to the realist, was that there was a *doubt*.

In these circumstances, where then could be found the best defence of the British Empire which would at the same time assure us some chance of counter-attacking an enemy? Plainly in a skilful diplomacy — as much unlike as possible that diplomacy that had got us into the South African war without ensuring to us the friendship of any of the great European military powers. This skilful diplomacy must bring us the alliance, on which we must be able to count in war, of one of those great military powers. To the imperialist it did not greatly matter which, and on the whole he preferred the Germans to the French. But an ally we must have. It was Grey's great service to the British Empire that his policy obtained it just such an ally, though he never knew while he was about it just what the outcome of his policy would be.

But while no formal alliance, except with Japan, existed, the soldiers continued their agitation about the state of the Army. No great changes had in fact been wrought in this. It was Roberts' opinion in 1911 that the Army was much as it had been in 1899. It was Wolseley's opinion in 1899 that the Army was much as it had been in 1888, when he had asked his question, what was it for? He had had to frame his own answers, which the Conservative Government of the day adopted in what came to be known as the Stanhope Memorandum.

According to this, the purposes of the British Army were four-fold. It must assist the civil power to maintain law and order, when necessary. It must supply the drafts required for Indian service. It must supply the colonial garrisons. And it must have available for service overseas two Army Corps and one cavalry division — some 70,000 men. (Lansdowne, at that time Secretary for War, had greatly exasperated Wolseley in the midst of his calculations by refusing to concur that for all practical purposes the 3,000 men stationed in Egypt constituted a further permanent military commitment which had to be taken into account.) South Africa had proved the inadequacy of the allocation of 70,000 men for oversea service. The militia, the Volunteers, and the yeomanry had all had to be summoned to supplement the Regulars — and it had been clear that in these auxiliary organisations too there was a great deal amiss. Wolseley, giving evidence in 1903 to the investigating Royal Commission, held to his previous opinion that the colonies were still all undermanned, and that it was only with the greatest difficulty, by constantly robbing Peter to pay Paul, that the Indian establishment — which was anyway inadequate — was kept up at all. As for the Army's chances in a European war, matched against a professional mass army, they hardly bore thinking about. Wolseley still thought of the French in the way he had been trained, as the likeliest Continental enemy: and did not France have 600,000 men with the colours, and another one and three-quarter million in the reserve? To be sure, they were at the other side of a ditch twenty-one miles wide at Dover: but he could quote Wellington, Napoleon, and Nelson himself in confirmation of his own opinion that an invasion of Great Britain from the Continent, although a

difficult, was a feasible project. If we had an abler Admiral than
Nelson at the Admiralty at that moment he, Wolseley, was yet to
meet him.

To such a jibe, of course, the Admirals could return as good as
they got. The Army and the Navy knew nothing of comparative
strategy or joint co-operation, and when Generals and Admirals
exchanged views they welcomed, as evidence of their own superiority, the marked divergence which was at once revealed. Not even
war made much change in this: in 1917, Admiral Beatty at the
Rosyth naval base had no information, and was not disposed to enquire, concerning the plans and dispositions of the Home Defence
Forces in whose area of deployment the Rosyth base lay.[1] Admiral
Fisher's comment on the Army in 1903 may stand for an accepted
and continuing opinion in naval circles:

> One does not wonder at South Africa when one sees every day the
> utter ineptitude of military officers. Half the year they are on leave and
> the other half of the year everything is left to the sergeant-major and
> the n.c.o.'s.[2]

Civilian appraisal was much the same. Lord Esher, whose committee accomplished some very speedy spring-cleaning of the War
Office that same year, noted that it was all very well to set up
some new form of efficient Army organisation, but where were you
going to find the officers who would be able to run it? Junior
officers had indeed more charm than their seniors, but, if this
quality were subtracted, it was plain that the subaltern in no way
compared in efficiency and knowledge of his job with the ambitious
young man in every other profession. Indeed, the further the investigation probed, the more remarkable it appeared that British
imperialism should so far have so successfully asserted itself. It was
becoming clear even to the noisiest patriot that it could only have
done this so long as its activities were underwritten by the tacit
consent of the Powers of Europe — for the British Empire had
never had, and did not now possess, any engine of power to match
those of the militarised Continental nations. Now it had lost that
consent, our obvious military weakness cast shadows over the
whole future of the Empire.

---

[1] C. a'C. Repington, *The First World War*, (London, 1920), II, 15.
[2] 6 June 1902; A. J. Marder, *Fear God and Dread Nought*, I, 242.

That a modern Empire would demand land as well as sea forces for its defence had of course been a point made, and shuddered away from, by anti-imperialists from the start. One Conservative Government had appointed a Commission to enquire into matters of imperial defence in 1879. Another had begun a more detailed enquiry in 1890; the evidence put before this Hartington Commission was indeed of such a damaging nature that the Government did not venture to print it. But little had been done to deal with the findings that were at both times presented. The recommendations that Wolseley had made in 1890, that both a Ministry of Defence and an Army Council should be instituted, had seemed less important than the retention of the Queen's cousin, the Duke of Cambridge, as Commander-in-Chief, who had never trafficked in reform and would not start now. Even when Cambridge was got to retire in 1895, Campbell-Bannerman as Secretary for War still balked at setting up a General Staff; a true Liberal, he 'instinctively shrank from giving a brain to the Army, lest it might think too much.'[1]

Nevertheless in 1903, although the institution of a Ministry of Defence was (as in 1938) too dangerous a political experiment to attempt, and the creation of a General Staff had to wait for another four years, an Army Council was set up, and important internal structural alterations made in the system. In the next seven years organisation improved, if only slowly. By November 1914 there were to be six Regular divisions in France, serving in the line — but these, equipped with two machine guns per infantry battalion, were required to encounter whole German machine gun batteries, and had also to cope with an absence of both high explosive shells and motor ambulances. Moreover, Esher's point — where were the able men? — was never to be adequately met. The South African War had ensconced the cavalry, an arm that was never able to be used effectively in France and Flanders, in the high places of the British Army. It was an arm whose tactics had not greatly changed since the days of Marlborough, and whose social position was such that it tended to look down on expert advice proferred to it by engineers and artillerymen who fought on their feet. General Sir William Butler's comment that the disaster of Colenso had been solemnly rehearsed for twenty years on the banks of the Basingstoke Canal[2] finds its sad echo in Amery's observation that the

[1] R. C. K. Ensor, *England 1870–1914*, (Oxford, 1936), p. 291.
[2] Royal Commission on Militia and Volunteers, 1903, Cd. 2061, p. 28.

tactics of the British Army on the Western Front in 1916 reminded him of General Sir Redvers Buller on the Tugela.[1] Since not much had ever been expected of British officers save courage, it was courage, in the main, that was most lavishly expended. In the interim public opinion continued to disinterest itself in the fortunes of the Army altogether, seeing it merely, in Esher's words, as a glorified national constabulary, an incidental instrument for helping out the local predicaments of the India and Colonial Offices. What the public far preferred to follow were the fortunes of the Navy.

The state and welfare of the Navy, always a part of the national consciousness, had been a lively political issue since the great naval scare of 1884. Naval scares were all based on the realisation by the public that the march of technology in naval armament and gunnery was constantly rendering obsolescent the proud battle-lines of a previous day, and that in no class of modern ship could we afford to be outstripped by a rival Power: the candidate for this role, right to the end of the nineteenth century, was always France, a nation which indeed has more naval inventions to its credit than any other. Yet at no time was the body of taxpayers prepared to vote sufficient money to bring about the desired state of affairs, and successive Governments of both parties were increasingly exasperated by the element of unreason. The Liberals were naturally the unhappier both because of their economic principles and because they sincerely doubted whether the desired end was anyway possible of attainment, putting aside all question of its moral propriety. The scare of 1884 had been largely concocted by W. T. Stead in his *Pall Mall Gazette*, with the aid of Captain 'Jackie' Fisher, R.N., and Alfred Milner. It had been punched home by the subsequent disclosure that when war with Russia seemed likely in the spring of 1885, we had no plans for mobilisation, naval or military, with which to meet the challenge. Since then Stead had acted as press agent to the Liberal-Imperialists, and his 'leaders' were quarried by the Jingo popular dailies as well. The Blue-Water School had therefore become an accepted political institution.

Moreover, in the American naval historian Captain Mahan, whose historical studies on the influence of sea-power on men and events began to emerge from 1890, amid storms of applause, all advocates of an overriding sea-power had found a heaven-sent publicist who could not be accused of having any political axe to grind.

[1] L. S. Amery, *My Political Life,* (London, 1953), I, 47.

It was indeed Mahan who was the architect of that lobby through which thereafter the Admirals and the Navy Leaguers and all big-navy advocates so confidently trooped, their most notable *coup* to date being the forced retirement of Gladstone himself in 1894. Far-flung Empire, far-flung trade demanded a Navy, and as other nations began to found oversea empires and to stretch their own networks of commerce abroad, it became plain that the Navy so demanded must be such as to be able to remain supreme superintendent of the intervening seas. Everyone in Britain applauded the concept of the two-power standard: that in British naval strength there should be a margin of ten per cent over the joint battleship strength of the next two naval powers. The French and German objection, that this was merely another brand of that militarism in international affairs which England so professed to dislike, was considered an argument not worth discussing, and it was not discussed. The perverse European and American view as to the meaning of the popular English expression, 'the freedom of the seas', elicited strong language from Fisher at the Hague Peace Conference, to which he went in great reluctance in 1899. Law and order, at sea as everywhere else, required its incorruptible policeman: as to the nationality of the policeman there could, again, be no discussion.

Secure in public favour, in the favour of Radicals, in the favour of Labour members representing dockyard constituencies, the Navy became the most formidable weapon in the imperialist armoury precisely because the foes of imperialism never saw it as an instrument of imperialism at all. Nobody needed to ask the question, what was it for? Cobden's response and Chamberlain's were the same: it was there to protect our commerce and to guard our shores. It was the bulwark of those British interests that Palmerston had declared to be eternal. Liberals could not forget the record of the Navy in the task of putting down the oceanic slave-trade organised by foreigners. They were always comforted by the thought that naval officers, by the very nature of their service, were precluded from annexing large tracts of unproductive and hostile hinterland. Blue-Water Admirals and those who followed them were considered more sensible guides than were discomfited Generals who, if given their head, would pillage the entire labour-market of the country for the sake of getting some mythical 'security' — for even if every man was pressed into uniform, we would still not have an army à la Prusse. The Navy, in contrast, gave to the country a genuine security, and played a vital part in the country's economy, whereas a standing Army was one that made men stand idle, a burden on the economy as a whole. Campbell-Bannerman when Prime Minister, at the time of the second Hague Conference in 1907, when the British attitude on the navy was as unbending as ten years previously, wrote an article in *The Nation* stressing the Navy's defensive role. It was nothing if not up-to-date. Indeed, up-to-dateness in naval construction had long been a sore burden to the Treasury, for the invention of the Dreadnought was only the last in a series of revolutions in the design of capital ships which at once made existing designs obsolescent. Thus the competing Germans, less cumbered with such arrears, were thought to be able very easily to get ahead of us in this ultra-modern type of construction, and it was this that kept the political temperature in naval matters at its height: Balfour indeed warned the Government that the Germans would have twenty-five Dreadnoughts by 1912. (In fact that year they had only nine.)

The Navy was thus a constabulary that everyone took pride in. That it was a factor in Britain's power of enormous importance was also so incontestable as to be frequently overlooked. In 1923 Amery, when First Lord of the Admiralty, had this in mind when he remarked to Mackenzie King, as the two men stood together overseeing the naval review at Spithead, that it was the existence of these battle-lines that had made King himself Premier of the Dominion of Canada and not, at best, the junior Senator from the American State of Ontario.[1]

Accordingly, there was a tacit bargain made between the political parties in the pre-1914 era. The Liberals would maintain the Navy — and thus the British Empire, within its guardianship — while the Tories would not press for any form of expansion. On the whole this bargain was kept. No British Government between 1890 (Heligoland) and 1919, when a piece of Jubaland was allowed to go to the Italians, gave anything away. And the Liberals, recalling that it was their own much-disputed 'Spencer programme' of 1895 that had helped fend off European intervention during the South African War, actually laid down eighteen Dreadnoughts in the three years 1909–11. Between 1907–08 and 1913–14 the naval estimates rose by 50%. Those who would not, by their conduct,

[1] ibid., II, 276.

subscribe to the terms of this bargain were considered by both sides as extremists: here Lord Roberts and Ramsay MacDonald may be said to join hands.

To Roberts, the whole concept of Empire as a static position, not as a dynamic force, was anathema; was not acceptance of it equivalent to that old policy, which had caused such trouble on the Indian border, of 'masterly inactivity'? Would other nations agree to let the British Empire live a quiet life? The Chinese Empire was disintegrating at that very moment, at the mercy of all comers, simply because she had neither the means nor the will to defend herself. Roberts raised the cry of 'the Empire in danger', but few people heard him: politicians, Conservatives alike with Liberals, turned a deaf ear. Soldiers, however eminent, were now as ever regarded as professional alarmists, men who, if debarred from extending the bounds of the Empire, would console themselves by extending the sway of their own administrative system over as many innocent civilians as possible. After 1906, it can hardly be said that the Army enjoyed any 'public relations' with the Government and electorate at all. Army leaders became more out of touch with general opinion, and fell into the habit of political intrigue of a restless, nervous character in which the acknowledged master was Sir Henry Wilson. The one link between the military organisation and the people — Haldane's Territorial Army — the regular officers ignored entirely: Kitchener, on becoming Secretary of State for War in August 1914, when told of the organisation which lay ready to his hand, said only, 'Yes, but what I must have now is more soldiers.'[1]

With a Government that had little confidence in the Army leadership, with an Army leadership that despised the pacifistic radicalism of the Government, it was unlikely that an Empire of consolidated power such as Milner and his friends were advocating in the *Round Table* could ever be fashioned. The incident at the Curragh in 1914, when the Government committed the extraordinary blunder of asking Army officers whether they thought it proper to carry out orders which had not yet been given, threw a dramatic spotlight on to the area of disagreement between the two. Although when war came party and Service ranks closed again, and the spotlight was switched off, the strife the Government carried on with the General Staff throughout their four years of enforced

[1] Amery, *My Political Life*, I, 24.

co-operation was only the continuation to the sound of shellfire of an already established quarrel.

Kitchener's comments supply good guides to Service feeling. You politicians, he told Churchill, have got the country into this mess: 'I have to get you out of it.'[1] On the doctrine of Cabinet responsibility, he was equally terse: he declared that it was repugnant to him to reveal military secrets to twenty-three gentlemen with whom he was barely acquainted. This opinion is well supported by Sir John French, Commander-in-Chief in France and no friend to Kitchener, who observed that if he were to tell Kitchener about his plans for the Loos offensive in 1915 Kitchener would have to tell the others in the Cabinet — and then it would be all over London.[2]

Until the outbreak of war, however, the public knew and cared nothing of Army quarrels, and nearly as little about foreign policy. As to imperial policy, this seemed to be again as shadowy as it had appeared to its critics in the seventies. A series of Colonial and Imperial Conferences, each hailed as more significant than the last, had produced nothing at all that could be called policy. Empire, once the shrine of all aspiring Tories, had become the temple of coteries only — powerful enough in the arcana of Conservative politics, but without public support. It was such a group that instituted Empire Day in 1904; another, the quarterly *Round Table* in 1909; but Sargent the popular painter risked no part of his popularity when he decided to paint satirical portraits of both Roberts and Cromer in those same years.

What absorbed the public interest was that old 'condition of England question' which Disraeli had deserted in order to go imperialising. Between 1906 and 1910, when the Liberal Government enjoyed so great a majority that it had no need to pay attention to the wishes, or indeed to the presence, of the Irish Nationalists, it was not evident that this re-emergence of the 'condition of England question' would ultimately bring about the return to the political arena of its twin, the 'condition of Ireland question' — an imperial issue if there ever was one, and one that was to revivify in a most remarkable manner the flagging imperialism of the Unionist party. In this noonday before the storm, Liberals and Radicals were determined to put in hand that renovation of social conditions that had

[1] S. Salvidge, *Salvidge of Liverpool*, (London, 1934), p. 142.
[2] R. Blake, *Private Papers of Douglas Haig*, (London, 1952), p. 101.

for so long, and so deliberately, been delayed. To the charge that this kind of policy was going to cost a great deal of money which the country could not afford, they had a riposte hard to parry: in 1899 they had seen an old-age pension scheme drop because it would have cost £20 million, on that very ground, that the country could not find the money — but since then they had sat back and watched the Conservatives spend £250 million of the country's money on a war in South Africa, which attained nothing. John Burns' opinion that 'Society' and the military caste had governed the country long enough was subscribed to by the mass of the electorate. Imperialism, said Labour members, now as since, begins at home: in the minds of readers of Rowntree's celebrated study of social conditions in the city of York (1904), the question easily arose, what kind of heritors are we breeding up in, and for, this great Empire?

The election of 1906 put out of power the hereditary governing classes of England. It took a major war to put them back in again. The House of Commons was no longer a club, where like-minded gentlemen enjoyed agreeable disputes: it was a battleground where contrasting ideologies about the nature of society and the duty of its leaders waged war with increasing bitterness and fury. The club that survived consisted of Balfour's hundred followers in the Commons and the entire House of Lords; the rest, including the Government Front Bench, were outsiders and wild men whose policies must be circumvented in the country's own interest. In a naval debate Balfour indeed bitterly upbraided the Prime Minister, Asquith, for daring to presume that he and his Government spoke for the nation. These were the years of political uproar, the volume of which has not been since repeated: the row over the Education Bill, the Dreadnought scares, the terrorist methods of the suffragettes, the protracted *mêlée* over the Budget of 1909, and the guerilla warfare between Limehouse and the shires over which Lloyd George presided with such gusto. By 1913 a Tory hostess might feel herself obliged to burn her carpet if Asquith's daughter set foot in her house, and J. A. Spender, editor of the Liberal *Westminster Gazette*, relates how a great lady stood at the top of the stairs and shouted epithets at him on his way down from the Ladies' Gallery to the lobby of the House of Commons.[1] Page, the American ambassador, was reminded of what he had been told of the electric social

[1] J. A. Spender, *Life, Journalism, and Politics*, (London, 1927), II, 3.

atmosphere in his own country just prior to the outbreak of the Civil War. He saw the issue as clearly as the embattled peers: conservatism was making (what looked like) its last stand.

It chose to make it on the boggy ground of the Irish question, once more miring the feet of English politicians. The Irish members returned to their position of dominance over the Liberals after the two elections of 1910. It was the Irish Home Rulers who had enabled the Government to pass through the House of Commons the Parliament Bill curtailing the powers of the Lords, and in return they expected the Liberals to put through Home Rule for Ireland. This simple bargain was denounced as unconstitutional, and the Unionists, as the constitutional party, demanded that the voice of the people be heard on this issue. Both Liberals and Unionists knew very well that the English people did not care a straw for the Irish question, and never had; but to the Unionists it was clear that a break-up of the United Kingdom was the first step towards breaking up the Empire itself. This they were determined to prevent. They played that 'Orange card' that Lord Randolph Churchill had discovered by accident in the political pack. Ulster was filled with loyalist constitutionalists, too, men who were not to be handed over to the mercies of a parliament on College Green: Ulster would fight, for the English Tories were going to see to it that she did.

The Conservatives now abandoned the traditions of Wellington and Peel, two of their revered ancestors who had always insisted on keeping resistance to change within certain definite limits. Certainly they lost sight of Wellington's famous dictum that the Government must be carried on, however much it hurt. The Liberals must either submit their Home Rule Bill to the people's judgment, or be prepared to face the consequences of civil war. This was the declaration of Bonar Law, the Conservative leader, and he was prepared to summon his party to amend the Army Annual Act in the House of Lords to exclude the use of the Army in Ulster against the patriotic forces being raised there by Sir Edward Carson. Law thought that the Liberals — notoriously men who had never had stomach for a fight — would knuckle down; Asquith for his part seems to have thought that the Tories were talking nonsense, that there was no risk of civil war, that Irish issues always generated a lot of spurious excitement which soon died away, as would this. With this blank incomprehension on both sides, with the mishandling of the Army in Ireland by a foolish War Minister and an incompetent General, plus the inability of Carson (whose appearance was the most formidable thing about him) to control the people in Ulster whom he called his followers, there is no doubt that war would indeed have broken out had not the European crisis supervened. In fashioning a compromise some kind of intelligence is required: but this was absent from the control of Irish affairs in all quarters. In hindsight the case looks no better. The young Leopold Amery was a powerful parliamentary fighter for the right of Ulster to rebel, with the blessing of the Conservative party; and no hint appears in his autobiography, written as late as 1953, that he and his party had anything to be ashamed of, or even that somebody, somewhere, would have done well to sit down and think out what it was he did.

Amid these events the cry of 'the Empire in danger' finally took on a meaning which Roberts ought to have been struck by, busy as he was in the summer of 1914 advising Carson in Ulster how to get himself an army with which to withstand His Majesty's forces and the lawful Government of the country. The Empire was in danger from the Conservatives, the imperialists, themselves. It might indeed have been true — no one could tell in 1914 — that if the Liberals were successful in giving Home Rule to Ireland it would bring disaster to the Empire; but for the Conservatives to break down the government of the country by fomenting an Irish rebellion, in the best style of King James II, was self-evidently a faster way of causing imperial ruin.

That such things were possible did not surprise the more cynical among the Radicals, who had always declared that imperialists were a public menace, and had no objection to being proved right. People who depended on power would use any methods to retain it when threatened: it was, after all, a very similar cry of Tory loyalism that had once burnt down the parliament-house in Montreal. Moreover, the example of insubordination from Ulster lighted the way to the ultimate establishment of the Irish Republic. It was the Ulster crisis of 1913–14 that broke the control of the Irish Nationalists over their own followers. The Irish members of the United Kingdom Parliament for sixty years had fought for the Home Rule cause according to the rules of the English game. When it seemed they were about to win that game, the English changed its rules. In 'Southern Ireland' a Sinn Fein party took note of Carson and his methods, and decided, in its own time, to improve on them. Plainly there was nothing to be got any longer from an English Government and Parliament which could not even keep its 'loyal Opposition' loyal.

Into these sands poured the idea of Empire during these first years of the twentieth century. Cromer, Curzon, Milner, no longer had the ear of anyone important, and the proconsular idea was on the wane. Milner had often insisted that no single class could harmonise the ideals of Empire and build a solid structure of imperial unity and strength; but in fact it was a single class, the Service class, to whom this task was left, and it was called to do it at a time when it was falling more and more out of touch with the public will and the notions of ordinary men. 'Empire' retreated from reality into a realm of thought and planning for the future where the bulk of Conservatives were unwilling to set foot. Problems of administration are neither communicable nor interesting to the majority of men, and more absence of mind was to be shown in governing the Empire than ever there was in getting one together. Ulster was an issue on which men could distribute their emotions freely without having to exercise their brains, but no other cause won attention. Hobhouse noted sarcastically that suburban villadom, from which Toryism drew its mass vote, was absorbed in one great mission only — that of keeping down the rates. Moreover, Empire cost money, and the returns on investment were disappointingly meagre. In some cases, no return could be expected at all; here was another lesson from South Africa, to which some £41 million, in addition to war costs, had to be given in the name of rehabilitation. It was no accident that the years between 1904 and 1914 saw British capital flowing prodigiously to foreign countries outside of the imperial ring.

Imperial administration, however, remained as complex as ever. The Liberal Government had not lost sight of ideas of imperial mission, and at first the situation in vanquished South Africa appeared to present it with an opportunity to put its theories into useful practice. To Liberals, the old nostrum of self-government, responsible government, was still the best part of the imperial tradition: 'We treat it not as an odious necessity,' Campbell-Bannerman had insisted to a Bradford audience in 1901, 'not as a foolish theory to which unfortunately the British Empire is committed. We treat it as a blessing.' Campbell-Bannerman as Prime Minister was resolved to bestow the blessing afresh.

The ground had already been prepared. The terms of the treaty of Vereeniging, arranged by Kitchener with the Boers in May 1902, had included a pledge to grant representative institutions leading up to full responsible government. In the interim Milner had set to work to build up a paternal despotism in the two annexed republics under British auspices: this interim, if the High Commissioner could have had his way, would have been a long one, for he disagreed both with Chamberlain and Lyttelton at the Colonial Office as to the degree of trust which could safely be extended to the Boer exenemy. On 31 March 1905, however, Lyttelton promulgated his 'semi-representative' constitution for the two States, and two days later Milner left South Africa. The Liberals in opposition handled Lyttelton's constitution roughly, and, as was expected, the King's Speech for the new Liberal Government in February 1906 announced the intention of granting full responsible government to the Transvaal. By December this was done.

Now, not for the first or last time, the doctrines of good government and self-government met in collision. The population of Southern Africa was, after all, a black population, and the fact that the two white races had just finished a fierce tribal war of their own was irrelevant to this main issue. There were, moreover, some 152,000 Indians to provide for. In February, soon after the new House of Commons met for the first time, a back bencher initiated a motion asking that in any dealings with the Boers on the question of the future government of South Africa the rights and interests of the natives should not be forgotten. The Government, still flushed from their enormous success in the country, were able to accept this motion, and went far along the road of stern principle before observing the bends in it. It was the Under-Secretary for the Colonies, Winston Churchill, who declared that, after all, self-government itself was not a moral principle, and when it collided with a moral principle, as plainly it was going to in this case, 'I think upon occasion it should be overborne.'[1] Moreover, self-government in South Africa, since it must come as a grant from the imperial authority if it came at all, depended upon our own reading of its extent and validity. Churchill — who, according to his colleague, Herbert Samuel, spoke the language of Liberalism with correctness, but 'perhaps with the careful articulation and the slight accent with which one may speak a language learnt a little late in

[1] 4 H 152, 28 February 1906, 1283.

life'[1] — paused here to remark that a self-governing colony was not, for one thing, entitled to say one day 'Hands off, no dictation in our internal affairs' and the next day to telegraph for the protection of a brigade of British infantry.

But when inspected, Vereeniging proved a tribal peace, written and subscribed to in European interests alone. Before it was agreed to, Chamberlain himself had urged that we could not consent to purchase peace by leaving the coloured population in the position it had previously held[2] — but the pace of events in South Africa, and the growing public distaste at home for the war, proved too strong for this opinion to be given weight. The peace declared that the franchise was not to be granted to the native population until *after* the whites had been given self-government.

This was, as has turned out, and as was plainly foreseen at the time by 'African' observers like R. H. Brand, Sir Harry Johnston, and Sir Frederick Lugard, to postpone the emancipation of Africans to the twenty-first century. The Liberals could indeed with justice profess that in this business they were tied to the terms so flatly laid down by their predecessors at Vereeniging. They were also able to defend the terms themselves, in company with the Conservatives, on the ground that, if they had not been given, peace would never have been got at all. The Boers would have been driven to suicidal desperation if they had thought that the victorious British intended to hand their country over to the natives. It was because of England's continual interference in the native question that the Boers originally had trekked out of the arena of British governance, and had fought the 'imperial factor' whenever possible ever since. An earlier generation of politicians had weighed this with care, and had on the whole decided that Boer hostility was to be preferred to any rejection of our trusteeship for the natives of Africa. In the venomous 'Majuba debate' of July 1881, this was the best point made: Hicks-Beach had declared from the Conservative Opposition that it was one thing to give the Boers self-government, as Gladstone's Liberals intended, but quite another to give them the natives, 'whom you are bound to care for in the future as in the past.'[3] A line was now drawn around this future, and for the second time in South African history, in the name of

[1] Viscount Samuel, *Memoirs*, (London, 1945), p. 91.
[2] Chamberlain to Milner, 6 March 1901; G. B. Pyrah, *Imperial Policy and South Africa, 1902–10*, (Oxford, 1956), p. 92.
[3] 3 H 263, 25 July 1881, 1770.

liberty the Liberals turned their backs on the idea of mission. 'Mission' by its nature was tutelary, was stamped indeed with Milnerism, than which hardly anything worse could be said.

The great thing was to hold the Empire together in South Africa, and this could only be done by placating the Boers. Here Liberals and Conservatives agreed as to the purpose, and when the Union of South Africa Bill was passing through the Commons in 1909, the many voices raised — from the Labour benches, from Sir Charles Dilke — concerning the second-class citizens which the Empire was about to get for itself in the name of Dominion self-government, made no impression on the two Front Benches. The Government indeed held on to the three native enclaves of Bechuanaland, Basutoland, and Swaziland, on all of which the Transvaal had long cast its eyes, retaining them under the control of the High Commissioner; but beyond this there was no concession.

Asquith had remarked — before arriving in high office — that a trust could not be delegated, and that in South Africa it was not any fatuous Tory notion of paramountcy that made our presence there essential, but this duty laid upon us to care for the native races.[1] The whole scheme of Union in South Africa would be wrecked, Asquith as Prime Minister now declared, were interference by the imperial government to take place in native affairs. Lyttelton, as one who had suffered much under Liberal attack when in office, here allowed himself a sardonic comment: 'You cannot raise great eulogies and paeans on the granting of responsible government without taking the full consequences of your action.'[2] It was known in advance in the Commons that the Government were going to accept no amendments to the Bill when it was discussed in committee: we might, said Byles, who had instituted the debate of February 1906, be the House of Lords discussing the Budget. MacDonald suggested that if the Parliament at Westminster was now going to rubber-stamp colonial bills, its members might as well go home. Where did this notion come from, anyway? For we had changed — or Chamberlain had — more than mere commas when the Commonwealth of Australia Bill was before the House nine years previously. He repudiated absolutely this doctrine that we had now no right to safe-guard native interest. A

[1] 4 H 130, 22 February 1904, 666.
[2] 5 H 9, 16–19 August 1909, 961 ff.

franchise restricted to men 'of European descent' would have excluded the vote from the founders of every one of the world's great
religions. Section 35 of the Union Bill, 'entrenching' the coloured
voters in Cape Colony on the common roll, did not appear to
MacDonald as excellent a safeguard for the future as it seemed to
the Colonial Office.[1]

The Bill, said Dilke, ignored entirely, or put to one side, or just
trusted to luck, the whole of the labour future of South Africa. He
echoed Disraeli, insisting that self-government should not, should
never, be given *gratis*, but on terms. The native question in South
Africa, as elsewhere in Africa and in Asia, was a genuine imperial
problem.[2] But we were burking it. We were throwing ninety years
of missionary endeavour to the winds. Nor could we complain that
this was a burden that had been laid upon us without our consent,
for it was one that we had ourselves sought to take up. It was our
justification for possessing an Empire at all. This was a negation
not only of moral principle but of will. We were allowing the Boer
principle of mastery to expand and predominate. Similarly Keir
Hardie urged — after commenting how no member of the House
had found himself able to rise in his place, on whatever side that
might be, to defend this measure — that this was the last chance
the Imperial Government would ever have to intervene for good in
the affairs of South Africa. Balfour, following him, made no defence
of the measure itself, but produced an argument to explain if not to
excuse it which made an impression at a time when one of the re-
current popular scares was a yellow or other coloured peril. You
cannot, he told what he himself described as a 'thin and weary
House', give the natives in South Africa equal rights with the whites
without threatening the whole fabric of white civilisation. Of this
argument much more was to be heard, both in Africa and elsewhere
within the imperial confines.

It needed no Conservative leader to tell the Liberal Government
that in the resolution of imperial problems Liberalism had its
limits and limitations. They were Liberals in the Colonial Office
who had already sanctioned the fierce white suppression of a fierce
black rebellion in Natal, and who had restricted for the use of
Europeans the highlands of Kenya. It was a Liberal Colonial
Secretary, Harcourt's son, who in company with the High Com-

[1] ibid., 1624–29.
[2] 4 H 188, 13 May 1908, 1229.

missioner in South Africa, Gladstone's son, defended the right of General Smuts to employ soldiers of the imperial garrison (still some 6,900 men in 1913) to break the strikes on the Rand. It was this kind of thing that Hobhouse had had in mind when he equated the processes of imperialism with those of intellectual dry-rot.

But if Balfour's argument was the soundest, if it were true that everywhere the white world must adopt a defensive position, it was also true that the British Empire — or that part of it which was white — must play its part by drawing together as a unit. If through imperial union lay strength, as imperialists on the Conservative side had long insisted, what was the best way to map its future accordingly? The Liberal Government of the day, and Liberal historians since, drew great credit from its settlement of European quarrels in South Africa, for the native question interested only a minority and was considered irrelevant to the main theme. The majority expressed a cordial agreement with the opinion of General Botha, who, become Premier of the new Union of South Africa, asserted in 1911 that it was the wise and enlightened policy of decentralisation that had made the British Empire what it was.

But what was it? Unity, imperial or other, could only be founded upon a common weal, in the manner of the young Commonwealth of Australia, whose foundations were based on the common interests of the component Australian colonies. But, if every self-governing colony was free hereafter to legislate without regard to the interests of others, or of the metropolis, or of the Empire as a whole, then in what sense could the British Empire be said to exist? Here was a question to which a further fifty years of applied thought could not supply a thoroughly satisfying answer: fittingly, since it was a problem with metaphysical overtones, it was the great political metaphysician Balfour who was to come nearest to dealing with it, at the Imperial Conference of 1926. But Balfour's thinking had always been *sui generis* among Conservatives, and in 1911 this boasted decentralisation seemed to the imperialists among them just another name for sloth. Plainly the Liberals would never stir to 'organise' the Empire — because they had no wish to, they didn't really care. In 1907 the Liberals were more interested in the forthcoming Peace Conference at the Hague than in any Imperial Conference, and although they did preside over some imperial discussions on defence in 1909, critics in the *Round Table* felt able to liken the ship of state, as then manned, as one which, although storm-threatened, had assigned no stations to its crew nor ever given them a boat-drill.[1]

Since 1887 Colonial and Imperial Conferences had been poring over rather than dealing with an agenda on which the three main items were always Imperial Defence, Imperial Consolidation, and Imperial Reciprocity. Reciprocity, wanted by the colonies, would have entailed a fiscal revolution in the United Kingdom. Chamberlain, but not his principal colleagues, had been prepared to convert himself to Reciprocity from his previous doctrine of an Imperial Free Trade — the establishment of which would have involved a fiscal revolution in the colonies. On the other two items the colonies had always expressed more or less polite disinterest. Contribution to any scheme for Imperial Defence was taxation without representation, and Imperial Consolidation was merely a new name for Downing Street Government. This disinterest the Liberal Government in England at no time tried to remove, and to imperialists this was a sin of omission as great as any expression of the old full-blooded Radical anti-imperialism would have been. All Chamberlain's ideas of centralisation, of creating a strong metropolitan executive for the Empire, ranging through Imperial Councils, a Defence League, a customs union, and Imperial Preference, involved *doing* something, involved action and planning and forethought, involved renovating and reconstructing the traditional machine of administration in the United Kingdom itself. But *laissez faire*, at least in the fields of imperial and foreign policy, still had its grip on the Liberal mind. Lyttelton's idea, circulated to the colonies in 1905, that an Imperial Commission should be set up as a permanent body, with United Kingdom and colonial representatives upon it, charged with the investigation of imperial facts and the framing of imperial policy, had been broadened out so far that its outlines were no longer ascertainable.

The Colonial Conference in 1902 had seen colonial Premiers conferring with the Colonial Secretary, and pressing ideas of imperial preference on him which he afterwards improved upon. But the Conference of 1907, under Liberal auspices, was just a general get-together between the Dominion Premiers — the word 'Colony' as a description of self-governing communities was now officially dropped — and members of the British Cabinet, among whom the Colonial Secretary was not the most important. The

[1] *RT*, March 1917, No. 26, p. 237.

colonial statesmen learned more of what was going on — indeed Grey in 1911 was to tell them more of the state of foreign affairs than his own Cabinet colleagues knew — but policy-forming was beyond their powers. Asquith was firm on this: one thing that could not be decentralised, or delegated, was the foreign policy of the United Kingdom, which was the foreign policy of the British Empire. Indeed, responsibility in this difficult field was beyond the Dominions' inclinations. English Conservatives regarded Canada's Liberal Premier with some suspicion for his lukewarmness, surmising that, had he been able to, Sir Wilfrid Laurier would have contracted out of any obligation at all, while gaining every advantage from the entire imperial defensive system. But English Liberals could not fail to sympathise with Laurier's unwillingness to involve his country in obscure British Foreign Office disputes based on unknown European circumstances: this, after all, had always been a main plank in their own stand against imperialism, that it committed its constituents without their knowledge and normally against their will. They believed it true, that every community knows best what it does for itself. Laurier had no desire to be consulted, either — although Chamberlain, always like lightning when he saw a concrete advantage, had once taken him up on a loose remark he had made as to the desirability of being 'called to council'. For consultation implied, if not consent to, at least some sort of responsibility for the decision ultimately taken. Laurier, like all Canadian statesmen walking the narrow ledge between the prejudices of two Canadian races, preferred not to know and thus not to commit himself in advance. Compromise had never been, in Canada, an amalgam of policies; it was always a policy in itself.

Moreover, the Liberals believed in democracy. So did the self-governing Dominions. If the peoples of these territories showed no interest in imperial federation, imperial unity, organic machinery, and the rest of it, then these matters did not belong to practical politics at all. If the people did not want an imperial union, or wanted other things more fervently, then nothing could be done about it. England's duty in the matter — as Derby had remarked back in 1875 — was to maintain goodwill and promote cordial relations. Loyalty was not something that was owed, as imperialists dealing with native races seemed inclined to believe: it could not be conscripted, or elevated into a political institution.

Colonists were more interested in alliance than in union, federal or other. The *pax Britannica* was an umbrella that sheltered all colonists, one which they neither wished nor could afford to dispense with. Australian national pride, and a logical desire to carry responsible government to its conclusion, had brought that new Commonwealth to float its own naval squadron in 1908, and to pay for it; but this was but a contribution of an adult son to the family savings bank. Canada, in contrast, was older and so less enthusiastic for the broad gesture. Canadians saw no objection to allowing the United Kingdom taxpayer to continue paying for the upkeep of the naval base at Halifax, Nova Scotia, while still insisting that contingents of the Canadian Army were strictly Canadian forces, not to be considered by British War Office strategists as so many additional available drafts in time of crisis.

Chamberlain's efforts to interest the Dominions in his imperial economic insurance scheme thus won no colonial support. Common interests in present or future economic relationships could not be conjured up just by constantly talking as if they were there, and Canada who in fact enjoyed more trade with the United States and with Germany than she did with Great Britain, could not be reasonably expected to ring herself within imperial economic frontiers whose restrictions would injure both her present prosperity and her prospects of more. Thus Laurier, and in this he had Botha's support, always refused to put pressure on Great Britain to drop her long Free Trade tradition. One day, too, Canada might wish not only economic but external freedom, and command of her own destinies — here was another reason for Laurier's tip-toeing imperial activities, which baffled the English imperialists who contrasted them with the full-blooded and delighted cries for some concrete imperial policy which emanated from Premier Deakin of Australia, who knew well enough where the best Australian market lay. No imperialist but could applaud, and indeed Deakin was blandished to stop over in England and become a great man among the Conservatives.

Australia's interest marched with England's more than did that of Canada: but in recognising this, Australia no less than Canada put her self-interest first. Circumstances might change. Churchill made a remark in March 1914 that has thrown its echo far enough, too far indeed for many, even now. He warned that if ever the power of Great Britain were shattered on the sea, the only course of the five millions of white men in the Pacific would be to seek the protection of the United States. This same possibility had been noted by Richard Jebb in his book *The Imperial Conference* (1911). As in the field of economics, a perpetual union for defence presupposed a perpetual community of vital interests. What guarantee of such perpetuity existed, in a world in which the American, the Slav, and the Asiatic races had not yet had their day of power?

Ironically, it had been a South African politician at the first Colonial Conference of all, that held in 1887, who had suggested instituting an imperial tariff on goods entering the Empire from foreign countries, and devoting the revenue from it to the general defence of the Empire. He had suggested a rate of two per cent. So inspired, the Conference produced the first bout of genuine imperial thinking ever generated, and were given moral support for this *Kriegsverein* idea by Salisbury himself: the Australian colonies, imperialist in temper, on this occasion had contributed £126,000 per annum towards the upkeep of a British naval squadron in Australian waters. Twenty years later, to a succeeding Conference, Chamberlain declared that trade and defence were inseparable, but the colonies would not take the point, or, at best, they translated it to mean that so long as Britannia ruled the waves their own commerce and their own defence were thus secure, and so no further step need be taken. It is worth recalling that 'splendid isolation' was a phrase first coined by a Canadian politician. Certainly the self-governing Dominions were all imperialist, in a sense that they believed, that they knew, that the British Empire was founded on power. They lived by the light of this conviction, and had frequently acted upon it: Canada and Australia sent contingents to the Sudan fighting as well as 25,000 men to South Africa, while Australian colonies had gone imperialising in the Pacific further than the Colonial Office thought necessary.

In this outlook they were at one with so unlikely a coadjutor as Curzon. Curzon always looked towards the east for his illumination, for there he could see a tangible of power more intoxicating by far than any British Navy, namely, the *Raj* in India. Here was the true symbol of British supremacy, not merely in India itself, but throughout the eastern hemisphere from Suez to the Western Pacific. All our most vital fortresses lay somewhere along the imperial route to the East. All of them reflected the sun from Delhi. To attack British rule in India, or the concept of British imperialism in the East, was to attack the defensive system of half the world. Curzon wrote the future down as he saw it in 1908. If Radical democracy, the great enemy of the imperial idea, gained the ground it now believed it would, if India were to be overturned, then, depend upon it,

> Your ports and your coaling-stations, your fortresses and dockyards, your Crown Colonies and protectorates will go too. For either they will be unnecessary, as the toll-gates and barbicans of an Empire that has vanished, or they will be taken by an enemy more powerful than yourselves,[1]

and the ultimate state of England would be that of a glorified Belgium. But surely — surely? — this would not happen. England's own sense of self-interest, if nothing more honourable, would prevent her from squandering her hard-won heritage, and from scattering broadcast her responsibilities in the world.

Indeed the sense of self-interest seemed often to be stronger in Sydney or in Wellington than it was at Westminster — although this, as 1914 was to prove at the last, was an appearance only. Australasians had seen the imperial frontiers of both Europe and America enclosing island-groups in the Pacific too long to class the idea of *Kriegsverein*, some kind of defence league, as the same sort of armchair foolishness as all the schemes of federation for federation's sake. In the years before 1914 the symbol of Empire best understood by Dominion statesmen and citizens, as by the British public itself, was the Royal Navy. Here was an admirable engine of power, already in being, already unified, already fully prepared against emergency; the fact that it possessed no Staff, Imperial or other, worried only a few naval men themselves, and these junior in rank. British naval power, allied to the power of British capital — these were bonds neither loose nor sentimental, but of a kind easily grasped by the hard-headed. Curzon tended no doubt to think too much of rows of bedazzled natives, which had in fact passed into a dim history even as he wrote, but he may be excused for admiring his own brilliant stage management of Edward VII's Durbar, itself the model for that of George V: still, Durbars proved little save that Orientals liked now what they had always liked, a handsomely mounted stage show. Yet Australian politicians and publicists who thought such things flummery, and did not hesitate to say so, agreed with Curzon and the Anglo-Indians, that Great Britain's

[1] Curzon, 'The True Imperialism', *Nineteenth Century*, January 1908, 157 ff.

control of Egypt and the Suez Canal ensured to the Pacific, as much as to India, the protection of a formidable and essential palisade. Twice within the next forty years Australasian citizens were to fight and die in the Levant to give point to the validity of the old Disraelian assertion, that the 'Eastern Question' was more than an elaborate mare's nest constructed by restive European politicians with too little to do.

But by 1914 Disraeli's foresight was amply justified: England and her Empire, her power in the world, *were* valued at the rate she herself set upon it. The shortcomings in the military organisation of the Empire were known only to a few, but it was clear to everybody who weighed world affairs at all that imperial unity depended now, and would depend in the future, on the successful assertion of that power of England in any crisis when her interests were at stake. Had England kept clear of the Continent in August 1914 she must have resigned her position as one of the Great Powers of Europe, and would have had before her, in Grey's words, 'nothing but a miserable and ignoble future'.[1] Imperial England must make her presence felt when great events were taking place. It was necessary accordingly to become a belligerent in a 'cause' whose nature evaded accurate definition; but fortunately, as has been seen, Belgium proved to the public the case of necessity. In all the self-governing Dominions the attack on the European state-system mounted by Germany was taken as a personal challenge, simply because they instinctively understood that the success of that attack would displace England from her position of world control, and so leave the Dominions themselves at the behest of another master. They therefore sent one million volunteers to Europe to stop this coming to pass.

That there was already another master in the field, not indeed planning aggression or aiming at dominance in the German style, but still pursuing a manifest destiny whose implications no European statesman as yet clearly understood, had occurred neither to Australasians nor to any other member of the British imperial institute — or, if perhaps the Canadian questioned the future, he kept the question buried deep. The United States ambassador in London, Walter Hines Page, was in 1913 confiding a rumination to his diary, as he noted the force of the tide of on-sweeping democracy in England. What are we Americans, he asked, 'going to do with this

---

[1] Grey, *Twenty-Five Years*, II, 15.

England and this Empire, presently, when economic forces un-
mistakably put the leadership of the race in our hands?'[1] It was because Americans themselves preferred to delay a solution to this
problem for another generation that England and her Empire were
able to enjoy another lease of active life.

War is most clearly seen and understood as a struggle for obvious
strategic advantage, and because this is so it inevitably revives ideas
of imperial expansion in the national interest. In war the paths of
duty and advancement become the same — which was one reason,
as Cobden had long ago pointed out, why wars were 'got up in
India'. Moreover, the fact and challenge of war makes problems of
administration, imperial and domestic, communicable as at no other
time. Their magnitude can be grasped by the public, but, so great
is its degree that the public is quick to leave responsibility for control over all such issues to those who want to take it — usually, to a
few men whom it has not chosen and does not know. Esher's remark to Fisher, made in 1904, that changes of Government in England are of little significance, as the value of the dozen or so men in
the country 'who really count' is never affected by such things,[2] becomes in wartime an absolute definition of fact. The history of the
war, Balfour's biographer has remarked, is very largely a history of
personal combinations. The men who count number more than a
dozen, but it is certainly neither Parliament nor the democracy behind it who decides on their value or on the roles they play. Democracy is unable to wage effective war unless and until it surrenders
the substance of its powers.

Between 1914 and 1918 the democracy surrendered its power to
men whom in time of peace it had looked upon with a hearty distrust. Only in a major war could Milner, Carson and Curzon have
been allotted high Cabinet office. When the State is in battle, when
efficiency is at once the highest and rarest of virtues, an ideal in itself, it is the proconsul, the expert, the man on the spot, who becomes the most valuable public servant. His ignorance or dislike of
democratic method no longer acts as a leash on his powers. The
democracy is already committed to a task that he alone knows how
to tackle — the task of maintaining and operating the war machine.

In August 1914, the imperialist war machines took over control
of events from hesitant Foreign Offices all over Europe. Russia

---

[1] B. Hendrick, *Life and Letters of Walter Hines Page*, (London, 1923), I, 174.
[2] Esher to Fisher, 6 August 1904; Marder, *Fear God and Dread Nought*, I, 324.

mobilised because Austria-Hungary mobilised, Germany mobilised because Russia mobilised, France mobilised because Germany mobilised, and when all the mobilisation was complete hostilities began because no nation could afford to disregard its own military time-table and allow its neighbours to make dispositions or to carry out movements of troops which would threaten its own security or existence. The diplomacy of Europe was thus conscripted into war by the machines it had itself created. In this process Great Britain was the only volunteer. It had to gear its free society to the making of a similar machine in a hurry. The difficulties were great. The men who eventually learned, after painful errors, how to keep their machine running in control not unnaturally over-estimated their ability to keep the country behind them in support of the policies for which the machine was designed. The Germans' dictum was a wise one: it took one year to make an Army, but twenty to make a General Staff. They might have added, that it took several generations to make a military nation.

In war, Service interests as a whole — and such Service concepts as that of a 'Middle East', for example — become political and national interests. Service opinion becomes sacrosanct — or it does if someone is not careful. After the outbreak of war all the imperialists' frustration that had animated the whole series of passionate domestic rows was released, and the Liberal Government found itself backed — indeed, pushed from behind — by powerful and impulsive forces which it was accustomed to see, and far preferred to see, in Opposition — even in disloyal Opposition. These new allies Asquith had no notion how to control. He and they shared no common ground. Lloyd George who displaced him in December 1916 at least understood the ideas that motivated them, and indeed agreed with a great many himself. Yet it was he who, clinging to his Radicalism, waged the long dour battle with Service opinion from 1917 onwards; often on the wrong ground, usually with the wrong weapons, generally in an underhand fashion — but that he saw that this battle needed to be waged at all was a service to his country that has long, like most of Lloyd George's services, been forgotten.

For what was to be thought about the war? Was it merely to preserve the British Empire from the machinations of the German Empire? The phrase 'an imperialist war' was not yet in vogue, but many English Liberals felt acutely that war was inseparable from imperialism, was indeed its natural activity, and that under cover of appeals to their patriotism they were being dragooned into backing policies absolutely alien to their ideas. Only a man like Asquith, who was free of all taint of 'militarism' — this indeed was the reason why he was deposed later — could have managed to get a Parliamentary majority to accept the principle of national conscription at all, failing the actual arrival of the enemy at the gate. Or was the war a nobler thing than this: war for a cause, for the authority of public right, for civilisation, designed to rescue even the Germans from militarism?

These were great matters, but the men who were in charge of the day-to-day administration of the war, relieved from the pressure of public supervision, saw no great reason to tax their brains with them. They naturally concentrated on the more practical aspects of their task, which was formidably hard. 'Winning the war' was the easiest of war-aims to adumbrate. The official view on war-aims was that the future was not foreseeable, and therefore that to take out stock in particular aspects of it was foolishness. Accordingly, the Governments of Britain and France returned no answer to the early enquiries on ultimate policy sent them by the Vatican and the White House that was likely to reassure either Pope or President. Not until December 1917 was a major debate permitted in the Commons on the matter, and its nature was not such as to placate unhappy Liberals.[1] Herbert Samuel declared that our aim in the war was to bury imperialism: he used the older-fashioned term of Caesarism. But he was at once confronted by a phalanx of those who preferred rather to praise than to bury Caesar. Carson declared roundly that all this talk of war-aims was got up only to embarrass the Government, which was an unpatriotic thing to do. Balfour reiterated that war methods, rather than war-aims, were the things of importance. (But to say this was to give ground away of another kind, for by 1917 few Liberals or Radicals had much admiration for our war-methods, an attitude which, had they but known it, they shared with that fugitive from their own ranks, the embattled Prime Minister.)

Lloyd George, after he had become leader of the Coalition, was in no position to take any recognisably 'Liberal' step because he could never be sure whether he would be supported by the pure Asquithian Liberals with whom he had so bitterly quarrelled, or

[1] 5 H 100, 14–20 December 1917, 1574 ff.

whether his new Conservative allies would turn on him if he did. His 'War Cabinet' itself, in the views of many Liberals, was nothing but a group of irresponsible proconsuls, with Lloyd George the most irresponsible of the lot. So he was reduced to asking rhetorical questions about our aims, rather than setting out prosaic statements. Did anyone believe, he asked, that we had entered the war for sordid motives — in order, say, to get hold of Germany's colonies?[1] Perhaps no one believed this; but when in November 1917 he had been pressed by Colonel House, President Wilson's travelling personal representative, to say flatly just what it was the Allied Powers wanted, he had included the German colonies in a list whose other items set out the establishment of an 'independent Arabia' under British suzerainty, of a Zionist Palestine under either British or United States' control, of an independent Armenia and of an international regime for the Straits.[2] But this tally was not made public. It was principally because House was unable to get the Allies to say anything at all in public that Wilson on his side of the Atlantic thought the time ripe, as 1918 opened, to tell them the principles they ought to steer by to obtain the things they ought to want.[3]

Already the Bolsheviks had disclosed the diplomatic record of some very old-fashioned imperialist deals, made to cajole into active service this or that Power. It was from this source that the world public now learned, among other things, that the Allies had promised Constantinople to the Tsar and Dalmatia with part of Asia Minor to the Italians. The Arabs learned that they (or some of them, at any rate) had been toiling in the hot noonday for Turkish trophies already allotted to their Western protectors. This kind of thing was dismaying to those who wanted this cataclysm to purge away the evils of the old system. By February 1918 C. P. Scott of the *Manchester Guardian* was openly contemptuous of what he called 'an imperialist and reactionary Government', one which had presented more *faits accomplis*, of more lasting significance, to the English people than any hitherto.

In the Commons the vigilant Arthur Ponsonby, who had been railing for years at the Foreign Office for their conduct of secret

[1] ibid., 20 December 1917, 2222.
[2] C. E. Seymour (ed.,) *Papers of Colonel House*, (London, 1926–28), III, 240.
[3] Cf. Wilson to House, 21 July 1917: 'When the war is over we can force [England and France] to our way of thinking,' ibid., 54.

diplomacy, took some pleasure in quoting Lloyd George that we were not fighting for territory, or for any additions to our imperial responsibilities. Then for what were we fighting? A fight to a finish, was it? Till what was finished? How was a finish to be recognised? What began when this finish was attained? No answer was given: the questions, like Lansdowne's letter to the *Daily Telegraph* in November 1917, suggesting some exploration of possibilities for a negotiated peace, were thought improper, and the answers impossible. Yet although no official voice backed Lansdowne's, many felt with him that a negotiated peace — such as had ended every major war in which we had been involved in our history — was better than the continuation of the indiscriminate slaughter which was the only programme the military leaders seemed able to produce. That this should continue so that Governments might make off with spoils of war to which neither a name could be given nor a date set for their capture, seemed not only immoral, but lunatic. Echoes of President Wilson's remark of 1916, that he was unable to find out what the war was about, reverberated far and for long on the Left.

But the controlling minority in all countries, Britain not excluded, knew very well what the war was about. It was about the balance of power. No amount of invective directed against this stock target had yet toppled the concept, or replaced it with another fitted to do its task. Balance-of-power politics had in England been equated with wickedness since Bright's time, but neither Bright nor any of his successors had squared to the issue of the existence of power at all. As it happened, Gladstone's nostrum of a working Concert of Europe was very shortly to be realised in the shape of a League of Nations, but this League too was not equipped to face facts of force. Certainly the War Office, the Admiralty, the Foreign Office, the Cabinet secretariat, the Government of India, and the 'Arab Bureau' in Cairo were not fighting for the nebulous desires of a league of nations but for British interests. Should a league of nations turn out to *be* a British interest, they would fight for that, too. At the moment the major British interest was to defeat its imperial challenger, Germany. It was Germany who had broken the peace in Europe, maintenance of which had always been a British concern, and who had threatened to displace England on the seas, on mastery of which the existence of the British Empire depended. There was indeed an answer to Ponsonby's questions, even if it was not one that could be aired in a democratic assembly. The true finish, the one talked about in the mess, was attained when Imperial Germany was seen to lie dead on the battlefield, her grip on the balance of European power broken for ever.

These soldiers, thinking thus, were singularly favoured in their generation. Had a triumphant Tsarist Russia survived the war, they would have found control over the balance of power as far away as ever: as their successors were to find out on the morrow of another victory in 1945.

In the meantime the British Empire was able, once more, to expand.

IV

THE IMPACT OF WAR: (ii) 1914–18

THE adherence of the Ottoman Empire to the Central Powers in October 1914 made it essential for Great Britain to find and fashion, under extreme pressure and at high speed, a new policy for the Levant. Salisbury's 'wrong horse' had finally entered the wrong race, and we, its backers, were left looking for another animal to put in its place. In two Turkish properties where we were already bailiffs prompt action was taken to regulate the situation. Cyprus was annexed. In Egypt martial law was declared. There were many who urged that we should take this fine chance to put an end to the 'veiled protectorate' now thirty-two years old, and annex the country to the British Empire as a prize of war. This would have been a legal action, and the introduction of legality into the control of Egypt at this point could hardly have damaged our prospects there. The Liberal Cabinet indeed toyed with the idea, but decided that it was not one that could be adopted by a Government which had, since Cromer's retirement in 1907, heavily publicised its project for training the Egyptians to fit them for the eventual enjoyment of self-government.[1] So Egypt was, unilaterally, declared to be a Protectorate; and throughout the war it served the Allied Powers as an armed camp, a planning headquarters, and a leave-centre, taking on so exclusively imperial a colour in the process that by August 1919 Balfour as Foreign Secretary was able to note in a despatch, as a matter of course, that Egypt 'was English, as Tunis was French'.[2]

But what was to be done with the rest of the Ottoman domain?

Vistas were now opening which would have horrified Palmerston — but their very length held a fascination for strategists, amateur alike with professional, that no horizon in France or Flanders could

[1] Grey to Cheetham (Acting Consul-General, Cairo), 13 November 1914; Lord Lloyd, *Egypt since Cromer*, (London, 1932), I, 196.

[2] *DBFP*, I, iv, 11 August 1919, 343.

ever match. 'Side-shows?' exclaimed Lloyd George, always an 'Easterner' in his outlook, 'The British Empire has done very well out of side-shows!' His history was sound. No one outside of a study recalled the desperate struggles that had taken place in Europe during the great world war of the eighteenth century (1756–63), or could find the battlefields of Leuthen or Rossbach on a map — but who had not heard of the glorious victories of Plassey and Quebec? In this modern conflict, the course of events in the East once more proved the case for the side-show: for it was certain that Allenby's ultimate victory at Megiddo (September 1918), the British entry into Jerusalem, the thunderous collapse of the Ottoman power, were matters of pith and moment not to be compared in the scales of history with the winning of another thousand yards of Somme mud. The British in the east, presented with an opportunity whose magnitude they could scarcely gauge, found that their original and conservative intention of safeguarding the road to India led them into radical and indeed revolutionary fields of action. Setting out to do their best to improve an occasion, they did at the end what Palmerston had always rigidly refused to do: they obtained the lease of 'all the inns on the way'. Those that they did not want to occupy themselves they decided to give to a thoroughly reliable tenantry. Two such tenants found their favour. These were the Arabs and the Jews.

The Zionist movement was the favoured candidate in governing circles in Whitehall. It was supposed that Jews when inserted into Palestine would perform the same function that was expected of those Greeks whom it was also intended to insert into Asia Minor. They would act as injections of European culture and technology into a decaying Asiatic trunk. They would found new 'Latin kingdoms' in the Levant such as the crusaders had built. But the 'Arab Bureau' in Cairo was always impatient of such notions. The military staffs there preferred to square to practical issues, such as those that were posed by the attitude of the local inhabitants of the Ottoman Empire, who were Arab to a man. From the outset, therefore, almost as little love was lost between the two promoting groups as between their respective *protégés*.

The British Government's declaration, marked with Balfour's name, that in Palestine a 'National Home' for the Jews should be set up once the enemy had been defeated, was issued only one month before Allenby's forces entered Palestine, having defeated the enemy. Allenby, whose immediate problem was the pacification of the territory, refused to publish this policy-declaration at all. His Chief Political Officer, Clayton, warned Curzon in June 1919 that among the Arabs of Palestine fear and disgust of the professed Zionist aims were growing daily: if a British mandate for Palestine was established and pledged to carry out the Zionist programme, it could only mean that a British military force, considerably larger than that now there, would have to be kept in the country. This advice was coldly received. Both Balfour and Samuel took the view that Clayton and his administrators were unsympathetic to the larger issues that Zionism involved, and they constrained their colleague Curzon — no Zionist — to send a curt note to the Arab Bureau informing it that Zionism as a British policy in Palestine was a *chose jugée*. Clayton was replaced by Meinertzhagen.

Meinertzhagen was a strong pro-Zionist, but he too came exactly to Clayton's conclusions. The people of Palestine were not at present in a fit state to be told openly that the establishment of Zionism in their country was the policy to which the British Government was committed, and which it was determined to enforce. Accordingly, he had thought it best to withhold Curzon's *chose jugée* order from general publication. It was then September 1919 — but it was true, the thing was indeed judged. In December a Foreign Office memorandum was prepared and circulated, which envisaged with equanimity the eventual placement of three million Jews in Palestine.[1]

As early in the war as November 1914 Herbert Samuel — then Home Secretary, a Jew and a Zionist, unlike his anti-Zionist Jewish colleague Edwin Montagu, Under-Secretary of State for India — had discussed with Edward Grey the possibilities of bringing into being some autonomous Jewish state in the Palestine area. Chaim Weizmann, leader of the Zionist movement, was then looking for an Allied protector, but he found it politic to let his English friends know that the German Zionists were simultaneously urging the German Government to adopt the movement. Whoever did so would certainly equip himself with a potent engine of propaganda and influence in all countries, particularly in the neutral United States. The British Cabinet at that time had no agreed view. Many of its members had never heard of Zionism, and some saw no great

[1] *DBFP*, I, iv, 30 December 1919, 599 ff.

reason to hear of it now. Asquith thought and continued to think that it was so much romantic nonsense, providing material for yet another page of that baleful political text-book of Disraeli's, *Tancred*. Grey considered, and kept to his opinion, that some kind of internationalisation was the best fate that could be allotted to Palestine, for the French had been making clear their assertion of interests in that area, should its tenancy fall vacant, since the beginning of the war. But both Balfour and Lloyd George disliked the idea of internationalisation, as being too negative, indeed too weakening: for in the control of any international zone or sphere of influence, as African examples could show, too many people had always a say. Did we want to be bound to approve the construction, say, of a French or a Russian railway in areas whose security we considered vital to our own interests? Palestine was a strategic buffer of Egypt, and must therefore be in hands we could trust. Curzon, although complaining that any responsibility in Palestine opened 'a long vista of anxiety, vicissitude, and expense' could not be impervious to such an argument, but his trust in the Zionists was not profound. Whose hands, after all, were better than our own?

Such an opinion commanded ready applause in Cairo, headquarters of British imperial strategy in the Middle East. Searching for buffers had long been a lifetime's occupation for professional soldiers bred to Indian traditions of the 'country power' and the necessity to command that further horizon. Although Lord Robert Cecil was not alone in pointing out that to defend Palestine as a buffer we might have to go to Aleppo, and on to Alexandretta, and on indeed to anywhere else fancy might take us, he was a civilian, and civilian opinion was not of prime importance. Commanding the further horizon in the Middle East was however a difficult business. The horizon appeared to be limitless. No obvious natural barriers could be seen from any vantage-point, nor indeed was it a simple matter to find a vantage-point at all. The Mesopotamian campaign provided a fine illustration of the problem. The occupation of Basra at the head of the Persian Gulf, by the Indian Army in November 1914, took that Army ultimately, by inevitable if painful steps, to the shores of the Mediterranean. Cromer wrote in 1916 that it was likely that Mesopotamia would become a Dominion of the Crown, and so the British and the Russian frontiers would become coterminous, after a century of Anglo-Indian effort to prevent the occurrence of any such thing. It would then be forgotten that this would not be due to any prancing proconsul, but to the fact that, in purchasing the Persian oilfields in 1913, a Government and Parliament 'of marked democratic tendencies' had rushed into a very important undertaking without any due appreciation of the gravity of its proceedings or of the ultimate consequences which those proceedings would probably involve.[1]

But the intervening distances between Basra and the sea were not empty. The British had to reckon not only with the Turks, who garrisoned the area, and with the French, who still dreamed their old dreams of a Levantine supremacy, but with the Arabs who lived there. The issue presented by the Arabs was reckoned the simpler.

As, in the seventies, many people in England had taken a lot of convincing that the various Christian subjects of the Ottoman Empire who lived in the Balkan Peninsula were readily distinguishable one from another, and constituted in fact nations struggling to be free, so now English opinion was remarkably ignorant of the Islamic world that stretched from Sinai to the Persian Gulf. There were never any European promoters of an Arab 'cause'. There was no Arab cause. The British Government therefore prepared to deal with the Arabs under Turkish rule as with an inchoate mass: one which however, if carefully moulded in foundries of our own construction, might prove a serviceable weapon in the Allied cause. One assumption could safely be made about Arabs: they did not like the Turks, because nobody liked the Turks. Thus the Anglo-French, or 'Sykes-Picot' agreement of May 1916, which dealt out destiny to the Arabs, never supposed that 'Syria' and 'Mesopotamia' were anything more than names on a map — and Latin names at that, for what the Arabs themselves called these lands no one in Europe had as yet troubled either to discover or to remember. On the Turkish map of the area, with its arbitrary boundaries, new and equally arbitrary boundaries were to be laid. These territories were certainly nowhere assumed to contain 'nationalities', even in chrysalis stage. Middle Eastern experts, even when their heavily-subsidised 'Arab Revolt' was well under way, saw no reason at all to change their view of this, because for every Arab who revolted there were a hundred who did not. Arab chiefs, like other European chiefs, had their ambitions. These could be flattered and used. Arab chiefs had as much to lose from a genuine Arab nationalism as had European interests, and as time went on they were to make

[1] Cromer, *Political and Literary Essays*, (London, 1916), III, 4–5.

painful discovery of this. It was not they, but the Allies, who began
to make nationalist propaganda.

For, when addressing the Trades Union Congress on 5 January
1918, two days after the American President had published his
charter of Fourteen Points to the world, Lloyd George as Prime
Minister was determined not to be outdone as an authentic democrat. He declared that Arabia, Mesopotamia, Syria, and Palestine
were 'in our judgment, entitled to a recognition of their separate
national conditions'. He insists, in his *Truth about the Peace Treaties*,
that this judgment he referred to was that of the Cabinet and not
merely his own: but much other evidence shows that this judgment
was in fact far in advance of that of his War Cabinet colleagues and
their private staffs of advisory experts. Moreover, even in Lloyd
George's list Palestine was an odd inclusion. The insertion of
Zionism into an exclusively Arab territory debarred application of
President Wilson's principle of self-determination from the outset,
for no Arab, then or since, was going to *vote* for his own political
and social extinction, which was what he was convinced would be
the natural outcome of any establishment in Palestine of a Jewish
state. Curzon was only the first of many to ask what a 'National
Home' meant. The French were not the only nation to have no
word for home in their language. But Balfour, Zionism's strongest
crusader in the British Government, had faced this point and was
determined to dismiss it as secondary. Zionism, he wrote,

> be it right or wrong, good or bad, is rooted in age-long traditions, in
> present needs, in future hopes, of far profounder import than the
> desires and prejudices of the 700,000 Arabs who now inhabit that an-
> cient land. . . . I do not think that Zionism will hurt the Arabs; but
> they will never say they want it.[1]

Arabs were to meet greater sympathy from other Englishmen
than Balfour found time to allot to them. But no Englishman in an
official place thought for a moment that their aspirations, whatever
these might be, should be allowed to interfere with high policy.
Arabs were useful in so far as they conformed to the British pattern
for the area. So were the Zionists. As presumably both the Arabs
and the Jews had the sense to see that in conforming to the British
pattern they were themselves making new progress in the world,

[1] *DBFP*, I, iv, 11 August 1919, 'Memorandum by Mr. Balfour (Paris), respect-
ing Syria, Palestine, and Mesopotamia', doc. No. 242, p. 345.

they would play their role of client not only with acquiescence but with gratitude. To the official mind it was the French who presented the severer problem. They were harder to manipulate, and would not rejoice to see themselves considered as clients. But fortunately for the freedom of British movement the French were absentees throughout the war, for very few French troops got further east than Salonika. The Governments of the Republic could not afford an imperial strategy: it distrusted most of its own generals, who had monarchist tendencies, and agreed with them only in their conviction that the German invader must be hurled from French soil. In that task the assistance of Great Britain was an essential, and the French imperialists who looked over their shoulders at events in the Levant were accused by their own countrymen of inattention rather than hailed as grand strategists.

The Anglo-French *entente* of 1904 had carefully skirted the question of the various aims of Britain and France in the Levant, as neither Government was then clear what in fact these were. There was, moreover, the point that at that time the entire area was still under the governance of that sovereign state, the Ottoman Empire, and thus could hardly figure legally as disposable property in an agreement between two other sovereign states. Partition in Poland, in those old, more confident times, had thrown its shadow far into the political conscience. Accordingly the long-standing rivalry between the one imperialist aspiration and the other had continued since the *entente* was arrived at, being fought out in embassies, consulates, religious missions, schools, and newspaper offices. France's recognition that we possessed a base in Egypt had in fact cut away the practicability of their mounting any new Syrian adventure that did not command our support: but soldiers like other men are happiest dealing with issues whose significance they have long grasped, and are slow to note that circumstances alter cases. Both Kitchener and T. E. Lawrence, who were otherwise not much of a mind, agreed that it would be a great advantage to England to hold Alexandretta, and both disliked the thought of any expanding French influence in the Middle East not much less than they objected to the similar German control of Turkey.

When in 1914 Britain and France had become not merely cosignatories of an *entente*, but firm Allies whose troops fought side by side on the soil of one of them against a common enemy, French generals and their friends in the French press still agonised lest the

British, while French manpower was pinned down on the Western Front, should steal some eastern march upon them. Grey at the Foreign Office was well aware of this, and was himself genuinely anxious to prove to the French how groundless, how outmoded, were their fears on this point. It was this determination that led him to give his sanction, if not his blessing, to the Sykes-Picot agreement, and to see to it that the French were kept informed of the negotiations which the Arab Bureau in Cairo had set on foot with their prospective *protégé*, Husein, Sherif of Mecca and ruler of the Hejaz. Dealt with thus so openly by the British Foreign Office, French officialdom came to trust it: but they were not long in perceiving what the Foreign Office could not afford to admit — or perhaps never realised — that the initiative in such questions, and thus all subsequent political planning, lay in the hands of the soldiers and strategists at Cairo, and to some degree too in the Political Department of the Government of India. These were people who knew and cared little for French susceptibilities and interests, and who had been bred to believe that the French, with their great Army, their great Navy, and their great oversea Empire, were a likelier and probably in the long run a more formidable enemy to the British Empire than any other nation in Europe. The French on their side remembered from their experiences in Africa just how far a determined British agent could draw a surprised and genuinely reluctant Foreign Office after him, and thus their suspicions could not be laid to rest by anything that Grey, or his successors Balfour and Curzon, could do.

Yet while the Russians were still a factor which must be considered in any rearrangement of destiny in the Middle East, France could feel some reassurance that her position there would not be mined and sapped entirely. She felt able to bargain with some confidence, using as her counters the traditional hostility of her two Allies in the 'Eastern Question'. France knew well enough that although England might be irked by the propagation of French aspirations in that theatre, anything of the same sort coming out of Russia would cause in England's governing circles something not far from panic. The latter were already beset with claims which, in the days of their splendid isolation, they had been resolved never to hear, let alone meet. But what Grey sadly called 'the logic of an imperial position', what anti-imperialists had always called a snare of entanglement, led him now to concede in wartime to both

France and to Russia Middle Eastern 'spheres' which, in peace-time, England would have gone to war to prevent them from taking. Constantinople had already, in 1915, been promised to the Russian Ally. Now, in 1916, France was granted out of the Turkish lottery what she wanted in Syria, including Alexandretta itself, Cilicia, and the Taurus. These things were done in the name of compensation. They were reflections of the pre-war deals over Persia and Morocco, but grown to monstrous size. Nevertheless, Grey, anxious not to lend his name and that of the Liberal Party of England to a partition of the Ottoman Empire in a style that mirrored the old partitions of Poland — and in company with one of the prime movers of those notorious crimes — insisted that there must be left, or created, an independent Muslim political unit somewhere. Grey did not know where, as his knowledge of the Middle East was never extensive. But something there must be, to play the role of 'Congress Poland', and to mark a virtue that circumstances un-fortunately did not allow to be given any wider illustration.

Prior to the war the Arabs of the Hejaz had already produced what, with difficulty, might be called a liberal revivalist movement, modelled, if remotely, on that of the 'Young Turks'. This move-ment, like the Turkish, had not been thought by the Liberal Government of England as worthy of any encouragement. The Young Turks found another backer, but the Arabs continued to market their wares. In February 1914, Abdullah, the second son of Husein Sherif of Mecca, had called on Kitchener, then High Com-missioner in Cairo. There he drew attention to himself and to his ideas of hostility to the Turks, whose continuance as a paramount Power was known to be a subject then under pessimistic discussion by the Powers of Europe. Kitchener heard him out, but could not encourage him. But when war came and the Turks joined with the Germans as enemies to the British Empire the matter appeared in a very different light, and the attitude in Cairo naturally changed. In-deed it was in September, a month before the Turks made up their minds definitely to throw in their lot and their future with the Central Powers, that Ronald Storrs, Oriental Secretary in Cairo, reopened the *pourparlers* with Abdullah.

This was done on the orders of Kitchener, now translated to London as Secretary of State for War. To a soldier there were good strategic reasons for extending political control to the Hejaz, on the eastern shore of the Red Sea. The Germans, working from their base in Tanganyika, might establish submarine depots in that Sea, and at the same time realise those well-publicised schemes of their Kaiser for setting up some protectorate over Islam in general and the Arabian peninsula in particular. Moreover, it was from the Hejaz that the Turkish garrisons in Arabia drew the bulk of their camels. Maxwell, British Commander-in-Chief in Egypt, laid more stress on this concrete issue than on the fact that the ruler of the Hejaz was also a descendant of the Prophet, and custodian of the Holy Place of Islam. Whitehall however showed attachment to this more spiritual consideration. The India Office assured the Foreign Office that we could not afford to ignore the susceptibilities of the 70 million Muslims who lived subject to our rule in India, nor indeed of those other 60 million who were the responsibility of the French in North Africa. Muslim resentment that Britain and France were in arms against the Ottoman Sultan, Caliph of Islam, was an issue that no British or French Government was ever able accurately to gauge, either then or later. Thus, to get a high religious potentate on the Allied side who would offset our enmity to the other religious potentate on the German side, was reckoned a shrewd move.

There were of course two views on this. (What the Muslim view was, if in fact there was such a thing, is still remarkably difficult to ascertain.) But certainly British officials in Cairo, who often found a great deal that was odd and more that was impossible in the views on Eastern questions held in Whitehall, liked to dwell on the point that the Sherif of Mecca was a Sunni Muslim, while the Arabs of Mesopotamia were Shi'ia. Storrs commented that therefore the name of Husein was likely to be as glorious a talisman to them as Alva's would have been to the Protestants of the Low Countries.

But these were small details only in the great strategical concept, which were not permitted to mar it. For whatever else they were, the Sherif and his ambitious sons were genuine indigenous inhabitants, whose forces, guided and maintained by us, would help pin down the Turks in a theatre of war vital to our security. The attack mounted by the Turks on the Suez Canal on 2–3 February 1915 was ineptly mounted, and parried without trouble, but who was to say that another, planned and perhaps carried out by Germans, might not be successful?

Husein of course was looking for an ally rather than a protector. He did not have Weizmann's clear conception of what was and what was not immediately practicable in the Middle East, and he never arrived at a full comprehension of what role this area, invented by military geographers, played in the diplomacy of the Christian Powers. (His sons Abdullah and Feisal, who were later to learn their lessons in a hard school of experience, arrived at a shrewd enough estimate of this.) But in 1915 Husein held good cards in his hand. To get him to play them, England had to make pledges to him of a kind smaller in scale but similar in essence to those which that same year she found herself constrained to make to Russians, Greeks, and Italians in regard to other parts of the Turkish inheritance. For by July the British position in the Levant was very much a defensive one. By October Sir Henry MacMahon, High Commissioner in Egypt, was pledging to Husein that, in return for the latter's mounting of an Arab rebellion, to be paid for in gold by the British Treasury, Great Britain would ensure to him that 'independent Muslim state' of which Grey had spoken. Husein was to note that 'portions of Syria lying to the west of the districts of Damascus, Homs, Hama, and Aleppo' could not be said (by the Allies) to be purely Arab, and must thus be excluded from any such Arab state. Moreover, our own especial interest in Mesopotamia was reserved, and the French claims in the areas around Alexandretta were underwritten.

In this curious correspondence, in the conduct of which both MacMahon and Husein studiously kept avoiding each other's concrete points, no mention was made of Palestine, or even of Jerusalem. The correspondence itself, although published by *Le Temps* in 1919, was not officially laid before Parliament by a British Government until another 20 years had passed.[1] In the interim it was easy for both the British and the Arabs to provide their own interpretations of the various ambiguities that studded the correspondence, and to hold to them with a sincerity which might be suspect, but which could not be easily impugned. For what was 'Syria'? Where did it stop and where did 'Mesopotamia' begin? What anyway was Mesopotamia? How great was the area around Alexandretta meant to be? How large were 'portions'? What was a 'district'? How exactly could a district be said to 'lie to the west of'? Neither the British nor the Sherif troubled to probe these points in 1915, as no very gainful result could have been expected to emerge from a debate on the imperfections of territorial boundaries every

[1] Cmd. 5957 (1939), docs. 1-8.

M

one of which was still to be drawn, and whose suzerain lord was yet to be displaced by a force that was not yet in being. Husein asked only that, if the projected revolt was unsuccessful, he and his Arabs should not be left alone to face the fury of the Turks; and that, if successful, the value of the Arab services and the extent of the Arab claim should not be overlooked when a peace conference was summoned. Even to these reasonable provisos he got no clear answer. It was all bazaar-trading: and as such it was put in the shade the following year, 1916, when the real protagonists on the Middle Eastern stage, Great Britain and France, came together to do what they could not have done in 1904 and squared to the problem of the future of these Arab territories of the Ottoman Empire.

The resultant 'Sykes-Picot' partition of the Middle East was arranged in London, and not in Cairo. The officers of the Arab Bureau did not hear of it until all was completed, and Mark Sykes, head of the 'Middle East Department' at the War Office and one of many Cabinet *factotums*, came to tell them about it. Neither the Sherif nor Weizmann were ever informed of the Anglo-French plans officially, and out of this both were glad in future times to make a considerable amount of capital. Neither, certainly, could be expected to accept at its face value the excuse that amid the pressure of great events the English had not found the time to let them know of the arrangement.

'Sykes-Picot' has always had a bad press. Lloyd George described it as an 'egregious document'.[1] Curzon condemned it as a 'fancy sketch', which made the singular error of assuming that Mosul was not an integral part of Mesopotamia. Some official commentators, and historians following their lead, still speak of it as if the whole thing was self-generated behind the backs of responsible statesmen, something for which the Foreign Office ought not to be held accountable. In fact it was a Foreign Office responsibility. Something can be made of the excuse that since the Foreign Secretary was not even a member of the War Cabinet, he was hardly to blame if large decisions on policy were there taken by men who knew nothing of diplomatic tradition and who only called in Foreign Office expert opinion when they felt so inclined. Certainly, at a time when no one was absolutely certain what his colleagues were doing, areas of re-

[1] Lloyd George, *The Truth About the Peace Treaties*, (London, 1938), II, 1023.

sponsibility became blurred, and the customary departmental loyalty normally given to a policy-decision was grudged. The blame for what went on could therefore be laid later not on the innocent departments but on Lloyd George and Milner, who were for different reasons looked upon as expendable by the Conservatives who kept the Coalition Government in power. Yet Maurice Hankey, who had best reason to know, stressed later how Lloyd George took particular pains to let those who were not in the War Cabinet know what was going on, and this is likely enough: Lloyd George had enough trouble with the Army to want to go looking for more among his colleagues. 'Sykes-Picot' was no worse an arrangement than the Treaty of London which bribed Italy. It was an example of frank imperialism, so ambitious that only two years later, before the fighting had stopped and while President Wilson's principles were still the commonplaces of popular sentiment, it had become a distinct embarrassment — one that was the more embarrassing in that it was given out, in the public interest, by those friends of the people, the October Revolutionaries in Petrograd.

'Sykes-Picot' was a mapmakers' exercise that is best appreciated from a study of their own map. It allotted Acre to Britain. It allotted the coastal strip of Syria, a strip that included Haifa, Tripoli and Alexandretta and indeed lay 'to the west of' Aleppo and Damascus, to France. Cilicia, the Taurus, the town of Diarbekr, all went to France also. To Britain was allotted 'Central and Lower Mesopotamia', with the two cities of Baghdad and Basra. In the hinterland two enormous zones A and B were laid out. In these zones independent Arab states were to arise, but the division between A and B was also to mark the division of the spheres of interest of Britain and France, as the protecting Powers. Britain also obtained permission, which both France and Germany together had denied her in the spring of 1914, to construct a railway from Haifa to Baghdad. Palestine was to be an internationalised area. Its boundaries, like all other boundaries mentioned in the agreement, were to be later defined.

British imperialism was thus setting out to get what it felt it needed in the Middle Eastern theatre. What this consisted of was well defined by Leopold Amery, in 1916 the secretary to a 'Territorial Changes Committee' of the Cabinet, and, with Sykes himself as colleague, assistant political secretary to the Cabinet under the authority of the omniscient Hankey. It was: 'continuity of territory

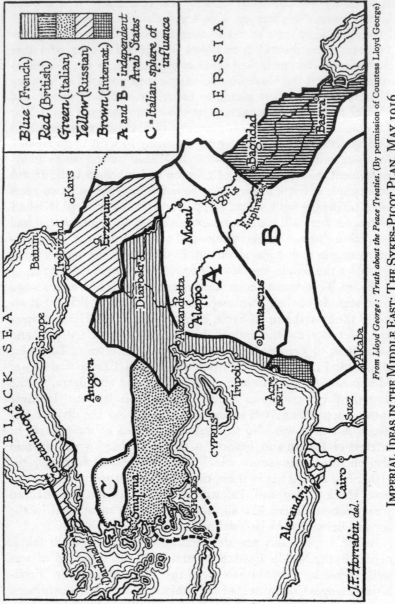

From Lloyd George: Truth about the Peace Treaties. (By permission of Countess Lloyd George)

IMPERIAL IDEAS IN THE MIDDLE EAST: THE SYKES-PICOT PLAN, MAY 1916

J.F. Horrabin del.

Legend:

Blue (French)
Red (British)
Green (Italian)
Yellow (Russian)
Brown (Internat.)
A and B = independent Arab States
C = Italian sphere of influence

or of control between Egypt and India'.[1] This was the corner-stone of British policy thereafter, though 'Sykes-Picot' itself was demolished and other strange things happened later which no Territorial Changes Committee, however farsighted, could then have reckoned on. One receives the impression from Amery's own book, *My Political Life*, that to ensure first the inception and then the maintenance of this imperial policy he, Hankey, and Sykes pulled more strings than any of their masters, save Milner, were aware of. He notes how Hankey would always insist that Cabinet minutes must end with a definite decision. 'This was not easy,' is his comment,

> after some particularly woolly discussion. But my experience was that, if one invented the best decision one could think of, it was rarely queried by those concerned.[2]

Self-importance is not necessarily accompanied by pomposity, and perhaps this observation need not be taken too seriously: but anyone with experience of committees at a lower level may consider that there is some truth in the point. Certainly the significance of these able and purposeful *aides* in formulating ideas for a policy, even if not the policy itself, is not to be underestimated.

For example, Storrs, when secretary in September 1917 of a Cabinet committee whose members consisted of Balfour, Milner, and Curzon, busied himself with writing memoranda on the affairs of Egypt in the sure knowledge that 'Milner will correct some things, Curzon will rewrite the whole document, and Balfour will not read it at all.'[3] It was Amery who wrote a memorandum for another Cabinet committee, consisting again of the three staunch imperialists Curzon, Milner, and Smuts, on the subject of 'security', that most elusive of all imperial goals. Amery also sat as secretary to Curzon on a committee for 'Territorial Desiderata', and it was he who drafted the final version, after Milner had tried his hand, of the Foreign Office paper on Zionism issued on 2 November 1917 and known to the world as the Balfour Declaration. Balfour as Foreign Secretary, when challenged by critics in the Commons to state like a man what game he was playing, may perhaps often have wondered what kind of cards he had been dealt, and by whom. Nevertheless he knew the rules of the game perfectly. He was the most clear-sighted of all Disraeli's imperialist successors. He lacked the emo-

---

[1] Amery, *My Political Life*, II, 102.   [2] ibid., 94.
[3] Ronald Storrs, *Orientations*, (London, 1937), p. 304.

tional drive of Joseph Chamberlain, but he was always fascinated by power and its use, and he could assess it with a sureness of judgment that outclassed that of better-publicised imperialists like Curzon.

Certainly by 1919, when he was delegate to the Peace Conference, Balfour had made himself fully master of the wartime imperial deals concerning the Middle East. Their intricate convolutions appealed to him aesthetically, and their contradictions did not deter him from arriving at a clear view as to the aims of Britain and France in that theatre. 'Neither of us,' he wrote,

> wants much less than supreme economic and political control, to be exercised no doubt (at least in our case) in friendly and unostentatious co-operation with the Arabs —

adding, 'but nevertheless, in the last resort, to be exercised.'[1] Always a realist, he took some pleasure in dispelling those clouds of romantic rhetoric that had already gathered and which were to remain as an envelope around the story of the 'Arab Revolt'. Discussing that shadowy 'adviser' who appeared in the Sykes-Picot documents with the role of assisting the Arabs to set up their independent states in those Zones A and B, he commented, in terms much the same as those in which Granville had guided Cromer in Egypt back in 1883,

> Now, by an adviser, these documents undoubtedly mean — though they do not say so — an adviser whose advice must be followed.

On the concept of Arab independence, Balfour again had something sharp to say: 'No State,' he insisted,

> can be described as really independent which has habitually and normally to follow foreign advice supported, if the worst comes to the worst, by troops, aeroplanes, and tanks.[2]

This has a note of platitude, but it was not a platitude to his colleagues Curzon and Milner. It made them wince, and its language was of a kind they were unable to bring themselves to use. Yet it was a simple fact enough, and one whose reality no subsequent 'Treaty' arranged between any European Power and any Arab 'State' was ever able to mask from the Arabs who inhabited those

---

[1] DBFP, I, iv, 9 September 1919, doc. No. 265, p. 374.
[2] ibid., 344.

States. They could not be expected to share the Balfourian detachment, but they knew where the truth lay. Feisal, third son of the Sherif of Mecca, the warrior of the Arab Revolt and T. E. Lawrence's candidate for honour, who had led it, under Allenby's eye, to Damascus itself, saw Balfour's point plain. Feisal had heard of independence in the Middle East before, and knew what it connoted. The Arabs in Syria, he pointed out, knew it too. They knew that 'independence' for them would mean the introduction of 'capitulations' and extra-territorial privileges, legal and commercial, for foreigners; would entail the protection, by foreigners, of the Syrian Christians; would bring about the granting of foreign concessions, and, in the train of such grants, corruptions and intrigues innumerable. This was not inviting, but, even so, Feisal insisted that the Syrians would prefer all this to the establishment of a mandate, and a French mandate at that, over them. This would only be regarded, could only be regarded, as national death.

Since independence therefore meant one thing in Europe and another in the European perimeter, it was not a matter for surprise that the language of the Covenant of the League of Nations, designed to suit the longitudes of Washington, Paris, and Prague, should, when employed in the longitude of Damascus and Aleppo, get its users into trouble. From the first the British and the French confidently expected nothing else from President Wilson's declared wish to ascertain the views and opinions of the Levantine populations. His deliberate choice of two American commissioners to examine this matter, Messrs. King and Crane, men who knew nothing of Syria or of the Middle East as a whole, was a direct rebuttal of the entrenched British official theory that only a Middle Eastern expert, a member of what Storrs called the 'great club', really understood what an Arab actually was, or could weigh the great strategic principles that were visible, to the initiated, in the desert sands. Churchill's comment on the King-Crane Commission was more vividly expressed than Balfour's, but the two statesmen held the same view:

> To stroll around among masses of disorganised, infuriated people, asking them what they think about it and what they would like, is the most sure and certain method of breeding strife.[1]

The outcome of this private expedition was as had been foreseen.

[1] W. S. Churchill, *The Aftermath*, (London, 1929), p. 364.

The King-Crane report — which was not officially communicated to the British Government nor laid before Parliament — considered that the three things to which the British were already committed in the Middle East were either mistaken in aim or impossible of fulfilment. Syria, it advised, should not be sundered from Mesopotamia. No French mandate over Syria should be granted. It would be impossible to establish Zionism and the 'National Home' amid the Arabs of Palestine without the use of force.[1]

There were many in the British Government, and many serving it, who agreed with 'King-Crane', though it was not politic to say so. Balfour himself had by May 1919 come to the conclusion that in face of the present hostility of the Arab majority in Palestine the British Government would not be able to fulfil its pledges of any form of political preference for the Jews. Steady colonisation, he noted, would have to precede the granting of political favours. Similar adjustment would have to be made in regard to all those other pledges to all those other people, which the exigencies of wartime had compelled us to make. After a careful examination of the records of wartime diplomacy, Balfour came to the conclusion that the literal fulfilment of all our declarations was impossible, partly because they were incompatible with each other and partly because they were incompatible with the facts. Five documents competed for the solution of the Syrian problem, to begin with. There was that odd correspondence between Sir Henry MacMahon and the Sherif, on which the latter and his principal spokesman, his son Feisal, were now putting the most embarrassing interpretations. There was the now notorious Sykes-Picot agreement, which never mentioned the Sherif at all. There was what was called the 'Declaration to the Seven' of 1917, which consisted of a statement made to a committee of Syrian Arabs, issued in Cairo and instigated by Lawrence, that the pre-war Arab provinces of the Ottoman Empire, and any other Arab areas freed by the military action of their own inhabitants during the war, should become entirely independent. There was Lloyd George's ebullition of January 1918; and, surpassing this in scale, the heady Anglo-French declaration issued four days before the Armistice of November, which promised the complete and final liberation of the peoples whom

[1] The report is printed in *Papers relating to the Foreign Relations of the United States: the Paris Peace Conference 1919*, XII, (Washington, 1943), 745 ff., 848 ff., — which includes a confidential appendix, 'for the use of Americans only'.

Turkey had oppressed, with the setting-up of national governments and administrations which should be chosen by the indigenous populations. Finally, but not before the camel's back was already broken, there were the firm statements to be found in the Covenant of the League of Nations, to the effect that the same right of self-determination should obtain in the fallen Ottoman Empire as in the fallen Empires of Europe.

In Balfour's view, the best thing that could be salvaged out of all this was the spirit, if not the precise letter, of the Sykes-Picot agreement. Britain and France must remain in the Middle East and continue to play the roles they had played throughout the nineteenth century — but this time, if possible, in harmony. London and Paris should be the capitals of the Middle East, the two places where Middle Eastern policy had its proper home. Palestine should be permitted to extend across the Jordan, and perhaps it might be well to connect Mesopotamia with the Mediterranean by means of rail and pipelines which must however pass through British-protected territory. Lawrence and his band, regarded in the Foreign Office as Feisal's bearleaders, outsiders anyway, and not members of the 'club', must somehow be prevailed upon to stop embarrassing this sensible British policy.

How this was to be done did not at present emerge, for Lawrence was even then confiding his view to Curzon that it was his great ambition that the Arabs should comprise 'our first brown Dominion, and not our last brown colony.'[1] What this meant Curzon did not enquire, but its implications were disturbing enough in that they harmonised remarkably with those of the arguments produced by the delegation from the Hejaz which was at that moment, in company with a dozen aspirants from the four quarters of Europe, pacing the *coulisses* of Versailles. Lloyd George had already been bluntly told that the plan to separate Syria from Mesopotamia was 'imperialistic', a word not long minted but one soon to dull with overuse. Nuri es-Said, ahead of whom spanned a long future in the lee of British power, was assured that the imperialists wished first to divide and then to rule the Arabs lest some single Arab state should develop ambitions of its own which would conflict with grand policy and strategy. He suggested himself that some form of federation of Arab states might provide a solution that would neutralise the suspicions of both parties.

[1] *DBFP*, I, iv, Lawrence to Curzon, 25 September 1919, p. 423.

This kind of talk won no favour in either Paris or London. In Downing Street itself Feisal put his case with considerable skill.[1] He pointed out that Arabs had not fought Turks with the intention of dividing the Arab territories between France and Britain. He warned the Cabinet that the future government of the Arab provinces would prove to be the last lesson that Europe had to give to the East. What sort of lesson was it to be? No one had an answer to this searching question. Lloyd George's mind still reflected the confusion which the various papers from the Foreign Office had instilled in it. He declared roundly to Feisal — what Balfour had confided was an impossibility — that he was bound to keep to both sets of engagements, those to Husein and those to the French. He might have added that by the same logic he was bound also to keep the engagement with the Zionists, which conflicted with the pledges made to both Husein and the French. In fact, now as always, if it was a question of weighing France with the Arabs in a scale of power, it was France who tipped the balance. This was certainly Lloyd George's view, though a number of his colleagues saw little to recommend it. It was not Feisal alone who was unable to understand why we had to pay any attention to French susceptibilities, and to French claims in the Levant; for Russia was now gone from the scene, and was unlikely to return in the foreseeable future. Balfour, too, wondered just what the French claims were based on, while Curzon considered the French attitude over Syria — which after all had been wrested from the enemy by British imperial forces — to be insufferable. But in this Lloyd George's word was law. He felt we could afford to be generous, and in Clemenceau he had to deal with a man who cared as little as he did himself about the French *mystique* of power in the Levant.

Clemenceau, always a 'European', an unreconstructed Radical and therefore a natural enemy of the aristocratic clericalism which governed French ideas in the Levant, was absorbed in the problem of the security of the French frontier: oriental trophies such as Mosul were nothing in significance compared to the Rhine. After a year of bickering, which permanently soured relations between British and French officials in the Levant, he and Lloyd George were able to come to an accommodation by which the British retired from the French 'zone' in the Middle East, but retained Mosul. The conference at San Remo in April 1920 arranged the matter of

[1] ibid., 283 ff.

mandates to both nations' satisfaction, and the frontiers drawn around the new state of Palestine were in fact the frontiers of the two Great Powers in the Middle East.

Mandate — a concept invented by the American historian George Beer, who had also invented 'the Old Colonial System' — was all things to all men. Statesmen in power tended to look on it as an escape-hatch. Grey had thought of internationalising Palestine in 1915, and even 'Sykes-Picot' had provided for a 'special régime' there. The Independent Labour Party, to scotch the snake of imperialism in Africa, had suggested in 1917 that all that continent's tropical territories should be placed under an international control. No firmer enemy of this idea existed than Smuts, who in other spheres supported the notion of mandate, and gave it an intellectual content it had not previously enjoyed. Empires, in his view, were breaking down, and subject peoples and provinces could not be left amid the ruins and the rubble. It was for the League of Nations to take them under its responsibility until they were able to govern themselves. President Wilson supported this view, suggesting in December 1918 that all the German colonies should become the common property of the League of Nations, and that they should be administered by small Powers. It was Lloyd George's comment — 'the Dominions won't like that' — that revealed the divergence of view on this matter between Britain and her powerful 'associate'. Cromer on his side had pointed out that international control had bedevilled rather than helped the good administration of Egypt; while Colonel House commented darkly that he suspected that beneath Lloyd George's suggestion that the United States should accept the mandate for German East Africa lurked a motive of another colour. This was, that the United States should take the thankless, while Britain took the lucrative, responsibilities. House's thinking was shared by many of his compatriots. The 'King-Crane' suggestion that the United States should take the mandate over all Syria and Palestine, together with the older idea that Armenia would thrive best under American protection, were both to be thrown over by the United States' Senate.

Neither on Left or Right in Britain was mandate a popular idea. The Liberal historian H. A. L. Fisher was content to leave in his *History of Europe*, throughout all its many editions, the comment that 'the crudity of conquest was draped in the veil of morality'. But others saw in conquest nothing to be ashamed of, and the veil entirely unnecessary, as no moral question was involved. They considered its imposition upon us as a device of American theoreticians, indeed as an insult: Lloyd George was quite right about the Dominions, who had firm convictions as to the rightful heirs of Samoa, New Guinea, and South-West Africa. But the important thing to be borne in mind about a mandate was that, however liberal it might be in other aspects, it always put the control of the particular territory's foreign relations firmly in the hands of the mandatory, as the protecting Power. Three peace Treaties — those of Sèvres, Lausanne, and Versailles — ceded the ex-enemy territories to the Allied and Associated Powers, and in these territories it was their word that was law. Curzon tacitly agreed with those who considered mandate merely another name for a sphere of influence, for he took some credit to himself in the House of Lords for never having suggested that Persia should be placed under mandate. He always took pains to point out that mandates were supervised by, but did not originate with, the League of Nations. The gift of a mandate, he explained, rested with the Powers who had conquered the territories, which it then fell to them to distribute.[1] Mandate, Balfour concurred, was a self-imposed limitation by the conquerors on the sovereignty which they exercised over the conquered territory. The Covenant of the League of Nations indeed stated in regard to the Ottoman Empire that the wishes of the communities within it must be a principal consideration in the allocation of mandates — but at San Remo no attention was paid to this, and Syria was forced under France. Amery meanwhile was writing briskly, in his capacity as Under-Secretary of State for the Colonies, of 'fixing up' a mandate for German East Africa (Tanganyika), and while doing so he inserted a clause providing for Tanganyika's right to a closer union in the future with the other British possessions in East Africa.[2]

From the imperialist point of view, therefore, the existence of the concept of mandate did not fundamentally alter positions of power. Confirmation of the correctness of this diagnosis came with considerable force from the subject-races who were involved. The old *pashaliks* were gone, they had become mandates, that was all. The attitude of the Mesopotamians may be taken as an illustration. Iraqi nationalists saw little to satisfy their aspirations in the Anglo-

[1] 25 June 1920.
[2] Amery, *My Political Life*, II, 181.

Iraqi Treaty of 1922, or in subsequent ameliorating arrangements in 1926–27. Mandate meant in this case that there were two governments in the country — one national, and one foreign. There were many Iraqis who genuinely believed that Arab and British interests were reconcilable, but the Mandate got in the way of both. An official British report on the Government of Iraq, submitted to the League of Nations in 1928, admitted as much. 'The Iraq Government,' said this Report,

> controls and administers the railways and the Basra port, but does not own them; can declare martial law, but, under the Military Agreement, cannot administer it; and has an Army, but cannot move it except with the concurrence of the British High Commissioner. Foreign Governments can discriminate in tariff and other matters against Iraqi subjects, but the Iraqi Government has no power to retaliate; foreign subjects have special judicial privileges in Iraq while Iraqi subjects have no reciprocal advantages abroad.

Accordingly, unable to defend such a state of affairs, the incoming Labour Government opened negotiations with Nuri es-Said in 1929, and a new Treaty was signed in June 1930. This arranged a close alliance between Britain and Iraq, made the Iraqis responsible for the internal administration in all its branches, and obtained the recognition by Iraq that the maintenance and protection of British communications in the country was a common Anglo-Iraqi interest. Britain was allowed her air-bases at Habbaniyah and Shu'aybah, 'on the understanding that the presence of those forces shall not constitute in any manner an occupation, and will in no way prejudice the sovereign rights of Iraq.'

Understandably, many Iraqi nationalists failed to understand this understanding. To them, the presence of alien bases on Iraqi soil went ill with proclamations asserting that Iraq was now fully independent of foreign tutelage and control. To imperialists, proclamations asserting Iraqi independence undermined the sense of security the continuance of the bases should have brought them, and the wrangling in Iraq before the treaty was ratified had its counterpart in the House of Commons. Had the Mandate been given up for no very well-defined *quid pro quo*? Was not Baghdad, in Churchill's words, still the Clapham Junction of the Middle East? These fears were, in fact, illusory: from the imperial point of view a good bargain had been struck. The British not only had the bases, but the right to use railways, rivers, ports, aerodromes and all other means of communication. All Iraq's war-material and equipment was to be purchased in Britain, and only British officers were to be granted posts as military instructors in the Iraqi Army. An Advisory Military Mission soon took up its residence, and it was the British Ambassador who enjoyed diplomatic precedence.

So, Mandate or Treaty, power was still asserted. But, since neither Mandate nor Treaty had been the original goals of imperialists, they tended to behave rather ungraciously about their benefits. For it had seemed, when the war drew to its close, that great opportunities were theirs — that not since the eighteenth century had Great Britain been presented with so great a field in which to extend her imperial power, absolutely, as that which lay before her in the Middle East. Winston Churchill indeed begins his book *The Aftermath* with the statement that at the end of the war England was raised to the highest position she had yet attained. British and Dominion troops, to the number of 400,000, still garrisoned the lands of the Ottoman Empire — although this great number was itself but the remnant of the total of one and a half million men who had been employed on the campaign, and whose activities had cost their country some £750 million. Feisal still flew his standard in Damascus, still drew a monthly salary of £150,000 from the British Treasury. Imperial caissons were already set down in the soil of Palestine, Mesopotamia, Egypt, and Persia (where the Shah had to be content with £120,000 a year), on which might be reared a new imperial structure. Its outworks we already held British troops were still in those towns of Central Asia whose very names had long been fabulous, long acted as a magnet, in the minds of ambitious Anglo-Indian frontier officers. Established there and in the Caucasus, they could safely command what a later generation of British strategists was to call the 'northern tier' of the Middle Eastern world. Had the British people wished to answer this new call to a new but plainly manifest destiny, there was no external force to hinder them. Those who had organised the opportunity, set the stage for another imperial drama, thus waited for an enthusiastic audience to come and applaud their play. They waited in vain.

Yet the drama was fashioned out of the old materials, well-tried, long approved. What Curzon said of the case of Persia could have been said of all the lands we now bestrode. If it were asked, he wrote, why we should undertake the task at all, and why Persia should not be left to herself, to be allowed to rot into picturesque decay, the answer was that her geographical position, the magnitude of our interests in the country, and the future security of our Eastern Empire combined to render it impossible for us now — just as it would have been impossible for us at any time during the past half century — to disinterest ourselves in what happened in and to Persia.[1] The course of the war just over itself proved this without a doubt. It was to counteract Turkish and German intrigues at Teheran, the Persian capital, that the Indian Army had occupied the southern zone of the country which had been allotted to us by the Convention of 1907 with Russia. After the fall of Baghdad, the Mesopotamian capital, a British force had pushed up towards the Caspian Sea to seal the northern doors both of Persia and Mesopotamia. Admittedly the Turks and the Germans were now accounted for, but in the areas they had left were now encamped the Bolsheviks in unknown quantities, and our troops at Kasvin still provided Persia with her only shield against the expected incoming horde. That these troops should remain there, that we should reinforce them in strength, was plainly in Persia's own interest, for what forces could she herself produce to deal with the Russians, who, whether Tsarist or Bolshevik, would continue to threaten the very existence of Persia as a national state?

The terms of the Treaty with Persia that Curzon drew up in 1920 underlined these points. What Persia needed now and in the foreseeable future was money and stability. The British Treasury should supply the first and British advisers the second of these necessities. Moreover, did it not say distinctly, in the first clause of this Treaty, that His Majesty's Government were bound to respect absolutely the independence and integrity of Persia? (Balfour's candour about the reality that lay behind these 'masked words' was never emulated by his colleague Curzon, who would probably have denied that Balfour's point was valid. Curzon found it hard enough to bring himself to mention the word 'oil', which was well supplied with masks from the outset of its career in international politics.) Finally, when we took into account our new responsibilities in Mesopotamia, it was clear, to Curzon, that we could not allow 'a hotbed of misrule' to exist in Persia, or in any part of that territory which lay between Mesopotamia and the Baluchi frontiers

[1] Memorandum, 9 August 1919; *DBFP*, I, iv, 1119 ff.

of India. Assessment of the issues in this sense was by no means the same as the promotion of 'spread-eagle imperialism over the wastes of Central Asia'. It was a statement of policy based on obvious commonsense. Great Britain's task now, in this new era, was not only to seek peace, but to make peace, and to ensure peace. Only our continuing presence could do this in the Middle East. It was our duty to stay there. We had no right to replace commotion with chaos.

This was the kind of language and reasoning that had been used to explain the non-retirement of British forces from Egypt, forty years back, and which was still being used to explain our continued residence there. But the volume of criticism directed against Curzon's policy was greater than anything the Gladstone Government, or successive Governments, had had to contend with in relation to Egypt. What Persia wanted, composed a catalogue from out of which every other nationality that wished to declare itself a nation was to take and adapt items. She wanted representation at the Peace Conference. She wanted abrogation of the partition of 1907. She wanted compensation paid for the damages that had been wrought by, or at any rate might be put to the account of, the forces that had occupied her territory during the war. She wanted cancellation of all foreign extra-territorial rights. She wanted the revision of foreign concessions. She wanted the revision of her frontiers. Above and beyond all these things, she wanted recognition. Curzon's 1920 Treaty reflected the 1907 Convention in this: it did not recognise Persia, it only dealt with her.

Arguments of this kind were in the long run to prove more powerful than all the British forces that ever left their native shore. Even now, in 1920, Persia's voice raised echoes in Washington, where self-determination was still the creed of the State Department. The parallel that Curzon carefully drew between England's relations with Persia and the United States' relations with Liberia was viewed with cold disfavour. The Americans, as Curzon confided in a gloomy minute, 'really seemed to have gone out of their way to be nasty' on the business of Persia. In this they were being abetted, it also seemed, by Grey himself, who was now British Ambassador in Washington. Curzon suspected that Grey had a sore conscience, remembering 1907, about the affairs of Persia, and grumbled that his distinguished predecessor in the Foreign Office had not been sent to the United States with a view to making trouble about the Persian Treaty, although he seemed to regard that as his main preoccupation.[1]

Grey was not alone in fearing that this kind of protecting policy, if it were to be seriously pursued, would cause us to drift into an extension of our frontiers from the Himalayas to the Caucasus: 'spread-eagle imperialism' would not be stayed merely because imperialists chose to deny its existence. Its administrative roots were beginning to go deep. The suggestion was already being sounded out that a Middle Eastern Department should be created, possibly with a full Secretary of State at its head, which should draw its officials from a specialist service not dissimilar to that which at present governed in the Sudan. Drift and confusion already existed: it seemed that the War Office did not know or greatly care what the Foreign Office was doing, and certainly it would have been hard to explain to an inquirer why it was we abandoned a control of forty years' standing over the Afghans while we were working to establish exactly the same kind of tie with the Persians, and had such grandiose plans for the Arabs of Mesopotamia. But Crewe, leading the Liberals in the House of Lords, told Curzon flatly during a debate on policy in Mesopotamia that the people of this country were not prepared to play fairy godmother to all undeveloped parts of the world.[2] The country simply could not afford to pursue such a policy, at a time when the annual national expenditure was in excess of the 1914 figure by £950 million. We had to make up our minds collectively that we could no longer undertake to be either the rulers or the protectors of the whole of the world. The task was an impossible one. Look at the events in Mesopotamia as an example: between 1918 and 1920 we spent over £50 million in setting up a grandiose Crown Colony system of rule in that territory, run by enthusiastic and inexperienced Anglo-Indian officers. (Of the 233 officers in Mesopotamia, only four were over the age of 45.) And what had been the result? A dangerous outbreak of Arab feeling in July 1920, which only the inability of imperialists to call things by their right names prevented being designated a rebellion. T. E. Lawrence exclaimed at this, how a hundred thousand Arabs, men whom we had been glad to blandish while the Turk was still in the field, had been sacrificed to a type of colonial administration which could benefit nobody but the administrators: it seemed that the Indian Government were intent on turning

[1] *DBFP*, I, iv, 1195, 1205.   [2] 5 H of L 40, 25 June 1920.

N

Mesopotamia into some kind of Punjab — not the modern Punjab, either, but the Punjab that Henry and John Lawrence had ruled in the early eighteen fifties.

The charge was over-emphatic, like a great many of T. E. Lawrence's charges against officialdom of all kinds. But his words carried far, as nothing that the English hero of the Arab Revolt had to say about the Arabs could yet safely be ignored. Colonel Josiah Wedgwood, now in the Labour ranks, diagnosed from his point of view the flaw in all these one-man, proconsular policies, most of which had neither been originally sanctioned nor indeed ever brought to the notice of Parliament. Whether these policies concerned the Sèvres Treaty with Turkey, promptly jettisoned by the Turks, or Curzon's Persian Treaty, promptly jettisoned by the Persians, or Winston Churchill's intervention in Russia, which had cost the country over £100 million for no returns at all, they had all collapsed or were in the last throes of collapse because their collapse had been inevitable from the first. For they were based on no firm political principle. They all needed, for their proper operation, a military basis which they did not have. They depended on the continuation of military conscription, and military conscription was a policy that had been bodily thrown out by the electorate of the country in 1918. And rightly, in Wedgwood's opinion. Why, anyway, should we be asked to erect a system of 'elaborate palisades' around India? Who was going to attack India? Who was a worse enemy to India than ourselves, with our outmoded ideas of imperial control?

The war was over, and the days of power of its managers seemed numbered. A new day had dawned. Up till 1914 both the United States and the Dominions had been able safely to devote themselves to absorption in domestic affairs, and to the development of their democratic systems to a pitch far beyond that reached in Great Britain, whose time was mainly occupied maintaining the *pax Britannica*. But now the democracy in Britain for whose sake the war had been fought — had it not? — was going to have that say in the control of political affairs which had been denied it while the mysteries of high policy, grand strategy, and the like had been the private perquisites of a few determined men. And even if, on any one subject, the democracy preferred to give no hint of its preference how it should be dealt with, silence should not be taken to mean consent. Blunders, disguised in war, would in future be committed in open forum. Thus the Coalition Government between 1918 and 1922 was left to deal with issues that the war had poisoned, and in which the electorate took little interest. It was Government's task to make the best arrangements possible in the circumstances. It was no time for mission. It was no time for calls to be made for effort, for shoulders to be summoned to a wheel, for ringing phrases in the leader-columns. There had been something too much of all this. Thus the Coalition had to face the Irish question, grimly, in the knowledge that no political dividend could possibly accrue from dealing with it. It was to be left to the Unionists to put through a form of Home Rule for Ireland in which they had no confidence. In February 1920 Birkenhead as Lord Chancellor frankly declared, when introducing the second reading of the Government of Ireland Bill in the Lords, that he would have preferred to see established in Ireland 'twenty years of resolute government' all over again. But he knew, and said as much, that we had neither the machinery nor the popular support necessary to put any such policy into operation. Not in Ireland, not anywhere. It was no time, assuredly, for Winston Churchill as Secretary for War to pilot a Naval, Military, and Air Force Bill (6 March 1919) which would have retained nine hundred thousand men in arms.

It was necessary therefore to cut down the Middle Eastern schemes of the imperialists to scale. The system originally envisaged in Mesopotamia alone would have required to be backed with military and air forces which Parliament would never agree to supply. It was Churchill's work, at the Cairo Conference in March 1921, to reshape the Middle East according to a lesser plan, but even so he saw to it that to Mesopotamia was awarded the protection of eight squadrons of the Royal Air Force, based on Baghdad — a force that accounted for one-third of the whole R.A.F. Nevertheless the idea of the bomber as a policeman did not emerge on to the international stage without criticism. Was the bomber to become, enquired the *Round Table*, a regular instrument of our administration? If we took to governing from aerodromes and to bringing in our revenue by hovering planes, 'our rule will have become Oriental and its end will be seen'. For our power in the Middle East was not (surely not?) founded on force, but 'on the contrast in the minds of our subjects between the justice and rationality of our methods and the terrorism of their former oppressors'.[1]

[1] *RT*, December 1919, No. 37, p. 110.

Rule over Mesopotamia was given as a consolation prize to Feisal in October 1922. Whether this was a proper diagnosis or not, the arrangements made at Cairo implied a tacit admission of defeat by the imperialists. Feisal, who had been homeless since his ejection by the French from Damascus, was expected to be, and did in fact prove, 'loyal': but hopes bred in wartime of making this great bastion of India another bright jewel in the diadem now died, and were not resuscitated. The Mesopotamian adventure, declared Asquith in some rancour, had been one of the worst investments that we had ever made in our lives. It seemed a symbol of the finality put to imperialist hopes that the Arabs' own name for Mesopotamia — Iraq — was now accepted into English speech.

Yet Asquith was wrong. Although the degree of control in the Middle East was not all that had been hoped for, control was none the less established there, and 'the Middle East supply services', established on a separate supply-vote from September 1921, was one branch of the public expenditure on which the 'Geddes Axe' was not allowed to fall. The Protectorate established over Cyprus was terminated in 1925, and the island became a British Crown Colony. Egypt, another Protectorate, became a kingdom in 1922, but one whose external policy still remained in British hands, as did the destinies of the Sudan and the responsibility for its defence. The extent of our control over Iraq has already been described. Although Persia was given over to internal disorder, our economic interests there remained secure so long as we controlled the Persian Gulf. This we did. The power of Ibn Saud in Arabia, who had himself conquered the Hejaz, was frankly recognised by a Treaty made in 1927, but we could afford to do this since we could keep watch on his southern shores from our possession of Aden and the protectorate in the Hadrhamaut. We owned the mandate for Palestine both cis- and trans-Jordan, for the area east of the river had been given to Feisal's brother Abdullah, as the emirate of Transjordan, in 1921. They were British officers who trained Abdullah's Arab Legion, British bombers which controlled the tribal areas from Amman. The entire Middle East, with the exception of Syria, was held in the grip of Great Britain; and Syria could be discounted, as the French were no longer considered as imperial rivals. So long as Britain was resolved to maintain this grip, no Great Power could enter the closed world of the Mediterranean and the Levant. It was a resolution that was proved when Mussolini's Italy sought to enter that world, and the British made a new treaty with Egypt (1936); when in 1940 the British fleet destroyed the French fleet, a possible pawn in other's hands, at Mers-el-Kebir; when, again that same climactic year, British troops were sent to Egypt even while absolute military collapse threatened the United Kingdom itself.

It was a grip not unwelcome to all Arabs. The generation of Feisal in Iraq, Abdullah in Transjordan, even of Nahas in Egypt, realised that for all practical purposes England was the 'country power' in the Middle East, and that England would continue to protect the countries of the Middle East both from internal and external disorders. She would do this, of course, for her own purposes: but she would do it, and it was a thing that needed to be done. The strong hand was respected. What was to poison the hand, and forfeit the respect, was England's support of Zionism.

In Zionism England considered she had as serviceable a *protégé* as Arab nationalism, although it was very seldom that any individual Englishman could be found prepared to declare that he wished ultimate success to both these clients. Zionism was itself an imperialist movement from the beginning. It was in 1922 that the British Government laid it down, again as a *chose jugée*, and through the medium of a White Paper issued by Churchill as Colonial Secretary, that the Jews were in Palestine by right, and not simply on Arab sufferance. This view was emphasised by another White Paper issued by the Labour Government in 1930, which stated that the obligations of Great Britain as the mandatory Power to both the Arabs and the Jews were of equal weight, and were in no sense irreconcilable. Between 1921 and 1936, under the Colonial Office's Crown Colony régime, the Jewish population in Palestine increased by 343%, until the Jewish proportion of the population of the country had risen from 11% to 28%. As a result, by 1936 Palestine was their one sphere of influence in the Middle East where the British had found themselves unable to encourage any form of political emancipation. In Palestine alone would such a development have proved actively dangerous to British policy, for in Palestine alone did the protecting Power play a double game, doing its best for each community and ending hated by both. A generation of Arabs which had been fed on the stories of the iniquities of the Colonial Office and of the Mandate was coming of age, and could not be expected to see the logic of the policy of the 'country power'. Indeed it was hard to see. The Arab view was

underwritten by the Peel Commission of 1937, which spoke sadly
of the development in Palestine of 'an irrepressible conflict' and
declared the Mandate, with its commitment to the Jewish National
Home, to be unworkable. The Commission proposed in its place
a scheme of partition: a Jewish state and an Arab state should be
fashioned, with Great Britain left as mandatory only in the Holy
Places and in the strategically essential points of the port of Aqaba
and the airfields of Lydda and Ramleh. How this story developed
will later appear.

Certainly no greater disservice was ever rendered to the cause
of British imperialism than by its own support of the Zionist
movement. The British aim for the Middle East was the establishment of a *pax Britannica* — a Victorian conception, it might seem,
in the twentieth century, yet one which circumstances in the area
singularly favoured. But their insertion among the Arab *protégés*
of an alien foster-child was to prove fatal to this hope, and to make
nonsense of policies that were framed along ambitious and genuinely idealistic lines. The Labour Party was always a strong
supporter of Zionism: but it was left to the Labour Government of
1945–50 to deal with the wreckage of a policy that had in truth
been 'unworkable' from the day it was propounded.

Yet on the whole, between 1919 and 1936, it could have been
said that British imperialist policy in the Middle East had proved a
success, for it had obtained for the British Empire an exclusive
position of power in the area. This was not emphasised, not because
no one was aware of it, but because imperialism was not in favour,
and British statesmen pursuing British interests in the older imperial theatres took care not to call them British imperial interests.
The reputation of British imperialism, having got off to a bad start
in the post-war era, indeed never recovered. The errors that were
committed were more obvious than the benefits that accrued, and
were always swiftly underlined by the Government's vigilant opponents. Plainest of all items was the cost, at a time when the
National Debt exceeded the 1914 figure by £6,600 million and
when taxation per head had increased sixfold. Although the swinge-
ing taxation Budget of 1920 had cut down Services expenditure by
£386 million, this was still, at £230 million, reckoned far too high,
and Middle Eastern contribution to it far too extensive. Critics
pointed out that the call for economy so often made by members of
the Coalition Government could not but seem a little insincere,

since by 1922 they were all responsible for spending some £300 million of the country's scarce money on policies that had not only not succeeded, but which had never had any chance of success.

All our policies seemed to be set on foot by engineers who were blessed neither with luck nor judgment. Turkey was resurgent, had thrown the Allies' Greek *protégé* out of Asia Minor, and had followed up this feat by threatening to attack the British forces at Chanak in 1922. Persia seemed more than ever inclined, after its dose of old-fashioned Curzonian medicine, to turn for political guidance to the Communist International. Our invasions of Russia had earned us the undying hostility of the new leaders of the new Soviet Union, and nothing else. The contradictions inherent in our support for the Zionist 'adventure' — Balfour's own name for it — were becoming plainer every day. It was no Radical, but Admiral of the Fleet Lord Wester Wemyss, who in a maiden speech in the Lords — traditionally an innocuous occasion — informed Curzon that in Palestine we were trying to set up a community which, by all the laws of economics and by all the laws of psychology, from the force of reason and from the lessons of history, could neither maintain itself nor live in amity with its neighbours. At the same time we had in Syria succeeded in manoeuvring ourselves into such a position that the fulfilment of our promises to one ally had entailed the breaking of our moral obligations to another. Curzon was reduced by this naval broadside to asking that feeblest of all questions that can come from a Government Front Bench, what would you have done?[1]

Moreover, the history of turmoil in Egypt since 1918 would have been remarkable had it not been surpassed by that in Ireland. It was on 16 January 1922, the year we were content to play king-maker in both Egypt and Iraq, that we finally resigned our responsibility for the Irish problem, and the Lord Lieutenant handed over to Sinn Fein. The case of Ireland made it clear to everyone that the British Empire could no longer be assumed to stand foursquare on a basis of unchallengeable power. For the Sinn Fein movement had challenged that power, and had challenged it successfully. They won Home Rule, denied to generations of Irish Nationalist parliamentarians, in a campaign of terrorism and crime. They won it by what Curzon called 'revolution by murder'. They won it not because they had superior military force. For England to 'hold' Ire-

[1] 5 H of L 40, 4 August 1920.

land in 1922 would have required the tactics of Strongbow, Essex, and Cromwell combined. England had bigger forces at her disposal still than ever Strongbow, Essex, and Cromwell had possessed: but employment of their tactics was not a practicable imperial policy. What was, then, a practicable imperial policy? The implications of the Irish action, the implications of the British reaction to it, were clearly written on a wall for others besides the Irish to see. Indians, Egyptians, could read as they ran. 'How could such a state of things,' Balfour asked himself, 'be said to fit in with the scheme of the Empire?'

What this scheme of Empire was, whether in fact there was one at all, was once more a matter for debate. It was discussed this time not merely among the imperialist seers, but between the Dominion leaders themselves. These politicians still feared lest the seers, with their ideas of organic unity, should push the discussion to some conclusion arranged in advance, and it disquieted rather than calmed Dominion opinion to find Milner still a figure of power even when the war was over. A scheme of Empire? The metaphor implied that someone was doing the scheming. It would be better, averred the general opinion among the Australians, to have no scheme at all, than for Churchill as Secretary of State for the Colonies to open the Imperial Conference of 1921 with some far-reaching and resounding plan in the style of the late Joseph Chamberlain. After four years of living at crisis point, none of the Dominions were in a mood to go adventuring, or to underwrite the large ideas of British proconsuls who were reluctant to loose their grip on the engine of administration that had been constructed to carry the Empire safely through the war. Zionism was one such adventure, a piece of imperial policy which was left by the Dominions strictly within the sole care of the United Kingdom. Ottawa and Canberra always viewed the whole British policy towards the Turkish Empire with some alarm, and preferred to steer clear of the complications which were foreseen and which duly took place. Canada in particular, from the time she put her hand to the peace Treaty at Versailles, was not at all anxious to see her signature attached to anything else. The Treaty of Sèvres of 1920, which was supposed would settle the Turkish account, was part of the Versailles settlement as a whole and as such was signed by the Dominions: but they were gladly absent from the protracted and rancorous negotiation that preceded the Lausanne treaty of 1923, which displaced the Sèvres Treaty and its arrangements, which the Turks had by then successfully violated. Thus, while thirteen signatures for the British Empire embellished the Versailles Treaty, Lausanne was graced with one alone, that of Curzon as British Foreign Secretary. He signed for the Empire — but Canada refused to ratify Lausanne, after a long and bitter wrangle in the Ottawa House of Commons about status and commitment.

Although realists in all the Dominions continued to point out that the frontiers of the British Empire still lay on the Rhine, the possibilities of German aggression in the future now seemed remote to the average Canadian and Australian, who were not at all anxious to subscribe to any of the French schemes for getting some cast-iron security in that area. In Dominion opinion, the adjective best derived from Empire was not imperial, but empirical. The Dominions would deal with matters that concerned them as these matters arose. They wished neither to commit themselves and their course of action in advance, nor — this above all — to be themselves committed and to have their course chosen in advance by the United Kingdom, whose imperial policies it had been that had involved the whole Empire in war in 1914, whether its members willed or not. The fact that they had so willed was beside the point as they now saw it.

For the impact of war had made the citizens of the Dominions, just as much as the citizens of Egypt, very much aware that there was such a thing as national status. It was not fitting that sacrifices of such an order as had been made should be made at the behest of others. The policy put forward by Laurier before the war, the policy of non-involvement in European quarrels, now became the direct aim of all the Dominions. And it seemed a perfectly feasible policy. The menace to British sea-power, and thus to Dominion security, had now vanished. Britain was now involved in clearing up the débris of Europe, but the nature of the European state-structure was not now, and never had been, a matter vital to Dominion interests. Dominion statesmen were not clear just why Britain chose to spend those £300 million on abortive policies in Egypt, Iraq, Palestine, Ireland, and Russia; but they were clear enough on the point that all such policies contained elements of danger and commitment. The argument thus centred, not on schemes of Empire, but on the status of its individual components. Smuts had drawn the start-line: 'Whatever we may say, or whatever we may think,' he had told the Imperial War Conference in 1917, 'we are subject provinces of Great Britain.' The phraseology was strange, even shocking, to the ears of Hughes the Australian Premier. But divergence of view here was natural enough, for no Australian had fought, and lost, a war of independence. Smuts later underlined the point. 'When I went to England in 1917,' he told his constituents, 'I found there was a totally wrong movement afoot, a movement to establish an Imperial Federation', and added that it was largely as a result of his attitude that that view of Empire had been given up.[1]

The South Africans, like the Irish, frequently produced this disconcerting trick of switching on a glaring light amid the pleasant and companionable gloaming. Much ink had been poured as a joyful libation on the formation of the Imperial War Cabinet, but in fact the policy pursued was the policy desired by the United Kingdom, and the actual direction of the war and its strategy never left the hands of the British War Office and of No. 10, Downing Street. At the peace conference at Versailles the British Empire Delegation made up a formidable *bloc*, which impressed itself on Europe: but the Delegation died thereafter, because it did not suit the Dominions that it should be kept alive. The Dominions made an impressive showing, too, at the Washington Conference in 1921, but it was again Smuts who pointed out that they had not been invited to Washington as 'international persons' but as part of the British delegation: 'and a United Kingdom delegation does not become an Empire Delegation merely by slipping in some Dominion Statesmen through a back door.' It was therefore proper that a British statesman, Balfour, should act as their spokesman. Proper, perhaps, but hardly heart-warming. It was pleasant to be in harmony with one's friends, but it might be still more exciting to have an opinion of one's own and be free to express it in mixed international company without causing shock or dismay. It was surely time to set on foot that constitutional overhaul of the imperial system that had been adumbrated in the ninth resolution passed by the Imperial War Conference of 1917.

Something would have to be done, Milner had declared when Colonial Secretary in 1920, if we were not to separate from one another and go different ways even without knowing it. We were all partner-nations, certainly, we had all equal status: but, he added,

[1] *RT*, December 1919, No. 37, p. 350.

we must all speak with a single voice. To give this voice the power it must have, some new instrument of government was needed. His invitations to the 1921 Imperial Conference dwelt on these urgent problems of common interest which called for co-ordination and action by the different Governments of the Empire, while *The Times* spoke hopefully of establishing an Imperial Peace Cabinet. But the Conference when it met, although it spoke in its Report of the necessity of concentrating the whole weight of the Empire behind 'a united understanding and common action in foreign affairs', kept clear of the question of new machinery. Lloyd George himself saw no need for any new machinery. He said in effect what Asquith had said in 1911, that foreign policy could not be decentralised, that the instrument of this foreign policy — the foreign policy of the British Empire — was and must remain the British Foreign Office. Joint control of foreign policy implied a joint responsibility, and as it suited neither the United Kingdom nor the Dominions to have either, the matter was shelved; and the subsequent 1923 Imperial Conference was content to recommend nothing more epoch-making than a preference on canned salmon and dried fruits. And here a mould was formed. The *Round Table* was to comment ten years later how much evidence the critics could assemble for their reiterated view, that 'post-war Imperial Conferences have been donkey-engines pumping water from a hull which fills twice as fast as they empty it, and which must eventually sink.'[1]

Empire statesmen themselves found this somewhat unheroic. Empire and attitudes had long gone together, but Lloyd George's declaration that liberty must be the binding principle, and his fellow-Welshman Premier Hughes' contribution to the effect that, if nobody did anything concrete, the 1921 Conference might prove to be 'the last magnificent flare of a dying illumination', seemed somehow to lack the authentic imperial note. Moreover, if liberty was a binding principle, it ought surely to be respected. For liberty surely implied freedom *not* to do anything, if one did not wish to do anything: and if one were in reality a partner, then as a partner one had a right to object, if one saw fit, to the policy of speaking with a single voice. The incident at Chanak in 1922, when Turkish forces under Kemal came near to attacking British forces — and so involving the British Empire once more in war in the Levant — tolled the bell on the arguments for an entire imperial

[1] *RT*, December 1933, No. 93, p. 42.

unity. Lloyd George and Winston Churchill did not even consult their own Foreign Secretary, Curzon, before making public their defiant attitude on Chanak. It was too much to hope for, therefore, that the Dominions, who as signatories of the Sèvres Treaty would inevitably be involved, should be consulted. Too much to hope for now: but it should not be too much in the future, if the Dominions had their way. 'Foreign Office responsibility' began to look too much like irresponsibility to be comfortable, or even tolerable. It was time to loosen, not to tighten, the bolts of the imperial structure. It was time to have the areas of policy and of commitment to policy closely defined. It was time to assert the idea of partnership as more than a piece of dinner-table oratory: it was time to get rid of the idea of the 'single voice'.

So Milner's dreams remained dreams, and the plans of Amery, his Under-Secretary, for instituting the first rational imperial economic policy were inevitably frustrated by what Amery called political and financial prejudice. It was the more vexatious in that the economic argument of Empire had never before had so many of the figures on its side. How Joseph Chamberlain would have rejoiced — for in 1923 the value of British exports to the Empire stood at £285 million, a sum only £15 million less than that of exports to foreign countries. But few, exasperatingly few, drew Amery's eager deduction, that we should proceed to invest in Empire until the figures drew level, and then again until the imperial investment drew ahead. Many, regrettably many, argued instead that the figure of foreign investment was shockingly low, and that every effort must be made to increase it. No long-term imperial policy could be put in train against a background of one million of unemployed, of continuous labour unrest, and of the absolute dependence of Europe for economic aid on the United States.

It was also the case, and one soon evident, that Great Britain could not maintain her former world position, and that therefore an overhaul of imperial strategy was necessary. This was a difficult decision: but the country was not, in 1921, so weak that her pride forebore her to take it. During the war both the United States and Japan had increased and developed their power. Both were now Great Powers, in direct contact with the British Empire and its interests. In naval building Britain had now been outstripped by the United States, and it was neither economically nor politically possible for her to mount another naval race similar to that of the pre-

1914 period. Lloyd George's outburst in 1919 was instinctive —
that we would spend our last guinea on maintaining the Two-
Power standard in naval affairs:[1] but he curbed the instinct by his
realisation that, since we were physically unable to undertake the
naval defence and policing of both the Atlantic and Pacific Oceans,
we had better keep our last guinea for some better purpose. But it
was his firm resolve, and here everyone agreed with him, that although it might be necessary to abandon the Two-Power standard,
a One-Power standard was the least that could be allowed to replace it. We could not afford to be less than equal in naval strength
with any Power.

With this sentiment the Dominions cordially concurred. In 1917
Canada's Conservative Premier Sir Robert Borden had indeed cast
his eyes to the future of naval supremacy, and had commented that
if a day came when Great Britain no longer assumed the sole responsibility for imperial defence on the high seas, that day she
would no longer be able to assume sole responsibility for foreign
policy in the Empire either — for imperial policy and imperial
defence were and must always be inextricably linked. The Admiralty, alarmed, had produced a scheme for an Imperial Navy in
1918, and Jellicoe had toured the Empire to win friends for it. But
although he never won enough, anyway now that peace had come
Borden's point did not seem so unanswerable as in fact it was. At
any rate no one troubled to try to meet it, and the 1921 Imperial
Conference accepted the principle of the equality of navies. Thus
the British delegation to the Washington Conference fulfilled what
had already been agreed to as an imperial policy in regard to naval
matters. The Conference had been summoned by the United
States Government in order to put an end to the naval race, to limit
armaments, and to stop that imperialist competition for China and
the Chinese market in which the Japanese, providentially relieved
by the events of the war of all Russian and German competition,
had forged dangerously far ahead. In such circumstances it was no
longer a major British imperial interest to maintain the Anglo-
Japanese alliance, which had last been renewed, for ten years, in
1911. If it had been renewed by Britain in 1921 it would have been
construed by the United States as an unfriendly act.

Nevertheless during the war Japan had served the purposes of
the Alliance loyally. They had been Japanese cruisers who had

[1] Seymour, *House*, IV, 190.

escorted New Zealand's forces to the theatres of war in the Middle East. It was therefore not easy for Britain to shrug off the Alliance with the excuse that times had changed, that Japan was no longer a valuable friend because Russia and Germany were no longer pressing against China, and because the United States, with whom it behoved us to stand well, was now deeply suspicious of the role that Japan had been playing in the room of Russia and Germany in the Far East. Australia indeed considered the Alliance as valuable now as it had ever been, but Canada in contrast was now beginning to look uneasily across the Pacific at the power of the rising sun, and thus was content to make common cause with the continental American viewpoint as a whole. Premier Meighen, having swung the 1921 Imperial Conference round to the Canadian viewpoint, thus did not mind accepting for Canada at the subsequent Conference at Washington an international status distinctly inferior to her rank at Versailles and Geneva.[1] The Washington Conference, after some bargaining back and forth, thus saw the Anglo-Saxons, as Dilke would have been pleased to call them at this crisis in their joint affairs, presenting a common front of policy to the Japanese. The battleship tonnage of both Britain and the United States was not to exceed 525,000 tons. Japan should limit hers to 300,000 tons. As one Japanese cynic commented, these were explicable proportions — Rolls Royce: Rolls Royce: Ford.

In return for her consent to this limitation, Japan insisted that the *status quo* should be maintained in the Pacific in regard to fortified naval bases east of longitude 110°. The British and the Americans agreed to this. Twenty years later the consequences of this consent were to be made painfully clear, for both Hong Kong and the Philippines were left at the mercy of the Japanese Navy, in 1941–42 twice as powerful as the combined Anglo-American naval strength in the Pacific. Even the short-term gains made at Washington were shorter than even the pessimists had supposed. It was American policy to allow no spheres of influence to be carved out in the Far East after the model of the Middle East, and nine Powers under American guidance subscribed accordingly to a self-denying ordinance in regard to the affairs of China: Britain indeed in 1926 returned both the Boxer indemnity and the useless imperial trophy of Wei-hei-wei to the Chinese. But the chief result of this high-

[1] J. B. Brebner, 'Canada and the Anglo-Japanese Alliance', *Political Science Quarterly*, v. 50 (March 1935), p. 45.

minded policy was that a power vacuum was left in China. The self-denying ordinance cut both ways, as many British imperialists sought to convince the State Department. If no outside support was granted to the Chinese Government, it would fall, either before internal or external attack. And so it did. China's last state would be worse than anything previously known, even in the bad old imperialist days. And so it was.

Indeed this whole 'Washington policy', which governed the naval policies of both the United States and the British Empire until the end of 1935, which entailed the scrapping of ships, which put this artificial ring around a dying China, and which left the British Empire without a berth east of Malta capable of accommodating and refitting a capital ship, was looked on with considerable misgivings by British statesmen from the outset. There were ways around it, which could be taken, but it was an obstacle to imperial planning and strategy all the same. In fact as to scrapping, the Empire did not suffer very greatly, for whereas the United States, to the dismay of American naval officers, scrapped nearly 755,000 tons — two-thirds of which was of shipping under construction — the Empire's figure amounted only to some 180,000 tons, none of which was new, although it did include Australia's only battle-cruiser. Moreover, the Washington decisions were concerned with capital-ship tonnage only, and had laid down no limitations concerning cruisers, destroyers, and submarines. By 1927 Britain had 11 post-Washington cruisers on the stocks, and a naval race in this type of ship and in submarines thereafter proceeded, studded here and there with naval conferences wherein Anglo-American amity was not the principal feature. It seemed a *coup* to the Baldwin Government in 1935 to obtain Hitler's agreement to limit the German navy to 35% of the entire Empire strength, and indeed in its limited way it was, else it would not have encountered such savage criticism from both the United States and France. Nevertheless the major factor lay in this, that naval protection of the British Empire and its lines of communications existed under sufferance of the United States, and it was not to be supposed that imperialists had forgotten Balfour's pre-war dictum, many times repeated, that if we failed to maintain our sea-power as a nation then we should have ceased to count as a Great Power. They remembered, too, with nostalgia, that in those days the Empire had had 59 ships-of-war in the Pacific, including five first-class battleships. Now that great ocean was the exclusive chequer-board of the naval power of the United States and Japan.

It was this feeling of undefinable — indeed unutterable — future menace, coupled with the desire to reassert prestige, that animated the Conservative Government in 1923 to bring before Parliament and the nation a scheme for making Singapore a base capable of taking capital-ships. To critics who declared at once that such a policy could only be directed against Japan, a friendly nation recently in firm alliance with ourselves, Amery as First Lord of the Admiralty made only the tactical reply — that Singapore could in no sense be construed as a danger to Japan, as Singapore lay no nearer to Japan than did Gibraltar to Boston. Was the policy then, he was at once asked, directed against the United States, which was simultaneously setting about to make Pearl Harbor their impregnable base? To this no answer was possible. Imperialist policy, now as previously, in fact was necessarily isolationist: Japan and the United States were not our enemies today, but tomorrow they might be. Charges of cynicism imperialists continued to shrug away. Power was power, after all, and the fact that the United States was not a member of the League of Nations was surely a point worth noting and putting away in the strategical files. For what was Great Britain's principal weapon, if ever a 'sanctions policy', as prescribed by Article 16, had to be put in train? The Royal Navy. But if sea-power was used to interfere with neutral commerce, in order to deprive an erring belligerent of that commerce we should inevitably come face to face as we had in our past wars with the hostility of the United States, now a Great Power. In fact the United States' abstention from the League of Nations had immobilised the British Navy, and paralysed the effectiveness of Article 16 as a security for European peace.

Other strategical points which might have been put in these files were not given the consideration they also deserved. In the Commons a soldier and a sailor — Spears and Kenworthy — both pointed out from different sides of the House that Singapore was likely to be attacked from the landside, from the north, if ever it was attacked at all.

Still, the Conservatives' determination to proceed with the Singapore base, after the Labour Government of 1924 had decided to drop it, was cordially hailed by the Dominions as a genuine imperial (as opposed to imperialist, by this time a bad word in the Dominions also) policy. It was a balm to the fears of Australia and New Zealand, and a comfort to the remaining members of the Blue-water School at home. An observation made by Premier Massey of New Zealand — to the effect that it might turn out to be a pity the League of Nations was ever invented if the defence of the Empire was to be left to it alone — was much quoted by Conservatives at those Labour idealists who wanted to drop the project, as a gesture to the world that we were sincere in our quest for disarmament, and in our intention to put the affairs of the world on some better basis than that of military power alone. It was not, said Sir Robert Horne, a gesture to the world at all: it was merely a backward nod by Ramsay MacDonald to the people who sat behind him.[1] But not everyone, even apart from those sitting behind MacDonald, disagreed with the latter's point of view. Smuts declared that the Commonwealth had indeed its genuine mission to play in the world, and felt that the authority of the British Empire, as the leader of 'the great cause of appeasement and conciliation among the nations', must be undermined if the Empire diverted its attention to matters of sheer self-interest, like the building of a base at Singapore. But then, Smuts was always a privileged person.

The Singapore question served to focus attention on the new facts of power in the world. This very need to create a new naval base underlined the major fact, that the Empire was no longer shielded by unchallengeable sea-power. The naval defence of Canada, and in all probability of Australasia as well if Britain were elsewhere hard pressed in time of war, had become an American responsibility.

A responsibility, but not a duty. Here lay the danger.

Certainly no one saw the United States playing the role of aggressor against the British Empire, but in the 1920's it was equally hard to see her in the role of its rescuer: indeed in 1920, while de Valera had an English price on his Irish head, the freedom-loving citizens of New York and New Orleans honoured him with the freedom of their respective cities — an action hard to equate with sympathy for the policies of imperial England. The United States could not be relied upon by anybody except Canada. It was because of this hard fact of geography, which had been as valid in Laurier's day as now, that Canada got more annoyed than any

[1] 5 H 171, 18 March 1924, 1174.

o

other Dominion at the many suggestions that she should contribute to the naval defence of the Empire. The many carefully-
worked-out tables that were drawn up by amateur statisticians
and strategists, stressing that while in 1924 citizens of the United
Kingdom were contributing £11 per head towards the costs of
naval defence Canadian citizens were contributing only £3 11s. 11d.,
drew the irritated reply from Ottawa that it was pointless to pretend that the British Navy existed in order to protect Canada.
If Canada had not been there, the Navy would still have to be paid
for. To be sure it was true, that British sea-power protected
Canadian shipping and commerce, but equally was it true that
it also protected the oceanic trade of such countries as Sweden
and Belgium — and no suggestion had yet been made to Swedes
and Belgians that they should have an immediate whipround among
themselves to cover the costs of the British Navy. Such an argument struck the *Round Table* as particularly ungracious. It was a
farce, it declared, that Dominions which made so much to-do
about claiming independent status through the League of Nations
— and with it the right to negotiate treaties — should nevertheless continue to expect Great Britain to provide the force without
which treaties were scraps of paper. This was true, but the Canadians were facing truths that lay in a different direction, and had
ideas about them that would never square with *Round Table* imperialist preconceptions. In this new age it was the imperialist pre-
conception that had to give ground.

The British Government thus geared itself to its somewhat
thankless task of meeting the Dominion claims for status. To those
foreign Governments that troubled to watch this process in operation, the task seemed more than a little academic, for what would
come of all these nice readjustments and fresh juxtapositions of
constitutional convention within the British imperial structure?
The structure might find for itself a new facade as a result, but behind it would stretch the old imperial building and its outhouses.
Canada's Mackenzie King was himself prepared to admit that
status was not the same thing as stature. Nobody in Europe supposed it was. Thus, while devising formulae to soothe Canadian,
Irish, or South African *amours-propres* was doubtless an occupation
worthy of the attention of an intellectual statesman like Balfour,
could these ever alter the fact that the control of imperial defence,
and therefore the ultimate decisions in foreign policy, still lay

where they had always lain, in the hands of the Cabinet of the Government of the United Kingdom? The average American's belief that King George V governed Canada as King George III had once governed the thirteen American colonies was of course absurd, but was not this very absurdity only a truth perceived in a distorting glass? The Germans, too, recalling how effective Imperial solidarity had proved itself to be between 1914 and 1918, still reckoned it a factor in Britain's position in Europe, perhaps indeed giving it more value than it had precisely because German leaders before 1914 had so greatly miscalculated its potential strength. French diplomats continued on their part to incline to the opinion that the whole notion of the 'independence' of the Dominions, their separate status and their right to have their say in British policy as it affected the affairs of Europe, was one of those subtler inventions of the devious Lloyd George — whose efficacy his successors, although admittedly less astute, were still determined to exploit. Thus the Powers who foregathered at Versailles, and thereafter in the Assembly of the League of Nations at Geneva, recognised as a constant factor the existence of a British *bloc* whose various representatives never quarrelled, at least not in public, with whatever the British Foreign Secretary happened to be saying. If they proceeded to quarrel with him after he had said it, that was their affair: it could not affect whatever had been agreed upon.

From within the imperial structure this problem of status, as it confronted its inmates, seemed much less clear-cut. The Imperial Conference of 1923 had recognised that on each part of the Commonwealth fell the responsibility for its own local defence, but emphasised, too, that there were certain routes and areas whose security was vital to the whole group. Into this category fell the imperial chain between the Mediterranean and the east, via the Suez Canal: so, too, did the question of the Singapore base. The Conference did not state whose task it was to guard and maintain these lines of imperial communication, but in fact, as everyone knew, there was only one 'partner' who had the means to carry this out, and that was the United Kingdom. The Conference of 1926 affirmed this point. The principles of equality and similarity appropriate to status, it was now declared, did not universally extend to *function*. 'Here we require — ' the voice was that of Balfour, now adopting a 'masked word' in place of 'stature' — 'something more than immutable dogmas.' It was not stated however what this something more might be, but the immutable fact whose function was being referred to was presumably the British Navy, which rode the seas free from dogma, with a clear task to perform. It remained, moreover, the task of the British taxpayer to meet the bill for imperial defence expenditure, and it remained the obligation of a British Government to take action against any aggressor against any of the Dominions.

Although none of the Dominions was under any corresponding obligation to go to the help of the United Kingdom if that partner was attacked, and although this particular illustration of what status actually meant rankled with imperialists, in sum the position was not so different from that which had obtained before 1914. The Dominions could not be committed by overt action by a British Government — but they might still find themselves inevitably committed, none the less. An enemy of Great Britain would still be likely to assess the Dominions as so many appanages of British power, and to proceed to attack them in that conviction. This being so, it was still in the Dominions' own interest to underwrite the policies that emitted from the British Foreign Office: at least they must always hope that these policies turned out for the best, for if they failed, then their own security was at once menaced. 'In spite of the theorists', commented Australia's Robert Menzies in 1939, the foreign policy of the British Commonwealth was to a large extent in the hands, still, of the British Foreign Secretary of the day. He was convinced that

> the great issues of peace will be much more determined by the gentleman who sits in a room looking across the Horse Guards Parade than it will by my colleagues in Canberra or one of our colleagues in Ottawa or Pretoria.

'The nations of the world,' he added,

> would not be prepared to sit down for a few weeks or months while the members of the Commonwealth have an intimate chat as to what they are to do.[1]

That the point was well taken may be illustrated by the attitude of Canada, who as late as 1939 thought it necessary to have only three diplomatic missions representing her abroad: in France, in Japan, and in the United States.

[1] Quoted in Lionel Curtis, *World War: Its Cause and its Cure*, (Oxford, 1945), pp. 51–2.

Thus the great Conference of 1926, while indeed it did serve to assure the Dominions that their status as independent, equal, and autonomous powers was all that they wanted it to be, was not such a landmark in the evolution of both human and imperial affairs as the admiring press of the day, constitutional historians later, and all the theorists Menzies referred to, have combined to make it appear and no doubt genuinely assumed it to be. It did not stress the facts of power and the necessity for action, or with whom lay the ultimate responsibility for the security of that status to which so much publicity was being given: but these facts remained, which could be ignored over dinner-tables but had to be coped with in Dominion Cabinets. In the Report of the Conference Balfour took a typically oblique glance at this truth. 'A foreigner,' he wrote,

> endeavouring to understand the character of the British Empire by the aid of the formula about autonomy might be tempted to think that it was devised rather to make mutual interference impossible than to make mutual co-operation easy.

Balfour was here probably wishing upon the foreigner thoughts that had passed through, and no doubt stayed in, his own mind. (He had already privately confided to a friend, in a phrase that echoed one of Goldwin Smith's, that he had never had much love for wooden guns.) The public implication of the remark, of course, was that the foreigner, so thinking, would be wrong. But foreigners were anyway not tempted to venture down such blind alleys of speculation. The Empire, or the Commonwealth, as it seemed now to choose to describe itself, must remain together in a body, for the sake of its own security. Assured of their status, able to meet their own glance in their own mirror, citizens of the Dominions would be content to remain under the sheltering folds of the British umbrella. No one wished Neville Chamberlain's policy of appeasing the European dictators more Godspeed than did Mackenzie King.

Imperialists, theorists themselves, were however gloomily impressed by the paeans which rival theorists raised after the 1926 Conference, that the bad old days of Empire had gone. They feared that the Empire, under its new and rather meaningless name, would break up and vanish, and with it, the power of Great Britain. The Statute of Westminster of 1931 which gave legal force to the resolutions about autonomy and equality seemed to those bred in Milner's school of thought a sorry ending to the great project for imperial unity. Prior to the Conference of 1926 the *Round Table* had discussed, but only to dismiss, the view that the dilemma concerning the commitment of the Dominions to the actions and consequences of British foreign policy might be resolved by arranging for some formal notification to be made to all foreign nations that a declaration of war by Great Britain did not commit the Dominions to belligerency, and that no self-governing portion of the Empire would be in a state of war except as a result of a declaration to that effect by its own Government. 'On examination, however,' the article proceeded, 'this solution proved to be no solution, because it was seen to involve the dissolution of the Commonwealth itself.'[1] When the Conference went on to adopt that very solution, without apparently grasping the implications of what it was doing, the *Round Table* could only swallow hard and face the future in a spirit of resolute pessimism. The Dominions appeared to look on the League of Nations as an effective substitute for imperial co-operation both in defence and in foreign policy. The *Round Table* could only hope that the Dominions were right, but could not help doubting it, particularly as the same vague woolly notion had governed British opinion at home for so long.

Yet there was a bright side to see, even if it was not the side that the Dominions themselves wanted to have exposed. Hidden beneath the mountain of platitude about equality and status lurked certain facts of life. For, after all, freedom to decide whether to go to war or not must depend on whether one is physically able to make the choice. Throughout the period between the twentieth century's first and second world war none of the Dominions possessed, were given, or asked for, this kind of freedom. What Froude had said in 1880, that the right of people to self-government consisted and could consist in nothing but their power to defend themselves, was still true fifty years later. The Royal Navy was still, as Sir Edward Grigg put it, the Maypole round which, like coloured ribbons, twined and twisted the million varied activities of a Commonwealth that spanned the world. 'Take away the Maypole, and the ribbons, the world over, would flutter to the ground, or be seized by rude boys from adjoining villages.'[2] Empire was still based on power, and the imperial power-house was still the United Kingdom. It was just not in keeping with the spirit of these inter-war

[1] *RT*, June 1926, No. 63, p. 677.
[2] Sir Edward Grigg, *The Faith of an Englishman*, (London, 1937), p. 331.

years to remark on it. In Ottawa, the Canadian Minister of Defence caused a surprised furore when he commented in March 1938 that although Canada's status was all that the legalists thought it, the country was still in actual fact a political dependency — as it was still the case, in 1938 as in 1913, that the major deterrent against a major attack on Canada by a European Power was the existence of a British fleet in North Atlantic waters.[1]

Such a remark could not fail to give those who had pored over the language used at the 1926 Conference, and the phraseology employed in the Statute of Westminster of 1931, a considerable shock. Imperialists had always disliked the Statute for this very reason, that by putting on paper a constitution for the Empire it might lead the inhabitants of the Empire to think that all safeguards could be reduced to paper too. But Churchill's fear that this piece of repellent legalism might be fastened on by an army of colonial lawyers, anxious to extend their own influence by defining new fields in which status was king, was proved groundless. The Australians also thought the Statute unnecessary, and Menzies spoke for a great many when he gave his view that both the Imperial Conference of 1926 and the Statute itself had done the Empire 'a grave disservice': the whole 1926–31 process had been a misguided attempt to reduce to written terms something which was a matter of the spirit and not of the letter. The whole thing, his colleague Hughes insisted, had been arranged for the benefit of the South Africans and the Irish — and what good could anything be that was designed to suit the book of such a collection of anti-imperialists as those?

In the outcome, the only Dominion determined to take the utmost literal advantage from the Statute proved to be the Irish Free State. Irish leaders had made the well-calculated decision that their country could afford to be neutral in any future European war, as the United Kingdom could never afford to allow even a neutral Ireland to be attacked from Europe. The difficulty was that under the 1921 Treaty Britain was entitled to claim in war-time, or in time indeed of 'strained relations' with any foreign power, any facilities in Ireland that she might require, and de Valera had always consistently pointed out that with these terms there, no one in Europe would look on Ireland as a neutral at all. Ireland was just another Egypt or Iraq, which had treaties of much the same

[1] 24 March 1938; Mansergh, *Documents*, I, 436.

kind. But it was a difficulty that was removed in 1938, when Neville Chamberlain cancelled the offending articles of the 1921 Treaty. Ireland could now afford her neutrality — and could also afford to remain encamped under the British umbrella, which would be extended over her if the rains ever came. It might also be said, of course, that Australia and New Zealand were camping under this same umbrella: but Ireland's offence was a rank one, for the Irish, shrewd judges ever of power, called things by their right names, and made no bones about exploiting the imperial power of Great Britain for their own republican, self-regarding ends. When de Valera spoke with a sneer about the non-existence of a Commonwealth foreign policy, whose activities were so much spoken about 'by people who should know better',[1] he struck a note in complete contrast to that so often sounded in the Dominions, which liked to be able to hail British causes as their own, and spoke more often of 'our Commonwealth unity, which no formula could imprison nor constitution express' than did British statesmen themselves. Imperialists noted with satisfaction how in 1933 students of the Universities of Melbourne, Toronto, and Cape Town all passed the motion that students in the Universities of Oxford and Glasgow had rejected, 'That this House will fight for "King and Country".'

Thus, although the hard impact of war had greatly altered, it had not destroyed the imperial idea. Dominion loyalties were still kept burnished bright, and Great Britain, while relinquishing the remnants of political power over the Dominions, retained their strategical control. She had also successfully established it in the Levant, as heritor of the Ottoman Empire. Her power was still asserted without self-consciousness in that vast dependent Empire which was the particular realm of the Colonial Office — shorn in 1925 of its former responsibilities towards the Dominions. In this sphere questions of status were not discussed, and were not supposed to arise. 'Colonials' in dependent territories were still indulgently regarded as inhabitants of a vast and unkempt kindergarten, whose pretensions to self-importance did not even require the notice of a reprimand. In India the British *Raj*, although confronted with forces whose strength it did not yet recognise, still stood in apparent splendour. It was still the centre of that great sphere of British influence that spanned from Gibraltar to the Pacific. Im-

[1] 16 February 1939; Mansergh, *Documents*, I, 440.

THE IMPACT OF WAR: (ii) 1914-18

perial shipping, imperial airways, still had the use of all those imperial bases which Curzon had described as the necessary barbicans of Empire. It was an era when the Suez Canal was still, to use the words of a young Conservative back-bencher, Captain Anthony Eden, in 1929, 'the swing-door of the British Empire.'[1] Britain was living on her imperial capital, but she was living on it in some style. It was no longer politic to wave banners over her property, to use a vaunting tone, to draw attention to this or that aspect of prestige: but the British Empire, as an entity, as an idea, was still part of the public consciousness. The fact that its continuing existence could arouse bitter opposition still among 'intellectual' Englishmen testified at least to its continued vitality. School atlases still had their maps, largely coloured red: the middle classes were brought up to believe in some curious way that the Empire was indeed some kind of geological structure, which the normal processes of time and change could not alter. It was true that, while ideas about the Commonwealth, and the free partnership of equal nations, grew in public favour, the older imperial ideas faded, and no new crusader was arising to take the place of Churchill or Amery, now well into their middle-age. But in the iron age of the 1930's the bonds of sentiment and loyalty still held, the more deeply prized because the world outside had grown so dark and menacing.

No overt challenger to the power of the Empire had yet appeared on either side of that swing-door at Suez. But the forces of the future were already preparing to move into position.

Three attacks were now to be mounted on the British imperial power. There was the attack whose strategy was drawn up on old imperialist lines, the attack from the rival empires of Germany and Japan — an attack which, though physically it was cripplingly difficult to deal with, turned out to be the easiest psychologically to tackle, as it left no scars on the mind. There was, further, the attack on the domestic front, made by a triple combination of the old-style Radicalism, the new-style Socialism, and the apathy of the democracy.

And then, there was the attack whose deploying levies had long been seen in the distance: the attack that came from those who lived within the imperial ring itself.

[1] 5 H 233, 23 December 1929, 2046 ff.

V

THE IMPACT OF NATIONALISM

BECAUSE it declares itself in action, nationalism is more easily recognised than defined. Indeed it contains static elements which are easy to identify, elements such as a common descent, traditions, customs, religion, language, and territory. But no one can predict correctly where or when or how these elements are going to coalesce, or what will happen if they do. Nor are all of these elements necessary to nationalism: and even when all these elements are present the one essential, the driving impulse, may still be lacking.

It was the French Revolution that internationalised the idea of democracy. Soon afterwards the growth of industrialism created the 'operative', the man who tended the new machines, and set him to work at the base of the new society. Democracy and industrialism made everywhere a natural alliance: Marx's call in 1848 for the workers of the world to unite, to realise in union their enormous social potential, was foreseeable from the start. Such movements acted as a groundswell beneath the foundations of the ordered society, and in so doing presented a common problem to the governing and employing classes. The promotion by the latter of exclusive, nationalist sentiment was as good a method as any of preventing the dry, destroying wind of the 'Internationale' from blowing where it listed. Workers who were convinced that they were the natural enemies of other workers — foreigners — became willing supporters of that balance-of-power system constructed by their betters and of whose details they knew nothing: in 1914 the German Social Democrats, convinced by the military argument of encirclement and the honour of the nation, threw in their lot, sadly but conclusively, with the Hohenzollerns. Hitler was later to call his totalitarian fascism a National Socialist movement, well aware that both these adjectives logically cancelled each other.

For whatever else it is, nationalism is a divisive element in human society, cutting athwart the values of the community, fostering particular and peculiar ideas. Mazzini always thought of nationalism as a calling and a mission, a sign in a people that it recognised and respected its own personality and rank. That it could lead to a disrespect for the personality and rank of other peoples he would have denied — but this was the road it took.

It was indeed the road it had already taken in Mazzini's own time. The French Revolution itself became a nationalist movement of the Right. Freedoms made in France were originally designed to be put at Europe's disposal. But as Europe's aristocrats would not accept them they had to be imposed by French armies, eventually under a leader who thought little of liberty or equality or fraternity. Frenchmen in Germany, Frenchmen in Spain, Frenchmen in Russia aroused not enthusiasm for their superior code but detestation for their presence: and German, Spanish, and Russian nationalism roused to eject them. This is the simplest of all aspects of nationalism to understand and recognise: for, when it represents the hatred caused by the presence of the foreign soldier at the street-corner, patriotism *is* enough, and many a 'resistance movement' has made respectable men who in no other form of activity would have won anyone's respect. Palmerston, with the backing of the British public, supported nationalist movements in Europe because he was convinced that all nationalists were natural liberals, natural constitutionalists: but this was never the view of men who were close to the problem. The British public's adulation of Garibaldi, and Cavour's cordial distrust and dislike of that freebooter, may be set in contrast to illustrate this point.

That nationalism was by its nature an enemy to all forms of imperial governance was a lesson that had long been taught to those Great Powers which could not afford the degree of detachment enjoyed by an island-kingdom. Metternich saw it for what it was, a disruptive force which must be imprisoned if it could not be executed, lest it should destroy not only the Austrian Empire but that concert of Europe which had been so painfully attained at Vienna after the overthrow of Napoleon. For a generation, coalitions of the European Powers had waged war on the entire French and revolutionary principle that there could exist such a thing as a *nation en masse*, able beneath the banners of its victorious armies to propagate ideas that would lead to the downfall and spoliation of the society that all European states held in common.

Metternich was not personally successful in his long battle with this force. It exhausted him in the end, as the task of stemming it was always too great for any one man. But his purposes survived him, and men less pessimistic about the way of the world than he were soon to improve on his strategy. When all the storms of 1848 and 1849 had cleared, it was seen that the forces of the Right, reinforced by consciousness of their own successful self-assertion, continued to rule in Europe. Their leaders discovered that radical jacobinism, which Metternich had always assumed to be an integral part of any nationalist movement, was in fact detachable from it. The residue of patriotism could be poured into a different mould. Thus Bismarck made nationalism the foundation of his militarist Imperial Germany, and his success allowed the Powers of Europe to enjoy forty years of peace, forty years of confidence that the old radical menaces to society had finally been scotched. Both the Austrian and the Ottoman Empires, congeries of races, staved off the nationalist peril to their existence: it was China, home of a homogeneous race, that foundered like a whale full of imperialist harpoons. When ultimately both Austria and Turkey went down too, their disappearance was brought about far more by the follies of their professional militarists than by any enthusiastic impulse of the racialist, nationalist 'patriots'.

The European catastrophe of 1914 convinced liberals everywhere that the balance-of-power theory had been its primary cause. The long years of peace it had gained for Europe were forgotten, only the militarists' ultimate excess of folly was remembered. This was natural enough. It was natural, too, that the great ideas of the French Revolution should once again be looked on with a roseate respect as the great alternative. President Wilson's support for the doctrine of 'nationality', his desire to suit boundaries to nationalities — forgetting that every nationality has its own Ulster — consecrated the claims of nationalism thereafter, and they were everywhere regarded as so self-evidently right that little argument was brought forward against them. Those who spoke, with Norman Angell, of Balkanising Europe did not command a public ear. In England a National Government was later to hold the view that Hitler's invasion of the Rhineland was not an invasion at all, but only a 're-entry', an act of natural justice which unfortunately happened to cut athwart certain European agreements. In such a case justice was preferred to law. Again, the 'cause' of the Germans of the Sudetenland area of Czechoslovakia was one that met much sympathy: Englishmen could, and indeed should, do nothing to prevent Germans from joining Germans, even if it meant conniving at the destruction of a state whose territorial integrity they had underwritten as a signatory of the Versailles Treaty.

Extreme nationalism, Lord Hugh Cecil once observed, 'is a sense of the beauty and passion of living made a destructive vice or crime.'[1] Rabindranath Tagore denied that it had any spiritual quality. It was in fact an enemy to the spirit: 'a nation is that aspect which a whole population assumes when organised for a mechanical purpose.'[2] Nationalism was a cruel epidemic of evil, the iron coffer which bound the true spirit of the West, which in Asia had scattered seeds that were immortal. But must Asian peoples become 'nations' in self-defence against the evil? Nationalism brought with it a natural distrust of humanity, was always sounding a bagpipe of righteous indignation, was a moral anaesthetic, a prolific weed. But the weed grew as fast as the fertile shoots, and it was still not clear, in the mid-twentieth century, whether or not it would choke them. Europe suffered earlier than Asia, as Tagore foresaw, because what barriers against anarchic nationalism had not already been knocked over in war were removed by the peacemakers.

These barriers were by no means flimsy. In Christendom the aristocracy and the peasantry had always held respectively more in common than in contrast. So, too, had the European intellectuals, one with another. The merchants, although naturally at rivalry, had followed a like code of trading and dealing, and had set high the interests of the community because those interests marched with their own. It might seem that only one caste or group has depended for its prestige and power on the assertion not of what was held in common, but of what was held in dispute: that it has been the professional soldiers — sharing a code, indeed, but one mainly related to the proper conduct of war — who have made it their business to take advantage of any disruption in society, sometimes to promote it, in order to carry dispute to the point of war, thereafter to justify their argument with an appeal to some concept of national honour which they themselves have invented. This can only be

[1] 5 H 217, 10 May 1928, 490.
[2] Rabindranath Tagore, *Nationalism*, (London, 1917).

cautiously accepted, for while officers were still aristocrats, their cosmopolitan connexions crossed the frontiers, and their status did not depend at all on military glory. The really dangerous men were the military careerists whose status depended on nothing else, such as Napoleon's Marshals, men from the lowest ranks of society. It was his conviction that this was true that caused Palmerston to continue his support of the practice of the buying and selling of commissions in the British Army. Aristocratic officers might be inept, but at least they were not a public menace elsewhere than on the battlefield. Similarly, the struggle for power in Hitler's *Wehrmacht*, between the professionals who were also Prussian aristocrats and the professionals who, like Hitler himself, were nobodies from nowhere, had to be fought to a bitter end indeed.

Nevertheless, that nationalism should be best esteemed and most easily recognised as a weapon in the soldier's armoury is not surprising. Every people that has an ascertainable past at all can boast a hero who exemplifies the virtues of the warrior, someone who has fought the alien invader of his home-ground. King David, Robert Bruce, Tyrconnel, the Cid, Joan of Arc, Owen Glendower, Ivan the Terrible, Scanderbeg, William the Silent, Kosciusko, Kossuth, Kemal — all these are honoured names on a famous roll. From it two nationalities are missing. No German and no English name appears there. The Germans in times of nationalist ebullience must fall back on forest deities and Wagnerian gods. In England, although many attempts were made in the nineteenth century to rekindle life in and enthusiasm for such long-lost dissenters as Boadicea, Hereward, and Alfred, these have remained still-life figures, embalmed in the textbooks. The foreign yokes put in turn upon the inhabitants of the fertile areas of the British Isles by Romans, Angles, Saxons, Danes, and Normans were never bodily rejected. No great national uprising marks the English story, and only in England could the date of a conquest be thought of, when thought of at all, as occasion for a mild joke. (Compare the overtones sounded north of the Border by the name of Flodden Field.) It was perhaps the felt need, to have a hero of the approved type, that has in England underlain the entire mysterious myth about King Arthur.

The islanders, then, accepted what came to them, assimilated most of it, and improved on almost all of it. This was a sensible, if non-heroic, course to pursue.

It is perhaps because of this past, because English patriotism has never been racial, that accounts for that insensitivity to and non-comprehension of the very different feelings of other races on just such a matter which the Englishman has so often displayed in most of the far places to which his enterprise has taken him. As he had himself never found it wise, and therefore necessary, to flaunt and promote an assertive racial nationalism, he has never understood the depths that this emotion can stir. Intellectually he may have been able to gauge it, and politically he has very often been able to make allowance for it. But it is only an allowance: and that a man of another country can genuinely feel his own English presence in that country to be a blight and an insult, is something the Englishman has found it often impossible to take into his emotional account. Times changed, indeed, from the 1860's, when Charles Dilke found notices in all the Indian hotels he stayed in, that 'Gentlemen are requested not to strike the servants', and when the conversation in many an Indian Army mess ran mainly on loot,[1] but Curzon always insisted that a successful dealing with Orientals must involve the use of the understanding as well as reason. Cromer held that to obtain the sympathy and the goodwill of the Egyptians was as important as to be honest and just. King George V and Keir Hardie, alike brief visitors to India, were amazed at the almost incandescent effect of 'a little simple kindness'. But these were lessons that were remarkably difficult for Englishmen in general to learn.

At the very moment when Professor Seeley was warning his Cambridge audience that an Empire which took over the control of unassimilable races was weakening itself ineradicably, Sir Auckland Colvin, the British Agent in Egypt, was making a few comments on the nature of the liberal and national movement which he had observed was gaining ground among the younger educated generation in that country. (This was in January 1882, six months before the English invasion.) Precisely because he wished this movement to succeed, Colvin wrote, it seemed to him essential that it should learn from the outset within what limits it must confine itself.[2] Here Colvin, an able and upright official with long administrative experience in the East, may be said to represent the ingrained attitude of his class and type towards the subject-peoples in the British Em-

[1] Dilke, *Greater Britain*, pp. 222–4.
[2] Memorandum, 2 January 1882; Sir Edward Malet, *Egypt 1879–83*, (London, 1885), p. 216.

pire. Nationalism in such peoples might indeed contain elements which were deserving of encouragement, but only so far: it was not itself a thing to be encouraged. Since its aspirations, coming from such a source, must necessarily be of a lower order than those of the imperial protecting Power, in no case could they be allowed to interfere with or to obstruct the latter's authority.

Thirty years later Cromer pronounced on this subject with his usual thorough, English, commonsense. Those who cried 'Egypt for the Egyptians' on the house-tops had gone off on an entirely wrong scent — because, even had they attained their ends, nothing approaching to Egyptian autonomy would have been realised. The existence of the Capitulations — which constituted a legal Alsatia for Europeans — would still have barred the way to all important legislation and to the removal of those defects in the administrative system of which the Egyptians most complained. The only possible method by which the country could be provided with a workable legislative machine was to include in the term 'Egyptians' all the dwellers in Egypt, and to devise some plan by which the European and Egyptian elements of society would be fused together. The true Egyptian patriot was not the man who by his conduct and language stimulated racial animosity in the pursuit of an ideal which could never be realised, but rather one who recognised the true facts of the political situation. To Cromer, the dominating fact of that situation was that Egypt could never become autonomous in the sense in which that word was understood by the Egyptian nationalists. Egypt was, and would always remain, a cosmopolitan country. The real future of Egypt therefore lay not in the direction of a narrow nationalism which would only embrace native Egyptians, nor in that of any endeavour on our own part to convert the country into a possession on the model of India or Ceylon, but rather in that of an enlarged cosmopolitanism.

It must always be, accordingly, the duty of the imperial Power to see to it that liberty among its subject-races was not allowed to degenerate into licence; for men who began by asking for some minor reform might well end determined to engineer a revolution. It was Cromer's principle that we must do what we conscientiously thought to be the best for a subject-race, without reference either to any special interests of our own, whether military or commercial, or to those of the subject-race itself — whose ideas on its own interests, although worthy of attention, might very well not be worthy of respect. If this principle was applied, then, although we could never create a patriotism akin to that based on affinity of race or community of language, we might still perhaps foster some sort of cosmopolitan allegiance grounded on the respect men always accorded to superior talents and unselfish conduct, and on the gratitude derived both from favours conferred and from those to come. There might then, at all events, be 'some hope that the Egyptian will hesitate before he throws in his lot with any future Arabi'.[1]

It was from this same angle, always, that the Irish question had been viewed and judged in England. The Home Rule issue was as emotional a matter on this as on the far side of St. George's Channel. Men so different as Hartington and Chamberlain, Tennyson and Randolph Churchill, held the same views. They were moral views. Irish nationalism was not thought a proper political issue at all, and Gladstone when he made it such affronted the conscience of politicians as well as their party positions. The Irish claim that Ireland was a nation was one that was bitterly and passionately refuted by the late-Victorian Englishman and the generation he trained, who saw in it only a deliberate rejection of his own standards, which were, he was genuinely persuaded, the highest that men had yet attained to. An Irish State, with a Foreign Office of its own! — declared Curzon late, late in the evening of this sad story — was a contingency which he was sure no British statesman worthy of the name would ever be rash enough to propose. Curzon was thinking not only of the practical issues involving the security of the United Kingdom, vital as these were — he was thinking that anyone who caused such a rent in the United Kingdom itself would commit an act so wicked as to constitute madness.

Englishmen of the best kind talked little of their superiority to others, they were content to assert that superiority in action. They did talk a great deal, however, of their responsibility to others, and among those others was generally included world interests as a whole. On an imperial Power, so Lugard asserted with reference to African governance, lay a dual mandate: a mandate of trusteeship towards the subject-people, and a mandate of responsibility to the civilised world. We had a responsibility of this sort towards the people of the Sudan, so declared Austen Chamberlain when Egyptian objections to this same principle were being discussed in 1929, which must be retained for ever. He was cross-questioned.

---

[1] Cromer, *Political and Literary Essays*, I, 12, 13.

P

For ever? Yes, he asserted stoutly, for ever. It was the same case in Egypt itself. Anthony Eden in this same debate declared frankly he was not content, and felt that none of us should ever be content, to leave the protection of a vital artery like the Suez Canal to the goodwill of the people of Egypt. He added, in words he was to repeat in 1946 and reiterate in 1956, that we should not be justified for a moment in leaving the defence of the Canal to the occasion of that goodwill.

This point about justification is of the greatest importance in assessing the imperialist outlook. Cromer laid it down that the main justification of Imperialism was to be found in the use that was made of the imperial power. If we made a good use of our power, we might face the future without fear that we would be overtaken by the Nemesis which attended Roman misrule. If the reverse was the case, then the British Empire would fall, and would deserve to fall. There was truth in the saying — although it was not the whole truth — that the maintenance of Empire depended on the sword. Law and order required its own armouries. But so little, indeed, did Empire depend on the sword alone that if once we had to draw the sword, not merely to put down some local effervescence, but to overcome a general upheaval of subject-races which had been goaded to action either by deliberate oppression or by (what was far more likely) unintentional misgovernment, we would find that the sword would be powerless to defend us for long, and the days of our imperial rule would be numbered.

Here Milner added his testimony. He saw it as the duty of his generation of Imperialists to hold the fort during the long, and indispensable, process of education. It would be for another, a more fortunate generation, to build the great Imperial edifice itself. No matter that this duty was a formidably difficult one, so difficult indeed that 'Laocoon wrestling with the serpents' was no unfitting symbol of the desperate struggle which imperial patriotism had to wage against the hydras of particularism and the party spirit that everywhere threatened to throttle it. Maintaining the *pax Britannica* was maintaining also civilised conditions among a fifth of the human race. But true imperialism involved something more than this task of maintenance. It was not by what it took away, but by what it gave — not by depriving alien races of their own character, language, and traditions, but by ensuring them the retention of all these things, and at the same time opening new vistas of culture and advancement — that Imperialism sought and should always seek to win these races to itself. Might not even the Indians themselves become Imperialists, if changes were made, changes that gave a wider scope to native abilities and ambition, changes that removed those 'disabilities and indignities to which even the most highly civilised Indians are at present liable in some of the white communities of the Empire?'[1] Milner had told a Cape Town audience in 1900 that they could only justify the rights that white men in South Africa claimed over black men by using those rights for the benefit of the subject-race, and not merely for their own convenience. It was a position from which he did not swerve. (Or not knowingly: for he confessed himself always 'totally unable to see' any moral stain attaching to the programme of Chinese labour.) Imperialism must thus preserve its moral content, its imaginative range, and its grip on the imaginations of its own subjects.

Justification was therefore a term used emotionally. The moment an imperialist began to use it rationally, he could not but see himself — in his private moments at least — as his enemies had always seen him: as a cynical power-lover who would make use of any humanitarian or sentimental argument that happened to suit his book at the time. Winston Churchill, staunchest of the imperialists of the inter-war period, himself asserted that our national self-confidence in the imperial mission we had set our hand to *was* the sole justification for our presence in the East. For if we did not believe in what we were doing, then we deserved all the epithets of bully and oppressor that Egyptians and others so constantly hurled at us. 'Once we lose confidence in our mission in the East . . . then our presence in those countries will be stripped of every moral sanction, and cannot long endure.'[2]

Emotional imperialism on the one side thus kept regular rendez-vous with emotional nationalism on the other. It is not surprising that there were many love-affairs as a result: that T. E. Lawrence (and a whole school of officials who thought Lawrence's other ideas absurd) idealised the Arabs; that Gandhi and Nehru alike deeply respected the English liberal tradition; that a modern Army Mess in Pakistan is today (1957) the exact replica down to the slang of that of a good British regiment; and that Asians who have known British imperialism at first hand still set standards for British in-

[1] Milner, *Nation and the Empire*, p. 493.
[2] 5 H 233, 23 December 1929, 1995 ff.

ternational conduct that they do not think of applying to the behaviour of other nations, as was clear from their differing reactions to the British invasion of Egypt and the Russian invasion of Hungary in October-November 1956. It was always the calculating element in imperialism — or what is more conveniently called 'colonialism' — that drew down the hatred and contempt of the nationalists. It was never difficult to see through those strategic arguments that disguised themselves as safeguards for civilised values; through those British interests that wrapped themselves in the dogmas either of Free or of Fair Trade, trade neither free nor fair in the subjected customer's view; through those men who said they were working for someone else's good when in truth they were interested only in themselves; through those officials who talked a lot about their duty to the people of India but who contrived to exchange as few civil words as possible with the inhabitants of the country. Many indeed had a conception of service, but always it was service of the Empire, with India a bad second.

It was always difficult, on the other hand, for aliens to penetrate the mask of reserve that even some of the best English officials thought it right to wear. If good is to be done, if favours are to be conferred, there are ways of doing these things — and when high principles conceal themselves behind a stern countenance and a haughty demeanour, they have sometimes as bad an effect on the beholder as would be caused by plain evidence of vicious intentions. Moreover, Englishmen whose principles were not high were inclined to look on everyone and everything east of Suez as 'below stairs' — an area inhabited by wogs where, as Kipling reported, the ten commandments themselves had no writ. Perhaps they no longer required public warning not to kick their servants; but they still often gave themselves a great deal of credit for exercising so considerable a self-restraint. A moment's loss of that restraint, by just such men, was enough to ruin the record of the high-minded imperialist himself.

Such men of course were not imperialists in the sense in which this term is being used in this book: they were democrats too rudely transplanted, and there was always much less sympathy between the patrician official and the plebeian commercial than there was between the former and the native subject. The Scottish captains of industry and commerce at Calcutta, the *Round Table* noted, attended to their trade in and manufacture of jute with scarcely more

reference to public affairs than they would have bestowed if their
business had been situated in Brazil or the Dutch East Indies.[1] But
the true imperialist searched long and earnestly to discover a high
principle in nationalism itself — a thing he would never have
troubled to do had he had either some actual experience, or some
over-riding race-memory, of its nature. (It was a matter he spent
no time at all investigating in 1940, when the national essence of
England was itself directly threatened by an alien.) He wished, if he
could, to do nationalism justice, but it could only appear to him re-
gressive and reactionary where it was not positively anarchical.
Moreover, nationalists themselves were not generous of justice,
and would see no motive anywhere that was not a bad one, no edict
that was not an insult, no plan for the future that was not a chain
binding them to the past. Long campaigns of vituperation and
calumny soured the imperialist's temper, and it was with a feeling
of righteous bitterness that he poured scorn on the dogma of self-
determination. How was India a nation? Surely, he argued, the test
of national capacity was neither oratory nor history, but the capacity
in the here and now to conduct an orderly government wherein a
sane public opinion ruled, law was obeyed, and the rights of the individual were effectively secured. This admirable definition could
have emerged only from an Englishman. Tagore answered it, that
peace was good but not better than life, which was God's own
boon. He reminded the English that people who possessed political
freedom were not necessarily free, they were merely powerful —
there is an echo here perhaps of what the Devil, an Irish critic, says
of the English in Shaw's *Man and Superman* (1903).

That Anglo-Saxon mould, which Rosebery had urged his
countrymen to export, had never in fact fitted the human materials
of the outside world. Neither Canada, nor Australia, nor the United
States, modelled their social, as distinct from their legal, conventions on those of their mother country. In the East the legal as
much as the social conventions caused bewilderment. There it is
not the institution, but the personality, that is of importance. This
was something the English themselves were well able to assess:
Balfour commented in 1910 that the East had indeed a great history, a splendid history — but not a history of self-government.[2]
Not a history, he might well have added, of law and order, of

[1] *RT*, June 1918, No. 31, p. 571.
[2] 5 H 17, 13 June 1910, 1141 : see also Appendix II, *infra* p. 359.

equality before the law, of a rigid budgetary system, or indeed of anything which the English, having in their gift, wished to distribute and impose. It needs to be recalled — for it says a great deal for the reality of England's prestige, and refutes Goldwin Smith's assertion that it was all a baleful imposture — that the countries of the East took, and tried to use these gifts; submitted to, and sought to understand, these impositions; and after they had taken them, asked for something else which would put life into them, asked for some key to their meaning, only to find that the English had no idea what they were talking about. Even when nationalist feeling rose to its peak, and the English were looked on as so many evil magicians, the power of their magic was never denied. When ultimately the imperial yoke was thrown off, still in the Indian midst the old imperial institutions stood, awaiting entry and use by new masters.

That such a thing could come about was thought impossible. Balfour and Morley, perhaps the two keenest intelligences in the Edwardian Houses of Parliament, agreed that it was impossible. Parliamentary institutions were native to English idea, English soil, English tradition. Morley as Secretary of State felt indeed it would not merely be misguided, it would actually be wrong, to set such institutions up in an Indian setting. India had her own destiny to discover, and she could hardly do this wearing an English mask. His own legislative reforms of 1909 Morley considered as 'a sop to impossible ambitions'. But the ambitions were there, and had thereafter to be reckoned as political factors. The nationalist outlook on this matter was simple enough: if parliamentary institutions were England's pride, and the reason she had made herself so great a name in the world, then Indians too must have these institutions, and they were not to be fobbed off with something else, something clearly inferior, something deemed suitable only for benighted orientals who did not know any better. This feeling of weakness and inferiority — the same corrosive that had burned so deeply into Anglo-Irish relations — simultaneously galled and stimulated the Eastern spirit. Indians and Egyptians agreed with the aphorism, that colonies were not weak because they were colonies, but were colonies because they were weak. The only remedy was to gain strength, and the only method of doing this was by the method of politics. The method of military force was not possible — or not practicable yet, although Adowa and Tshushima, battles humbling

European civilised powers at African and Asian hands, had already begun to cast their shadow down the years towards Manila, Singapore, and Rangoon.

Accordingly, the people whom Balfour chose to describe as

those ingenious native lawyers, whose delight and pleasure and perhaps whose road to fame and income, consists in embarrassing the administration, in respect of which they are absolutely independent[1]

continued to increase, until by 1918, after four years of assisting in a fight for freedom and democracy, they faced the *Raj* in confident expectation. The Western-educated in India had by now fully converted their movement from a desire to assert class privileges to a struggle between the forces of popular control on the one hand and bureaucratic government on the other. The 'interpreters' had come of age: what was it they had to interpret? Was the solution to make such people at last dependent on the system of government, a part of it, responsible for some at least of it? Would this ameliorate the position? Or would it only add fuel to the nationalist flames, make the cry for self-determination, complete Home Rule, *swaraj*, the louder? Either way it was a gamble, and imperialists who were not gamblers by nature inclined to stand pat and die hard. Somehow the British had to reconcile this rising nationalist spirit and the desire for self-government with the maintenance of their own power, and with the maintenance, too, of constitutional progress, of law, and of imperial unity. This they had to do in the face of racial and religious fanaticism, and in the teeth of a domestic public opinion which was fast being converted to Wilsonianism. Too many issues pressed too hard and too fast: India, Egypt, Ireland. Imperial problems had once been readily soluble by firm action, but this appeared now to bring in few tangible results. The *Round Table* lamented in 1923 that, looking back at the course of events since the war, and particularly bearing in mind that heart-breaking Irish 'settlement' which had been got at pistol-point, the Egyptians had every excuse for thinking that the British would concede anything to persistent clamour so long as it was persistent and clamorous enough. The writer drew the conclusion that unless we were able to harden our hearts and to ignore resolutely demands which, however persistent, were clearly unreasonable, we should lose the Empire — and we should have deserved to lose it.

[1] 5 H 3, 1 April 1909, 65.

Imperialists accepted that here we were reaping where we had sown. It was we ourselves who had supplied to our subject-races the materials which were now being used to weave the imperial winding-sheet. We had done this deliberately, not swerving from the stance adopted by Macaulay in the 1830's when he had pressed for the adoption of an English educational system in India, under whose discipline Indians should be trained to become fit to take responsibility for their own affairs. In time, in a long time: for Macaulay's aim had been the creation of a class of English-educated 'interpreters' in India, who should act as sergeant-majors for the *Raj* in dealing with the illiterate mass of the peasantry. He had considered, in 1833, that for India's own good the admission of natives to high office was a process that would have to be effected by slow degrees. But effected it should be. When the fullness of time had come, when it was plainly in the interest of India that this change should be made, no Englishman should refuse to make that change simply on the grounds that to do so would endanger his own power. That was a doctrine, said Macaulay,

> of which I cannot think without indignation. Governments, like men, may buy existence too dear.

His argument had sunk deep into the conscience of his posterity. The possession of Empire never in fact wrought that sea-change in British thinking which its Victorian critics, like the Duke of Argyll and Herbert Spencer, feared might come about. Great Britain remained a liberal country, a free country, devoted to the doctrine of government by consent, suspicious of the standing army. India, with its government by dictation, based on its Army, remained as a perpetual challenge to the English liberal conscience. It seemed that it could not for much longer be possible to combine the principle of self-government and that of perpetual dependency in the same political system.

What was power worth, Macaulay had asked, if it was founded on vice, on ignorance, and on misery? What was it worth, if we could hold it only by violating the most sacred duties that governors owed to the governed? Surely we were free, we were civilised, to little purpose, if we grudged to any section of the human race an equal measure of civilisation. Were we to keep the people of India ignorant in order that we might keep them submissive? Were we foolish enough to suppose that it was possible to give them know-

ledge without awakening their ambition? Or, worse, were we going
to be so crass as to awaken ambition and then to provide it with no
legitimate vent? It might be, he added, that the public mind of
India would expand under the English system until it had out-
grown that system. It might be that by good government we should
educate our subjects there into a capacity for better government. It
might be that, having become instructed in European knowledge,
they would, in some future age, demand European institutions.
Macaulay had no thought like Morley's, that this would involve any
perversion of the native genius. He did not know whether such a
day would ever come — but he declared that he would never try to
avert or retard it. Whenever it came, it would be 'the proudest day
in English history'. To have found a great people sunk in the lowest
depths of slavery and superstition, to have so ruled them as to have
made them desirous and capable of all the privileges of citizens, that
would indeed be a title to glory all our own.

No one could tell what the future held. The sceptre of power
might pass away from us. Unforeseen accidents might derange our
most profound schemes of policy. Victory might be inconstant to
our arms. But there were triumphs that were followed by no reverse. There was an empire exempt from all natural causes of decay. Those triumphs were the pacific triumphs of reason over barbarism; that empire was the imperishable empire of our arts and
our morals, our literature and our laws.

No British patriot was ever impervious to the force and attrac-
tion of this ringing and celebrated argument. The dilemma facing
the imperialist was not one of morals but of method. In fighting
against nationalism he felt he fought for the right, for imperialism
was a wider, grander concept than any that narrow racial passions
could ever aspire to. In the twentieth century he denied that the
point in time whose coming Macaulay had hailed in advance had in
fact arrived. He denied that we had educated our subjects to a
capacity for better government, for self-government for the Indian
millions was still an unthinkable absurdity. He answered the assertions from the Left, that Indians rioted because the *Raj* remained in India, with his own assertion that they would riot a great
deal more if the *Raj* quit. What but the *Raj*, after all, kept the
Muslim from the throat of the Hindu, or the Hindu knife out of
the back of the Muslim? Our moral duty in India was still as great
as ever; but it was not a moral duty to go, it was a moral duty to

stay. He recalled how India had fallen to the alien English in the first place because it had been a political vacuum. Clive might have been an adventurer, indeed, but behind him and his like had stood the stable society of Whig England, which had intervened, if belatedly, to put an end to such private adventuring. But suppose it had not been Clive and the English, but Avitabile the Italian adventurer in the Punjab, or any of the notorious 'free lances' of Hindostan, who had gained control? Suppose in 1857 the Delhi mutineers had managed to raise all India by means of the native army? Would not all the old tyrannies, and worse, have returned? To be sure they would have: and who could say even now that India was not the same political vacuum it had always been? Who could say that the venom unleashed in 1857 had not improved with keeping? Who could say, therefore, that it was time for the *Raj* to go, when it was the *Raj* that held the whole artificial structure of 'India' together?

It was indeed dangerous to stability, a cause itself of Indian unrest, to propagate any such notion. The *Edinburgh Review* had put this point of view as early as 1884, the year the first Indian National Congress convened. If the English, wrote the reviewer, were content to declare that they held India by a just and valid title, and that they intended to preserve and improve their heritage, that was a position plain and profitable to us all. But if they propounded for academic debate any thesis as to the moral justification of their government, and if they persisted in asserting that they only desired to stay in India so long as India required their good offices, they might soon get worsted in argument, and later might find themselves elbowed, more or less politely, altogether out of the country. Fifty years later Winston Churchill, attacking the National Government's Bill 'to make further provision for the government of India' in 1935, echoed these sentiments. 'We hope,' he said,

speaking for the entire imperialist tradition, to kill once for all the idea that the British in India are aliens, moving, with many apologies, out of the country as soon as they have been able to set up any kind of governing organism to take their place.[1]

Such an idea was too dangerous to be borne. For, to Churchill as to Curzon before him, the *Raj* was still the symbol of British power and influence throughout half the world.

[1] 5 H 297, 6 February 1935, 1663.

The Trojan horse in this struggle was of course the process and progress of Western education. Macaulay's clear-sightedness concerning the significance of the relationship between a man's education and his ambition had become blurred, by the time the twentieth century came in, partly because education itself had moved at so slow a pace. When Ripon succeeded Lytton as Viceroy in 1880, resolved to replace the latter's distinctly imperialist policy with one as distinctively Liberal, there were perhaps some 50,000 educated Indians in the sub-continent. This was a number which, in the eyes of the non-official, commercial Europeans in India, was anyway too high. It was Ripon's aim to make this educated class a friend to British rule, to continue indeed Macaulay's programme of producing interpreters; for by so doing the *Raj* would be able to govern, and to go on governing, in accordance with a growing public opinion which this intermediate class would nourish and guide. Ripon's principal *aide* in putting this policy into action was his financial expert, Major Evelyn Baring (not yet become Cromer and as yet unknown to Egypt) who was a firm supporter of plans to introduce better forms of local government, to be administered by the Indians themselves. We should not subvert the British Empire, he remarked, by allowing the Bengali *babu* to discuss his own schools and his own drains. Indeed, keeping the Bengali busy about such tasks would supply a safety-valve, by directing his political energies down fruitful channels.[1] But this was to see the matter in terms somewhat too simple. Minds trained to read, if not always fully to understand, the doctrines of Burke, Mazzini, and Mill, were unlikely long to be content debating issues of schools and drains. The urban councils and parish boards with which the *Raj* began to dot the Indian plains accordingly made little appeal to the graduates who were now coming out in ever-greater numbers from the colleges and Universities. Cromer himself commented thirty years later that the reason Indian towns were tolerably well governed lay in the fact that chairmen and presidents of the local councils were generally Englishmen.

The result was that, while nobody put forward the case that we should stop the education of Indians, anyone who actively encouraged it met with an opposition whose strength varied in proportion to the opposer's sense of security. As the ranks of Indian politicians, lawyers, and journalists swelled with those who had

[1] S. Gopal, *Viceroyalty of Ripon*, (Oxford, 1954), p. 96.

been destined by their educators for the peaceful tasks of local administration, the official found himself more and more on the defensive. Ripon was vilified in his own time for seeking to dethrone the European in India, and the *cause célèbre* of 1884, centring on the impropriety of permitting Indian judges to try Europeans, left him a marked man. Both Lord Randolph Churchill and Lord George Hamilton, who were subsequently Conservative Secretaries of State for India, used language about Ripon whose intemperateness showed the depths to which they and those who thought as they did were stirred. In Hamilton's opinion, expressed fourteen years after Ripon had ceased to be Viceroy, anyone who knew anything about India knew that Ripon had contrived to raise up a racial feeling there, and from that day forward no question in India was judged on its merits, but as a question between race and race.[1] As a result, the main difficulty that confronted every government was the allaying of those racial sentiments that Ripon's administration had aroused. This opinion passage of time did not weaken. As late as 1915, when it was proposed to erect a statue to Ripon in Calcutta, it had to be financed (and it was financed) by funds contributed by Indians alone. No European in India put an anna into it.

Ripon, as a convinced and active Liberal party politician, was fair game for embattled Conservatives. But this could not be said of his successors in the Viceroyalty — Dufferin the non-party Whig, the respected Whig-Unionist Lansdowne, the imperialist Curzon. Yet these men too were charged with misconceiving the serious issues presented by the fact of rising articulacy in Indian public opinion. It hardly mattered whether they and their subordinates were accused either of encouraging the movement too far, or of not giving it enough support (of the right kind): they were, in some indefinable way, selling the pass. This was, Ramsay MacDonald stressed in 1910 — a year when the Indian population stood at 237 million, on which three-farthings per head was being spent on education — *the* great problem of India, and those people who, like Sir Francis Younghusband, went on protesting that these Western-educated natives, 'exotically-educated young men, without weight or influence,' were not representative of the people of India, though what they said was perfectly true, were missing the vital point. It must be with this group, and not with the illiterate

[1] 4 H 53, 17 February 1898, 996.

mass, that the *Raj* should establish a *modus vivendi*. But how could it do this, since it continued to deny any value to the aspirations of that class?

In this impasse the *Raj* came finally to a halt. We were in India, H. G. Wells wrote in his *New Macchiavelli* in 1911, 'like a man who has fallen off a ladder on to the neck of an elephant, and doesn't know what to do or how to get down.' In India we made nothing happen; at the most we prevented things from happening. It was idle to pretend, as Milner pretended, that the British Empire gave to its constituent peoples any high and rewarding civilisation, when all it gave them was the services of an honest, unsympathetic and unattractive officialism. We not only suppressed our own literature in India, but made it difficult for ordinary English people to go even to see this great English possession. The periodic and rapid visitations of 'Pagett, M.P.' had to be permitted by the authorities, but they would not allow any Cook's tour of British India by, say, a collection of Manchester operatives. Our flag, spread over the continent, was nothing but a vast preventive. Of course everyone had heard of that apocryphal native ruler in the north-west, who, when asked what would happen if we left India, replied that in a week his men would be in the saddle, and in six months not a rupee or a virgin would be left in Lower Bengal. That was always given, by the imperialists, as our conclusive justification. But was it really our business to preserve 'the rupees and virgins of Lower Bengal in a sort of magic inconclusiveness'? Better plunder than paralysis, better fire and sword than futility.

Wellsian fireworks of this sort could of course be discounted in 1911 by the ruling classes, the 'old Macchiavelli', but Gandhi's language thirty years later was directly derived from it. In 1947 Churchill quoted to the Commons what the Indian leader had said when rejecting the 'Cripps offer' made in 1942. He had told the British to go, to

> leave India in God's hands — in modern parlance, to anarchy: and that anarchy may lead to internecine warfare for a time . . . from this a true India will arise in place of the false one we see.

No imperialist could listen to such sentiments without a sense of total dismay. To accept what Wells said, to accept what Gandhi said, was to accept the death of every British aspiration for the good ordering of the world. When Wells wrote, imperialists still did not think it too late for imperial governance to leave the impasse, to take another route. It was because he knew the dangers that lurked in the impasse that Cromer insisted that 'free institutions in the full sense of the term must for generations to come be wholly unsuitable to countries such as India and Egypt'. If it were denied it was actually impossible, it must surely be conceded that it was at least a lengthy and tedious task to make a Western silk purse out of an Eastern sow's ear. Our primary duty as an imperial power lay not in giving sops to impossible ambitions — and so encouraging them further. It lay not in introducing a system which, under the specious cloak of free institutions, would enable a small minority of natives to misgovern their countrymen. It lay in establishing a system which would enable the mass of the population to be governed according to the code of Christian morality. Who was to say that in an Egyptian 'Parliament' the slave-dealers would not have a powerful lobby, or that in a Rajputana 'Parliament' *suttee* might not again be legalised?

It was well, Cromer insisted, to be clear at this difficult juncture just what sort of risks the Empire was running. Our present system tended to turn out demagogues from our colleges, to give them every facility for sowing their subversive views broadcast over the land, and at the same time to prepare the ground for the reception of the seed which they sowed. Now this was the very reverse of a sound imperial policy. We could not, certainly, effectually prevent this manufacture of demagogues — not unless we adopted measures which would render us false to our acknowledged principles of government and to our civilising mission: for Macaulay's doctrine was, after all, still the only one worthy of a civilised nation. But surely we might govern in such a manner as to give the demagogue no fulcrum with which to move his credulous and ill-informed countrymen and co-religionists?[1]

If there was indeed a recipe for this, no one discovered it. Wells made a point that no one could shrug away, the same point to which Milner returned again and again. Wells asked, what would hold the Empire together? And answered his own question, that if most of the intelligent and active people in the Empire wanted it to continue then it would; but if a large proportion of such active and intelligent people became discontented and estranged, then nothing could save it from disintegration. India was now, as it had ever

[1] Cromer, *Political and Literary Essays*, I, 50–1.

been, outside the domain of public consciousness: and as a consequence, the *Raj* remained at its halting-place.

Imperialists still insisted that benevolent despotism was a duty
laid upon them, and that all these clerks, with their half-assimilated
knowledge of truths whose essence they would never perceive, were
not the kind of people to whom the destinies of the sub-continent
could be entrusted. Not now and not ever. What imperialists were
saying about the Congress party in 1910 they were still saying in
1935, when a largely Conservative Government was trying to build
a breakwater on ground which the tide had already submerged.[1]
Their Government of India Bill was designed as a treaty between
one sovereign nation, Great Britain, and a large number of sovereign, or at any rate dominant, Indian princes. It was a belated return to the principle of aristocracy: it could only appear that the
Raj, unable to stand fast alone, was summoning up its creatures.
As a result, Josiah Wedgwood remarked, all politics in India would
be poisoned, and directed towards hating somebody else. The keynote of the Bill, Clement Attlee insisted, was mistrust, and the one
thing that was missing in all its enormous length and bulk was the
Indian people themselves. For the imperialists Sir Edward Grigg
was still asserting Cromer's point and Milner's view — that there
was no possibility whatever of India's developing on the same lines
as the Dominions, and it was folly to suggest there was. Churchill,
attacking Front Bench policy, castigated the Bill as a piece of weakness and folly, and went into the same division lobby as the Labour
Opposition. On this the Prime Minister, Stanley Baldwin, was reminded of what the ostler had said to the duke:

> 'The beauty of 'unting, yer Grace, is that it brings together people who
> would not hotherwise meet.'

Since concessions to nationalism had always to be made under a
joint, but never a co-ordinated, attack from both Right and Left,
Governments that either wished or felt it essential to make such
concessions tended to make them in a halting and ungracious
fashion. This style of performance at once made it clear not only
to the imperialists but also to nationalists that what Government
was doing it was doing mainly for reasons of expediency. While
the debate continued — and it did so for forty-five years of the

[1] Debate in 5 H 297, 6 February 1935.

twentieth century — governance by principle tended to go by default, and the energies of a whole generation of British administrators were too often deflected into the task of putting down unrest,
subversion, sedition, disloyalty, terrorism, violence and all the
other euphemisms for rebellion that were in contemporary use.

The pronouncements of aim that were made were often ad-
mirably phrased; but, as Edwin Montagu, Secretary of State for
India, pointed out when his particular Bill for the better governance of India was going through Parliament in 1919, no one had
any use for pronouncements which took geological epochs to fulfil.[1]
In Montagu's Bill there was indeed more of principle than expediency, and it passed in a flush of enthusiastic Parliamentary gratitude
for the contributions India had made in money and manpower towards the war in Europe: certainly Churchill, a Cabinet colleague
of Montagu, said no word against it in public.[2] Indeed the Radicals
of the day hailed this 1919 Act as the most important piece of legislation that had been passed since the Reform Bill of 1832. It was
hardly that, and its consequences began no new epoch in India,
geological or other. Its passage had the misfortune to be sand-
wiched between two acts based on expediency alone: the execution
of the Rowlatt Acts against sedition in India, carried out in a
manner that seemed exceptionally oppressive, and the action of
General Dyer in the Jallianwallah Bagh at Amritsar, which world
opinion condemned as murderous. Amritsar — an event which, in
Churchill's words, stood 'in singular and sinister isolation'[3] in the
British imperial record — supplied Indian nationalism with all the
martyrs it was ever to need.

Moreover, the principles in the 1919 Act were hard to discover
— and, when discovered, not hard to impugn. The doctrine that
one had to govern in the East or go — once propounded at a Guild-
hall dinner by Theodore Roosevelt, to the embarrassment of his
Liberal Government hosts and to the delight of many imperialists
present — was heavily disguised in the system of 'diarchy' that the
Act instituted. It seemed that the British were neither governing
nor going: they were doing something else again, presiding over a

[1] 5 H 116, 5 June 1919, 2298.
[2] The India Bill was however drafted by Montagu while the War Cabinet, of
which Churchill was not a member, was still in being. Normal Cabinet Government was not resumed until 3 November 1919.
[3] 5 H 131, 8 July 1920, 1725.

manner of governance unknown to political science, for which Lionel Curtis had had to invent a Greek name. Diarchy was an attempt to preserve to Parliament and the Indian Executive the control over the essentials of administration, while giving to Indians a field in which they could exercise the practice of government. (It was the same system, although it was never called by that name, that was soon afterwards adopted throughout the Middle East.)

Imperialists disliked the system because it was not an honest system, honest in the sense that it made plain where authority lay. Nationalists detested it for precisely the same reason, and Congress accordingly took little interest in those 'transferred subjects' in the government of the Indian Provinces which were now allocated to its members, but a very great deal in that Bluebeard's chamber where the non-transferred or the 'reserved subjects' were confined, as property of the *Raj* — law and order, external relations, defence, and finance. Was this the responsible government that had been spoken of by Montagu himself back in 1917 — when, of course, the war was still being waged? Was this democracy? Was this, or anything like it, the system of governance that had made the British Empire renowned? What was diarchy, after all, but a reach-me-down garment hastily cobbled together to cover the nakedness of a poor relation who had, unfortunately, a legitimate claim on the imperial tailor?

A stout answer to this type of attack came, somewhat surprisingly, from Lloyd George, of a kind that momentarily raised his standing even with those Conservatives who were beginning to feel it was time to dispense with him. Democracy, said the Prime Minister, was only a recent experiment in the West. It could not be put, fully-fledged, into India. No matter what was said, or how vituperatively, India remained a trust — and no honourable man got rid of a trust the first time the beneficiaries lost their temper with him, and thought they could manage the thing better themselves.[1]

Naturally this did not meet, or even see, the nationalists' point. They asserted that by now they had seen how hollow were the imperialist pretensions. The true imperialists of Macaulay's day had laid down principles in regard to India which their false posterity were refusing to follow, and why? Because if officials were to follow those principles the road would lead them to a place of oblivion and

[1] 5 H 150, 14 February 1922, 965.

Q

the extinction of their own careers. Nor did nationalists often contend that they matched the West in political expertise. They asserted instead that it was time they developed an expertise of their own. This they could not do while the *Raj* throttled their aspirations.

They denied, moreover, that there was any trust, in much the same language as Hobson had used in 1902, and which Lenin had already improved upon. They denied, further, supposing for the sake of argument there was such a thing as this trust, that they were its beneficiaries. India, Nehru noted in his *Autobiography* (1936), was treated as a kind of enormous country-house, with the Indians in the servants' hall, pantry, and kitchen. 'Sometimes we were treated to a rare honour — we were given a cup of tea in the drawing-room.' So alien a governance of India, 'which is as little touched by human hand as possible', could hold out no promise to its inhabitants. The basis of the Hindu religion was the desire to get in touch with the infinite: it was unlikely that any Hindu could receive guidance how best to do this from any hard-pressed, overworked District Commissioner, the product of an English public school. They objected that the physical problems of India were not tackled at all. What was it that struck all visitors to India like a blow in the face? Its condition of grinding poverty. Only a high death-rate prevented the multiplication of the people to the point of starvation: in 1921 in Bombay it was 667 per 1,000. Of all modern states, India had the weakest of economic foundations, and how many of the 4,000-odd British in India could honestly call themselves expert either in industrial questions or in tropical agriculture? It was this charge — that the British did not understand either what India was or who India was — that supplied a powerful link between Gandhi, busily trying to defeat the Western industrial system by appealing to sentiment and calling for a return to the cottage spinning-wheel, and a magnate like Patel, who was only too anxious to modernise what industries India possessed. At least such men had *theories* how to improve life and living for the Indian masses. The British had no such theories. Once, indeed, they had had the self-confidence to attack and put down *suttee* and *thuggee*, but they had never faced the problem how to abolish the sacred cow. If they were told that what was wanted in India was less emphasis on law, order, and justice, and more ruthless efficiency, some kind of Soviet five-year plan, they would have been shocked.

The Indian Civil Service, thus accused of occupying its time and energy in the pursuit of irrelevancies, had no effective answer to make. On all sides its uprightness, honesty, and integrity were admitted and admired. No one doubted, as Labour members conceded, that future leaders of India would probably compare most unfavourably in these respects with the British officers, civilian and military, who now controlled the country: but they did not, they insisted, urge self-government for India because they thought it would be better government, but because, as Wedgwood put it, no human advance could ever be made save through freedom and self-respect. A period comes, added MacDonald, before a country is really fitted to obtain the best results from self-government, when its political forces compel it to get self-government.[1] He was reminded once more, as so many were in this age of questioning, of Macaulay: 'If men are to wait for liberty till they become wise and good in slavery, they may indeed wait for ever.' In this at least Attlee agreed with MacDonald, for he declared in 1937 that a Labour Government would always prefer to err in being too soon rather than too late in the grant of self-government.[2] For there was an inevitable tendency, even in the best of colonial administrators, to lay too much stress on the deterioration in administrative standards which was almost certain to come, and not enough on the need for enabling backward people to learn to govern themselves. Some time-table had to be drawn up, and adhered to, otherwise these doubts and dubieties, the fear of making mistakes transmuted into the fear of doing anything at all, would rule the political scene for ever. Ten years later in India, Attlee was to show he had kept to his opinions.

It was just this kind of reasoning that cut so deep into, and so hard against, the imperialists' grain. It appealed to emotions they did not share. It appealed to reasons their hearts did not subscribe to. But it troubled them, as the whole concept of Indian nationalism troubled them, because they could not deny that certain echoes were awakened by it. This language that was being spoken, was like a language half-heard, in a foreign tongue. In India the fact that it was Gandhi they had to deal with, and not a man like de Valera, made their task of comprehension the harder. At least the Irish

[1] 5 H 186, 9 July 1925, 631 ff.
[2] C. R. Attlee, *The Labour Party in Perspective*, (1937), quoted in G. Bennett, *The Concept of Empire*, (London, 1953), pp. 404–9.

were definable: rebels who used methods imperialists could well understand, methods of power. Although the Irish defeated the imperial cause in unfair fight, at least there was a fight of sorts and nobody could say that there was anything mysterious about Irish aims and tactics. Gandhi on the other hand used as his principal political weapon theories of passive resistance and non-violence that were unknown to the West. Although he could be hindered, headed off, imprisoned, imperialists still could gain no inkling of his mental strategy, and could lay no successful plans to circumvent a man who was prepared to adopt starvation as a policy of moral blackmail.

Smuts had already warned his age that humanity had struck its tents and was on the march. That this march might well set a good deal of humanity on a road that led through the portals of British rule was fast becoming clear. To be sure, one might lock the gates and build the walls higher. But imperialists knew that a man can always build a ladder as high as the highest wall, and in the meantime they searched about for some means to translate their views on moral responsibility into terms which nationalists could understand. Behind their resentment as they pursued this thankless task — in 1933, for example, jailing 128,000 people in Bombay Presidency and another 124,000 in Bengal — lay a deep confusion and trouble of the spirit. For it was the imperialist, after all, who felt most strongly, who had always taken the greatest pride in the fact, that the British race had not won its name and fame in the world as a builder of prison-houses. Churchill's innate generosity of character often allowed him to penetrate beyond his own prejudices and preconceptions. He was prepared to admit that he would have been a Sinn Feiner had he been born an Irishman, a militant Congress man had he been a Hindu. Nehru he dubbed in 1947 as 'an enemy of this country' — but he added, 'as he had every right to be, if he chose.'[1]

The moral dilemma of the imperialist was not the less real because very few, as the half-century wore on, were prepared to consider he had any right to claim a moral position at all. Churchill recognised bitterly that imperialists were always cast in the role of dullards and reactionaries, men unable to move with the times or to understand modern ideas — a sort of inferior race, mentally deficient, composed principally of colonels and other undesirables

[1] 5 H 434, 6 March 1947, 663 ff.

who had fought for Britain. Why should it be so easily assumed that virtue and modernity were the monopoly of the Left and its nationalist friends? What was digging in along the Suez Canal but a dereliction of our duty to Egypt, 'whose improving civilisation was once our pride'? Why did Irwin as Viceroy so consistently adopt an attitude of apology to Gandhi? Who was Gandhi, but a seditious Middle Temple lawyer, 'now posing as a *fakir* of a type well-known in the East'? If control were handed over to Gandhi and his friends, it would not be 'India for the Indians' that would be the outcome — only India for some Indians, for a very few Indians. These Brahmins, 'who mouth and patter the principles of Western liberalism', who posed as philosophic and democratic politicians, were they not the same men who denied the primary rights of existence to nearly sixty millions of their own fellow-countrymen whom they called 'untouchable'? They did this,

> and then in a moment they turn round and begin chopping logic with John Stuart Mill, or pleading the rights of man with Jean Jacques Rousseau.

Britain had no need to apologise for the exercise of her material power in India. The shame was that our moral and intellectual guidance should not have been exerted as firmly. Now the orb of power had been dangled 'before the gleaming eyes of excitable millions', we would find we had entered into a struggle in which our rule would be shorn of all its argument and of half its apparatus.[1]

These were arguments of solidity, so solid indeed that they seemed to block all paths. The imperialist was therefore most often accused of seeing things too much in black and white, now outmoded terms. Almost literally, this was so. Nothing had come of Cromer's suggestion that in Egypt an enlarged cosmopolitanism might be fostered. Nothing much came, either, from Walter Elliott's idea, which he put forward in 1922, that a racial partnership might be established in the Empire. He felt himself that this was too far-reaching a suggestion for his own time, and that the French example was not one that the British imperialists would follow. They would rather lose the whole of the Empire, Elliott felt, than endure the spectacle of a negro sitting in the House of

---

[1] For these viewpoints, cf. W. S. Churchill: *India: Speeches and an Introduction* (London, 1931), p. 126, *et passim*.

Lords — a negro whose countess, perhaps, was white.[1] Here
Elliott touched on an issue that was seldom aired in public at all,
either then or later. That colour prejudice, like anti-semitism, was
an emotion found in persons and places at a distance from Great
Britain was frequently emphasised — Kenya was frequently cited
as a good example — and this was of course quite true. What was
not emphasised at all was that both these things existed also in
Great Britain. It was Norman Angell's opinion, expressed in 1932,
that if Britain lost India it would not be because of a failure in dealing out political or economic justice, but because of 'the caddish-
ness of a certain British tradition, an attitude in dealing with
"natives".'[2] The Round Table's India correspondent, commenting
on the reception in India of the Government's White Paper of
1933, noticed how even responsible European officials had been
heard to remark that so far as the statement's manner and phraseology were concerned, it could scarcely have been more offensive to
Indian sentiment if it had been expressly designed for the purpose.[3] A recognition of Indian aspirations, one clause remarked,
while it was the 'necessary preface to any study of Indian constitutional problems', was 'an insufficient guide to their solution'; and
there was a great deal more — much of it, of course, true — to the
same effect. Harold Laski, devilling for Samuel Hoare while the
latter, as Secretary of State for India, was preparing his volumin-
ous Bill of 1935, reached the conclusion that the true reason why
this Bill was so long in the making, why it contained so odd a
mélange of so many once-good ideas, was that the predominantly
Conservative Cabinet felt a genuine repugnance to making a contract on equal terms with men of colour.[4] If Laski was right about
this, and responsible statesmen had to wrestle with such a feeling
before they could master it, then the damage wrought by irresponsible Englishmen who allowed the feeling to master them must
assuredly have been so much the greater. Gandhi warned the
British at the Round Table Conference of 1930–31 that it might
turn out, if such an attitude were persisted in, that the British connection itself would prove to be inconsistent with national self-
respect. So it proved, when nine years later Linlithgow the Viceroy

[1] 5 H 150, 14 February 1922, 940.
[2] Norman Angell, The Unseen Assassins, (London, 1932), p. 221.
[3] RT, June 1933, No. 91, p. 563.
[4] Holmes-Laski Correspondence, ed. Howe, p. 1336.

committed India to war with Hitler by *fiat*, as Wellesley had once
committed Bengal against Napoleon.

India, unlike Canada, Australia, and New Zealand, had always
been more preoccupied with stature than with status. Here India
stood on common ground with those other countries that had in
their time endured a British subjugation, Ireland and South Africa.
Yet the concept of Dominion Status, of which so much was heard
during the 1920's, was one that commanded nationalist respect. It
had won Hertzog, it had made de Valera pause. It had drawn
flattering praise from the outside world, and for a time it seemed
therefore necessary to India's self-respect that she, too, should
attain this status within the British Empire.

India's eventual attainment of this status had been foreshadowed
in the Montagu-Chelmsford Report of 1917, a statement of policy
by Secretary of State and Viceroy which had spoken of the increasing need to associate Indians in every branch of administration,
and of the gradual development of self-governing institutions with
a view to the progressive realisation of responsible government in
India as an integral part of the British Empire. This statement was
never debated in the House of Commons, and the subsequent Act
of 1919 never mentioned Dominion status, or responsible government either: throughout the 1920's it was left to the Labour Party to
include the magic phrase in their own policy-statements at their
annual conferences. Indians observing the treatment meted out to
their fellow-nationals by other British subjects in Kenya and South
Africa soon began to doubt whether the concept held any validity
for them anyway. In November 1929 a Conservative Viceroy,
Lord Irwin, on his own initiative asserted that it was indeed the
goal at which the *Raj* aimed, but whether Irwin or his ex-Secretary
of State, Birkenhead, was to be believed was the moot point.
Birkenhead had seen fit to declare in public speeches that the
British did not hold India for the Indians, but as the finest outlet
for British goods in general and Lancashire goods in particular anywhere in the world. We had conquered India by the sword, and by
the sword we would hold it. Certainly no one with any commonsense could envisage a state of affairs coming to pass in a generation, in two generations, in a hundred years, in which Indians
would be competent to govern themselves.[1]

These were cries of the die-hard imperialist at bay, and repre-

[1] 5 H of L 75, 5 November 1929, 405.

sented an attitude to imperial policy which was known in the Conservative Party as 'the wreck of the Birkenhead'. But Indians could not assess matters thus. They could only draw deductions from such facts as these: that no Indian sat on the Simon Commission of 1929–30 that examined the workings of the diarchical system; that despite Irwin's declaration the Commission's Report made no mention of Dominion status; and that, in that enormous Bill of 1935, the words 'Dominion status' were not permitted to appear even in the preamble. Although this omission was challenged at once by Attlee, who asked for explicit recognition of it as the aim of the Government, and urged again that we must lay down a time-table for the Indianisation of the public services,[1] Indians watching for this particular light in the distance finally gave up the effort. They felt always that the imperialists for whom they assumed Birkenhead had spoken would always be strong enough in party politics in England to emasculate, if not entirely to prevent, those measures that were taken for Indian betterment, including the process of Indianisation of the public services.

Attlee warned the Government in 1935 that it was going far to identify the Congress party, the extremists, with that cause of nationalism which now had the instinctive support of all the educated classes. It was a warning he had made before:[2] and one that Indian representatives of those classes had themselves made at the London Round Table Conference five years previously. Sir Tej Bahadur Sapru, a liberal Hindu, recalled that never before in the history of India, even in the India of the Mūghals, had the country been governed by agents and sub-agents as it now was. The Mūghals or the Muslims might have come as invaders, but they settled down and became men of the same country, Indians themselves, part and parcel of the social system. This could certainly not be said of the British *Raj*, still halted in its impasse. To be sure there were difficulties in transferring the business of government, but difficulties were there to be faced. The *Raj* spoke always of the necessity of maintaining law and order, but could an impartial observer of its record these last twenty-five years since Curzon's partition of Bengal truthfully say that law and order had in fact been maintained? Surely no native Indian Ministry could have made graver blunders than had been made. The *Raj* should not say to Indians at this Conference, that because these obstacles existed they

[1] 5 H 297, 6 February 1935, 1172.   [2] 5 H 262, 29 February 1932, 841.

must go back home and tell their countrymen that the utmost they had been able to achieve, after travelling 6,000 miles and after talking to British statesmen of all three parties, was provincial autonomy. The *Raj* could still do great things in India, for India, if only she would pluck up heart, find courage, and have faith.

Jinnah for the Muslim League read his masters a second lesson. They told him that Congress, that large and influential party in India, stood for wrecking or misusing the future constitution. He asked them this question. Did they want those parties who had checked, held in abeyance the party which stood for complete independence, to go back with this answer — that nothing at all could be done just because there was a strong party which would wreck the constitution? There were seventy million Muslims, there were Sikhs, Christians, the bulk of the Hindus themselves, who were, as Jinnah spoke, not behind the Congress in their political ideas. Did the *Raj* want them all to go back and get behind it?

Gandhi read the Conference no lesson at all: he told them the truth as he saw it, 'whilst there is yet a little sand in the glass.' He did not know an instance in which nations had attained their freedom without having to go through an incredible measure of travail. He was told that civil disobedience was a method that no government in the world would tolerate. Well, of course, no government in history had ever *tolerated* open rebellion, but open rebellions none the less had taken place. Yet a nation like India, a nation of 350 million, did not need violence to attain its ends. It simply needed a will of its own, an ability to say 'No'. His nation today was learning to say 'No'.[1]

To this the *Raj* could only return its own negative. Responsible Government, towards which Indian aspirations were mainly directed, was not an automatic device which could be manufactured to specification. It was not even a machine which could run on a motive power of its own. What could it mean in a country like India, where Jinnah and his Muslim League kept insisting that they would never submit to the rule of a Hindu majority? Where the Princes had their solemn treaties of protection from the British *Raj*? Where responsibility itself was an alien and ill-understood concept?

These difficulties, and others, were still emphasised when Linlithgow in February 1940 assured Indians of the British Government's earnest desire that India should attain Dominion status at

[1] Mansergh, *Documents*, I, 209–29.

the earliest possible moment. In riposte came the resolution of the Congress that it considered the British Government's declaration of India as a belligerent country, without any reference to the people of India, and the exploitation of India's resources for the purposes of the war, as an affront to them, which no self-respecting or freedom-loving people could accept or tolerate.[1] Congress hereby declared once again that nothing short of complete independence could be accepted by the people of India. Indian freedom could not exist within the orbit of Imperialism, and Dominion status or any other status within the imperial structure was wholly inapplicable to India, was not in keeping with the dignity of a great nation, and would bind India in many ways to the British political and economic system, from which she was determined to be free. Even when the *Raj*, in August 1940, offered seats to Indians on the Viceroy's Executive Council itself, the centre of Indian governance, and assured Indians again that after the war was over a constituent conference would at once be summoned, the Congress noted only the reservation made by the British Government: that it went without saying that the United Kingdom

> could not contemplate transfer of their present responsibilities for the peace and welfare of India to any system of Government whose authority is directly denied by large and powerful elements in India's national life.[2]

In other words, Congress charged, this reservation was the true heart of the matter: the *Raj* was still prepared to hold on to India on the principle of divide and rule.

Thus in March 1942, when the Churchill Cabinet sent Sir Stafford Cripps to India to make a definite pledge of Dominion status, it was already too late. For some indeed in the British Cabinet it was much too early: Lord Salisbury admitted in the House of Lords that the decision to send Cripps had been come to 'rather precipitately', while Churchill later frankly conceded that only the compelling war-interest induced him as Prime Minister to give his consent to the terms Cripps offered. These conditions laid down the attainment for India of Dominion status after the war, 'under a constitution to be framed by Indians by agreement among themselves and acceptable to the main elements in Indian national

[1] 20 March 1940; Mansergh, *Documents*, II, 604–7.
[2] Mansergh, *Documents*, II, 613.

life,'[1] but this was to be subject to the fulfilment of British obligations to minorities, including the Depressed classes, and of British
commitments to the Indian States. If this was an eleventh-hour
act of repentance, as some in the House of Lords thought it at the
time, to Indian nationalists it could only appear as if the clock had
stopped altogether.

Congress considered, anyway, that the offer was being made for
all the wrong reasons — made because the Japanese Navy was then
in command of the Bay of Bengal, made because the *Raj* was clutch-
ing at straws to maintain any semblance of its former power.
Gandhi tersely described the Cripps offer as a post-dated cheque
on a bank that was obviously failing. The nationalists could not find
in the offer any vital changes in the present structure. It had been
made clear that the defence of India would in any event remain
under British control. At any time defence was a vital matter;
during wartime it was all-important and covered almost every sphere
of life and administration. Therefore to take away defence from the
sphere of responsibility at this stage was to reduce that responsibility 'to a farce and a nullity'.[2] Thus the offer — to the great relief
of the Princes — was rejected on 10 April, and in July Congress put
forward its celebrated 'Quit India' resolution, which, when passed
in August, resulted in the last firm step taken by the *Raj* in India:
the outlawing of the Congress party and the internment of its
leaders including Gandhi and Nehru.

Churchill still took some comfort from the fact that even
after this grave step was taken, three million volunteers came forward to swell the ranks of the British forces. It was indeed a remarkable fact; but these three million did not constitute the 'creative
minority' of that generation in India. In 1914 Britain had committed India to a 'war for freedom', and, for whatever reason, whatever excuse, on whatever principle, the promised freedom had not
materialised. To do exactly the same thing again in 1939 was to
tempt fate too far. Britain might fight for her own freedom, but in
India British freedom wore a different face, and it was one that the
articulate Indian had long since turned from. 'The opinion of Con-
gressmen' — so ran the 'Quit India' resolution —

is that British rule in India must end immediately, not merely because
foreign domination even at its best is an evil in itself and a continuing

---

[1] 5 H 122, 11 March 1942.
[2] Mansergh, *Documents*, II, 619-20.

injury to the subject people, but because India in bondage can play no effective part in defending herself and in affecting the fortunes of the war that is desolating humanity.[1]

This is certainly the language of a people that had learned to say no. Admittedly, it was not hard for the Indian nationalist, once this lesson was learned, to go on repeating it, as he might be confident that the British *Raj* would not shoot him down. Indians would never have made so much of Amritsar had they not at once perceived how much it galled and seared the English liberal conscience. The ruled felt themselves able to retort on their rulers that contempt of which they had so long been the recipients. This was an intoxicating experience.

War strips power naked, and the *Raj* in India felt ashamed of its self-exposure. War makes expediency master, and imperialists who had long laid emphasis on service and mission found it hard to adapt themselves to this reality. Macaulay's principles might remain the only ones worthy of a civilised nation, but unhappily when nations go to war they have to leave a great deal of their civilisation behind them, and cannot afford to live up to principles which they have in the past respected and which in the future they will respect again. India was too full of critics to allow the imperialist to adapt himself in privacy. Egypt, however, where the same process was made necessary by events, allowed him more latitude. Imperialists indeed acted in higher confidence towards this sovereign state than they ventured to show towards the subjects of their own legal dependency. 'Strong pressure was needed', remarks the historian of *Grand Strategy* during the second world war, 'to induce King Farouk in June 1940 to send away the Italian diplomatic staff and to appoint a Prime Minister in whose co-operation the British could feel confidence.'[2] In other words, the assertion of British power in Cairo and on the Suez Canal took place as if there had never been any change since Cromer's day: proved, in fact, that there *had* been no change since Cromer's day, despite thirty years of *blague*. Once again, in the twentieth century's second war as in its first, Egypt was made an armed camp by foreign soldiers, once again were Egyptian Ministries made and unmade by the British Agent — disguised though he might now be under the title of Ambassador.

[1] 14 July 1942; Mansergh, *Documents*, II, 633.
[2] J. R. M. Butler, *Grand Strategy*, II, (London, HMSO, 1956), 301.

It had also been in a time of war, in 1799, that Pitt's principal lieutenant, Dundas, had written that 'the possession of Egypt by any independent Power would be a fatal circumstance to the interests of this country.' Nothing had happened in the subsequent 140 years to alter this opinion.

Cromer left behind him in Egypt a machine of government: and to English Liberals, a legacy of a curious kind. How best in future was this machine to be lubricated? And with what lubricant? Cromer himself considered that his major achievements during his 24-year sway were four in number. He had ensured that the state of tension with France had never got out of hand, so that an amicable arrangement about the role of Egypt in Anglo-French relations was possible of achievement in 1904. He had averted bankruptcy and put the finances of the country on a sound footing. The Sudan, which had been abandoned after 1885, had been successfully recovered, and set up in 1899 as an Anglo-Egyptian 'hybrid state of a nature eminently calculated to shock the susceptibilities of foreign jurists',[1] where British officials could be given a free hand to put the house in order. His fourth success, Cromer considered, was that, by relieving taxation in Egypt and by putting in train other reforms which remedied any really substantial grievances, he had cut away the ground from under the feet of the demagogues whom it was easy to see would spring into existence as education advanced. But here he was mistaken: perhaps because demagogues do not need solid ground to stand on, anyway, and do not miss it if it is removed.

It was not until 1904 that extensive funds for Egyptian education had been made available, but already in 1907 Sir Eldon Gorst, Cromer's successor, was noting in his annual report how it was that the pupils in the schools constituted the chief prop of the nationalists. His only comment on this was that it was a somewhat frail reed for a political movement to lean upon. This was not a very profound judgment, as children, in Egypt as elsewhere, grow up. Sir Edward Grey, whose opinion it was that we could not abandon Egypt without disgrace to ourselves,[2] in the House of Commons spoke approvingly of the training in the arts of government we were giving, and made particular mention of the talents and enthusiasm of the Egyptian Minister of Education, one Saad Zaghlul. In

[1] Cromer, *Political and Literary Essays*, II, 220.
[2] 5 H 17, 13 June 1910, 1153.

Egypt Ministers were, of course, men who were bound not to give advice but to take it. That this was a paradox did not occur (or not often) to civilian politicians in England, but the British soldiers whose imperial business took them to and fro in Egypt had no doubts in what light this paradox was viewed by the educated classes there.

Egyptian nationalism was in fact older than the British occupation. Originally it had emerged as a radical social movement directed against Khedivial misrule, and when the British propped up Khedivial government between 1882 and 1914, they took on themselves the onus of this hostility. When in 1914 they replaced Khedivial rule entirely, they met its full impact. Till then the situation remained as Dilke had described it: no one of weight in Egypt wanted us there, save our own officials. He had remarked that we could not allow a National Assembly to meet, for we knew what it would say.[1] When, in 1913, we did allow it to meet, it said exactly that, and we closed it up again the following year.

Some thinking about the future had always been done by British officials in Egypt, but in the nature of the case, since Egypt was not British in the first place, and had never been admitted into the ranks of the conquered colonies of the British Empire, it was hard to do any concrete planning. The outbreak of the European war, and the taking over of Egypt by the British military machine, made planning of any kind impossible, for if Egypt was not a conquered colony, what else in the name of commonsense was she? Cromer's 'Egyptians', an idealistic body of men, were replaced by soldiers who saw Egypt as just another military garrison, if more comfortable than most, where ideals were not spoken of.

Cromer's own massive commonsense had at least placed the ideals in perspective. 'The Englishman as imperialist,' he wrote in 1912,

is always striving to attain two ideals which are apt to be mutually destructive — the ideal of good government, which connotes the continuance of his supremacy, and the ideal of self-government, which connotes the whole or partial abdication of his supreme position.[2]

It was his own opinion that Egypt must eventually either become autonomous, or else incorporated within the British Empire. He

[1] 4 H 11, 1 May 1893, 1646.
[2] Cromer, *Ancient and Modern Imperialisms*, (London, 1912), p. 118.

favoured the first solution, although he stressed always that the period when it might be attained lay far away in the distance. But, thinking along such lines, he never attempted to awaken among Egyptians any feeling of loyalty towards the British Empire. Loyalty to good conduct, to high standards, to the moral code of the upright English official — all these things might, with devotion, be inculcated: but loyalty to a foreign abstraction like the British Empire was too much to look for. A realist himself, Cromer assumed always (and sometimes incorrectly) that the men he had to deal with were cut from his own cloth. The bulk of imperialists shared Cromer's opinions, but not his *rationale*.

Nevertheless, although British power in Egypt could not expect to be popular, it could not on that account alone, he was assured, lay down its responsibilities. It was the greatest of illusions to think that England could shake herself free of the 'Egyptian Question' merely by withdrawing the British garrison. While England was a Great Power, she must maintain herself in the Middle East. In Palmerston's time she had been able to do this by her influence merely: but since then the days of imperialist competition had come, and she must now do it by her actual presence. Politicians might speak of withdrawal as their aim, but it was never their policy, because they could not afford to adopt any such policy. Both Gladstone and Salisbury for different reasons had bemoaned the tie to Egypt: Gladstone because we had better moral grounds for leaving than for remaining, Salisbury because the Egyptian commitment obstructed all his diplomacy. He likened the irregular position of England in Egypt to the difficulty 'a man has in getting credit from the neighbouring tradesmen when he is only staying at an hotel'.[1] He sought in 1887 to arrange a Convention with the Turks that pledged the withdrawal of British forces within three years — but they would not withdraw 'if there was any appearance of danger in the interior or from without'. Of this danger England was to be the sole judge, and her right of re-entry, if she saw such danger pressing, was to be safeguarded. Drawn in these terms, this convention was not one that could expect to meet the approval either of France or of Russia, and it was a dead letter. A Convention made in the following year, that the Powers did approve, was to suffer much the same fate. Wolseley's expedition of 1882 had used the Suez Canal as a base for its military operations.

[1] Quoted in H. S. Edwards, *Sir William White*, (London, 1902), p. 229.

It was this action that had attracted the attention of the Powers —
for suppose Wolseley's operations had dragged on indefinitely?
They tried in 1885 to agree to internationalise the Canal, but could
not agree how this was to be done; and so in 1888 they decided instead to neutralise it. But the British Government however stated
that it reserved its own rights, and did not ratify this 1888 Convention until the French withdrew their Egyptian pretensions in
1904. But Convention or no, in 1914–18, in 1940–45, the Suez
Canal was once again an exclusively British and Allied line of communication.

Since Egypt was such an essential to the British imperial system,
why not annex it when its Turkish suzerain became an enemy of
the Empire? This logical imperialist argument was overruled by a
Government that had always hesitated to call imperial policy by its
right name, and, as already noted, the Protectorate was established.
This in no way improved relations. Since a Protectorate is the result of a bilateral agreement between protector and *protégé*, it was
certainly playing with words to call Egypt a Protectorate when in
fact it was operated under martial law by a Power that had carried
out no negotiation of any kind with any Egyptian leader, and who
laid it down that the foreign relations of the Egyptian Government
must henceforth be conducted through His Britannic Majesty's
representative at Cairo. Moreover, that a protector should set about
instituting a scheme of compulsory labour for the *fellaheen* was
thought, and not by Egyptians alone, to be an odd comment on the
benefits of protection.

In 1917 Gilbert Clayton, chief of the Arab Bureau in Cairo,
drew up a paper on the future political status of Egypt. He advised
annexation. As it was quite clear that control of Egypt was essential to us, we had better get that control of it in a firm and unmistakeable manner when victory was attained. But his superiors considered that the pro and con of the Egyptian problem might wait its
time. This was a parish matter which was far surpassed in its importance by other Foreign Office business. Thus, when the war closed,
and the English officials in Egypt took from the file the various
schemes for some better establishment of a more representative
type of government, they found that what Zaghlul and his friends
wanted was not representative but responsible government. Zaghlul indeed might give his assurance that special facilities would be
'conceded' to Great Britain in regard to the Suez Canal — but who

was Zaghlul, and what right had he to assume he was in a position to concede anything, or to deal with British statesmen as with equals?

In the democratic world of 1919 it was however necessary to explain oneself. Making explanations about the position in Egypt proved a task of considerable difficulty. The British might still claim that their position in Egypt was a temporary one, but as after forty years it was plain that they did not believe this for a moment themselves, they could not expect to convince foreign critics. They could not claim, either, now the Germans and the Turks had been laid low, that Egypt was menaced by an enemy from without. Nor was it easy to argue that the chaotic type of administration which had operated in the 1860's and 1870's would in fact be restored if the restraining British hand were withdrawn from the governmental machine. It was one thing to say, as the imperialists stoutly said, that we were in Egypt because we chose to be, because we had to be, because it was military necessity that retained our forces in position on this highroad to the East. That was true. But it was quite another to say that we were in Egypt by the consent of the governed, that all that we had done for Egypt had built up a store of affection and goodwill in the hearts of Egyptians which we could safely draw upon and live upon the rest of our imperial days. That was not true at all. Since it was the doctrine of consent and self-determination which now made the greatest noise in the market-place, the Egyptians were not to be told by distant politicians in Whitehall that the British were in Egypt with the consent of the inhabitants. They stated at once loudly and clearly that nothing of the sort was true. On the other hand, the British Government was not imperialist enough to take advantage of the sensible suggestion made to it by Allenby, their scourge in the Middle East, that it should insert into the treaty of peace due to be made with the Turks a clause by which the Sultan transferred to Britain his sovereignty over Egypt. The British Government insisted only that the Sultan should renounce his rights over Egypt, but made no suggestion what should then be the fate of those rights.

Egyptians had, on the whole, recognised the Protectorate cast over them by the British as a necessary evil in wartime, but they had confidently expected that when the war was over so also would be the Protectorate. Egypt in her own eyes was still a sovereign state, the state Mehemet Ali had founded and maintained — fallen perhaps on evil days, but still with a place in the comity of nations.

R

As these nations now gathered in Paris to clear up the wreckage caused by the war, it seemed natural to Egyptian nationalists that they too should be there. Now therefore was born that delegation (*Wafd*), which was to put the Egyptian case before the Powers at the Peace Conference. If Armenians, Albanians, every type of Ruritanian, and even people like the uncivilised desert Arabs of the Hejaz (for whom Egyptians had a hearty contempt), could do so, was there any valid reason why Egyptians could not?

Indeed there was — the same reason why the Irish Question was missing from the European agenda. Zaghlul and his delegation were not permitted to go to Paris, although Wingate, High Commissioner in Egypt, urged the Foreign Office to receive the delegation in London. 'We should indeed have been quite ready,' was Curzon's comment,

> to have heard Zaghlul Pasha and his friends, if they had not opened the proceedings by demanding our complete retirement from the country. This was not a basis for reasonable discussion.[1]

He refused also to grant time to Rushdi Pasha, the Egyptian Premier. As a result the Egyptian Cabinet resigned on 1 March 1919, giving Cairo over to Zaghlul, riot, and confusion.

It is hardly likely, had the *Wafd* been allowed to go to Paris, that any serious damage to British power in the Levant would have resulted. The victorious Empires of France and Japan had their own preoccupations, among which the rights of small 'nations' did not play any great part. The would-be imperialist Powers, Italy and Greece, had to rely on British support if they wanted to see any of their dreams come true. Self-determination might win for itself a large area of application in Europe, but it was not for export, as none of the Powers who had the chance to export it had any intention of doing so. Britain had indeed loosed her physical hold on Afghanistan, after an Afghan revolt, which the British promptly crushed: but the Afghans, now as ever, had a card in their hand denied to Egyptians and others within the British Empire — the presence of an alternative protector, Russia, on their frontiers. Nevertheless, by not allowing the delegation from Egypt to go to Paris at all, Britain presented the nationalists with a grievance more potent in its ultimate effect than Amritsar on the Indians. Egyptian nationalists thereafter kept *Wafd* as their party-label, and

[1] 5 H of L 34, 15 May 1919, 677.

with good reason. The British miscalculation was soon exposed. Allenby was sent to replace Wingate in Cairo in April 1919, and released Zaghlul. The Pasha then did proceed to Paris, but he cut no ice there at all, and had to suffer President Wilson's acknowledgement of the existence and the rights of the British Protectorate in Egypt.

In the meantime it was still British martial law that ruled Egypt, a state of affairs that no screen of Egyptian Ministers could mask. The Cabinet therefore sent out a Commission of Inquiry, with Milner at its head,

> to enquire into the causes of the late disorder in Egypt and the existing situation in the country, and the form of Constitution which, *under the Protectorate*, will be best calculated to promote its peace and prosperity, the progressive development of self-governing institutions and the protection of foreign interests.

Seven valuable months were however allowed to pass before the Commission arrived in Cairo, by which time the opposition to it was solidly organised. No one, Milner remarked, was prepared to be perfectly frank with him; but, despite this, he was still convinced that between the honest pro-Egyptian nationalist and an honest British imperial statesman some good and permanent alliance, profitable to both, could be made. It seemed a faint hope. The nationalists rejected a Mission that had come, on its own showing, not to get rid of but to perfect the Protectorate. Milner saw the point himself. He continued parleys with Zaghlul in London in the spring of 1920, and in August announced that he would advise the British Government to abandon the Protectorate, to remove British troops from Cairo, and to make a settlement whereby the independence of Egypt would be recognised — Egypt, of her own will, conferring upon Britain 'such rights as are necessary to safeguard her special interests'. Many Ministers and large numbers of the public regarded Egypt as an integral part of the British Empire and were astounded that Milner, whose imperialism was unimpeachable, should have proposed what they regarded as a surrender and abandonment of British territory. (But Milner, an old 'Egyptian official', had never for a moment thought of Egypt in those terms.)[1] Curzon and the Foreign Office in particular objected to being the recipients of such proconsular treatment, and nothing came of this. The

[1] *RT*, December 1936, No. 105, p. 110.

nationalists, who had always considered Milner as a plenipoten-
tiary — for was he not a famous imperialist? — were even further
embittered.

Thus at the close of 1921, three years after the end of the war,
martial law still governed Egypt, and it was found necessary to
deport Zaghlul to the Seychelles. But Allenby shared Milner's
view that the existence of the Protectorate was the great stumbling-
block. It reduced the Egyptians' stature and status in their own
eyes, and for whose benefit? Allenby saw the facts of power
straight.[1] Did it matter what stature or status Egyptians were permitted to pretend to, after all? Could we not give them shadows,
retaining the substance? After all, our most effective guarantees of
the security of Egypt as an imperial link were our military and naval
strength. Threatening resignation, he forced his view on Curzon
and the Cabinet, and on 28 February 1922 the Foreign Office issued a celebrated memorandum declaring that Britain was willing
to recognise the independence of Egypt and to put an end to the
Protectorate. Pending a final treaty between the two Powers certain
points were to be 'absolutely reserved to the discretion of His
Majesty's Government'. These were, clearly, the external relations
of Egypt and the defences of the country: the position of foreign
interests and minorities: and the affairs of the Sudan. A Note to the
Powers in March established a Monroe Doctrine in regard to
Egypt. Egypt, now as ever, under this new dispensation, remained
Britain's particular business.

Milner in his Report had said he wanted to establish the independence of Egypt and to secure the essential interests of Great
Britain. Since the essential interests of Great Britain excluded the
independence of Egypt, it seemed a task liable to tax the ablest.
Egypt, with a new sovereignty, new internal autonomy, and Zaghlul as its first Prime Minister under a new Constitution modelled on
that of Belgium, was given concessions: but they remained concessions, and what can be conceded can always be taken away.
Lloyd George laid it down that Egypt was a corridor country between east and west, and, since the British Empire was the most
concerned with a corridor of that kind, it had devolved upon us to
take charge of it.[2] Austen Chamberlain declared that Anglo-
Egyptian relations were not a matter of choice at all, and Ramsay

[1] A. P. Wavell, *Allenby in Egypt*, (London, 1943), pp. 70 ff.
[2] 5 H 217, 10 May 1928, 471.

MacDonald, becoming Premier in Britain at the same time as Zaghlul in Cairo, underlined the wisdom of this sentiment by agreeing at once with Allenby about 'our irreducible requirements regarding the Sudan and the Suez Canal'.[1] The *Wafd*'s outright claims went underground while its leaders tasted some degree of power. but it never consented to any doctrine that declared that Egypt had no choice at all what role she should play in the world. Independence had a certain meaning in the dictionary — but it was not the meaning it had in Cairo.

The 1922 agreement had its critics at home. Grey, now become the Liberals' senior statesman, deplored it — but he saw why it was done. It was done, he felt, because the Government of the day had come to the conclusion — a little belatedly, it seemed to him — that the work Cromer had done in Egypt did in fact rest upon force, and it became more and more evident after the war that this sort of position could be continued only by the use of force to an extent that was not to be contemplated. This was one position, certainly, though it was odd to find Grey taking a stand on it. Allenby adopted the middle position, that the use of force was not in fact necessary, and therefore need not be contemplated — if he had thought it necessary, he would certainly have used it.

Lord Lloyd, for the imperialists, took up a third stance on the Right. He argued that the main problem in Egypt had always been more one of administration than of politics, and that a self-governing Egypt, friendly to Britain, would have protected British interests because it was, after all, in Egypt's own interest to do so. (This was an argument of which a great deal more was to be heard in another post-war period twenty-five years later.) But to Lloyd the 1922 agreement was neither fish nor fowl. While it did not make Egypt self-governing, it also threw over our responsibility for the welfare of the Egyptians, and thus after forty years of imperial rule discarded all justification for that rule. Why should we so heartily congratulate ourselves on getting rid of what was now, it appeared, to be labelled Cromerism? In so doing we were ridding ourselves of a responsibility we had no right to relinquish. We were responsible not to the intelligentsia of Egypt, but to the unfortunate peasantry. What were we putting in the place of Cromerism? Independence with safeguards! — hardly a ringing avowal of a great cause. 'Independence with safeguards,' Lloyd urged,

[1] 7 October 1924, Cmd. 2269 (1924).

is to my mind a policy which fully justifies the criticism that all the enemies of our imperial history heap upon us. It appears as an attempt to shirk the responsibilities of Empire, and at the same time to take the profits.[1]

We had thrown over principle in order to rely upon expediency. In future we should have to fight a rearguard action to maintain our precious safeguards, and in that action we should be driven from one expediency to another. Constitutional safeguards could anyway never be safe. If they were enforced by the Imperial Government, constant friction was likely to make the constitution unworkable. If they were relaxed (as they were later in Ceylon) the representative body assumed powers (as in British Guiana in 1953) that its sponsors never contemplated. Probably it was the Hilton Young Commission on East Africa (1927) that set out the issue most squarely. Once an unofficial majority was permitted, Government was likely to pass from the representative to the responsible stage much faster than the imperial authority thought desirable.

But although Lloyd saw his particular Egyptian problem emotionally, he saw it clearly enough. Yet his argument seemed oversubtle to many at home, and to the Egyptian nationalists themselves, who had never perceived the principle of Cromerism, as Cromer had never gone out of his way to explain it to them. They assumed that imperialism was all power-politics, and would have made nothing of Lloyd's indignation at a settlement which seemed to give Great Britain all the really important victories. But Lloyd was quite right about the uneasy stance on which British policy had now to make shift. New constitution or no, Allenby presented an ultimatum to the Egyptian Government in 1924, holding it responsible for the assassination of Sir Lee Stack, the British commander-in-chief of the Egyptian Army. To Allenby, Egypt was always a military and not a political problem. In contrast the Foreign Office, whether presided over by a Conservative or a Labour statesman, was driven to tortuous courses to explain itself. When in 1924 Zaghlul asked MacDonald to remove British troops and British advisers, to annul British control over Egypt's external relations and the British claim to protect foreigners and minorities, and to abandon the British 'claim to share in any way in protecting the Suez Canal', he got an answer singularly free of Radical bias.

[1] Lloyd, *Egypt since Cromer*, I, 358 ff.

MacDonald found himself assuring Zaghlul that the presence of
British forces in Egypt, under treaty 'freely entered into by both
parties on an equal footing' would be in no way incompatible with
Egyptian independence.

A young Tory making his maiden speech, Alfred Duff Cooper,
accurately pointed out the nature of the problem, but left the solution unstated, as well he might. We were never going to get the
Egyptians to consent to a British government of Egypt. On the
other hand, we could not govern, in these modern days, by ulti-
matums and machine-guns.[1] It was a Conservative Government
that called for Allenby's resignation; a Labour Government that
called for that of his successor, Lord Lloyd himself — but this
issue remained, to trouble and confuse. It was all very well for
Arthur Henderson to state, as Labour Foreign Secretary, that any
interference in the internal administration of Egypt was utterly
incompatible with our recognition of Egypt in 1922 as an independent sovereign state. Incompatible though it might be, the plain
truth was that Egypt was not an independent sovereign state. Yet
no British Government could say this out loud, lest it be accused of
Macchiavellian imperialism of the worst kind in the arranging of
the 1922 Treaty itself. That independence in fact *had* no
safeguards was not a fact that anyone in power in England could
look straight in the eye.

The policy of force, Henderson said, was hardly worth a
moment's discussion. Nevertheless it was just this policy — the
policy not of using force, but of having it there to use, as it was
used in 1924 to expel the Egyptians from the 'Anglo-Egyptian'
Sudan — that occupied so many moments of the discussions and
negotiations with Egyptian leaders that trailed on during the 1920's.
The British proposal of 1927, that there should be a formal Anglo-
Egyptian alliance, but that British troops should remain in Cairo
and Alexandria for the next ten years, was at once denounced by
the *Wafd*, whose leader Nahas replaced the Egyptian Premier,
Sarwat, who had been negotiating with Austen Chamberlain along
those lines. In 1929 Henderson proposed to withdraw the troops
from these two cities, and to concentrate them in a 'zone' around
the Canal. This plan was greeted with great hostility by Lloyd
and Churchill — if troops left Cairo it would be noted by history
'like the recall of the legions' — while Eden was of the opinion

[1] 5 H 179, 15 December 1924, 706.

that it would take twenty years to make such a zone habitable. But even then the negotiations with Nahas broke down on the issue of the Sudan, round which a *cordon sanitaire* against the influence of all Egyptians — in an 'Anglo-Egyptian' Sudan — had been thrown since Stack's murder. We were trustees, Government and Opposition agreed, in the Sudan, and such a responsibility could not be given up to Egyptians.

It was found possible in 1936 to make a treaty of alliance after all, for by that time Mussolini's Roman Empire had set up its outworks in Libya and in Abyssinia, and rather than suffer from the machinations of a new imperialist the Egyptians made terms with the devil they knew. Article 8 of the Treaty arranged between Eden and Nahas provided that, whilst the Suez Canal was an integral part of Egypt, it was recognised by the two contracting parties not only as a universal means of communication, but also as an essential means of communication between the different parts of the British Empire. Eden stressed that even when in twenty years' time (1956) this treaty came up for review, any revision then made must still provide for the continuance of the alliance — whether such revision was made by the League of Nations, by arbitration, or by the two parties themselves. Thus, he declared, 'the Canal will be adequately protected by the Alliance for all time.'

The conclusion of this Treaty was an act warmly supported by the Labour Opposition, whose spokesman Hugh Dalton pointed out that this was substantially Henderson's draft treaty of 1929, which the Tories had then violently opposed. This new unanimity was to be welcomed. Was it possible that in our relations with Egypt we had arrived at mutual respect and moral equality, so that no further remarks like that of Austen Chamberlain in 1929 — 'it is really ridiculous to say that the foreign policy of the British Government and the British Empire is to be governed by the interests and the circumstances of the kingdom of Egypt' — would ever be heard again? At least something had been gained in that Eden had accepted the idea of a Canal Zone as the main base for British troops hereafter. This was, indeed, a notable concession, and it was unfortunate that as the international tension mounted Middle East strategists did not think it advisable to move the troops into their new home, and they were in fact still in Cairo when war broke out in 1939.

The war that broke out in 1939 was another war for freedom, for the overthrow of military tyranny and alien domination. These terms of reference applied to conditions in Europe. In Indian and Egyptian translation they could not but look a little strange, particularly as this war was the second that had been started for these same ends within twenty-five years: the senior generation of nationalists remembered the days and hopes of their youth vividly still. Imperialism it seemed was destined not to march forward but to go round in circles. In the war of 1914–18 it had been possible for the imperialist to seize hold of strategy and design his own world with its aid. In the war of 1939–45 the same task, still as essential to him, fell to him again — but this time he was aware that the world was not his to make, and that it was necessary to take some thought for the morrow even while, by means of the superior force he still commanded, he was bending recalcitrant inhabitants of areas strategically vital to the British Empire to his imperial will.

In India he found it necessary to outlaw the opposition, the Congress party; but he knew well enough that there was no Sherwood Forest to which it could be for ever banished. In Cairo in 1942, to keep the king 'loyal', he found it necessary, through the agency of his Ambassador accredited to that king, to surround the royal palace with a posse of armoured cars, in order to browbeat this independent ruler of an independent country into a proper state of dependence on British policy and strategy. Egypt under the 1936 Treaty was an ally of the British Empire, and must act as one, and quickly. It was the duty of the Empire to protect Egypt from her enemies, the Germans and the Italians. Whose enemies, precisely? Egyptians knew little of Germany and Italy save the pleasant fictions that were relayed to them over the Axis Radio in the Middle East, but they knew a great deal about the British Empire, and preferred to keep their powder dry. Loyalty was anyway not something that could be got by force: a nationalist viewpoint with which Cromer himself would have heartily concurred. The British Empire was fighting less for freedom and democracy than for its existence: it was fighting in fact for a *status quo* which subject-races had no interest whatever in seeing restored.

In the calmer days of 1950, Nehru, become Prime Minister of the sovereign independent Republic of India, was to reflect on the nature of nationalism. In the case of a country under foreign domination, of course definition presented no difficulty. 'It is anti-foreign power.' England's necessity had once been Ireland's opportunity, and the Irish story had always been required reading for Indian and Egyptian nationalists. But Nehru, by now in charge of a series of domestic issues which nationalists had never had to face, was aware that nationalism itself contained many elements that were, in fact, negative. Was nationalism in a free community a blessing, or a curse? When did patriotism in fact become the last refuge of the scoundrel? There were rational, not emotional, problems, fit to be worked out, or at least examined, in the calm of the study. Yet, in the British imperial structure itself, elsewhere than among what might be described as the professional subject-races, he might have found material which would have helped him to a conclusion.

For the nationalism that had grown, and on the whole grown unobtrusively, in Canada, was the nationalism developed by a free community, nationalism of a positive kind not devoted to hatred and contempt. This kind of nationalism too had made its distinctive impact on the imperial idea. It too had restored its strength during times of war. Canada, a country conquered by the British in the eighteenth century, indeed held its subject-race, the French-Canadians. It was they who from their own centre were to spread the idea of Canadian nationalism as one fit for the allegiance of all who thereafter made Canada their home, whether they were of British or of other European stocks. French-Canadians were always doggedly *Canadien* in their outlook and sentiment, because, stranded in life, time, and geography as they were, there was nothing else, save American republicans or British imperialists, which they might be. These of course were not alternatives at all, they were simply two forms of spiritual death. The French-Canadians were not absorbed in an English tide, as Durham when in 1839 he recommended the political union of English Ontario with French Quebec supposed they would be, because they set their minds and hearts against any such occurrence. The 60,000 French who had surrendered to the forces of General Wolfe in 1759 were some 4 million in number two hundred years later — a population which, never augmented by immigration from France, had indeed been lessened by a considerable amount of French-Canadian migration to the New England States. Partnership was wished on the English by the French, by force of this circumstance.[1]

[1] But by 1966 the French-Canadians were exploiting the fact that political partnership had not brought with it equality of social and economic opportunity.

Mackenzie King was to comment, in March 1939, that a strong and dominant national feeling was not a luxury in Canada. It was a necessity, for without it the country could not exist. The fact of Canada denied the facts of North American geography, denied the fact of what many in the nineteenth century held to be the manifest destiny of the growing United States: to become territorial sovereign of the whole continent. It was the link with the British Empire that prevented this from happening: and both the British in Canada and the French-Canadians saw this clearly. It was therefore in Canada's own interest to remain a member of the British Empire, because it was the power of that Empire alone which saved her from absorption by her powerful southern neighbour. Thus she fought, and gave the lie to, all the Cobdenist opinions that she intended to separate and go her own way as soon as she had attained self-government, as soon as she had federated together her diverse parts. She could not afford to do anything of the sort, and no sensible Canadian ever proposed that she should.

But, as Cobden had to be fought, so too did Joseph Chamberlain, with his ideas of imperial unity. For what was imperial unity but another type of absorption? British imperialists with all their grand ideas too often seemed to the self-governing colonies to be only British nationalists, always talking about the Empire's interest and the Empire's policy when all they meant was the interest and policy of Great Britain. Sir Wilfrid Laurier took care to insist at the Imperial Conference of 1897, amid a lot of London clamour about Imperial Federation, that colonies were bound to become nations, and he saw to it that although 7,300 Canadian volunteers were allowed to go to fight for the British cause in South Africa two years later, they did not constitute an official Canadian contingent, as Chamberlain had hoped. Nevertheless Laurier's rather chilly attitude won a further success for his country, as the Canadians fought in South Africa as a unit, in contrast to the treatment given to the Australian volunteers, who were attached to British regiments. Chamberlain and his supporters made a great point of this loyalty of the Empire in the South African case, and the British public did not learn of the considerable degree of heart-searching in the Empire that actually went on — nor did it find out, for example, that in several Australian parliaments the issue whether or not to contribute anything or anyone had been closely contested and in one case was carried only by the speaker's vote. French Canada was solidly hostile to the Boer War, not merely because they thought it a piece of piracy, but because they dreaded, as Laurier expressed it himself, seeing Canada 'sucked into that vortex of militarism which is the curse and blight of Europe'.

In Whitehall it was not thought that the existence of an interpreter of Canadian opinion was either necessary or proper. The remark of Sir John A. Macdonald, the redoubtable Canadian Conservative leader, that he was born a British subject and intended to die one, had been construed not as a piece of electioneering eloquence, which it largely was, but as the solid and lasting sentiment of public opinion in the great British dominion across the sea. Minto as Governor-General endeavoured as best he could to point out to Chamberlain that this was not an accurate impression, and that although Canadian loyalty to and affection for Britain was a very real thing, it was not something that must always be taken for granted, as bound to operate whatever the circumstances might be. On the issue of Canadian contribution to the Boer War, Minto himself argued that from the point of view of a Canadian statesman he did not see why Canada should commit herself to the expenditure of lives and money for a quarrel not threatening imperial safety — a quarrel which was moreover being conducted directly contrary to the opinion of another self-governing colony, the Cape of Good Hope. Later, Minto cautioned the Colonial Office against leaping to further conclusions: although a recent speech of Laurier's had been very eloquent, his 'call-us-to-your-councils' phrase appeared to have been accepted in England as indicating a *wish* to be called — the very last thing that Sir Wilfrid would want, and the speech itself did not justify that interpretation of it.[1] But neither Chamberlain then nor imperialists later paid attention to this: to Sir Edward Grigg, writing his *British Commonwealth* forty years later, Laurier's famous phrase was still a notable landmark in the history of the great cause of imperial unity.

Largely due to the Canadian attitude, the 1902 Colonial Conference did little of importance, blighting the high hopes Chamberlain had set on it. No one came to the rescue of the weary Titan. Instead, a resolution affirmed the impracticability of Free Trade within the Empire, and a scheme drawn up by the Admiralty and the War Office, which envisaged the setting apart for general imperial service a special colonial force that would for all practical

[1] Mason Wade, *The French Canadians* (London, 1955), p. 484.

purposes be under the absolute control of the Imperial (or, British) Government, was simply construed as an attack on responsible government, and had to be shelved.

French-Canadians who did not have Laurier's responsibility of walking the tight rope between the two races at home, were able, and very willing, to speak out more roundly about the trend of affairs. Henri Bourassa thought the presence in Canada, as 'Canadian' commanders-in-chief, of British officers like Hutton and Dundonald — 'South African' heroes — a menace, as they were all strongly imbued with the ideas of attaining better military efficiency as a first step towards the organised Empire, and used their control of the Canadian militia to insert themselves into local politics. He pointed out frequently that under an imperial tariff union Canada would lose the right to make her own commercial treaties. He declared himself 'a Liberal of the English school, a disciple of Burke, Fox, and Gladstone' just at a time when in England itself it was hard to find, at least in the field of imperial and foreign policies, any such disciples at all. He commented that Chamberlain's doctrines of 'what we have, we hold' required an addendum, 'what we don't have, we take'. British imperialism Bourassa saw resurgent, and he feared its wiles more than its physical power. As dangerous as the idea of military contributions from the colonies was the imperialist plan to have some great imperial council in London, for, as Cobden had long ago pointed out, London dinner-tables had their insidious attractions for the simple-minded. From Canadian experience of the influence that was now exerted from afar by the British authorities over colonial Ministers, Bourassa declared, it might safely be inferred that for the British Government to keep under the yoke men in close touch with them, 'and upon whom the whole weight of their favours and seductions could be brought to bear', would prove no difficult task.

Laurier, though he sympathised with a number of Bourassa's views, found it politic not to express them in that tone of voice. The nature of the dilemma facing any Canadian Premier was well exemplified in the struggle that attended the passage in 1910 of Laurier's Naval Service Bill. This constituted a Canadian naval force of five cruisers and six destroyers, which was to be under the command of the Canadian Government, but in wartime might be placed under imperial control by order-in-council, subject to the approval of the Canadian Parliament. Laurier made no bones about the main issue involved. 'If Great Britain, to which we are subject, is at war with any nation, Canada is exposed to invasion: hence Canada is at war.' (This was another Laurierism which later suffered considerable misquotation: it was frequently bowdlerised as 'When Great Britain is at war, Canada is at war', which struck a note of emotional enthusiasm for the imperial policies of the mother country which was in fact distinctly absent.) It was just this plain fact that was such gall to men like Bourassa: that Canada, while legislatively independent, was in fact still politically the dependency she had always been. He charged furiously that Laurier's Bill was the most complete backward step Canada had made in half a century. Britain neither could nor would defend Canada against the United States, which was, if facts were going to be faced, her sole possible enemy. Canada was putting her flag at the feet of a Chamberlain or a Balfour, and she would be drawn into all the wars of England — which in the past century had averaged one every four years. Collaboration in imperial defence would lead inevitably through an imperial tariff to an imperial council, and so to the full realisation of Chamberlain's dream.

The leader of the Canadian Conservatives, Robert Borden, had misgivings of another kind about the Bill: he wanted Canada, if she was going to contribute to an imperial navy, to have some say in matters of imperial defence. It was just this that Laurier did not want, and he took his opportunity, at the Imperial Conference the following year, to oppose an Australian motion that the British Government should consult the Dominions before signing treaties that bound the British Empire. For the giving of advice implied that if necessary that advice would be backed with armed strength. Laurier wanted no such commitment to be made, and thus he was assailed by both Canadian imperialists and Canadian nationalists because he appeared to belong in neither of their camps. 'In Quebec,' he remarked ruefully, 'I am branded as a jingo, and in Ontario as a separatist,' and when he fell from power in September 1911, it was indeed hailed in Quebec as a triumph for the nationalists, and in Ontario as a great victory for the cause of the British Empire. Certainly Canadian Conservatives under Borden established a more amicable relationship with the British Liberal Cabinet in London than Laurier's Liberals had done. Winston Churchill promptly offered Borden his assistance in drafting Canadian naval policy, and Borden, although not losing sight of his wish to be consulted as to imperial defence, proposed a grant of $35 million as a contribution to Great Britain for naval purposes. His emotional supporters in the Canadian House of Commons at once rose to sing 'God Save the King' and 'Rule Britannia' — a piece of patriotic ebullience that had had no match in the mother-of-Parliaments in London, even at the highest point of the imperial tide.

But Laurier and the Liberals, standing by their policy of a Canadian navy, opposed this, and a largely Liberal Senate saw to it that Borden's Bill was killed in May 1912. Bourassa and the nationalists rejoiced at the entirely negative outcome: there was to be no Canadian navy, no dreadnoughts for Britain, no money contribution, and no imperial squadron, based on Gibraltar, at the mercy of Winston Churchill's nervous system.

Yet the events of August 1914 brought out a wave of imperial patriotism in both Ontario and Quebec. Bourassa found himself an isolated critic, although he admitted that Canada, 'as an Anglo-French nation', had a vital interest in the maintenance of France and England, and of their prestige, power, and influence. By 1916, however, when it was plain that the war would be a long one — and when it was at least arguable that British strategy was not all that might be hoped for, and that Canadians were often laying down their lives for no very clear objects — considerable hostility between the viewpoints of the two races in Canada had arisen. This hostility Bourassa did not fail to exploit. Simple statistics of recruitment caused as much bad blood as anything else. By February 1916, a quarter of a million Canadians had enlisted. Of these, 62% were British-born, and 30% Canadian-born. Of this last group, 28% were English-speaking. Those of British stock accused the French of unpatriotic behaviour, while the French accused the British of both twisting the figures and keeping all the best commands and appointments in their own hands. Bourassa's voice was now more loudly raised, and had he said what he said in England he would certainly have been interned at the least — a fate that a great many British Canadians would have been glad to mete out to him. Some of his wild words had wings nevertheless. He objected, he declared, to fighting for the British Empire not because it was British but because it was Imperial. All Empires were hateful, for they stood in the way of human liberty and true progress, intellectual and moral. Nations had to choose between British ideals and British domination. For himself, he stood for ideals against domination — though he might be shot for it in the name of British liberty, as a number of Irishmen had recently been in Dublin. Lionel Curtis' book, *The Problem of the Commonwealth*, published that same year, irritated Bourassa immensely, with its bland assumption that the store of British wisdom and experience of rule would need to be freely drawn upon after the war by all the Dominions, in their own interests. Bourassa underlined a problem of Empire that had not caught Curtis' attention, in language in which there was an echo, at least, of what Gladstone had once said about a 'galling presence':

> In spite of his remarkable faculties for government, and the general humanity of his proceedings — when cupidity and the desire of domination do not push him to brutalities — the Anglo-Saxon does not know how to gain the confidence, much less the affection, of the peoples that he dominates, nor even of those with whom he associates. Now, when confidence and love are missing, good understanding is difficult.

Moderate opinion in Canada never approved of Bourassa's Gallic fires, but it found itself taking up, if much more quietly, some of his positions. Hardly a week went by, the *Round Table* pointed out in March 1917, without some public man in Britain expressing 'his deep gratitude for the noble sacrifices which the Dominions have made in coming so loyally to fight for the Old Country in her time of trial'. Such language only irritated Dominion opinion, for in so far as the Dominions conceived themselves to be engaged at all in chivalrous adventure, they were thinking of Belgium, France, and Serbia.[1] Moreover the Canadian Liberals did not view Sir Robert Borden's membership of the Imperial War Cabinet, for example, in quite the same light as Borden himself. Laurier pointed out in the *Manchester Guardian* that this was merely a consultative body, and that he still felt that the Dominions could have no real voice in questions of peace or war. They would do well to keep out of War Cabinets now and Peace Cabinets in the future. *La Presse* of Montreal described Canada's signature of Versailles as a piece of 'pure political bragging'. This was a sentiment which chimed with Canadian public opinion as a whole as the war ended, and Meighen, Borden's successor as Conservative leader, dished the Whigs and scored a triumph for his party when he managed to get the British Government and indeed the whole Empire to under-

[1] *RT*, March 1917, No. 26, p. 220.

write a peculiarly 'Canadian' policy for the Pacific at the Imperial Conference of 1921. Thereafter, Canada retired further from the orbit of British foreign policy than she had ever been, and it was a faithful disciple of Laurier's, Mackenzie King, who presided over the years that saw Canada's autonomous status made statutory and her presence in the councils of Geneva become accepted by the British Government as well as by the European nations themselves.

King took up a consistent, Canadian attitude from the beginning of his Premiership in 1921. In 1924 he refused to submit to his Parliament the Lausanne treaty that Curzon had arranged with Turkey, on the ground that as Canada had had nothing to do with its negotiation she could have nothing to do with its results, and therefore it required no ratification from the Canadian people. In all things the supremacy of the Canadian parliament was vital, and everything must come before it, including issues of peace, war, and neutrality. King could now afford to go much further than Laurier in his public statements. There was now no possible menace from the United States, and in a world that was meant to be safe for democracy, in a world where a system of collective security under the auspices of the League of Nations was supposedly in force, the assertion of national outlook and feeling was quite in keeping with the trend of the times: for no doctrine of self-determination could be supposed to exclude Canada's own right to share its benefits. The existence of the United States, the *Round Table* noted sourly in 1930, served the purpose for Canada that his brother James served for Charles II.[1] King stressed, for more than it was probably worth, 'the unparalleled complexity of our position, as a member of the League, a member of the British Commonwealth, and one of the nations of the American continent,' but his native cautiousness always kept him from such robust pronouncements as were made by his own Governor-General, Tweedsmuir — the erstwhile John Buchan, disciple of Milner — who declared publicly that a Canadian's first duty was not to the British Commonwealth of Nations but to Canada and to Canada's King. This last reference (to King George) could be construed any way his audience pleased, and it perturbed the Prime Minister for that reason.

Politically he was well advised to go so slowly, towards some goal of 'North Americanism' that really defied any very close or accurate

[1] *RT*, December 1930, No. 81, p. 117.

s

description: for, as his own Minister of Defence, Ian Mackenzie, exactly pointed out in March 1938, it was still the fact that the only main deterrent against a major attack on Canada by a European power was the existence of a British fleet in North Atlantic waters. He never openly quarrelled with what he called the imperialistic school — those in Canada who took the view that the British Empire was one and indivisible, and that in matters of defence there should be a common policy, which of necessity meant a common foreign policy for the Empire.[1] But he suggested, steadily, patiently, that the really creative minority in Canada were those who thought on different lines — who were distinctly Canadian in their outlook, believing that it was right to decide questions relating to defence or foreign policy by reference solely to what was in Canada's interests. All decisions must be made by Canada according to that criterion. He thought it therefore 'extremely doubtful', in 1937, that any of the British Dominions would ever send another expeditionary force to Europe.

Not only the activities of a British Government might still mortgage the Canadian future, so too might those of the League of Nations. Here King was again careful to point out that Canada had her free hand even in regard to the behests of the Covenant of the League. After all, since European states had not themselves obeyed that Covenant in disputes that took place outside of the European continent itself — in Manchuria, in the Chaco, in Abyssinia — Canada need not accept obligation in European disputes. Occasions might indeed arise where military action might become advisable, or even essential, but so far as Canada was concerned, that would be for the parliament of Canada to decide in the light of all the circumstances at the time. By 1937 it was plain that the system of collective security had obvious gaps in it, and Canada might find it necessary herself to slip out through one of those gaps. Accordingly the Imperial Conference which met that year, although it was designed to be devoted to the field of imperial policy, was remarkably inconclusive even for an Imperial Conference, and the *Round Table* had some harsh comments to make on the 'verbal generalities' to be found in its 'jejune pages'. ('Self-determination,' it gloomed, 'may end in disaster for the Commonwealth as it has in Europe.')[2]

[1] 25 January 1937; Mansergh, *Documents*, I, 392–3.
[2] *RT*, September 1937, No. 108, pp. 708, 713.

Such Conferences, said the British Prime Minister, Neville Chamberlain, were not summoned to solve any particular problem or to achieve any specific result. If he really believed this he was well satisfied. No attempt, said the official report, was made to formulate commitments, which in any event could not be made effective until approved and confirmed by the respective Dominion Parliaments. The Dominions did however agree that they approved of peace, the League of Nations, and disarmament.

New Zealand's Premier Savage, reporting to his Parliament, threw a little wry light on these proceedings. They had had to be content, he said, with agreeing that our objective should be peace throughout the world. Everyone was bound to agree to that; and the New Zealand delegation, in common with other representatives at the Conference, felt there must *be* a Commonwealth policy, whatever it was like. It was no good just getting a policy for New Zealand or Australia — it was a matter of hammering out a policy to which everyone could subscribe; 'and those who have been present at Imperial Conferences know that there is no royal road.'[1]

There was no royal road principally because the senior Dominion had long ago decided that it was not in its own interests that there should be one. King spoke more strongly out than he had ever done when Great Britain guaranteed the integrity of Poland on 30 March 1939. He stated that he could not accept the view that, regardless of circumstances, Canada should say here and now that she was prepared to support whatever might be proposed by the Government at Westminster. Had British foreign policy deserved such blank confidence? Canada's national interests were here at stake. Canadians must henceforward, to a greater or less extent, choose between keeping their own house in order, or trying to save Europe and Asia. The idea that every twenty years or so Canada should automatically and as a matter of course take part in a war overseas for democracy, or for the self-determination of other small nations,

— that a country which has all it can do to run itself should be called upon to save, periodically, a continent which cannot run itself ... seems to many a nightmare and sheer madness.

In September 1939 King still left the door open in case public opinion preferred to adopt a stance of 'aggressive neutrality', in ac-

[1] 29 September 1937; Mansergh, *Documents*, I, 178.

cordance with the inclinations of the United States, but on 9 September, six days after Great Britain declared war on Germany, the Canadian Parliament made its own decision of a different kind.

But, just as Indian and Egyptian nationalism resented being committed to British imperial war by force of law, Mackenzie King's Canada regretted being committed by force of circumstance. Bourassa's point was still true: in the scale of power Canada was still a dependency, and the Ogdensburg agreement negotiated in August 1940, which was little short of a Canadian-U.S. military alliance, only served further to underline Canada's precarious status in a dangerous and still imperialistic world. For though 'there'll always be an England', as a gloomy politician commented, 'would there always be a Canada?' Canadian nationalists — or, as they now. described themselves, Canadians — must make it their task for the future to ensure that there would be, indeed.

It was with these realities in mind that Canadians set out to fight in the line with and for their British friends. The moral tie still held, but it was not a tie so much to the British Empire as to Canadians' own sense of what was right and fitting. It was a tie that the Nationalists in South Africa did not consider binding at all, and Daniel Malan angrily opposed Smuts' argument that South Africans were interested in what became of Europe. It was an argument, he declared, that ought logically, if Smuts was right, to apply in all wars in which England was involved. If it was so, quite apart from constitutional ties, if it was really the case that moral ties were to draw South Africa into all England's wars —

> then I say, talk of freedom as much as you like, but we are a country of serfs!

It was a tie whose propriety had caused previous questioning in the Australian Labour Party, whose leader Curtin had echoed Mackenzie King when he declared his conviction that Australia was not big enough to act as a police force in Europe, keeping order there. It was a tie flatly ignored by Eire, whose leaders had no reason to doubt that if her security was attacked by a European Power, she would still be able to call on Great Britain to come to her assistance.

Nevertheless, with the Irish exception, the citizens of the Commonwealth rallied in 1939, as twenty-five years previously their fathers, imperial subjects all, had rallied, and came to the aid of the mother country in its struggle to keep the liberal and democratic tradition alive in Europe. But they did this without experiencing the same happy confidence that what they did was completely in their own interest, for it might be (what had not been thought of in 1914) that in fact no effort anyone made in Europe could possibly preserve the liberal and democratic tradition there, and that therefore democrats who had the luck to live at a safe distance might do better to keep their powder dry. To this view, for two vital years, the greatest democratic power in the world, the United States, gave a silent leadership. But in 1939 the authority of Great Britain was still the power-house of any world-wide system, whether it was called by an imperial name or by any other, and the validity of the imperial idea was emotionally still strong enough to keep the majority of men who were of British stock loyal to it throughout the world. Yet the force of the nationalist argument, whether it came from a subject-race impatient of political constraint or from dissident and self-interested opinion within the white self-governing Dominions, was now of such appeal that it could not be written off even by the most convinced imperialist as so much bubble agitation of a merely traitorous kind. It was a new moral issue, and as such represented an attitude of mind which statesmen would have to try accurately to assess.

In such fashion did nationalism fight its various battles, in such ways had it made its salients into the lines surrounding the imperial fortress. Although the faith within the fortress still burned strongly, its believers were none the less convinced that these dangerous salients would not have been driven in so deeply, or on so extended a front, had not the forces of the enemy nationalist faith been succoured from within the imperial lines themselves. 'The great ship', Churchill had exclaimed in 1931, when the Indian nationalists were winning powerful political friends, when the Statute of Westminster was being hailed as a piece of far-sighted statesmanship, 'is sinking in a calm sea'.[1] How, then, could it expect to keep afloat when the waters grew rough? And how were its officers to prevent members of its own crew from opening the remaining sea-cocks?

For, since early in the day, the imperialist had realised, in a mounting dismay, that the last enemy he must encounter was democracy itself.

[1] 5 H 259, 26 January 1931, 702.

VI

THE IMPACT OF DEMOCRACY

DEMOCRACY, like nationalism, has suffered for want of a working definition. Its ideals are not hard to affirm: but their translation into practice demands a political expertise which by its very nature must be looked for among the few and not among the many. A code of conduct, a way of life, an act of faith about the dignity of man and the worth of his soul, democracy needs to be powered with a determination to build institutions that will fulfil that nature and uphold that dignity. But who is best fitted to fire this determination, and what kind of institutions in fact ensure its successful application? Who, moreover, is competent to judge any answers that may be given to these questions? Rousseau's remark, that the British democracy was truly free only once in seven years, and then only for a week or so, might well be turned against him by the governors of a democratic state, who can say the same thing of their own situation. They work as best they may in the half-light of a popular opinion, whose depths and shifts they can never accurately gauge. They are not free to go their own way according to their own judgment. So it comes about, that a man like Milner, declaring a political programme of full speed ahead in everybody's interest, is not able to make his mark or to show his skill in party politics — just because he cannot bring himself to accept the limitations imposed on this decisive course of action by the nature of a democratic system of government.

Since imperialism is nothing if not a decisive policy, Froude and Milner always saw it as a vice in public life that unthinking democracy should be able to curb thoughtful imperialism, a creed designed for the universal benefit. When Ramsay MacDonald and Gilbert Murray insisted — and saw it as a matter for congratulation — that imperialism and democracy were incompatible, Milner was bound to agree with them, given the present circumstances of the case; but he denied that this incompatibility was inevitable and intrinsic, for the same reasons as he objected to those who asserted that imperialism and nationalism were of necessity enemies one to the other. People who made an absolute distinction between imperial and domestic questions were blind to reality. For surely, both true imperialism, and the condition-of-England question which Radicals were always proclaiming to be of the first importance, were at base aspects of one and the same thing? Taken together they set a common problem: how best to rear, house, distribute, co-ordinate, and train for peace and for war the peoples of the Commonwealth.

But the deduction from such an argument, that therefore there must always be a group of experts in charge — the distributors, the co-ordinators, the trainers — was just the one to which democrats took such strong exception. Democracy was, if it was anything, government of the people by the people; but imperialism entailed the government of one people by another. In fact it had at its heart a contradiction which must ultimately wither it away, for John Stuart Mill had declared that it was impossible that one people could govern another, and the entire Radical tradition agreed with him. Radicals indeed reserved their most colourful denunciations for imperialists like Milner, who was always asserting that he was working for genuinely democratic ends: they handled far less harshly cheerful and confident exploiters of Empire like Rhodes, who did not pretend to misunderstand the difference between the bond and the free.

Accordingly, Radicals were for ever proclaiming that if democracy ever got into the saddle in Great Britain, British imperialism must come to its end; for no people — and certainly not the British people, bred to the liberal tradition — would *wish* to hold another people in subjection for a single day. In 1908 Curzon rued the future, just because he felt this was a self-evident truth. Intellectual Socialist leaders, like MacDonald himself, indeed realised that power was a principal factor in the governance of the world's affairs, but they regretted this sincerely, and were assured that when their day dawned they would be able to dispense with it, and build a Concert of Europe anew on the foundations of international socialism, amid the débris of the destroyed system of the balance-of-power. How it was proposed to do this, they never clearly stated — and certainly they never envisaged circumstances wherein they themselves might find it necessary to make use of the balance of power, necessary *not* to destroy it, so that their ideals might have some faint chance at least of being brought within the range of practical politics.

Imperialists never failed to point out and to rub in this element of the impractical in their opponents' case. It was all very well in this imperfect world to say that love, or universal brotherhood, or whatever, would find a way. But what way, and how would it find it? Contempt for the intellectual processes of Socialism thus early entered the minds of men of the governing and employing classes because, in their view, these processes made no contact with everyday, workaday commonsense. If democracy did arrive at political power, that event alone would not bring Utopia into being. The democratic system, a Socialist system, would, like any other, require an institutional form of government. It would be compelled to have an executive, and that executive if it was to have any duration would have to have powers, and be strong enough and confident enough to use them. Attractive doctrines about the brotherhood of man would not cause these simple facts to fly out of the window.

It is fair to say that most of the invective thrown at Socialists, by the class that called itself hard-headed and was in return called hard-faced, was thrown after no very prolonged study of the doctrines that the principal English Socialists were trying to propound. It is also worth remark that many who spent their energies attacking the capitalist system had no clear idea what that system was, although they were convinced they knew all its implications in the social field. In fact a great deal of nonsense was retorted on a great deal of nonsense, so much so that the conflicting views as to the proper role and function of man in society were less often debated than dismissed. The jargon used on both sides grew more brutal, and contempt rebounded on contempt; and while this was going on the cleavage between domestic and imperial affairs, which Milner was so anxious to bridge, grew ever wider.

Lecky, a conservative Irishman, had remarked how the public opinion of a nation was something very different from the votes that could be extracted from all the individuals who composed it. The landlord, the clergyman, the local agitator, the publican, would each direct the votes of a large number of people — secret ballot or no secret ballot — so that in a 'pure' democracy the art of winning and accumulating votes in this fashion would become the main preoccupation of all practical politicians who were determined to make politics their career. Did anyone pretend that such a pre-occupation was thoroughly admirable, and that this was the best way for a nation to go about its business? Was public opinion — or Rousseau's menacing concept of a general will — anyway ascertainable? And, even if ascertainable, was it bound to be worthy of respect? Politicians of course paid it enormous lip service. Lord Randolph Churchill might declare his ringing conviction that the people of England were incapable of going wrong on any great question for any appreciable length of time[1] — and this view was shared and declared by so un-Churchillian a political descendant as Stanley Baldwin — but suppose that, even within a short length of time the people did go wrong, might not some irreparable damage be done? Was it to be a statesman's duty to wait till the people went right again? Or ought he to set to and try to put them right, no matter what became of his own platform of popular support?

These questions, and others like them, were particularly irritating to harassed men in the political arena. Bernard Shaw has described journalism as the art of posing grave problems without having to solve them, and the politician, beset by such artists, found it harder than ever to maintain both his balance and a sense of direction. (The most commonsensible, like Salisbury, never looked at newspapers and avoided the company of the editors of the quarterlies.) Certainly the people's own elected representatives often knew less of public opinion and the sway of the public taste than they found it wise to admit. The Labour Member who, during the emotional 'Suez crisis' of November 1956, was amazed to discover there was such a thing as 'working-class imperialism' was, however, merely confirming the fears that had long ago been expressed by Cobden, Bryce, Morley, and a whole host of lesser Victorian seers.

In 1866 Robert Lowe, who never forgot the buffets he had received during his early political apprenticeship amid Australian democrats, had declared that he had no doubt that the democracy would prove 'a terrible and warlike power'. Thirty years later it was clear to Wilfrid Lawson that Lowe was quite right, as the working man was obviously as keen on spending an increasing amount of money on the military and naval estimates as were Chamberlain and the Unionist Government; and indeed, it was the vociferous popular support for the South African War that gave Lawson's

[1] Churchill, *Lord Randolph Churchill*, II, 155.

Radical conscience a profound shock from which it did not recover. For it was not the educated and the reflective who were influenced by ideas, but the half-educated and the irreflective, of whom it seemed to pessimists there were more than ever about after the extension of the franchise, the broadening of the educational system, and the rise of the empires of the halfpenny and penny Press. A new public had arisen, to sway the fortunes and to mould the principles of the aristocratic and middle-class parties; it was an ironic comment on Lowe's experience that it had been also among Australian democrats that Rosebery, during his antipodean tour of 1883–84, had first imbibed the doctrines of Liberal Imperialism.

There were many, accordingly, who accepted the growth of democracy and the propagation of its public opinions in the same spirit wherein they recognised the lessons of the Darwinian theory or the existence of an Irish Question — the spirit of exasperated distaste. The democracy was always calling for a 'programme' — as later it was to assume its right to grant to its rulers a 'mandate' — but in fact the politicians whose elbows it crowded found it impossible to plan any far-sighted or long-term policy. Particularly in the field of Empire was it impossible to do any planning at all, because the great generality of the public was clearly never going to have the time, nor the inclination, nor — if imperialists were going to be frank — the intelligence to understand what it was that their leaders, in the people's own best interest, were about. Noisy jingoism at one extreme, apathy at the other — these two manifestations of the public attitude towards the Empire were, to the true worker in this field, equally depressing.

When Englishmen, or educated foreign observers, spoke of 'England' in the years before the first World War, they were speaking of an image of England that had been fashioned by the great middle class. This was true, whether the English or the foreign observer was defending or attacking the English social and constitutional polity. When the Radical thinker L. T. Hobhouse commented that democracy was cheapening and vulgarising the national ideas, he was referring to those ideas which the middle class, of which he was a member, had imposed on the rest of the nation, including the aristocracy itself. But it was known that, below this kingdom of the middle class, stretched a huge and unexplored region, areas of which were penetrated less often indeed and certainly to the accompaniment of a lot less publicity than the Congo or the Hindu

Kush. Now and then the inhabitants of this region surfaced where they could be seen. Seen, and deplored. In 1887 a mob ran riot for several hours in the West End of London; in 1900 the celebrations over the relief of Mafeking revealed a state of public witlessness that caused a shiver even in the most patriotic of club members. People in the mass were unpredictable, and would always be so. It was because they believed this strongly that Liberals and Radicals had, since Disraeli's day, resented the reckless inculcation by the imperialists of an unthinking jingoism — the lust of the spectator — in the masses. Emotions excited to serve one cause were easily transferable. Not only was it dangerous to beat on a big drum — any big drum, whether that of patriotism or another — but such activity was, in the full sense, anti-social. It was a dereliction of duty, the duty that was owed by the governors to the governed.

For what else was the British people — in 1908 a population of 36 million, of which only 1½ million earned above £3 a week, and wherein some 30,000 gentlemen owned 96% of the land — but the largest 'native race' of which imperialism had cognisance? The British people deserved to be educated, converted, and protected as much as any tribe in Central Africa. That the true imperialism began at home, was a Radical dictum from the start. It was one of Cobden's own. It was one that was echoed in the mid-1930's by George Lansbury, exclaiming his despair that in London, at the very heart of that great and greatly publicised Empire and Commonwealth, there should be a mass of people decaying mentally and physically because their rulers could not find them a livelihood. It was with similar evidence before him that Attlee was to declare that, if Indians were to be adjudged as incapable of self-government, then *a fortiori* we were also.[1] The same conviction brought him later to speak of the chief task of his first Labour Government as one of clearing up 'the mess of centuries'.

Radicals and imperialists were in fact closer than they allowed themselves to suppose in their views on the nature of the political task. They both propounded programmes of their own: they both had a philosophy of action. They were both always looking for room to manoeuvre, and were both uneasily convinced that they would never be able to accomplish all their best-laid schemes for human betterment if they were constantly being deflected from the

[1] 5 H 298, 5 March 1938, 1802.

course they had set by the necessity to pander to a public opinion whose content, whatever else it was, could never be classified as 'advanced'. It is not surprising, therefore, that Joseph Chamberlain, who was both a Radical and an Imperialist, should have been among the most autocratic statesmen produced in Great Britain in the nineteenth century; certainly far more autocratic than his aristocratic chief, Salisbury, who once pointed out where the weakness of his truculent colleague lay: 'No one,' Salisbury remarked, 'ever loved Joe.' (No one in politics loved Salisbury, either — but then, he did not profess to be a man of the people.) Even by the 1930's, when the leading imperialists were generally held by public opinion to be 'Die-Hard' and reactionary to their bones, it was still among their group that the most far-reaching ideals of social progress, as conceived by Conservatives, were to be found. How to reconcile the need for leadership with the fact of democracy, whether this leadership came from the Left or from the Right, was to emerge as one of the twentieth century's major problems. English political thinkers early noted its existence, and some of them hoped to find the time to trace all its implications, but this time was never easily found.

The emergence of an independent Labour party on the political stage did not, in the general opinion of both Liberals and Conservatives, solve the great issue of predictability. For the earliest Labour leaders were either men not of the working class themselves, or, if from that class, men who were inevitably sharply distinguished from the mass of its members by the very fact of their leadership. Many of them were Scots, and there was a formidable gulf dividing the traditions and the aspirations of the English from those of the Scottish proletariat. Furthermore, many of the leaders were at once pious, teetotal, and of intellectual leanings, whereas the mass of the working class were thought to be far more akin to those middle-class back-benchers in the House of Commons whose general philistinism in such matters was so strongly deplored by the best men on both Front Benches. Certainly there was no room for doubt that English Socialism itself was entirely the invention of middle-class men, people who might have been content to call themselves Radicals had they ever been able to accept the commercial premises on which, by the turn of the century, the house of English Radicalism had become so firmly established. Not, indeed, that they would have been allowed so to call themselves without protest from the old-style Radicals: for Charles Bradlaugh the great extremist declared all his life that Socialism would destroy all intellectual incentive and so cause the decay and degradation of the professions. In their place would arise 'an enormous army of Socialist officials'. Morley said the same thing.

Political Liberals found it hard to turn themselves into social Liberals, because they had been bred to a tradition that believed that political liberty was an all-inclusive liberty, and even when it was pointed out to them that there was in fact no such thing as freedom of contract between a rich Liberal employer and a poor labourer they could not set about revising their political philosophy for such an argument as that. It was therefore from Conservatives, taught by Disraeli how to dish Whigs and steal their clothes, that some of the most forward-looking Radicalism thereafter came. Lord Randolph Churchill might have developed, had he been given the chance, that scheme of political ideas he launched under the name of Tory democracy — although when he launched it, as he once explained to an enquiring Wilfrid Blunt, he had no idea what it meant. It might have turned out to be some kind of paternal society, garnished with bread and circuses, but it would also have moved along the path of social reform which Disraeli, Churchill's model in these matters, had laid down for his followers to take. (Certainly Churchill, once his Burmese days were over, debarred himself from adopting his master's other mantle, imperialism, by beginning a campaign to cut down on military and naval expenditure.) But as it turned out, the aristocracy that Disraeli had hoped to influence, and which in turn he had hoped would influence the tradesmen of England, grew idle, grew richer, and gave up the political ambitions that Disraeli had wished upon them. Thereafter no one from the ranks of the gentlemen of England stood forth to be recognised as an accepted leader of the people until 1940, in the person of Churchill's son.

The genuine goodwill that had been built up in the course of the English past between squire and tenant was gradually dissipated amid the rancours current between landlord and lodger. Arrived on their plateau of success between 1895 and 1900, the Conservatives thereafter found themselves no domestic policies worthy of the name, and poured their best energies into the causes of Empire and Ulster — causes which the people, in the long run, were to turn from as irrelevant. The only domestic policy that did run a course was one that was sixty years old, after all. Even to propagate Protection, the Unionists had to call in the assistance of a quite remarkable number of outsiders, many of whom were actually aliens, but the majority of whom were members of the professional classes, lawyers, journalists, and professors, who took up a cause like a brief and expected to be paid for their trouble. It was to this same class that the burden of imperial administration was left: in so far as aristocrats set foot in the outer reaches of Empire, it was most frequently in the guise of the remittance-man younger son, the kind of man Canadians had in mind when they stuck up on billboards their celebrated cards advertising jobs for which 'no English need apply'. Ulster was to prove the last cause wherein the gentlemen of England displayed a genuine corporate enthusiasm.

Still, in a society so constructed as that of England, the aristocracy was always able to get its interpreters. It was certain that this task of interpretation would become one of greater and greater significance — as the democracy made its progress felt, its voice heard, and its aspirations the louder. Someone — as in that British *Raj* which Macaulay had envisaged — must keep his ear to the ground, and pass on the messages received to headquarters. It was because they doubted the ability of the Socialist leaders to perform this vital task that Conservatives and Liberals paid more attention to Keir Hardie, a definable figure, than he actually deserved. His (fittingly) ostentatious presence in the Commons was a symbol of the wide-minded liberalism of the governing class, just as, in 1884, the calling together of an Indian National Congress by the *Raj* had been the subject for well-deserved self-congratulation. But the presence of these others, who were not working-men and who did not wear the correct uniform, the cloth cap, was a symbol of something else, something unseen and therefore dangerous. What could be made of MacDonald's assertion — that the Labour Party was not the product of national circumstances, but of the stage of civilisation that the world had now reached? Was it to be assumed that, before the advent of the Labour party in its midst, political life in Britain had existed in some state of barbarism? These pretensions were as absurd as they were alarming. It was wrath at the absurdity, defiance of the danger, that caused Winston Churchill in 1922 to make his notorious avowal that 'Labour was not fit to govern': a *gaffe* that had to be delicately explained away by his colleague Austen Chamberlain, that it was not labour that Churchill had had in mind, but Labour — Labour as represented by its regrettable Socialist leaders.[1]

But it was with the arguments of these leaders, who were the only articulate representatives of the unseen people, as Indian nationalists were the only representatives of their millions, that the imperialists were compelled to deal. The same exasperation that prevented them from sifting what was sense from what was nonsense in the Indian nationalist case, as expressed in the years before the first world war, hindered their understanding of the Socialist attitude, and in both spheres it was too readily assumed that all criticism was subversive and all critics unpatriotic and disloyal. (Both Cromer and Milner, in strong contrast to many of those who counted themselves their admirers and disciples, gave assiduous study to the Socialist literature that dealt with imperial topics.) English Socialists, like Indian *babus*, without responsibility, with no hope of obtaining political power unless some explosion took place — something not, in 1909, confidently awaited — could afford to keep up a running moral commentary on all actions of government. They could relate these actions to some high ideal of international dealing which they themselves had never had to live up to, and which, in the opinion of the embattled rulers, they never would. They set themselves up as keepers of the national conscience, far more confidently than the older Victorian Radicals — whose leaders at least had had experience of office — had ever ventured to do. The constant assumption that all government not based on Socialist principle must inevitably stagger from one blunder to another, if not indeed to actual crime, was one that was particularly hard to bear by a Liberal Government which felt that it had, from its own record in the past, some right to the role of protector of the public weal. To be sure, this Government could expect to command Labour votes in the division lobby — but how galling it was, to see oneself considered as merely the lesser of two evils.

Anti-imperialism as now expressed developed most of the older Radical arguments, but gave them a more colourful production and a sharper edge. Since the South African War, it was possible for critics to adopt a patronising, rather than a hectoring, tone. The error of the imperialist, the stupidity of the courses he favoured, had been clearly shown up, as all sensible men were aware — but the patient was clinging to his old assumptions because he feared

[1] 5 H 150, 8 February 1922, 193.

he would be cold without them. He was, in fact, going through a phase. Nothing is so infuriating as to be told by someone whom one detests that one is going through a phase. It was the attitude of the governess in both Shaw and Wells that chiefly maddened those who reluctantly, but compulsively, opened these sages' books. Nevertheless both writers knew that their audience was, though sensitive on the surface, tough at the core, and they were aware that ingrained complacency was not to be removed in a day.

Wells however always found his target more surely than Shaw, who as an Irish outsider was quicker in seeing the more clearly ridiculous aspects of the English *ethos* than in gauging those items in it whose exposure would prove most actively embarrassing to the Englishman himself. For example, it was not more dreadnoughts the Navy wanted, Wells averred, but brighter officers. Would a 'one-eyed, one-armed adulterer', rather fragile and prone to sea-sickness, nowadays get to the top in the Navy? It was not more men the Army needed, but more sense: had it not been revealed that in the Tibet campaign very few rifles had been fit to fire because we had not thought to take glycerine with us? It was not more planning the Empire required, but less. They had been outcast eccentrics who had built the Empire: what had Westminster ever done for it, outside of founding the United States of America? It was not a new policy that was required, but a new kind of politician. The present type was no better educated and very little better informed than his equals fifty years back. The chief difference was golf. The British reading and thinking public probably did not exceed 50,000 people all told — considerably less than the number of those educated Hindus whom imperialists were always denouncing as unrepresentative. What was modern imperialism, anyway, in practice? It resolved itself into a vigorous resistance to taxation and an ill-concealed hostility to education — as well it might. Wells fastened on the story of the sinking *Titanic* and used that as a microcosm of the society he was attacking. It could not have been easy to read of this comparison with a smile of dismissal.[1]

Shaw's cascading criticisms were more easily disposed of, and Shaw knew this well enough. In his *John Bull's Other Island* (1908) he makes the Victorian Englishman, Broadbent, cheerfully impervious alike to the passionate denunciations and the apocalyptic visions of the Irish patriot and seer, Keegan. ('All very true. And

[1] H. G. Wells, *An Englishman Looks at the World*, (London, 1914), pp. 33–44.

excellently put. Reminds me of poor Ruskin.') One of the surest signs of the faith of the Victorians in themselves was indeed the licence they had always permitted to destructive critics in their midst. Shaw and Wells were only the last of a series of denunciatory prophets that included Carlyle and Arnold. But Shaw and Wells deliberately cast themselves as entertainers — roles neither Carlyle nor Arnold would have wished, or indeed would have been able, to play — because they realised how massive were the foundations of the structure they attacked. It was better to be listened to in startled amusement than not be listened to at all. (For who had listened to Carlyle and Arnold?) Thus their very denunciations struck a note of paradox which indicated that they neither meant nor expected to be taken with absolute seriousness. They knew that so much, but just so much, had been gained for the critical cause: the capitalists had lost some at any rate of their confidence, they now resented the aspersions on their moral character that they had previously shrugged away, they were now aware that the future held its serious social problems, at least. Perhaps then, if the critical barrage was expertly maintained, they could be headed off from committing all over again the more obvious kinds of blunder — perhaps they could really be brought to realise, for instance, the basic absurdity of the imperialist pretension.

Heavy and various were the implements hurled at the imperialist's head to drive this point home. 'The old imperialism,' Brailsford accused him, 'levied tribute: the new lends money at interest.'[1] Imperial patriotism had by now become shaped into a convenient mask for the plutocracy to wear, so that it might continue to spread its materialist influence among the young and the simple, among University students and the readers of the *Daily Mail*: as a token of this policy, the South African magnates Rhodes and Beit, the newspaper magnate Alfred Harmsworth, all within a few years of each other set moneys aside for the endowment of chairs of imperial history at the Universities of London, Oxford, and Cambridge. Imperialists must still be exposed as enemies of society, creators of an international anarchy. They were men who had no neighbours, only allies and enemies — allies and enemies who, with a shuffle of the pack, might change places any time. (This, one of MacDonald's charges, was frankly admitted as true in Roberts' imperialist handbook, *Fallacies and Facts*.)

[1] Cf. H. N. Brailsford, *The War of Steel and Gold*, (London, 1914), throughout.

T

The men who governed the British Empire were, it was plain to see, drawn from the most narrow-visioned of all our social classes, men who were cut off both by inclination and by education from any deep understanding wherein lay the wellsprings of the current of human idealism. Now, if the British Empire was to exist at all, if it was to thrive and grow, it must represent a richness of life for all whose who lived in it. It must express a moral truth, and try to illustrate Burke's great principle — that the principle of all true politics was that of morality enlarged. Radicals like Morley and J. A. Hobson had agreed together that the governance of India was the noblest and most beneficent task ever undertaken in the history of the world. This might indeed be true; but how was this task being tackled? Could anyone say, in this time of violence and 'unrest' in India, that nobility and beneficence were the two qualities most conspicuously displayed by officials of the British *Raj*?

Imperialists, it seemed, were ready enough to produce closely-argued plans for the construction of some new emporium, but how half-heartedly they squared to their task of mission! Even Cecil Rhodes, dreaming of his Cape-to-Cairo sphere of influence, had followed an ideal of a sort, but he had no successor among the magnates of South Africa, none of whom now lifted his eyes from the gold reefs and the diamond pipes. What had become of another of Burke's principles: that power exercised over a native race must ultimately be exercised for the benefit of that race? Had imperialists any native policy at all? Conservatives had long ago given up paying even lip-service to the idea of trusteeship, while it was a Liberal Government that committed the Bantu, long the *protégé* of British Imperial Governments, to the mercies of the whites, in the name of colonial self-government. Self-government was not necessarily and not always a moral solution to a political problem. On how trusteeship was best fulfilled, MacDonald indeed took up a position not far removed from that of Balfour, Churchill, Morley, and Cromer. Like Milner, he objected to the Liberal Government's throwing up their cards in the South African game. It was our fundamental mistake in native policy, he believed, to regard the native as a Briton in the making — and as one who would, when made, turn out to be a second-class British citizen anyway. This was an error often fallen into by Radicals themselves, MacDonald emphasised, when they too readily assumed that the proper end and object of our native administration must be the self-government of the people. For what did this entail? Natives had governed themselves before, and in so doing had hardly advanced the cause of civilisation. Self-government and barbarism were old acquaintances, as Livingstone and the whole generation of explorers in Africa had testified. If our mission of guidance and example was to be well accomplished, we needed fewer Crown Colonies, fewer settlers, fewer Governors, and more Native States with British Residents.

Empire, in other words, was being mismanaged — as Great Britain, under capitalist régimes, was itself being mismanaged. Good principles of government had become stultified. Men of narrow vision such as governed the British Empire were not the men to shake themselves free of their traditional prejudices and preconceptions, not the men to lead other, more simple peoples into the future and towards a civilised destiny. It was not just that the imperial car had stopped on the rails: it was anyway on the wrong route. It was not the last task of the imperialist, to pioneer his road through the jungle. That was only his first. His real problem, the one that would test all his mental and moral resources — and the one of which he seemed at present to have little comprehension — then began.

This kind of reasoning explains why it was that two men of such dissimilar backgrounds and opinions as MacDonald and Balfour should both have been ardent supporters of the Zionist movement, and propagandists for the establishment under British protection of a national home for the Jews. Say what might be said about this, it was still a romantic, Disraelian scheme of a type far removed from the protracted subjugation of the Somalis, or from the subordination of Persian nationalist aspirations to the needs of the Admiralty for oil. It was later to be the bitter cry of the Labour party that the high mission of Zionism had been allowed to degenerate into 'the Palestine question', to fall into the hands of those same narrow-minded administrators who were not imaginative enough to meet effectively the challenge of Indian nationalism, men who could see no further than the nearest and stalest 'strategic argument'. Thus a great world issue was handled as though it concerned only a dispute between two insignificant rival tribes in a remote Asiatic province. The Radical Josiah Wedgwood was using Balfour's own language when he declared in 1926 that we could not *allow* the development of Palestine to be checked because a few Arab reactionaries preferred that territory to be in Asia rather than in Europe.[1] So — we had imperial power to allow, and power to disallow, for beneficent ends. This kind of old-fashioned imperialist thinking — Lytton's own kind — was to lead Wedgwood to deny hotly, during the India debates of 1935, that if Labour came to power it would hand India over to the Indians — hand over the Indian peasantry, in other words, to the control of capitalist magnates and princes.[2] A Labour Government, like any other, would have to assess the circumstances of its own day, and use its power to grant, or not to grant.

Conservative imperialists who accused Socialists of wishing to throw the Empire away were accordingly misleading themselves into a state of mind where possibly they preferred to live. It infuriated them to hear some wild agitator namecalling the British Empire as one vast slum; but the implication, even in this abuse, was that one day, if the agitator and his friends had their way, the slum would be cleared and its dwellers housed. The fact of Empire was still the plainest of challenges to all men of good will. Socialism, like Benthamite utilitarianism before it, might find there a fertile field wherein to apply itself. Socialists, missionaries in their own kind, recognised the nature of their mission. There was an economic need to control the tropics, and to introduce civilised values to lower races in the process. But such activities could not adequately be carried out by private agencies, or by the agents of one nation alone: they must take place under the auspices of the civilised world. In such an assertion there was of course some confusion of thought. One moment Socialists implied that power was innately nefarious, the next that, in the hands of upright men of proper principles, it need not necessarily be so — which was just the argument which imperialists themselves had always used to justify their actions and their existence. Indeed, Hobson and Lugard shared a great many ideas as to the correct way to develop tropical Africa. But the majority of Socialists were certainly not separatists like their Radical forebears, who had hailed self-government for colonial possessions because it would rid the mother country of a useless burden. They believed, with Kipling, that a white man's burden existed, and that it had to be borne. In fact they were Gladstonian imperialists: a school denied existence by the orthodox. They followed the great man's precepts, which he had got

[1] 5 H 200, 7 December 1926, 2009.
[2] 5 H 298, 26 February 1935, 1062.

from Macaulay, that the real task was to found a moral empire built upon the confidence of the nations, and not upon their antipathies, their passions, and their fears.

Moreover, Socialists were prepared to admit — although they had not yet learned how to manipulate — certain facts of life, capitalist in aspect though these facts might be. By the twentieth century the United Kingdom was an industrial state, depending for its prosperity — for its existence, even — on world-wide commerce and upon freedom from both fiscal and military burdens which would handicap it in competing with other nations. But it was also an imperial state, subject to indefinite liabilities for the defence of that Empire. There was, then, a double set of interests to pursue, and it must therefore be the objective of all British statesmanship to prevent these contending ideals from coming into conflict.

Socialists denied, however, that the orthodox imperialist was capable of coping with this formidable situation. He appeared to thrive on conflict, and not to wish to avoid it. Accordingly Socialists were for ever warning the democracy that it must put no trust in 'the man on the spot'. After all, on any spot there were always two men: had not Milner in South Africa found it imperative to dispense with General Butler, whose prognostications about the consequences of carrying a high paramount hand had subsequently proved to be entirely correct? All such experts were to be distrusted, for experts were men with an interest, though it was not one they declared: an interest in their own expertise. Diplomacy itself was still in the hands of a guild, not penetrable even in its lowest echelons by anyone who did not enjoy a private income of at least £400 a year. It was the last redoubt of the principle of aristocracy in government. Curzon, drawing on his great experience as an inquiring traveller, gave an illustration of this when he insisted that he had never set foot in any British consulate, ministry, embassy, or legation abroad wherein there was not rejoicing over Conservative and lamentation over Radical electoral victories.[1] Although this was at once denied by another member of the governing class, Rosebery, as casting a grave slur on the Civil Service tradition of impartiality, Socialists saw no occasion to give that tradition much credence and were glad to take Curzon's word for it. Rosebery was a Liberal — or so he said: and herein lay another lesson for the democracy, that it must take a greater care of Liberal

[1] 4 H 37, 11 October 1895, 34.

guile than of Conservative hostility, for Liberals masked themselves as friends of the people, while the more readily identifiable Tories had never troubled to make themselves uncomfortably conspicuous in this way.

In foreign policy least of all were Liberals to be trusted. Liberal Governments had had a lie in their soul ever since the occupation of Egypt in 1882, an action they now rationalised by assuring themselves that they had gone there in the first place to rescue not the European bondholders but the Egyptians themselves: an assertion that Gladstone himself had always taken particular care to deny. Since that act Liberal Governments had been forced to base themselves on Tory and imperialist principles in their conduct of foreign policy, and they had by now become reasonably skilful players of the game of the balance-of-power. And what were these principles, so contrary to the true principles of democracy? Why, that the real business of the nation was the maintenance of its imperial position, and that on such a business only the decisions of the knowledgeable, the committed, and the experienced were of value. Imperial questions were questions of power, and only those with a particular tradition of power, a particular view of it, and a proved ability to handle it, could decide them. But this was not true at all. Problems in foreign policy were basically not intellectual, but moral. When all information on a situation had been garnered, when all the opinions of the experienced had been taken into account, there still remained the simple matter of deciding which course of action was morally right. Imperialists who complained that we were not in fact free to pick and choose courses of action as we pleased were condemning imperial policies out of their own mouths, in thus admitting that our position had been so gravely compromised. Cabinet Ministers knew the force of this argument perfectly well, for did they not go to great lengths to make it appear that their policies — or those of them they were prepared to own to at all — were based on honourable premises, and planned for the common good? Imagine, for example (Lowes Dickinson urged his readers) that a Minister were to come down to the House of Commons and address the members thus:

'We are giving support to such-and-such an enterprise in Morocco or Persia or Turkey. We expect, by that means, to assist British capital in securing a good investment and further to gain a political influence and prestige which will open to British people in future further lucrative concessions and loans. In doing this, we shall probably be led to intervene by force in the internal affairs of the country concerned, and we may also find ourselves involved in trouble with one or two other of the Great Powers; but we think it worth while to take those risks for the sake of the profits to the British people involved.'[1]

If any Government dared come down to the House and say that, what sort of reception would they get?

The problem, therefore, was to get public opinion to bear more directly than it now did on all matters concerning imperial and foreign policy. What was wanted, was democratic control.

This was not merely a cry from men on the Left who suspected the worst of their rulers on principle. Prior to 1914 *The Times*, Rosebery, Austen Chamberlain and other public figures were making suggestions that this matter might at least be looked into more closely. *The Times*, in a leader on 23 November 1912, asked itself who were the war-makers in the modern world, and answered that the war-makers lived within the Chancelleries of Europe, men remote from everyday considerations of humanity, who had for too long played with human lives as pawns in their game. Wars would assuredly continue to be made while such a situation continued. Rosebery wondered, in a speech at Glasgow, whether any merchant who was in his audience

> would care particularly to do what we do in foreign affairs — that is, to engage in vast and unknown liabilities and affix his signature to them without knowing their nature and extent.

Austen Chamberlain approached the problem from another direction. He was reviewing, in a debate in the Commons in February 1914, recent events in Europe, the full gravity of which had certainly never been realised by the British people. He asked himself whether democratic government could be conducted on such principles. Could we — he spoke for the rulers — rely that the whole of the people would rise to the height of a great emergency when we called upon them to do so, if there had been no previous preparation of their minds, if they had not been able to follow the steps by which we had been driven to the conclusion at which we finally arrived? Could not the Foreign Secretary give at least once every year a reasoned review of our position in relation to world affairs, such as was 'accorded by the Foreign Minister of every other

---

[1] G. Lowes Dickinson, *The Choice Before Us*, (London, 1917), p. 240.

great State to the Parliament to which he is not more, but less, responsible than British Ministers are to theirs'?[1] To Chamberlain, then, the problem of democratic control was, how to attach people to policies, not how to attach policies to the people.

The catastrophe that fell that same autumn upon British diplomacy made this issue, from whatever angle it was seen, of immediate importance. A few days before war broke out *Punch* was ridiculing the idea of our fighting alongside such dubious devotees of freedom as Serbia and Russia. Yet secret diplomacy had arranged it — or at any rate was powerless to prevent it. 'Diplomacy,' Arthur Ponsonby declared in his pamphlet *Parliament and Foreign Policy*, 'cannot be allowed to add further to its series of failures while the people remain helpless and inarticulate.' What was secret diplomacy but a form of sleight-of-hand? One found Sir Edward Grey solemnly affirming that his actions must be guided by what the people thought — but prior to 1914 he had never taken any step to find that out. Such affirmations were dishonest, and it was easy enough for the Government to construe the inevitable popular clamour that arose at the actual outbreak of hostilities as approval for both all its previous and all its subsequent actions.

Under the shock of war, likeminded critics gathered themselves in a Union of Democratic Control. A body that included Hobson, Brailsford, Bertrand Russell, MacDonald, E. D. Morel, Charles Trevelyan, and Norman Angell, it was determined to see to it that the Government's subsequent actions were at least brought under a pressure that their pre-war doings had escaped. The U.D.C. wished irresponsible power to cease, and its programme for the aims of a peace settlement laid more stress on what it ought to avoid than on what it ought to obtain. Territory must not be transferred without a plebiscite being held. Treaties should not be made without parliamentary sanction. The old alliances should not be resuscitated, but must be replaced by an international Council or League or Society of the Nations. Armaments races should cease, and the nations begin to rid themselves of what armaments they had. Economic warfare should not continue in times that were professedly peaceful, and to prevent it the principles of Free Trade and the Open Door should be accepted by all.

These were views that could not be propagated *in vacuo*: assertion of them entailed attack on those who were clamouring for

[1] Quoted in Arthur Ponsonby, *Parliament and Foreign Policy*, (1915).

'all-out victory' and 'the fight to a finish', on the idea that Germany must be subjugated economically, on the opinions held by such people as Carson — 'I do beg and pray the House not to send out a message that the war is being waged not for the British Empire but equally for neutrals.' Accordingly the U.D.C., because it consistently attacked the political conduct of the war, was vilified as anti-patriotic and pro-German. As a result of this counter-campaign, and although it had disseminated its doctrines among trade unionists and members of the Labour Party, nearly all its adherents who were in Parliament were swept out of their seats in the general election of December 1918 — when the electorate, only 54% of which voted, was increased to twenty-one million, including six million women. This same election defeated Liberal leaders such as Asquith, McKenna, and Samuel. The war that should have been waged to end war and for the sake of the cause of democracy the world over ended in giving portions of the ex-enemy Empires to the victorious Allies. Brailsford and Gilbert Murray, writing while the war still raged, had warned of the dangers of an imperialist peace, a peace in which vengeance and caution would be tinged with a little idealism.[1] A very little, it now seemed: for what was Versailles but 'a masterpiece of predatory imperialism'[2], a treaty wherein — as Sir Ian Hamilton exclaimed — there was not a line to stand for 'the kindliness of England', not a word 'to bring back some memory of the generosity of her sons'. The Versailles settlement, in the opinion of the U.D.C., was thus an indefensible breach of international morality, and it was they who promoted that campaign against it that was to have so powerful a cumulative effect. The mayor of Stepney, one Clement Attlee, remarked two years after the armistice that serving soldiers had been too credulous, when they went to war. They had believed what the Government had said. They would have been wiser had they listened to the U.D.C. [3]

The struggle for a democratic control of foreign policy seemed however to have suffered tactical defeat. The Foreign Office changed neither its ways nor its personnel. The oligarchs were still in possession. No 'Foreign Affairs Committee', like that of the

[1] Gilbert Murray, *Faith, War, and Policy* (Oxford, 1918); H. N. Brailsford, *A League of Nations* (London, 1916), p. 88.

[2] Brailsford, in *The Daily Herald*, 21 May 1919.

[3] 11 November 1920; H. M. Swanwick, *Builders of Peace*, (London, 1923), p. 98.

United States' Senate, sat as a board of mentors to the Foreign Secretary. Cabinets kept their secrets still, and even that 'Front-Bench conspiracy', whose existence had been so denounced in pre-war days, seemed to survive intact, as neither Asquith nor Grey, though sympathetic to League of Nations' ideas and values, opposed Lloyd George on the peace treaties. The *Round Table* itself warned, in a remarkable article 'The Harvest of Victory' (September 1919) that unless Britain learned what democracy meant, so that she might be able to teach self-government to the peoples for whom she was responsible, 'the creation of that commonwealth of many nations, many races, and many colours, of which we have dreamed, may never come into being.'[1]

Yet it was not true to say that the struggle had all been for nothing. (It was a symbol of some kind of victory, at least, that it should have been the U.D.C.'s stalwart Morel who managed to unseat Winston Churchill at Dundee in 1922.) The Coalition Government in Britain, like the *Raj* in India, came ultimately to a halt. Strong spirited and forward policies in Ireland, Russia, Mesopotamia, and Turkey all came to nothing. The policies the Government did not pursue, the aims it did not propagate, the plans it left in the file — these bore the best witness to the impact of the democracy on the bastions of power. Ponsonby had declared in the Commons in March 1918 that he and his friends of the U.D.C. did not want the Foreign Secretary to lay his cards on the table; but they did want to know what game he was playing, because he played for such very high stakes — people's lives and the nation's money.[2] When the war was over the people were prepared to grant neither their lives nor their money to any card-player, however dexterous and experienced.

Moreover, a Government now beset with democratic opinion at home had to keep an eye on the forum it had built for itself abroad, at Geneva. The League of Nations was now an institutional fact. Indeed it was not the League that the U.D.C., the Fabians, or the Independent Labour party had set their differing hopes on.[3] It was not a League to *enforce* peace. It did not have the international police force at its disposal that the Quai d'Orsay, no less than

[1] Probably written by Philip Kerr (later Lord Lothian); *RT*, September 1919, No. 36, pp. 666–8.
[2] 5 H 104, 19 March 1918, 853.
[3] See H. Winkler, *The League of Nations Movement in Great Britain 1914–19*, (New York, 1952), p. 129.

Hobson and Dickinson, wished it to have. It was a League of victors, whose Covenant guaranteed the eternal existence of the new Europe that had been given recognition at Versailles. It was not made, as Brailsford had hoped it might be made, 'a possible instrument of fundamental change'. It was not a League of peoples, it was a League of Governments, and not even of all Governments. Three major Powers still roamed free outside it, including the United States, the greatest democratic state in the world. It did not represent the conscience of mankind, for it was soon clear that each man's conscience guided him differently. In Britain it did not command the support of the Conservative party or its organs, which, although the temperature dropped in which they were able to speak of 'exposing England's throat to the assassin's knife' (this from *Blackwood's*) never lost their distaste for this institution of an extramural board of guardians. Nor was this remarkable, as ideas for a League had always been far commoner among Liberals, Radicals, and Socialists while the war was being fought than among Conservatives.

Still, there it stood: a repository for the hopes of the many, a symbol at least of human aspiration if not of human achievement — something that could not be attacked on the hustings with that same virulence which was reserved for its political supporters in the other parties, something whose Covenant could be referred to with piety by politicians secure in the knowledge that few of those listening had ever read it either.

Carson no longer burst out that he preferred to hear talk of a League of *British* Nations, as it became clear that the Dominions themselves felt more at home in Geneva, and cut more of a figure there in their own eyes, than they could ever do coming respectfully to a conference table in Downing Street. Geneva indeed had a moral authority that nobody and nothing in Downing Street could match, and it seemed for a time as if the British public would become more familiar with the names of foreign statesmen than they were with their own. The League was a factor to reckon with, therefore — an unpredictable factor, but one which any Government promoting British interests in the post-war world, which must always be the duty of any British Government, must take into most careful account. The truth of some comments made in 1916 by Eyre Crowe, in a Foreign Office critique of a proposal emanating from Lord Robert Cecil for the establishment of a League, stood out in bolder relief than before. Crowe had emphasised that, if such a League system were to be set up, Great Britain stood to be more exposed to its vagaries than most, as a substantial majority of the Powers could be found almost at any time ready to League together to promote measures which might ostensibly be designed to further the cause of peace, but which in reality would be directed at curtailing British supremacy at sea and British power in the world at large.

British power after 1919 was not what it had been, but it was still generated at home, and not in Geneva. British diplomacy was not so free to operate as it had been, but it still operated according to its own codes and traditions — codes and traditions that were too deeply rooted to be removed by the mere impact of a war in Europe, however bloody and prolonged. Entrenched in the high places, wrote Gilbert Murray later, were the old traditional diplomatists, who thought always in terms of 'British interests', disliked the whole conception of the League, and resented the intrusion of a moral ideal into politics.[1] The League's historian agrees with Murray, that 'its deep and grave weakness' was that the experts did not want it.[2] These experts and the Governments they advised were more inclined to seek the friendship of the aggressors than that of the victims, because the aggressors were usually the stronger, and a strong friend was better — that is to say, of more use — than a weak. It was therefore not a matter for much surprise that the first aggressors against peace were not 'victims' of the peace treaties at all, but two of the conquerors, two of the imperialist Powers — Japan and Italy.

Thus, in their own estimation, the forces of virtue massed on the Left to confront the forces of materialist malevolence embattled on the Right. From the point of view of the Right, the battle lay between commonsense and cant about the nature of man and the motives of the societies he formed. Neither of these opinions was totally nonsensical, but neither of them was adequate either. It was certainly the case, that imperialists believed that it was 'Wilsonianism', with all its accompanying doctrine of self-determination, which, more than anything else, was weakening the fibre of assertive self-confidence that a great nation must retain if it were to remain a great nation. The idea that Jack should be assumed to

[1] Gilbert Murray, *From the League to U.N.*, (Oxford, 1948), p. 70.
[2] F. P. Walters, *A History of the League of Nations*, (Oxford, 1952), I, 16.

be and treated as if he actually were as good as his master, when candid observation made it clear he was nothing of the sort, was bound to prove as subversive in the international field as it had in the arena of domestic politics. Had Lincoln, the great democrat, allowed self-determination to the South? But now, it seemed, nationalism had now been promoted to the highest political status. Yet it seemed that at the same time its promoters believed that it would prove a suitable foundation for the international structure whose blueprints they so enthused over. They apparently thought that nationalist patriots, now that their dearest hopes had been realised, would at once consent cheerfully to reduce the scope of their immediate ambitions, submerging them for a common good: a common good that must certainly involve the good of those who had heretofore done their best to crush those hopes and kill those ambitions.

British imperialists could make nothing of this. Had they not themselves been reluctantly compelled to admit that all their own plans to establish an international community within the British Empire, to set up a broad-based imperial federal union, were too advanced, too far remote from the principles and emotions that were the natural heritage of a group of self-governing peoples? These peoples remembered — even although in their case the recollection was without the bitterness that seared relationships in Europe — how strong in their own colonial past, when they had not been their own masters, had been the degree of their determination to win status and dignity in their own eyes. Just as the Dominions and their statesmen retained an atavistic dislike of 'Downing Street government' and all its overtones, so too did the governors of the United Kingdom see Geneva as a similar symbol of danger for their country's future.

For what was Geneva, but a temple raised to celebrate those ruinous fancies so beloved by the Left: that a balance of power was something with which international society could dispense if it chose, that small nations had no need of protection, and that great nations — to whom the role of protector naturally fell — would be content to sink their individualities within some common pool of political wisdom, wherein El Salvador and Great Britain would be reckoned to have contributed an equal store? The idea that a board of guardians had a right to pronounce on the rights and actions of Great Britain in, say, Egypt and the Sudan, was anathema. There would always be, the fourth Marquess of Salisbury declared, out-side the confines of one's own country, or even of one's own Em-pire, certain regions in regard to which we had interests so import-ant and over-riding that we could not allow the interference of other Powers.[1] That was why, in 1922, we had informed these other Powers that the external affairs of the newly-created Egyptian king-dom were still our own particular concern, had in fact virtually promulgated a 'Monroe Doctrine' in regard to the area of the Middle East as a whole. No disapproval from the League of Nations, no adverse verdict of any self-constituted 'arbiter', could be ac-cepted by us as regards our rights in the Suez Canal and the en-vironing Levant. If the British people, misled by sentimental non-sense, ever came to underwrite any such verdict, such acceptance would inevitably bring about the downfall of the entire imperial idea and the British Empire with it.

Some, like Amery, might feel that the League was harmless enough so long as it made no attempt to be more than a standing conference bringing statesmen together at frequent intervals.[2] This could do no one an injury; indeed, it might do considerable good, as the statesmen so conferring might learn something of the facts of life, which were facts of power — or at least correct a few of their more ludicrous preconceived ideas. But all imperialists agreed that if the League sought to act according to the principles its propagand-ists professed it would succeed only in worsening any situation. The League was a scaffolding, not a structure: but if the plans got lost, it might not matter so much as the architects thought.

Accordingly, the Geneva Protocol of 1924 — an attempt by two Socialists, Arthur Henderson and Edouard Herriot, to inter-nationalise the principle of compulsory arbitration in cases of dis-pute — genuinely frightened both the leaders and the rank-and-file of the Conservative party, and caused them to state far more bluntly than they had ever ventured to do their instinctive dislike and distrust of League policies. Here was one of the principles of Cobden returned to haunt them — although, to do him justice, Cobden had never been a party to plans for having a Congress of Nations, with a code of laws, a supreme court of appeal, and an army to support its decisions. What else was arbitration but the in-terference by outsiders, aliens, in matters of whose background

[1] 5 H 233, 11 December 1929, 1125 ff.
[2] Amery, *My Political Life*, II, 163.

and tradition they could have no comprehension? Who could understand a British interest better than a British subject? What man in his senses thought that the use of courts and conciliation boards could do anything to 'solve' the Anglo-Irish question? For this country to give to an unknown group of men, responsible to nobody and representative only of themselves, the power to legislate in matters of vital importance to the world at large, would be to confront its own people with a worse menace than the rise of the Japanese Navy — a thing which at least was tangible, and which might be coped with by taking practical measures.

When the Labour Government fell from office in November 1924, the Protocol still lay on the table at Geneva. The incoming Conservatives, although anxious, as their Foreign Secretary Austen Chamberlain expressed it, not to live in short-sighted isolation, thought it wise not only to spend three months consulting the Chiefs of Staff of the Services — which MacDonald had not done — but the Dominions as well, since here was a question that concerned 'our influence and our mission in the world'.

Chamberlain was prepared to welcome the Dominion reaction in advance, knowing well what it would be. Nothing was so detested in Canada as a European entanglement. Already Canadians had taken as much exception to the tenth Article of the Covenant of the League of Nations as had their neighbours in the United States. For Article Ten, which stated that members of the League undertook to respect and preserve as against external aggression the territorial integrity and *existing political independence* of all members of the League, was nothing more nor less than a solid guarantee of the *status quo* in Europe. Who could assume that it was Europe's fate, from here to eternity, to remain in the state of petrifaction decreed upon it by statesmen in a hurry at Versailles? A Canadian delegate had already illustrated, in the League Assembly, the view held in places distant from Europe, and by many in England too:

> In this association of mutual insurance against fire, the risks assumed by the different states are not equal. We live in a fireproof house, far from inflammable materials.

To underwrite compulsory arbitration was to play with inflammable materials, there could be no doubt. The Dominions had all signed the Treaty of Versailles, wherein the Covenant of the League was enshrined, but by 1924 this action seemed to them, in recollection, an unguarded one. They could not undo what had been done: but at least they could see to it that they committed themselves no further.

Thus encouraged by this display of imperial solidarity, the Conservative Government gladly rejected the Geneva Protocol. They proceeded, in the following year, to give their assistance to the arrangement at Locarno of a series of treaties which were designed to maintain Western European security — treaties which were themselves a voluntary breach in the Versailles system. Locarno committed the United Kingdom, but not the Dominions, to the automatic defence of the Franco-German frontier by whomsoever violated, but not to that of any other frontier in Europe. Article Ten was not rescinded by Locarno, but its significance was dulled. Chamberlain and the Government were proud of Locarno, hailed it as a landmark, a signpost to the future. Distilled there was the celebrated 'Locarno spirit', and there was no doubt that popular enthusiasm believed in its potency, and many a dance-hall built in the next ten years used the magic name as a symbol for optimism. An opportunity was here given to the Left to make the charge that had been levelled in 1904, that under this arrangement the fate of Britain would again lie in the lee of French policy, which not two years past had thought it right to violate the Franco-German frontier by occupying the Rühr. But it was not a charge made either with confidence or with any accurate assessment of the future.

Many on the Left shared Amery's view of the League, that it had some therapeutic value, but what else it had they were put to it to say. The organisation known as the League of Nations Union had been founded in 1918 to propagate Geneva's cause in Britain. It had in origins been a non-party affair, and 538 candidates standing for election that December had found it possible to declare their entire concurrence with the principles of the League. But as thereafter Conservatives gave it little support, the literature and propaganda of the Union became, as Grigg put it, 'more and more saturated' with the political philosophy of the Left. Gilbert Murray, who presided over the Union for fifteen years, did not contest this finding, and indeed took pride in the great change that the Union and its agents helped to bring about in the language, attitudes, and assumptions of history textbooks in schools. But it was not by any deliberate design that the Union became both a conventicle and an organ of the Left. Murray indeed blamed the Con-

servatives themselves for allowing it to become so, for failing to
play their proper part in promoting the cause of international
organisation, Conservative speakers could have helped keep the
Union's feet on the ground of reality, could have done valuable
service in pointing out, for example, that no guarantee of collective
peace was practicable unless the nations concerned were ready, in
the last resort, to ensure the guarantee by using force against an aggressor. This point was one that Murray and other leaders of the
League of Nations Union did emphasise, but it was never the point
that its devotees expected to hear made or wished to pay heed to
when made. 'Any large political movement,' was Murray's comment, 'is sure to have an emotional fringe, and the prevalent
national emotion at the time was undoubtedly hatred of war.'[1] The
abstention of the Conservatives left this emotion more uncon-
trolled by reason, however, than it need have been.

Indeed, more positive assertion from the Right against not
merely the practices, present and potential, of the League but
against the fundamental assumptions that supported it, might have
done a similar service. At least it would have provoked the Left to
solid argument, and even in the resultant uproar the air would have
been cleared of a great deal of cant. The confessed imperialists took
their lead from Milner in this as in other things, and expressed their
honest objections: Milner had reported to the Cabinet in April
1917 that 'any too comprehensive or ambitious project to ensure
world peace might prove not only impracticable but harmful,' and
commented sharply on Versailles later — that in the victories of
freedom there was no room for revenge. His disciples had seen no
reason as the years passed to say that Milner, in either view, was
wrong. But imperialists were now on the far right of the Conservative party, and were considered by it often with a considerable
degree of embarrassment. Forthright outspokenness was not the
mode. Thus the rank-and-file, though never forgetting to include
the British Empire in their public speeches, kept off the difficult
subject of the League, beyond declaring they were 'for' it as they
were for virtue and the sanctity of the home. To set out positively
to instruct the democracy about this topic, to try to make it clear
that the 'country' — the Conservative expression — might not
always be able to afford the time taken by the 'people' — the term
used on the Left — in choosing the correct path, were tasks con-

[1] Murray, op. cit., p. 3.

U

taining too great a political danger, now that the Labour party was become His Majesty's official Opposition.

Imperialists were accordingly far more often impatient with the pusillanimities of their own party than angry at the follies of the Opposition. It was, now as ever, the duty of a governing class to govern, of leaders to lead. Those who were entrusted with this duty and did not carry it out would find that by such conduct they would not get even the peace and quiet they appeared to want more than anything else. For the country would find out in a pinch, when it came to one, that despite all the emotional attractions (admittedly considerable) of internationalism, it did not owe the same duty to Ethiopians as it did, say, to the inhabitants of the Isle of Wight. It was Edward Grigg's considered view, as expressed in his *Faith of an Englishman* in 1937, that any cult that either overtly or implicitly disparaged patriotism, that put duty to Empire and country no higher than that to the world at large, was bound to make all true Conservatives — not all of whom, by any means, were to be found within the ranks of the Conservative party — recoil instinctively from it. England had to remember, what Lloyd George and successive Prime Ministers had found it necessary continually to emphasise to successive French Governments, that she was the trustee in Europe for a system, an imperial system, infinitely greater than herself, and that her strength was the strength of that system.

Moreover, those enthusiasts for the League who also spent a great deal of their time and energy denouncing the iniquities of Versailles, seemed to forget too easily that the Covenant was written into the terms of that settlement, and thus that their constant denunciation of armaments was quite inconsistent with the possibility of carrying out those obligations of the Covenant which they were as constantly urging their countrymen to respect and revere. They preferred to ignore another fact, that the authority of the League represented the strength of the Alliance that had won the war rather than the conscience of civilised man. They might object that this Alliance, and anything it might have arranged to suit its own convenience, belonged to the bad old past when the balance of power was respected in Europe, but they could hardly deny that it was the military strength of the most unpopular member of that Alliance, France, that was the real underprop of the peace of Europe.

Raising their voices further against the clamour, imperialists argued that both the crisis in Manchuria in 1931 and that in Abyssinia in 1935 might have been settled short of war had the old-style balance-of-power system still been in unfettered operation, had not both China and Abyssinia felt themselves secure under Article Ten of the Covenant, which guaranteed to them as members of the League their existing territorial sovereignty. China and Abyssinia found out too late what the imperialists had always presumed would be the outcome, that this blanket guarantee was not honoured. Even the argument that it *ought* to have been honoured they were prepared to dispute. Grigg wondered whether Japanese energies in 'Manchukuo', Italian techniques in Ethiopia, might not do in the future for these backward territories what Western nations had done in the past in and for India and America. This of course was the justification Mussolini himself was using: but it also echoed the language Lytton had used in 1881, when he urged that conquest was and had always been a principal weapon of civilisation and culture, and that by no other means could the heritage of Greece and Rome have been spread from the Clyde to the Nile. It was never popular language, either in Lytton's time or in the 1930's, because its terms of reference cut athwart those that the liberal conscience would have liked always to follow. Nevertheless imperialists felt it worthwhile to point out to Left idealists who made every nation's cause their own, that if we in the British Empire were bound to die for the sake of the inhabitants of Manchuria and Abyssinia, then *a fortiori* while we were still alive we were bound to live a little less comfortably too, and jettison our domestic programmes of social welfare in the good cause.

Barbs like this struck deep. Geneva disillusioned more on the Left than ever it could expect to on the Right, which had long prided itself on freedom from any illusion at all. Very early in its career the League of Nations dismayed the Left, when it failed to assert itself — or, to put it more accurately than it was usually put, when League members failed to find any common ground of policy — in such questions as, how to eject the invading Poles from Vilna, or the Italians from Corfu, or the French from the Rühr, or how to make any mediation effective in the prolonged Turco-Greek quarrel. The very occasions that Amery thought useful and instructive — the conferences where men interchanged their views — were considered by many on the Left as simply disgraceful. At Geneva more matters were talked to a standstill than in many a democratic parliament, and it was more than ever obvious that what was best represented there was Government and not the People. Geneva certainly provided the more vociferous of European politicians with an adequate wailing-wall; but the great aspirations of justice and idealism seemed to perish somewhere down the long reaches of those antiseptic corridors.

Moreover, it was the older generation which seemed to think that 'taking it up at Geneva' constituted a step positive in itself. The young men of Europe joined either the Communist or the Fascist camps, not because — in the majority of cases — they were devoted Communists or devoted Fascists, but because to these iron choices there appeared no alternative. There was a democratic camp, assuredly, with Franklin Roosevelt as its guardian, but Roosevelt's America was far distant, and western democracy in Europe threw up no such dominant figure. Young men in Britain, whose tastes and emotions were expertly catered for and formed by the publications of the Left Book Club, turned their back on the League, accusing its professional devotees of a bourgeois cynicism whose consequences would prove more disastrous than the stupidities of imperialists and their like who did not know any better. Thus the symbol of collective action for the intellectuals of that generation was not any international conference, but an international brigade got together somehow to fight a confused battle in Spain. It was a symbol that proved to men on the Left that some at least of them were prepared to do more than talk about their ideals, that a man in twentieth-century Europe might still elect to die for a 'cause', that the doctrines of international brotherhood — disguised though they might be in the harsh colours of the Soviet Union — were able to find martyrs as gallant as any that the forces of militant nationalism had commanded in the past. Death on the Guadalajara, fighting the Fascists, proved that the politics of power were not the only politics that had reality. It proved not only that this was not true, but asserted that it was a treason to the human spirit to believe that it was true. It arraigned men who did believe it — like the imperialists — as men who were suffering from the symptoms of the same disease that had so many in Europe in its grip. The disease of fascism, which had beaten down so many bright hopes, was born of just such cynicism and distrust of the human spirit as was already (it was plain to see) infecting much of British right-wing opinion.

The Tories, because they were materialists, would never understand because they would never want to understand that the *same* cause was defended in Manchuria, in Abyssinia, in Madrid, as was defended by their hypothetical patriot in the Isle of Wight. 'Never send to find for whom the bell tolls. it tolls for thee.' It was the cause betrayed by Sir John Simon, when as Foreign Secretary he declared that no British Government was 'blindly fettered' by the Treaty of Locarno — their own vaunted triumph! — when he asserted that he would not risk losing a single British ship for the sake of Abyssinia, and when he made a naval deal with Hitler for the sake of something defined, forsooth, as British interests. It was the cause betrayed by Sir Samuel Hoare, when he concocted with the French a typical imperialist 'Sykes-Picot' partition of Abyssinia to suit the Italians' book. It was the cause betrayed by Neville Chamberlain, when as Prime Minister he set out on a stony road towards appeasement of the dictators, to sacrifice *en route* men who lived in far countries of which we knew nothing. These Tories were all dangerous men: whether they were crypto-Fascists or whether they were fools, they were materialists who did not understand the cut and the pattern of the materials they were handling. Rooted to ideas of conduct and convention which no longer had any validity, they would not comprehend that it was pointless, futile, to try 'to do business' with dictators, with whom in truth there was no business to do. Left-wing intellectuals could afford to admit what Labour politicians could not, that the mass of the people approved what was being done in their name. But this made the case the worse. Extreme Left agreed here with extreme Right: the first duty of a Government was to *understand* its duties.

As the death of Gordon at Khartoum in 1885 had been a symbol of victory for the imperial idea, so the death of Czechoslovakia at Munich in 1938 was one for its enemies. In neither case, on either side, was quarter given.

Men on the Right who were determined to face facts and discount theories were bound to be supporters of the policy of appeasement from the start. The absence of Russia and Germany from the roll of the active Powers of Europe made it possible for such men to assure themselves and the democracy that Great Britain had indeed a foreign policy that was based on an accurate assessment of the realities. But it became plain after the mid-1930's that Britain and France had been acting only as caretakers in Europe until the absentees returned. It was then obvious that the previous assessment was inadequate, and that it gave very little guidance how best to deal with these two vigorous newcomers, who not only thoroughly believed in but made a god of totalitarian power, whose prestige depended on continuous action in both the domestic and foreign spheres. Since 1920 the foreign policy of the British Empire had been to make the best of the League of Nations, and since 1922 of the Washington treaties, although the United States did not belong to the one and Russia did not support the other. By 1936 (just after the Japanese had denounced the Washington treaties) it was clear that a new world was emerging, and that new power-relationships would have to be established. For, styling themselves the 'Have Not' Powers, the Fascist Governments in Germany, Italy and Japan made it clear that they intended in no very long time to bring about a redistribution of the world's goods and the world's power which should make the title no longer applicable. Putting on one side the problems of Russia, beset by two militant imperialisms on east and west, it was plain that such a redistribution would be carried out mainly at the expense of 'the bloated pluto-demo-cracies' who had got hold of half the world at a propitious moment some fifty odd years ago, and who still seemed to think — like Tim Healy's Englishman — that they had a prescriptive right to it for the rest of time.

To this no answering challenge came from any Government of Great Britain. No official voice was powerfully raised to deny the contentions — though many went out of their way to deplore the methods — of the dictators. It was true, we had been somewhat too obstreperously imperialist in grandfather's day. It was true what the Germans said, they had been over-severely handled at Versailles: for how could there be peace in a European system which left both Germany and Russia without certain hope of rehabilitation except through overthrow of the settlement? It was true, that the principle of nationalist self-determination contradicted the continued existence of German minority-groups in states outside that great German Reich which Hitler, as a patriot, was anxious to build on a proper nationalist basis. It was true, that in entering the Rhineland in 1936 the Germans 'were only occupying their own back-garden' — and not, presumably, the front-garden of the French. The dictators were men overinclined, perhaps, to rough-and-ready methods, but they were the men of the future. It might be a grim future, and not the one which we, left to ourselves, would have selected for ourselves to live in; but nevertheless it was a future in which we too had a stake, and about whose shape we needed to have a say

While it was also true that Fascism and Fascist statesmen had their unpleasant side, at least it could not be said they were Bolsheviks, subverters of the entire order of society in Europe. Indeed, Fascist Governments were the sworn foes of Bolshevism, and, as such, potential warriors on the side of civilisation and its values. Winston Churchill, visiting Mussolini in Rome in 1927, declared that Fascism had rendered a service to the whole world. The great fear that had always beset every democratic or working-class leader, in Churchill's view, had been that of being undermined or overbid by someone more extreme than he. It seemed that a continued progression to the Left, 'a sort of inevitable landslide into the abyss', was the characteristic of all revolutions. But Mussolini's Italy had shown that there was a way of fighting the subversive forces, a way that could rally the mass of the people — properly led — to value and to wish to defend the honour and the stability of civilised society. Italy had provided the necessary antidote to the Russian poison. Henceforth, no great nation would be unprovided with an ultimate means of protection against 'cancerous growths', and every responsible Labour leader in every country would feel his feet more firmly planted in resisting levelling and reckless doctrines. After all, the great mass of the people, everywhere, loved their own particular country and were proud of its flag and of its history. They did not regard these sentiments as incompatible with a progressive advance towards social justice and economic betterment.[1] These were views that Churchill had not greatly changed ten years later, when he published his *Great Contemporaries*. Among these Joseph Stalin did not appear, but Mussolini and Hitler were both there; and the author did not think it was impossible that 'we might yet live to see Hitler a gentler figure in a happier age'.

But it was commonsense to realise that if we, the British, were indeed 'to do business' with Hitler and Mussolini, some of that business must be done, in part at least, on the dictators' own terms. It was certain that there would be neither a disarmament treaty, nor a restoration of the League, nor appeasement in Europe unless

[1] *The Times*, 21 January 1927; Emrys Hughes, *The Bolshevik Bogey in Britain*, (Glasgow, 1943), pp. 31-2.

Germany was given defensive security within a brief and specific period. Hitler's Germany, Lord Lothian informed *The Times* on 1 February 1935, did not want war. It was surely for us to see to it that Germany would never want it, for us to take the initiative in bringing Germany back to the comity of nations — by such steps as the signing of the Anglo-German Naval Agreement. Moreover, the British Empire could not afford to take risks, and to go out of its way to provoke Powers that had as yet given it no overt offence. The emergence of Italian imperialist ambition had thrown a shadow, the first seen there since 1918, across the whole Middle Eastern world where our word had been law; the expansion of a hostile Japan was taking place at a time when the Japanese had in their hands naval supremacy in the Pacific, with the consequence, as Eden when Foreign Secretary warned the House of Commons, that we could do nothing decisive anywhere in the Far East without the help of the United States — now more doggedly neutral in spirit, perhaps, than she had ever been. All these things were happening at a time when, after a decade of popular support for a policy of non-armament if not for the policy of disarmament, our Services were in a dangerously low state of efficiency. The Navy in 1931 had 74 fewer capital ships, 72 fewer cruisers, and even 40 fewer submarines than it had had in 1914. The R.A.F.'s front-line strength in 1918 had been 3,300 planes: by 1935 it was down to 850. The military strength available to defend 40-odd colonies was less than 30,000 men.

It was therefore not only pointless but highly dangerous to rattle an empty scabbard, forged in the League of Nations, at *arriviste* Powers just because they were inclined to use a heavier hand in their international dealings than we thought proper. Were Great Britain to be defeated in war, Canada would become of necessity a dependency of the United States, and all other parts of the Empire would henceforth live by leave of the strongest foreign navy within striking distance of their shores. Churchill had sketched out this possibility in March 1914: Grigg underlined it in his book, twenty-three years later. It was a forecast that bore repetition, for it was true.

It was the kind of truth that had to prevail — whether a British Government was imperialist in sentiment or the reverse. The experience of Labour Governments in 1924 and in 1929–31 bore this out. The voice of Ramsay MacDonald, laying stress on what he

called 'the confusions of an imperialist inheritance',[1] was often
raised at annual Labour Party Conferences. He warned his listeners
that the right policy for the Left was to create a transition period
between the conditions that had obtained before the war, and those
that were going to come into being before very long. Walking out of
India tomorrow, therefore, was really not feasible, nor indeed
would it be desirable to do so. But many Left stalwarts were as
firmly opposed to the doctrine of continuity in foreign policy as
once MacDonald himself had been. They therefore delighted to
assail their leader and his colleagues as men who had betrayed their
principles, who had been corrupted by power and seduced by
duchesses and dinner-tables, who had been overawed by the forces
of imperialism and capitalism as soon as they got to close quarters
with these. This was not an accusation that held much (although
perhaps it held some) water. It was not, that principle had been
betrayed. It was, rather, that principles proclaimed by Labour when
in opposition were exposed as unsound the moment Labour became
responsible for the government of the country and of the British
Empire. These principles indeed began to appear as unsound in
their own especial way as were those of the mischievous exploiting
'imperialism' against which they had originally been drawn up in
protest.

    Such principles had centred on the doctrine of self-determination
— of which imperialism was, by definition, a negation. But simple
self-determination, absolute nationalism, each nation being complete master in its own territory, solved no problems worth men-
tioning. They solved perhaps personal problems of *amour-propre*,
such as obsessed Hertzog and de Valera in 1926: but how many
people in the Empire ate the more or lived the better because some
words of Balfour's had been wrought into a magic spell? Yet it was
this absolute nationalism, this 'right' of everybody to be 'free and
independent', that was the nostrum which the Socialist critic usually prescribed as the only alternative to the soul-destroying imperialism he so detested. But if such ideas were to be relentlessly
pursued to their logical conclusion, an *International Anarchy*,
worse than any perceived by Lowes Dickinson in the old balance-
of-power system described in his celebrated book (1926), would assuredly result. For example, it was not just an imperialist incanta-
tion, it was true, that the Suez Canal was a highly important artery

[1] 5 H 217, 10 May 1928, 435–6.

of communication — even if, by 1957, the adjective 'vital' was proved to have been overworked. It was no imperialist, but Norman Angell, who insisted in 1932 that if the Canal were blocked, and trade with India and Australia made impossible, children in certain streets of Liverpool or Manchester would die. He suggested that, if 'rights' were going to be discussed, it might be remembered that these children had to be taken into account, that they too had rights needing as much attention as those more spiritual rights of

desert tribesmen who object to the presence within their 'national' borders of infidel contrivances like canals and steam-ships.[1]

It was therefore not just part of the imperialist smoke-screen, laid to conceal plans at which the innocent democracy would have choked in indignation had it discovered them, to say that there were indeed such things as British interests, and that British power — a British Empire, if you preferred, or even if you did not prefer — was necessary to maintain them.

It was because they were forced to understand this, when once in office, that Socialists continued to carry out the measures and policies that had been laid down by their bourgeois imperialist predecessors. They had no alternative, *positive* policy of their own with which to replace them. Nehru noted sardonically how George Lansbury, elected President of a Congress of Oppressed Nationalities held at Brussels in 1926, and also president of a sub-committee called the League against Imperialism, soon 'repented of his rash behaviour', for after all the Labour party was His Majesty's Opposition then, soon to blossom out as His Majesty's Government, 'and future Cabinet Ministers cannot dabble in risky and revolutionary politics.'[2] It was curious how all roads in England led to the maintenance of the Empire. Like other Governments Labour were compelled to deal with facts as they came, and the common problem in Europe and within the Empire itself — how to deal with disorder — was not one that had been created by capitalism and was not one that could be cured by the application of socialism. Angell did not deny his past: to him imperialism was *ipso facto* wrong and misguided, and required a remedy. But the remedy he prescribed was not nationalism, or self-determination, which threatened to balkanize the world, but internationalism. This in his

---

[1] Angell, *Unseen Assassins*, 198 ff.
[2] Nehru, *Autobiography*, pp. 419–20.

view was not a denial of nationalism but its enhancement, and here he agreed with Milner and J. A. Hobson. Internationalism was merely the orderly organisation of nationalism, involving quite properly the limitation of its 'rights' in the same way that in any civilised society the right of the individual to do what he pleased had to be made subject to the general interest in order that the individual could live at all.

Angell, like Murray, deplored the excesses of the emotional fringe. The war had generated a great deal of hot air besides a genuine resolve to do better, and it took some time for men to cool down. Admittedly, they did it quicker in our own cold climate than they did in, say, India or Egypt. When Gandhi exclaimed that he could not accept freedom as a gift, but that Indians must prove their right to it by suffering and self-sacrifice, he was only using language that had been taught him by the precepts of Victorian radicalism, plus the war propaganda for self-determination and democracy — a war in which, he recalled if we tended to forget, the British had invited the Indians to share, and in which they had shared. The tragedy of this was that Asians were adopting these Western principles just at a time when the West itself was discovering that they were inadequate.[1] But here Angell was mistaken, as Hitler, coming to power the following year, was to prove to him.

Between the two wars Labour Governments in Britain held office, but not power, as their members took care to point out. They had no 'mandate' to act according to the light of their own teaching, as they were dependent for their existence on political manoeuvre. Nevertheless, as the open and professed representatives of the aspirations of the democracy, it was their ideas, such as they were, that held the field. Haldane had commented, when the Government of Ireland Bill was feeling its uneasy passage through Parliament in 1920 — while Ireland was at the mercy of irregulars, both British and Irish — that he was deeply convinced that the people would not tolerate any system of 'law and order' that did not arise from their own goodwill.[2] Baldwin echoed him fifteen years later, when he answered Churchill's outburst that the great ship was sinking in the calm sea. If George III had been endowed with the tongue of Edmund Burke he might have made such a speech — and Churchill must surely realise that firm and strong government

[1] Angell, *Unseen Assassins*, p. 210.
[2] 5 H of L 40, 20 October 1920, 484.

such as he was always calling for, in India or anywhere else, was based on two assumptions. These assumptions were: that there was unanimity among political parties, and that, as a consequence, there was continuity of policy. It was just these two factors, Baldwin insisted, that had been missing throughout the long history of the Irish question in English politics. Inevitably, that question had ultimately posed the two alternatives, of war or surrender; and a British government, unbacked by any strong opinion in the British democracy, was compelled to accept the second of these. If the Empire today was loyal, as it was, it was largely because we had conceded with good judgment and in good time the reasonable claims of the units of that Empire.[1]

To Churchill this was sheer defeatism, and he could never stomach it. Reasonable claims! Who was to judge of the degree of reasonableness? 'What has struck me more than anything else,' he broke out, 'has been the amazingly small number of people who have managed to carry matters to their present lamentable pitch!'[2] How dared a Conservative Government present this doctrine — that the Socialist Opposition was always in power! For that, he insisted, and quite correctly, was what it amounted to. Conservative patriots and imperialists had lost faith in their own principles, and were following sheepishly in the wake of a set of other ideas that their forebears had long and tenaciously striven against. At this very time (1935) we were losing the situation in Palestine as we had lost it in Ireland, as we would lose it — if the Opposition had its way, or rather, if the Government spinelessly thought it had better be allowed to have it — in Egypt and in India; all through a lack of whole-hearted faith in ourselves and in our mission. 'Are we to conclude that British administration in Oriental lands is no longer capable of facing a storm?'[3]

Indeed British administration in Oriental lands was as capable of facing storms as ever it had been, but times had changed since Cromer had remarked that it would be hard to find a dozen people in England who could accurately tell you just what kind of administration operated in the Sudan. Now everything of this kind was done in the open, the privacy of Empire had been invaded, and the nature and extent of the responsibilities which Empire might at any

[1] 5 H 259, 26 January 1931, 744 ff.
[2] 5 H 297, 6 February 1935, 1659.
[3] 5 H 341, 24 November 1938, 1991 ff.

time call on the British democracy to face were far clearer now than ever they had been in the days when Sir Edward Grey had been able to contrive never to have his Government's foreign policy either accurately or closely examined at all. 'I have in mind,' Attlee pointed out in a debate on Iraq in 1926, 'the children that we have in this country, the children of the 1925 and 1926 classes, who may be called up in the event of war in the East.'[1] Imperialists, thinking constantly of power and strategy, were generally assumed not to have such things in their minds at all — or at least to have relegated them to that subconscious of whose existence Freud had made everyone conscious. When the question of abolishing the bombing aeroplane as a weapon of war came under serious discussion at the Disarmament Conference at Geneva in 1932, the Left did not fail to notice that it was the British Secretary of State for Air, Lord Londonderry, who argued most strongly for its retention — as the bomber was an essential means for policing the frontiers of the States in the Middle East that the British themselves had constructed.

In a deeply pacifist age, whose adults had returned from a four years' war 'with a certain scepticism as to the manner in which it had been conducted',[2] Empire and militarism were, now as ever, equated. But it was not an equation that commanded the unwilling respect of former times. Militarism was now vilified because it was assumed it would prove an inefficient instrument at best, rather than through any fear that imperialists, armed with might and drunk with glory, would use it to crush the democrats down. In the 1880's the 'modern major-general', personified by Sir Garnet Wolseley, had had his many admirers, even among Radicals; but by the 1920's and 1930's the modern major-general had been demoted in rank and degraded in name, now appearing in David Low's cartoons as the figure of Colonel Blimp — a brick-red countenance calling hoarsely for its tiffin when not voicing some fatuous admiration of Mussolini. The anger that during the war had been so often expressed concerning the remoteness of the Brass Hats and the Red Tabs from the dangers of the front line was easily transferred to the rulers of the political scene. Men in power would always be remote from the democracy, unaware alike of its day-to-day necessities and of its eternal aspirations. Democracy's cynical

[1] 5 H 191, 18 February 1926, 2278 ff.
[2] Grigg, *The Faith of an Englishman*, p. 291.

eye now demoted, debunked, all principalities and powers, cast doubt on official *communiqués*, and assumed that virtue was only paraded in order to conceal vice. The activities of politicians were suspect before they took any action at all, and the spirit of the observer was that of the tired soldier at the end of a bad day: if his superiors could contrive to get even one more thing wrong before nightfall, then that one thing wrong they would certainly get.

Accordingly, ageing social critics like Shaw and Wells, who before the war had been accepted as court jesters, were now promoted to a status of seer which neither of them strictly deserved. The structure of society at which they had loosed so many good-tempered thunderbolts of denunciation was now so shaken, so uneasy on its base, that any new attack was bound to leave its mark, and often do more permanent damage than the assailants intended. It was only now that Hobson's *Imperialism*, barely noticed by reviewers in the serious quarterlies when it appeared in 1902, began to find a wide and appreciative public. Yet Hobson, Shaw, and Wells were all positive, constructive thinkers: while they threw their spears at the enemy they continued to argue with him, and spoke of him still as a foeman worthy of their steel. The attack that came from another quarter was probably more damaging than theirs. This was the attack that found initial and famous illlustration in Lytton Strachey's *Eminent Victorians* (1918), a book which, unlike those of the older critics, was content to reduce, demolish, and deflate. It was a book that made iconoclasm the mode. It pioneered that type of literature which is best described as the literature of dissociation — well symbolised during the 1920's by the extraordinary rise of the detective story as the principal reading-matter for the upper and middle classes in their leisure hours. It is the literature that includes the disillusionment of Soames Forsyte, as described by Galsworthy in the last books of his *Saga*; the *Disenchantment* experienced by C. E. Montague, a reporter of the war; the private worlds explored in public by both T. E. and D. H. Lawrence; the promotion of Freud to the place Darwin had held in the public mind as a man casting a beacon-light on all human problems; Noël Coward's 'Mad Dogs and Englishmen', a brilliant irreverence which could not be cancelled out by any *Cavalcade*; and, in the same vein, all those deflating *contes* related by Somerset Maugham concerning the manners and customs of inhabitants of suburbia, promoted to membership of the imperial race in the East.

To be sure, John Buchan's Dick Hannay, now starred and gartered, still pursued his career of adventure, but he and his highly-placed friends were all growing older, and the only new man-of-action hero who found an enthusiastic public, Bulldog Drummond, was not the sort that Leithen and Lamancha would have admitted to their clubs. In this atmosphere it was quite fitting that it should have been a German book, Remarque's *All Quiet on the Western Front*, that was adopted by the British public as the only truthful guide to the emotions of the war.

In such an atmosphere, too, imperialism could only breathe with difficulty, and had to do even that as softly as possible. What if some of Colonel Blimp's views were not so fatuous on second thoughts: 'Gad, sir, Winston is right, we must have more armaments' (May 1934): 'We must have conscription if liberty is to survive' (1935)?[1] While power was thought of as an enemy of the people, a system of imperial government that was bound to call soldiers and proconsuls to its aid when natives grew hostile was not one that could expect to command warm support. Imperialists might urge in vain, with Grigg, that all this was false — that it was not the extent of the vast and varied Empire, not its wealth or its trappings of power, that stirred the blood: rather was it the immense responsibility for human welfare and the opportunity for human betterment that it represented. The answer always came that although indeed such opportunity might exist, as Socialists themselves had always emphasised, imperialists never had sufficient imagination to take it. Their delusion that Ireland was a part of England had led, as radical opinion had always held that it would lead, to a national dishonour — certainly inevitable from the time when we had put down the Easter Rebellion of 1916, unsupported as that was by the great bulk of the Irish people, with what the convinced imperialist Mark Sykes had himself described as 'a lumpish and idiotic violence'.[2] In Egypt after fifty-four years of rule our officials still transacted their business in bad Levantine French, and knew as little of Egyptian feeling as ever they had. In Palestine we had brought down on our heads the enmity of both races to whose protection we were sworn. In India — a country where we, the tax-collectors, drew fifty times more pay than the taxed — our coldness to the just aspirations of educated men would

[1] Quoted in Lord Elton, *St. George and the Dragon*, (London, 1942), pp. 34–5.
[2] 5 H 104, 12 April 1918, 1952.

before very long drive the entire control of the nationalist movement into the hands of extremists and demagogues with whom it
would not be possible to deal at all (was this what imperialists
secretly wanted?); while in Europe our lack of principle in the conduct of foreign policy, far from evoking storms of applause in admiration of our 'realism', had won us no new friends and lost us
our old ones.

It was therefore not true at all to say that the Empire was a wide
world. It was the narrowest world of all — the world of the clubs
and the shooting-boxes of a colonised Scotland. It was a world
whose very remoteness had its comic side, as a shrewd commentator
on many of its customs, P. G. Wodehouse, had long ago descried.
Did he not advise one of his heroes, fleeing from the wrath of an
irate General, not to go to the Rockies, to Yucatan, or the Congo,
places which the General would know intimately; but to catch a
tram to Balham or Dulwich, places of which the General would
certainly never have heard?

Against so strong a tide imperialists could make no headway. It
was all they could do to remain afloat. Those who knew the Indian
scene, for example, were well aware that the administrators of the
Raj were more often engaged in going through the motions of
governance than in governing. The charge Gandhi brought
against them at the Round Table Conference in 1931, that the
British were 'incompetent' to deal with the problems of India —
which were not primarily administrative at all, but social and religious — was probably the most wounding that anyone could have
made. There were not a few who were forced to the conclusion, or
who drove themselves there, that it was 'better' to be pilloried for
an action like Amritsar than ridiculed as ineffectual parasites. This
was what Bonar Law had in mind when he compared the inquest on
Dyer's action at Amritsar with that held fifty-four years previously
into the conduct of Governor Eyre in Jamaica: it was not so much a
question of argument as of temperament.[1] Power, it seemed, was
something that might with propriety be used against, but not by,
the British Empire — used by Irishmen, Egyptians, Indians, and
later by Jews, Arabs, Malays, and Cypriots. What kind of logic or
justice was this? There was therefore truth in what the Left said
about the Right, that many of them looked with some longing at the
efficient authoritarianism of European fascism. It was, of course,

[1] 5 H 131, 8 July 1920, 1806.

also true what the Right retorted on the Left, that many of them saw their ideal home exhibited in the inefficient authoritarianism of Russian Communism. But power has never lacked its admirers, on either side of the political scene.

Leaders of both sides shared a dilemma, in that they had constantly to take note of the ingrained pacifism of the people whom they wished, as democrats, accurately to represent. It was this preoccupation that betrayed the Labour leadership into calling for the enforcement of a collective security system and simultaneously inveighing against the rearmament policy which would have made such an enforcement possible. It was this that prevented the Conservative leadership in the National Government from 'unsealing its lips' and taking the country into its confidence about the dangers that were inherent in the situation in Europe. No one led the democracy because no one knew where the democracy wanted to go. One thing was known, that the democracy was opposed to war — and, it was supposed, to all types and all kinds of war, war for whatever reason. Closing the Suez Canal to Italy during the Abyssinian War, was Eden's comment on 6 May 1936, must inevitably have led to war, of which the British Government had a horror.[1] Certainly Baldwin's Government kept firmly in the forefront of its mind the lessons of a by-election at Fulham in October 1933, when a Conservative candidate, standing for a rearmament policy for Britain, converted what had been a majority of 14,000 for his side into a Labour majority of nearly 5,000. When the Government did introduce a measure in July 1934 to provide for an establishment of 41 air squadrons, the Labour Opposition at once tabled a motion of censure. The Government apologetically put up its defence estimates for the year 1934–35 by £10 million, only to be again promptly attacked both by Labour and by Churchill, who pointed out that Germany had now a front-line strength of 600 aircraft and a productive capacity of 125 per month. Conviction was still absent, and the naval agreement with Hitler, made after his announcements of the reintroduction of conscription in Germany and of the existence of a German Air Force, was only an attempt to make the best of a third world that did not in fact exist.

In the autumn of 1935 the British electorate roused itself remarkably to fill in a questionnaire put out by the Labour and Liberal parties through the agency of no less than 800,000 volun-

[1] *RT*, June 1936, No. 103, p. 52.

teer members of the League of Nations Union. Over eleven million people took part. This 'Peace Ballot' was thus a serious political lobby, whose only historical analogy, and that not a very good one, is the Anti-Corn Law League of the 1840's. Six millions voted for the application of military sanctions to curb an aggressor — although whether they were all quite clear that this meant war against that aggressor was at once angrily disputed. In November the Government triumphed at the election, and from 1936 squared more adequately to the rearmament question, Neville Chamberlain's Budget of that year being vilified by Labour as a war Budget and by Churchill as a peace Budget. A White Paper on defence issued in February 1937 dropped the usual pious reference to collective security and did state plainly that it would be imprudent to contemplate a total expenditure on defence during the next five years of much less than £1,500 million. But little was done to mobilise public opinion in favour of any such expenditure, and the rearmament 'drive' was less a drive that a backstairs backroom negotiation. Joseph Kennedy, the United States Ambassador in London, remarked that 'a boxer cannot work himself into a psychological and physical condition for a fight that he seriously believes will never come off'. Labour did decide, at its annual conference in 1937, not to vote in future against the Service estimates, but merely to abstain.

This backhanded acceptance of rearmament was followed by a continuous Labour resistance to any plans for military and industrial conscription which alone could have put teeth into the policy if it was to be a policy at all; the Trade Unions had never forgotten what had happened after 1918, when new and unskilled labour had been taken into the skilled industries and into the Unions, and could not afterwards be got out again. So hampered, and themselves not convinced of the necessity of rearmament, the Government pledged themselves not to introduce conscription in peacetime, and delayed creating Ministries of Supply and of Defence — Ministries which would have had to be given powers of compulsion if they were to function at all. The Secretary for War declared in March 1938 that the first purpose of the British Army was for home defence, a scale of priority that would have scandalised Sir Garnet Wolseley; and it was not until another eleven months had gone by, eaten by the locusts, that the Cabinet decided that any part of the Regular Army should be equipped on the scale necessary for warfare against a first-class Power.[1] This was in February 1939, when there was no single fighter squadron of the R.A.F. based in India or anywhere in the Far East. Without co-ordination, therefore, British rearmament lurched on its way — managing to get built just sufficient aircraft for the defence of the country, though no reserves by means of which an offensive policy could be mounted, and managing to send abroad in 1939 an expeditionary force which was, in the words of a competent commentator, 'worse equipped for the war of its day than any since that which once set sail for the Crimea.'

But it was not at all true, that the British people were so pacifist that they were determined not to go to war for any reason at all. Appeasement was one thing, a sensible and practical policy. Outright capitulation was another, even although the critics might say that the line of division was perilously fine, and inveighed against the peace that had descended on Czechoslovakia as that of the looted grave. Chamberlain believed he could achieve something positive by appeasement. Those to his Right hoped he would prove a true prophet, but always had their doubts — doubts that increased proportionately with the Prime Minister's complacence. Imperialists at least had never held so low an opinion of their own race that they could believe that it would have peace at any price. People might say such a thing, indeed — but they did not mean it, or indeed understand what it was they were saying, and the Government should not do the country an injustice by believing any such nonsense. Chamberlain, Hoare, Simon — did they really think it was not nonsense? Where did they stand? At what point would they stick? Nobody, in 1938, knew: and the doubts that they would stick anywhere were much the same on Left and Right. To the imperialist, patriotism was still the mainspring of the imperial idea, and he was emotionally convinced that, although this concept had been for so long under fire, the barrage would lift, and it would then be seen that the damage done had been superficial only. In the meantime how important it was that all Conservatives — men whose faith in Empire was traditional — should hold fast to their colours, so that they might be seen on high when the time of testing came![2]

For true imperialism was no party matter. It could (now) be conceded that some of its greatest triumphs were owed to the infusion

---

[1] Butler, *Grand Strategy*, II, 15.
[2] Grigg, *Faith of an Englishman*, p. 357.

of Liberal sentiment. Moreover, pride of race animated the working classes as strongly as any other section of the British community. Milner had always asserted this was so, and had foreseen, too, the danger that had actually come to pass. The ideals of national strength and imperial consolidation on the one hand, and of democratic progress and domestic reform on the other, had become dissevered, and people had come to regard as antagonistic objects which were essentially related and complementary to one another. Thus the imperialist could find a good deal of sympathy for the point of view of the Labour member who asserted that the main difficulty in regard to the development of the British Commonwealth of Nations was the fact that people did not know it, did not understand it, had not seen it, and were unlikely to have any very high opinion of a group of Dominions which seemed to want as immigrants only agricultural labourers and domestic servants: with the natural result that British people looked upon the process of imperial migration not as a privilege but as a last and desperate resource. ('What is the good of talking about our great imperial ideas if we are not able to clear up the muck which lies around our feet?')[1] The imperialist sympathised because he knew this was true, and he wanted it not to be true, for the Government to have the faith and the confidence to set about to make it untrue. Socialism itself, eaten into as it was by a vague cosmopolitanism, could give no helpful lead — only Conservatism could do it. The British democracy, the whole Empire and Commonwealth, would have to depend for resistance to the perils of the age upon the strength and vision of the Conservative and Unionist organisation.

To such as Churchill this must have seemed a perilous reed to lean upon. Yet, bent parallel to the ground though it was, it did not break. There did come a point — late, late in the evening — when Neville Chamberlain did come to understand something at least of the forces he was trying to do business with, and changed his course. He dropped appeasement to build up a belated collective-security and alliance system in Europe that had no chance at all of surviving the day of wrath. But he dropped it. It was true what Macaulay had said — that both Governments and men might buy existence too dear.

The perils of the age were, then, finally challenged, and leadership was ultimately forthcoming. But what had brought the country

[1] Haden Guest, 5 H 179, 15 December 1924, pp. 1112–17.

to such a pass, and how were we steered into such straits? Why had the natural confidence of the ruling group allowed itself to be so sapped, so that while it could criticise the negative views of the Left it could present no constructive programme of its own? These were the questions that called for an answer.

In a book he wrote in 1931 (*La Crise de l'Empire Britannique*) André Siegfried had pointed out that it was impossible for England to confine herself to her own insular interests without disaster. She had to follow a difficult way of life, one that demanded experienced pilots. No other political organisation, in his view, was able to produce and in the past had produced such great leaders and men of affairs. Similarly, no other organisation suffered so much from lack of leadership. England was not one of those countries which,

dowered with a natural equilibrium and a low centre of gravity, can be governed by mediocrities without suffering gravely thereby.[1]

As a courteous foreign observer, and a Frenchman, he did not say that England was suffering that condition now: but he meant that, and he was right. J. B. Priestley, describing an *English Journey* he made two years later, set out the straight indictment. Lloyd George had already set it out more straightly still. This country, he rasped, could not be saved by swapping footlers.[2]

The mediocrities, like the leaders of the past, were products of the public schools. Was it there, then, that the damage had been done? What had happened to what Dilke had called 'the nursery of statesmen and warriors'?

The public schools had never lacked their Radical critics, as has been already noted. Just before the first World War there appeared a penetrating account by H. B. Gray of *The Public Schools and the Empire*, which emphasised tendencies that promised, if they were left unchecked, to reverse the tradition on which the schools had been founded and nourished. It had already become clear by 1914 that it was possible to inculcate an imperial idea in the young without at the same time ensuring a corresponding growth of intellectual magnanimity. It was possible to educate them within a moribund curricular system, so that in time it might well be said that

[1] Quoted in Sir Edward Grigg, *The British Commonwealth*, (London, 1943), pp. 8–9.
[2] Speech, 5 December 1930; *RT*, March 1931, No. 82, p. 379.

Kennedy's Latin Primer had proved one of the winding-sheets of Empire. In an England bred in such a system there was no organised connection between the academic and the industrial sphere. Too often the only contact between mind and hand was signified by the beating of a ball with the foot or a stick. It was possible to breed more types than personalities, a dangerous development indeed when the survival of Empire as an idea might well depend not on strength or on kinship of race or on caste or on religion, but on mental adaptability. Sanders of the River, who no doubt had a way with natives, might have to be replaced by someone who could cope with the aspirations and assertions of a native intelligentsia: it was certainly hard to envisage Sanders himself doing any such thing. It was quite easy, too, to go on turning out from the public schools a contented and complacent race of pass-men to the Universities of Oxford and Cambridge, the kind of men who would find it difficult for the rest of their lives to rise into the region of general ideas — which was the region wherein all factors of power and prestige would in future be brought for assessment. Easy, but not of much practical use.

Of course, all these things and many more had been said by critics in the 1880's; and indeed, the source of most of these objections could be found in the Report of the Royal Commission on Public Schools which had been issued as long ago as 1861. This Report had concluded on the whole that public school education, as an education, was a failure, and had likened its obsessive devotion to the classics to 'long voyages in the belly of Jonah's whale'. Such things, no doubt, would long continue to be said. It was not these that upset devotees of the imperial tradition. They were not pedagogues, interested in curricular change. Public schools had not been built to equip the mind but to develop the character. Voyages in the belly of Jonah's whale were not to be sneered at, for such voyages might well be as gainful to those who undertook them as voyages to the Pole — that is to say, they gained nothing at all in any concrete sense, but the men who made them were men whose characters were tempered and hardened by the arduous experience. The doubts expressed in the 1920's and 1930's were of a different kind. It was feared that something had gone wrong with the process of character-building itself.

It seemed now that the public schools were inculcating a code not animated by any creed. (It was this code that felt itself offended by the Hoare-Laval pact that partitioned Abyssinia. Things were not done in that way. The same things might indeed be done, but in some other way.) Public school education was not implanting that constructive impetus, which must always be the background to faith and the spur to action. And if the public schools were not doing this, who else in the world of education could be expected to? Certainly not the elementary schoolteacher, whose arrival on the scene had been noted as a portent forty years before: for he was a man whose natural allegiance was to the Left, and whose approval of those new-style history books that Gilbert Murray was so proud of might be taken for granted. In the past the men who came from the public schools had been accustomed to make for themselves in the world not merely a living, but a place and a memorial. For a century and more British administrators, pioneers, and colonists had carried with them to their work a strong sense of the mission of their race, and accordingly of the value of the work they were doing. Of course it had always been easy to poke fun at this tradition: easy to poke fun at one of its exponents like Curzon — a great public servant indeed, but one who 'always seemed to live in spirit on the back of a highly-caparisoned elephant', and who had somehow managed to make everything in which he believed, 'including himself, faintly ridiculous.'[1] But such fun had been good-humoured, not savage or searing. The really serious critics of imperialism had been men of passion, men committed, who had shown their seriousness and high-mindedness by never using the weapons of satire at all, and who had had the courage to meet the imperialist on his own ground. Since the times of Clive, Empire-builders had come under fire, but neither Burke nor Macaulay, nor even Trollope nor Goldwin Smith, had doubted that there was such a thing as a mission laid upon Great Britain, chief exponent of the culture and values of western civilisation.

Now, however, the critical intelligentsia were drifting away from patriotism altogether. In their attack on capitalism they assumed that everything that was a product of that system, whether it was an institution, an idea, or a moral precept, was innately nefarious. These opinions they derived from a *mélange* of Marxian doctrine and the older Cobdenist criticism; it was certainly from the latter that they resuscitated the notion that the Empire was a narrow and private preserve for public school men, which they might use

[1] Grigg, *Faith of an Englishman*, p. 385.

as they pleased. Bertrand Russell's gibe could be taken as typical: thank God we had an Empire, for if it had not been there to act as a labour-bureau for the upper and middle classes, we would have had a lot more fascists at home. This was not good-humoured fun; it was meant to hurt, and it did.

This was the kind of virus that had eaten its way down into the ethos of the public school education. Nobody, plainly, could discharge a trust with advantage to his wards if he did not thoroughly believe in his own right and competence to discharge it, or if he looked on it mainly as a means for furnishing himself with a career and a pension at the end of it. Yet there were a lot of such people about, and George Orwell's *Shooting an Elephant* describes one such. Too many retained an attitude of 'public school superiority', which was based on nothing but good fortune in birth, money, or both. Such men had ceased to believe in the imperial idea and in the imperial mission, but they had not ceased to admire themselves nor to expect others, whether natives or rude mechanicals, to go on doing the same. A code of social convention was itself no passport either to political wisdom or indeed to political survival. It was no wonder, then, that the 'Old School Tie', symbol of a loyalty to a tradition that was fast losing all meaning, had become as much a music-hall joke as the old discredited jingoism itself. All the idols had to come down, to as noisy a chorus of mocking laughter as could be contrived. Some idols even seemed prepared to topple on their own, as the abdication crisis of 1936 illustrated.

The chill of the times seemed to penetrate to the stoutest of hearts. John Buchan, in his last and haunting book (published posthumously in 1941) turns Leithen's back on the codes of a lifetime, and takes that staunch companion through his last days in a puzzlement to die at *Sick Heart River*, busy about a dead-end task, amid a dying tribe, that yet seemed to promise him more personal fulfilment than any he had gained during his long pursuit of imperial service. Kipling even before the first world war had begun to sound a note that was to deepen during its aftermath:

> This season's Daffodil,
>   She never hears
> What change, what chance, what chill,
>   Cut down last year's:
> But with bold countenance,
>   And knowledge small,

Esteems her seven days' continuance
  To be perpetual.

So time, that is o'er-kind
  To all that he,
Ordains us e'en as blind,
  As bold as she:
That in our very death,
  And burial sure,
Shadow to shadow, well persuaded, saith,
  'See how our works endure!'

Sad times for the patriot, the imperialist, who noted how differently the spirit of the British public that went to war in 1939 manifested itself from the spirit of that first hundred thousand in 1914. *Il fallait en finir.*

Not until the summer of 1940, when the enemy was at the gate, did British nationalism, long denied, assert its presence, and zest return.[1]

[1] For a fuller examination of the domestic background, the reader is referred to A. P. Thornton, *The Habit of Authority* (London, 1966), Chapter 6.

VII

THE COMBINED ASSAULT

IN time of war, under the hammer of an enemy recognisable as
such, a foreigner from a camp outside the lines, the imperial
idea grew strong in confidence and temper. The British democracy rallied to the call of a strong leadership, and it was not just in
rhetorical enthusiasm but with considerable personal satisfaction
that Churchill hailed the year 1940-41 as the British people's
'finest hour'. He, with other imperialists, was delighted by the fact
that, when it came to the sticking-place, it was the old-fashioned
loyalty of the reactionary British Empire to all that was symbolised
by allegiance to Crown and country that came forward to save
European civilisation from utter overthrow by German tyranny. In
slogans and symbols, hitherto discarded, were suddenly discovered
things of value. Courage and honour and a disregard for personal
survival still seemed to hold their place. The attack of faithlessness,
was Grigg's comment, seemed largely to have worked itself out.[1]
Who could now discern either the *Munichois* or the pacifist, or the
collective-security man from the imperialist? From these motley
ranks it could be seen that there were not, after all, so many
embusqués.

The impact of war reverberated as it had done in 1914-18. But
there were some new echoes. A better-educated public opinion still
knew as little as before about the actual control of imperial strategy,
and this necessarily, as before, passed to the professionals. These
professionals were not, however, as their predecessors had been,
men of the same caste, all firm in their conviction that to them
alone had been granted both the secret of success and the right to
make use of it. Nor were they regarded by public opinion as the
men who must, in the nature of things, know best. Generals and
staffs, like anyone else, had spurs to win, and had to be plainly
photographed, out in the open, winning them. Everyone knew that

---

[1] Grigg, *British Commonwealth*, p. 12.

the winning of the war was no longer a matter of applying firm Staff-college principles — particularly after the ruinous *débâcle* of the summer of 1940, when it became plain that these principles had very little chance of application anywhere for a long time to come. In such circumstances trial and error had to be allowed for: and room was found for the bold eccentric, whether Orde Wingate or an unorthodox commando subaltern, who had an idea that might conceivably pay off. Such men, if they could not be given their heads entirely, might at least be granted considerable lengths of rope. The boldest eccentric of all was now in the highest positions of power, as Prime Minister and Minister of Defence. Churchillian ebullience however was always more than an expression of the Premier's own naturally optimistic temperament: it expressed a pleasure that once again the time had come when the power of the Empire, wielded with determination, had its own justification — a justification so clear that all the world could hail it as leader and beacon for the day of battle and the day that followed. 'If we have to quit Gibraltar,' we find in a minute, 'we must immediately take the Canaries.' Of what significance could it possibly be, while the armies clashed by night on the darkling plain that was now Europe, that the Canaries belonged to somebody else, a bystander? There ought to be no bystanders, for he who was not with us was against us. The days of showing the flag — even for only a momentary glimpse, such as was all that inhabitants of Greece and Crete and Dieppe had of it — had returned. The Empire was the Empire once more, and to 10, Downing Street returned that imperial control that two generations of Dominion opinion had combined to condemn as sinister. No departure in principle, Churchill informed the Secretary of State for the Dominions in December 1940, was contemplated from the practice of keeping the Dominions fully informed of the progress of the war — but in that practice 'there should be considerable soft-pedalling'.[1]

The Empire was on the march again. So intoxicating an idea was this that it often seemed to be secondary where exactly it was marching to. Churchill's conception of grand strategy often parted company with that of both his own staffs of strategists and of his American Allies, just because he laid such emphasis on the factor of British power, a factor that the facts of British power could not always support. The Americans considered, for example, the British

[1] W. S. Churchill, *The Second World War*, (London, 1949), II, 631.

invasion of Burma as a waste of time and effort, as it was plain enough that the best road to Tokyo did not lie through Burma. The historian of British *Grand Strategy* stresses how negotiations between the Allies in 1944 and 1945 turned on the employment of a British force whose presence in the main Pacific theatre of operations was judged both by the Americans and by the Russians to be not strategically essential; and in the event the British contribution in the Pacific was limited to a series of bombardments and air-strikes by a relatively small fleet, acting as one of two naval task forces under American command.[1] It was thus not surprising that suspicions that the British Prime Minister was fighting not so much against the evil forces of Hitlerism as for the resurrection, reassertion, and triumph of the British imperial power should have crossed the minds of Roosevelt and Stalin alike. The Russians objected because they had laid imperialist plans of their own. The Americans, ancient enemies of imperial ideas, had laid no future plans at all, and greeted with a dark dislike anyone who had. The Americans in Europe, as Eisenhower put it later, were there for the purposes of a crusade. The British were not noted as crusaders. Were they back at their old imperial games?

To the true imperialist this was a wounding charge. He had in himself more than a touch of the crusader: he used his new-found power as a means to an end. He could convince himself that with its aid he might attain the goal that had been denied to his predecessors in 1919–22. Could he not, this time, secure success, and this time with the democracy on his side, as it had never been previously? Surely, this time, when the victory was attained, the democracy would not let go? (How calamitously it would do this, from Churchill's own point of view, of course could not be foreseen, as he expected to find himself, like Lloyd George in 1918, the appointed architect of peace.) Thus imperial idealists, drinking eagerly the first draught of refreshment they had had since the great days in Mesopotamia, ventured out along those lines of imperial unity that Milner had so often laid down. Might not the time be coming that Milner had foreseen, when to a more fortunate generation than his own a great task of imperial construction was to be granted? So many signposts seemed to point that way. This time Canada, always so dour and withdrawn during the inter-war years, was giving not only her men but her money, $3,000 million

[1] John Ehrman, *Grand Strategy*, VI, (London, 1956), 220.

of which was devoted to the great imperial (and Commonwealth) cause between 1942 and 1944. Here was an exhilarating start towards that international economic co-operation which would prove so essential a feature of any post-war world.

For surely, if the war proved anything it proved this: that Britain's old and much abused role of guardian was in fact essential to the preservation of peace and civilisation, that *pax Britannica* was more than a trope on the lips of retired Indian Army colonels. To Great Britain fell both European and oceanic responsibilities. She had in fact a dual mission, not unlike that other, more localised colonial dual mandate, from which there could be no escape short of abdication and rapid decay. These responsibilities she had not shirked, or wished to shirk, as her conduct in war proved. This being so, Britain with her world role could surely claim, as confidently as she had done in the nineteenth century, imperial rights — under whatever name these might now have to be called. Among such rights were the retention of British sovereignty over the bridgeheads, landing-grounds, and channels which were indispensable to free communication between the peoples of the Empire — a sovereignty that necessitated ownership and operation of vital imperial routes. And what, when facts of geography and facts of power were faced, was not a vital imperial route? What argument against the retention of *Raj* in India by disinterested, *i.e.* British hands could really be worth consideration? What else but war could have welded the fissiparous Middle East together? What else but a confident use of power could keep that area henceforward at peace? Was it not a great thing that necessities of war had added to the roll of the British Cabinet a Minister for Middle East affairs (28 June 1941) — a dignitary whose War Council had among its members such authorities on the Middle East as the Premier of South Africa, the British Ambassadors to Egypt and Iraq, the High Commissioner of Palestine and the Governors of Cyprus and Aden? The Middle East was an appanage of Empire, and British peacetime strategy must ensure that it remained so. Egypt must be rendered independent, at least of others, like the Germans and the Italians. 'The interests of our two countries,' Anthony Eden was declaring in 1946, 'are as one.'

Power, then, was still to be exercised. But it must be power of a kind that could command applause, approval. Everyone admitted that Great Britain had rendered great service in wartime, applauded Churchill, hailed the finest hour, respected British courage and endurance. But all this was done in a highly emotional atmosphere, the atmosphere wherein men are killed and causes desperately gained. That it should continue to be done when the temperature fell, when diplomats not warriors came to the forefront, when the talk was once again all of frontiers and tariffs and displaced persons, was something too much to expect. But in war, when men are expending all their effort, they are liable to expect too much, and are not ready to listen to warnings. Imperial strategists were not slow so to warn, even while the war still went on. British imperial power must be properly consolidated: it was pointless, in peacetime, to beat on a patriotic drum. The future depended on this consolidation. Russia and the United States were now of age as world powers, working in the arena, no longer absentees as they had been during the 'twenties. Indeed, they were our friends today: but power-relations are not relations that have much to do with friendship. Once again, therefore, it behoved the British Empire, the Commonwealth of Nations, to look to its fences and to mend them — or to put them up where they had not previously run.

Part of this process of repair and maintenance involved a checking of some older notions and opinions. The post-war world this time would certainly prove no safer for democracy than the world after 1919 had proved. British vigilance would once again be necessary to ensure the world's liberty, and thus — the argument continued — the coming generation must be protected somehow from the cynicism that had gone far to destroy its seniors, and must learn to look upon the Empire not as an outworn and disreputable hunting-ground for aristocratic and plutocratic adventurers, but as a truly majestic responsibility with which its own future was inseparably connected.[1] Imperialism — or, at any rate, British imperialism — was too indispensable to the world's peaceful progress to be jettisoned just because there were a number of people about (as there always would be) who disliked the name and the thing. To be sure, its actions must always be guided by the forces of conscience, but surely this conscience was nowhere more strongly developed than in the school of experience? Away, then, with the thought that, in the world that war was now shaping, Britain's need of America would be greater than America's of Britain. That essential mutual respect could not possibly survive the spread of a be-

[1] Grigg, *British Commonwealth*, p. 70.

lief that the British, despite their brave tenacity, were an outworn people, or that they were clinging to an anachronistic imperialist system inconsistent with true democracy. And, if precedent was any guide, no one was more likely to spread such a belief than British people themselves — or some of them, the eternally disgruntled, the eternally critical, the men who were always prepared to comment on what other men did. Let it be seen to that theirs remained isolated voices, and that public opinion had too stout a mould to allow itself to be permeated by any such.

None the less Americans would, and quite rightly, object to the notion of underwriting a British Empire which was unable to defend itself. The post-war Commonwealth must accordingly combine and cohere. Certainly it was to the interests of the British Dominions themselves that this should come about, for had not all recent history shown how the United Kingdom had been driven into a hegemony which made it the arbiter in fact if not in form of imperial policy in matters of international concern on which the peace and security of the Dominions had ultimately turned? What Froude had said in 1880 remained true: the right of people to self-government consisted and could consist in nothing but their power to defend themselves. What Menzies had said in 1939 had now been given ample proof: it was, after all, the gentleman sitting in a room overlooking the Horse Guards Parade whose decisions meant life or death for half the world. Let the word 'status', which had too long hoodwinked the patriot, be reduced to that lowlier position it should never have been allowed to quit. Independence was never a question of status only, but of organised, and earned, security.

Organisation was the great thing. Imperial and foreign policy, Grigg suggested in his *British Commonwealth* (1943), should be in the hands of a single Minister. A clear and decided British policy, added E. H. Carr, in his *Conditions of Peace* (1942) would make the active co-operation of the United States and the Dominions more, and not less, certain. After all, the tradition of waiting for a British lead was one that was still firmly planted in American and Dominion minds. Britain, therefore, had only to see to it that her confidence was kept bright and burnished in peace as in war, in order to find willing helpers and followers in the great tasks that awaited her in the new world her efforts were winning for mankind.

Opposition to all this came of course from the quarter whence it might have been more confidently expected by imperialist publicists: from the Empire itself. The imperialists' facts were correct, but their deductions were considered amiss. The Australian Premier, Curtin, told his own Labour Party in 1943 that he for one did not believe that Britain could or should be allowed to manage the Empire on the old basis — of a Government sitting in remote London, moving Dominion destinies about the board as pawns in its own game of foreign policy, however ably and high-mindedly — or, for that matter, however fatuously and selfishly — that game might be conducted. Curtin believed that some imperial authority would have to be evolved in the future so that the British Commonwealth of Nations would have, if not an executive body, at least a standing consultative body.[1] That same November Smuts assured the Empire Parliamentary Association in London, in what he forewarned them was an explosive speech, that although in the postwar time to come Great Britain would indeed enjoy glory and honour and a prestige such as perhaps no nation in history had ever enjoyed, nevertheless from the material, economic point of view she would be a poor country. An Empire was based on power, and one engine of power was capital. After the war, where would Britain's capital be? She had put everything into the war, holding nothing back. She must not assume that she could take up where she had left off, and look round a similar scene with an accustomed eye. She was already a member of a strengthening group, the Commonwealth: would it not also be wise for her to strengthen her position in Europe, by working closely, certainly far more intimately than ever before, with the smaller democracies of that Continent? Here was a cold douche that caused to gasp imperialists who had always counted Smuts as 'one of us'.

Two months after Smuts' speech, Halifax, then British Ambassador in Washington, while addressing the Toronto Board of Trade, laid on a table in public for the first time the correct deductions that ought to have been drawn from Balfour's confidence trick at the Imperial Conference of 1926. At that occasion 'function' had been declared to be different from 'status', but where the difference lay had never been defined, and everyone for their own reasons had been content to leave it at that. Nobody had sought to equalise the position, or to define the function of 'Dominions', sovereign territories unable to defend themselves, in a dangerous world. The subsequent Statute of Westminster of 1931, in leaving

[1] 14 August 1943; Mansergh, *Documents*, I, 562.

to each and every Dominion complete self-government, perforce left unsolved the problems of foreign policy and defence. It was right and true to say that it was the moral tie that had held the Empire together as one in 1939, that had rallied Commonwealth opinion to the British cause: but it was right and true to say, also, that the strategic tie was one that could not for long have been ignored had the moral tie not existed. Dominion opinion had realised that, since nothing had been done to make the case otherwise, Great Britain was still their first line of defence. To be sure, their 'magnificent response' had not come too late to save the cause of Commonwealth and Empire — but a response, though it might be admirable in its nature, was not an initiative, and it was initiative that had been required if the peace was to have been saved. Saved in 1939, and saved, perhaps, in some year to come. How, Halifax asked, should members of the Commonwealth square to this problem, and to the future with it?

> Either they must confirm a policy which they had only a partial share in framing, or they must stand aside and see the unity of the Commonwealth broken, perhaps fatally and for ever.[1]

It was not to be supposed that the mind of Mackenzie King, not in 1944 and not ever, was likely to warm to this kind of argument, put so squarely but so late in the day, by an ex-Foreign Secretary of the United Kingdom whose policies were nowhere greatly admired. It was King who had seen to it that no Imperial War Cabinet — imposing in name perhaps, but of no great political significance — sat in London, as it had done in 1917–18. (Churchill had been anxious to repeat the precedent, while agreeing about the lack of a political significance.) It was better, King had remarked in 1941, for a Dominion Premier to be in his own place. And where was that? Why, clearly, at the head of his own Government, and at the head of the country that had elected him. A week after Halifax had spoken at Toronto the Canadian Premier reiterated his view on this. The objection he held, he said, to going over to London to imperial conferences to try and settle policies — if such was to be the object — was that he, as a Dominion Premier, must always find himself at a complete disadvantage in such circumstances. A Premier attending in London was liable to be confronted with an entire British Cabinet, its arguments expertly marshalled for them

[1] 24 January 1944; Mansergh, *Documents*, I, 575 ff.

Y

by a horde of civil servants. He could unmask no such batteries. To be sure, he, King, was one hundred per cent for close consultation, close co-operation, and effective co-ordination of policy on all matters of common concern between the different nations of the British Commonwealth. But let it also be remembered that there were other nations and other people to co-operate with, to consult with, and to co-ordinate policies with too, and that these others could not be ignored or relegated to a lowlier place if the sort of world organisation which Canadians hoped would prevail in the post-war world in fact came into being.[1] Organisation was certainly needed: but not an imperial organisation. Nothing of the sort.

After all, King urged, behind the ideas of Halifax and behind the forecasts of Smuts lay, or lurked, the idea of 'inevitable rivalry between the Great Powers.' Could a nation like Canada, situated as she was between the United States and the Soviet Union, the two mammoth Powers of the future, for one moment give support to such an idea?

King's voice, as not infrequently before, was to prove the voice of doom, so far as chances of success for an imperialist idea of some new 'Grand British League and Confederacy' were concerned. Before five years had passed Smuts was expressing his anxiety lest the Commonwealth degenerated to the status that had befallen the old Holy Roman Empire, lest it became 'mere verbiage, a mere term with no real meaning behind it.'[2] Jawaharlal Nehru, become Prime Minister of independent India, found it possible to say that the Commonwealth, itself and as such, was not a body. It had no organisation through which to function, and the King also, head of the Commonwealth though he might be, and as such recognised by India herself, could also have no functions.[3] It was all-important, the *Round Table* had declared in 1930, that the King should not himself be divided. He must not be transformed into a puppet pulled in seven directions by seven governments. But by the time that King's grand-daughter was crowned as Queen, a generation later, something of this kind had come about, for she had seven Crowns and seven names.[4] Prime Ministers' Conferences contin-

[1] 31 January 1944; Mansergh, *Documents*, I, 579–83.
[2] 11 May 1949; Mansergh, *Documents*, II, 873.
[3] 16 May 1949, ibid., 848.
[4] *RT*, December 1930, No. 81, p. 103.

ued to be held, and communiqués were as blandly uninformative as ever. But the Commonwealth had become thoroughly de-centralised and its member-nations had found at Lake Success a platform of more prestige than any ever presented them at Geneva. No British power, as envisaged so hopefully by wartime imperialists fired by British success, could in fact be exercised over Dominion minds and methods of behaviour. That particular pass had been sold too long ago for it to be redeemed now.

Nor could money make the mare go any further, for there was, as Smuts had predicted, not much money. None the less imperial ideas animated the use of British capital even in the lean times of the post-war era. The American loan of $4,000 million was pumped out by Great Britain, at the rate of some £200 million a year, in the form of grants and loans and investment abroad. One economist defined the whole concept of the sterling area, with its high interest rates, as the most important vestige of the old kind of authority exercised from London over the British Commonwealth, and went on to make a comparison with the attitudes of the French towards North African nationalism, since the military cost to the French of staying in North Africa was much greater than any econ-omic gain that could accrue to France by her continued possession of these imperial territories.[1] There was more a spiritual than an economic value in the whole notion that the pound should be able to look the dollar in the face, although this was yet another British opinion that Canadians, who kept out of the sterling area, did not share. It was a remarkable fact that ten per cent of Britain's total export earnings were expended on military expeditions abroad — £50 million a year, for example, was spent on keeping up British forces in Germany — on the colonies, and on investment. If the dexterous use of not very much money could make Great Britain an international power, then successive Governments were deter-mined to stretch the shillings as far as they could go in so vital a cause. It was another kind of imperial idea that urged Britain to make and pile stores of H-bombs for herself, although it was always urged by advocates of this policy that she would never 'go it alone' in the use of this weapon. For there was also considerable spiritual value in having the same shot in the locker not only as one's enemies, but as one's best friends.

Power itself was no longer so vilified as it had been. Facts of war

[1] Andrew Shonfield, 'The Pursuit of Prestige', *Encounter*, January 1957.

had proved that the use of power was not necessarily an evil thing, and that the theory of balancing it was not, after all, a wicked delusion perpetrated on the innocent by the cynical and conniving politicians. And if power was a good, a great deal of power was better, and the Great Powers were those to whom the destinies of the world might quite properly be given. In wartime the rights of small nations are not much canvassed: it is sufficient for the belligerent to say, and whether with absolute accuracy or not is beside this point, that the one side is an invader of the small nation and that the other side is its liberator. Neither side is likely to agree whom these particular caps fit; and certainly the small nation, caught in the indiscriminate shellfire of the forces of good and the forces of evil, may find some difficulty in giving its blessing in any direction.

It is therefore not surprising that war is a great breeder of nationalism: that a small country, whether invaded or liberated, should make a resolve to cut itself off in future from any *bloc*, whether confessedly imperialist or other, whose activities might well mortgage its own future existence. Egyptians and Iraqis were left in no doubt that they were regarded, in fact if not in law, as so many subjects of the British Empire, and even the Persians must have wondered what had become of that integrity and independence to which so many successive British Governments had paid lip-service. Imperial ideas had not changed at all, and what Balfour had once said about the flimsy nature of an independence that depended in the last resort for its protection on foreign guns and tanks was impressed with vivid force on a new generation, nationalist by training and inclination. In July 1940, when an entire British Army had just been bundled without ceremony out of the Continent of Europe, the War Cabinet of the United Kingdom was still absolutely determined to defend Egypt, and resolved to send 150 tanks and 100 guns and modern aircraft there forthwith. As Churchill remarked, 'writing about it afterwards makes one shiver.'[1] Others shivered too.

But there were some places in the world where British power, having no existence except on paper, could not be asserted at all, and the Australians, together with the 92,000 troops who surrendered at Singapore in March 1942, were the first to become aware of this. Neville Chamberlain had told Premier Lyons in March 1939 that the basis of British strategy in the Far East would

[1] Churchill, *Second World War*, II, 370.

lie in the establishment at Singapore, at the earliest possible moment after the outbreak of hostilities with Japan, of a battle fleet. Nineteen months later, although war with Japan had not yet broken out, it had become plain to the British strategical staffs that it would be impossible to establish any such thing, and the promise was rescinded. In the absence of a battle-fleet the Joint Planners reckoned that 22 squadrons of the Royal Air Force would be needed in lieu.[1] But they did not have these at their disposal, nor did they ever get them. No strategic plan for the Far East was in fact based on realities, for the realities were of a sort that made all planning futile: but this was not a thing that could well be told to soldiers and sailors and airmen who were expected to defend the British Empire with a will when politicians told them to. The one safeguard for British Far Eastern interests was the United States: but the United States had no tradition of any imperial idea, and Roosevelt, for all that he could see that the storm in the Pacific was blowing up, had to wait for the moment of deluge before he could move the American people in any direction at all. The bastions of the British Empire fell in the Pacific: a determined enemy could easily have sapped them at any time in the past two decades.

Japan retired — she was never ejected — from South-East Asia, and in 1945 the Europeans returned. The British thereafter endured ten years of trouble in Malaya, the French as much in Indo-China, while the Dutch had a shorter shrift in Indonesia. A damage had been done to the white man's prestige that no political reconstruction, no constitution-making was able to erase. The mystique of Empire had gone, and imperialists were left more strongly convinced than ever that they had been right all along: Empire depended on power, on the successful assertion of that power. Great Britain, having failed in this primary task in the Far East, had had to reap these sad consequences. The fault was our own, that men wilfully will not understand what is the nature of the task they set their hands to.

But in India the task had already become too great. Attlee's Government early resolved to wind up the British *Raj*, and the process was made the simpler since Indianisation of the services had proceeded at so rapid a pace during the war. His own Cabinet Mission was against the whole notion of Pakistan, and against handing over power to two separate states, recommending instead

[1] Ehrman, *Grand Strategy*, VI, 308 ff.

a Union of India, uniting British India with the Native States. But the initiative lay in India, and by March 1947 the British Government had agreed to draw a deadline, at which date power would be handed over to whomsoever was prepared to make himself responsible for it: the date was June 1948. The Conservative Opposition formally condemned this: had we any right to hand over to utterly irresponsible people problems that put those of Danzig and Trieste in the shade? What the Labour party called a tremendous experiment the Right called an unjustifiable gamble. Churchill and Amery argued that no one on the Right had thought, when in 1942 Amery as Secretary of State had despatched the Cripps Mission to India, that there was any possibility of an Indian Constituent Assembly's being invited to declare for or against separation from the British Commonwealth before the Indian Constitution had been accepted by the British Parliament. Surely it might have been possible to negotiate some Act of Parliament, say on the lines of the British North America Acts, granting full Dominion Status but still including in the Constitution some safeguards for the 'minorities' — including the 60 million 'depressed classes'? After all, nobody had (yet) set a time-limit for the evacuation of Palestine, where there were three or four times as many British troops as in India. Labour's Foreign Secretary, Bevin, was constantly declaring that we could not walk out of Palestine because we should leave behind us a war between 600,000 Jews and 900,000 Arabs. How then could his Prime Minister bring himself to walk out of India in fourteen months' time and leave behind us a war between 90 million Muslims and 200 million caste Hindus?[1] But the imperialist emotion could make little headway. Now as ever it could awake no corresponding feelings about India among the British democracy, which remained as blankly ignorant of Indian affairs as it had ever been. All the British democracy knew that it was not prepared to sanction the stationing of a great Army in India to preserve the *Raj* in might, and the Labour Government, bedevilled with man-power problems in industry at home, was in cordial agreement with this view.

Retirement from India was abdication of power. This, the imperialist view, was countered with the old Radical assertion, made by Attlee himself and with due mention of Macaulay's name, that withdrawal of the British *Raj* was but the fulfilment of the British

[1] 5 H 434, 6 March 1947, 663 ff.

mission in India.[1] Idealism and generosity thus saw themselves matched — and of course not for the first time — against discomfited reactionaries who saw power as an end in itself. The reactionaries however had some better points to make amid their discomfiture than any not among their own number was then prepared to allow them. A divided India, after all, was a sad comment to make on one hundred and fifty years of British consolidation. Moreover, an Indian bureaucracy that was the enemy of the princely houses did not promise well for the future of democracy, whatever was understood by the term, in India. They had been Radicals who in 1909 handed the Bantu over to the mercies of the Dutch in South Africa: they were still Radicals who in 1947 handed over the masses to the classes — a thing Wedgwood had declared could never happen — in the Indian sub-continent, and this in its turn set a precedent for the Tories six years later, when it came to winding up the Anglo-Egyptian condominium over the peoples of the Sudan. These deeds were all accompanied by a cry of 'scuttle!' from those who saw nothing but dereliction of duty in the whole process of decolonization.

The Left in post-war Britain could assume, it did not need to assert, that handing power over in India to the nationalists would meet the approval of the British democracy. The muted tone of the Right-wing protest at this same action bears further witness to the validity of this assumption, for, however much the imperialist's emotions were wrung at the death of the *Raj*, he knew well enough that no one not a plain fool could suppose it possible to maintain it save by a preponderance of armed force. As in 1919–20, a recently conscripted democracy saw no reason, at the conclusion of another war for freedom, to remain in uniform in order to hold in subjection peoples who plainly wished to be free. And democracy was now fairly in the saddle in Britain, as it had not been in 1919–20: it was, in the rancorous *argot* of the Right, 'Buggins's turn', and with a vengeance. The task facing Conservatism in the future would clearly be one of clearing up the damage that Buggins had done — always assuming he had left anything to clear up.

The democracy, in so far as it had any idea at all about imperial topics, shared (oddly enough) a popular Victorian delusion: that all nationalists were democrats. The delusion was of course a deal more crass than it had been in Victorian times, as a further

[1] 5 H 439, 10 July 1947, 2441 ff.

century of European experience had demolished whatever there had ever been of 'truth in the idea. At any rate, the popular opinion was that self-government was better than good government, even although it became progressively harder to maintain, as the decade passed in Indonesia, Burma, and elsewhere, that it was the same thing as good government. A further assumption accompanied this: that, even if new nations made mistakes, there was world enough and time for these mistakes to be made without inflicting damage on any circle wider than that of their own immediate, and unfortunate, subjects. The post-war world indeed did not assume itself to be safe for democracy in the same blithe self-confidence that had filled the years immediately following 1918: but it did consider, for at least four years after 1945, that under the auspices of the United Nations Organisation it would at least be safe from the old-style predatory imperialism. So, indeed, it might have been, had not the Soviet Union suspected the Western Democracies of the same intentions with which the Western Democracies credited the Soviet Union. Predatory imperialism was certainly back in strength following the Korean War which broke out in the summer of 1950, and it became increasingly clear that areas of the world without the ability to govern themselves properly or to protect their particular forms of governance would be drawn into the one *bloc* or the other. In such a world Right-wing ideas on the role of British imperialism were bound to come, if not into favour, at least into common currency once more. Six years of Labour rule in Britain were to be followed by thirteen years with the Conservatives in power — Tories who were assumed to have a better grasp of this kind of world (for it was the kind of world they had long been at home in, and indeed had helped create) than the idealists of the Left.

But making an inventory of the nature of British power was a harder task in the 1950's than it had been in Disraeli's time. To Curzon and to all imperialists, it had been the *Raj* that stood as the symbol for British power. But in a flush of enthusiasm this had been given away to others. What was left to take its place? There was, indeed, something: a last barbican of Empire, perhaps, but one where Britain's was a famous name and her preponderance was real. It had to be admitted that the forces of the British Empire had not been sufficient to 'win the war', either in Europe or in the Far East. No equivalent of Wellington or Nelson had arisen from the

British ranks to rout the villain on land and the villain at sea. In one theatre alone had British action been genuinely decisive, in both the strategical and political fields. This theatre was the Middle East, and Montgomery, Middle East victor, was the only British general whose status and prestige were everywhere admired. (The annual Alamein reunion dinner in the Albert Hall in London was the only celebration of its kind, a popular and democratic event.) Enthusiasms nourished by the excitements of war died without putting up much fight, and a lot of cold water helped to chill the fire of slogans concerning the finest hour when we stood alone, and to blur the figures on the Royal Air Force's Battle of Britain score-card: but from these misfortunes the record of the 'desert victory' remained free. The world of the Middle East remained a sphere of the old-style British imperial power, and still managed to arouse old-style British imperial emotions.

In doing so the area performed a function of some value. Bastions of British power were now so few. With the British economy itself underpropped by American money; with the Western Approaches under the command of an American Admiral; with the North Atlantic Treaty Organisation dependent for its life on American strategy and weapons; with the American Sixth Fleet the principal power in the Mediterranean; with the American A- and H-bombs the chief deterrents of war with the Soviet Union; with the failure to shore up imperial power in South-East Asia, Malaya, Indo-China, and Indonesia; with Australia learning the lessons of Japanese bombs on Darwin and constructing a defence pact with New Zealand and the United States without benefit of British participation at all (1950); with Hong Kong existing on sufferance of Communist China, and with Asian members of the Commonwealth pursuing policies of neutrality for what they were thought to be worth, symbols of power were hard to discern. Some emotion might be expended on Gibraltar, about which Spain was again restive: while the island of Cyprus, hardly heard of since Disraeli's achievement of 1878, was to become an imperial controversy by force of circumstance. Labour colonial policy busied itself in ac-celerating a programme already laid down, of granting self-government to colonies adjudged likely to make some decent use of it, and it was Africa, a continent still unthreatened by any out-side power, that witnessed the greatest development of this. The only imperial theme that aroused strong criticism in these years was the invention of a Federation for Central Africa — mooted by Labour and carried to a conclusion by Conservatives, against the wishes of those Africans who lived in the area and who had sufficient education to make their objections known.

On this, as on other matters, it often seemed that on both sides of the House of Commons more attitudes were being struck than principles expressed. Although debates in the post-war period on colonial affairs packed Parliamentary benches and drew full Press coverage as never before, the declarations of policy and principle that emanated from both Left and Right seemed more to belong to another era than their own. An imperial historian's comment, delivered some 40 years previously, was still apposite: 'British colonial policy may be summed up as an effort to harmonise what ought to be done with what has been said.'[1] Radicals read up on what Radicals had been wont to say about the British Empire, and said it again — but, remembering their responsibilities, said it in muted tones. Tories continued to strike the imperial note every so often, but more in nostalgia than from conviction. When Oliver Lyttelton, a genuine Tory Colonial Secretary in his father's tradition, spoke of the project of federating three British territories in Central Africa 'as a duty laid upon our shoulders as trustees',[2] and assured the House that one must go forward even when some of the beneficiaries of the trust were not in accordance with one's views, he not only echoed Lloyd George but at the same time considerably repelled the sympathies of a large number of Conservatives behind him. When James Griffiths, Labour's Colonial Secretary, waxed emotional about the plight of backward races, he managed to alienate a similar number of sympathies on his own benches. Left and Right in fact agreed that the Commonwealth — whether one called it a British Commonwealth or omitted the adjective was a debating point between the two — was a necessity of both a moral and a political kind in the modern world. It was therefore necessary to strengthen it, and this was best done by making possible the access to it of liberal communities with a say in their own affairs. The phrase 'Dominion status', although not, like some others, in the condemned cell, was not much in use: but this was the status that colonies in the British dependent Empire were expected to consider their final goal.

[1] C. P. Lucas, *The Empire and the Future*, (London, 1916), p. 18.
[2] 5 H 515, 4 May 1953, 50–8.

Some odd things happened that illustrated the essential sameness of outlook in Whitehall, whoever sat on the Front Bench. It was a Labour Colonial Secretary who deposed the chief of the Bamangwato, a Conservative successor who removed the Kabaka of Buganda. It was Labour that both sent to and later released from a Gold Coast gaol the political agitator Nkrumah. they were Conservatives who saw him installed in pomp as Premier of Ghana, and welcomed him to the conference of Prime Ministers of the Commonwealth in 1957. As 1957 ended it was anyone's guess whether it would be a Conservative or a Labour Government that would have to deal with a Cypriot Archbishop, not long back from the Seychelles, as Her Majesty's principal adviser in the last British possession in the Eastern Mediterranean. In the new Federation of Rhodesia and Nyasaland successive Premiers Malvern and Welensky saw to it that their impact in London was as powerful as they could make it: throughout 'white settler' Africa, Labour was suspect under their old title of 'Fabians' — a paradoxical term, as Labour were thought to be going too fast in pushing along self-government rather than too slow. But in truth there was not much to argue about, save these questions of method and timing. Both parties vied with each other in convincing the world, and in certain cases themselves, that if they were imperialists still, it was only in the sense that there was still such a thing as an imperial legacy to deal with, and that they were the only people available to deal with it. Labour's was the more embarrassing predicament, but the party had passed the stage when any but its very wildest men thought that idealism was everything in politics, and that if, say, they disliked the idea of there still being a British Empire in the mid-twentieth century, then they could abolish it. Ernest Bevin for the Foreign Office had put up the correct signpost to the future. It had always been accepted, he observed, that the party coming into office did not just tear up existing undertakings, but sought to change them by proper negotiation and by substituting another policy.[1]

But the harmony of view between Left and Right in colonial affairs proper was not reflected in the Middle East, where it was still necessary for Great Britain to have, and to be prepared to own to, an imperial policy proper. It was difficult to get matters into focus, for what Ramsay MacDonald had once called 'the confusions of an imperial inheritance' had always been more pro-

[1] 5 H 433, 18 February 1947, 1903.

nounced in the Levant than anywhere else. It was all very well for Bevin to declare that he aimed to substitute another policy by proper negotiation. Agreed, methods of negotiation could be improved, and now that the war was over it was not right or fitting that we, democrats all, should order Governments about and displace Prime Ministers with others more amenable. (After all, this was the kind of thing that went on behind the Iron Curtain.) But how could the policy itself be changed? Changed to what? What other policy was there? Attlee in 1946 could comprehend perfectly why it was that Egyptian nationalism should be determined to get the British to clear their troops out of Cairo, but at the same time he could bring no sympathy to the Egyptian assertion that Egypt had her own imperial rights in the Sudan. Bevin's negotiations with Sidky foundered on this very point: the Sudan was still, as Austen Chamberlain had expressed it, a trust of a particularly sacred nature, and if British imperialism had ever had a shop-window, it was surely in the Sudan, brought in fifty years from absolute anarchy to relative prosperity and absolute peace. Similarly, Bevin (and Eden with him) might believe that they had good grounds for thinking that the Arab League, hastily constructed before the war's end, would act as a *protégé* force for Great Britain, something like Brigadier Glubb's Arab Legion in the British-subsidised Transjordan — but this was never true, and before ten years had passed a day was to come when it was no longer true of Glubb's Arab Legion either.

The Indian Army, underprop of British might in the Middle East, had gone. Some other must be found, and fashioned. Genuine bases must be established. The soldiers were to wander, sometimes in imagination, sometimes in reality, from the Canal Zone to Kenya, from Cyprus back to Haifa, searching, somewhere along this inner circle, for security for the British Empire, for the protection of its communications and the safeguarding of its supplies of oil, two-thirds of which now came from the Middle East and 68 million tons of which passed through the Suez Canal in 1955. (1938's figure had been 5 million.) It was a task which had to be done, as it turned out, in the teeth of a nationalism that was at once self-righteous, militant, and incompetent, and it was not surprising that it was done with an equivalent degree of self-righteous incompetence.

Lynchpin of any settlement in the Middle East was, of course, agreement with Egypt. At the end of the war Egypt was, as in 1919, a vast military camp. Under the terms of the treaty that Eden and Nahas had signed in 1936, Britain was entitled to keep in Egypt a maximum of 10,000 troops, confined to the zone that bordered the Suez Canal. The delay in withdrawing what Nahas called the care-free khaki hordes — over 80,000 of them — caused Egyptian nationalist opinion to harden against the retention of even the agreed 10,000. The example set by Syria and the Lebanon, who with considerable dexterity and deft manipulation had succeeded in ridding their countries entirely of the French, had been carefully noted in Cairo. The Attlee Government, resolved to treat Egypt as an ally, and to consider the '*alliance* with Egypt as one between two equal nations having interests in common', proposed in May 1946 a withdrawal of all British forces from Egypt, and to settle 'mutual assistance in time of war or imminent threat of war in accordance with the alliance'. But Churchill adjourned the House: the presence of British troops in Egypt was something that served not merely a British purpose, or an Anglo-Egyptian purpose, but an imperial purpose and a world purpose. 'It is to keep the Canal open that we require troops on the spot.'[1]

Attlee in 1954 threw this back at him when Churchill, again Prime Minister, presided over the Government that did finally agree to take British troops out of the Canal Zone. The day had gone when we could put bases in other people's territory when the people did not want them.[2] That had been as abundantly clear in 1945 and 1946 as it now was, even to the Tory imperialists, in 1954. Labour policy was right all the time, and it was a pity for the Tories' own reputation and *amour-propre* that they had not decided to recognise this when there might have been some grace in their doing so. Of course, there was an immense difference between Churchill in office and Churchill in opposition. When he came into office he had to face realities: he had to take responsibility instead of indulging in merely factious attacks on those who were bearing responsibility. Attlee turned the knife in the wound, for Labour had not forgotten how Churchill had always held that Labour was not fit to govern, and had no idea what responsibility consisted of. 'We have borne for years these accusations, freely thrown about, of "scuttle".' If it was true that to keep the Canal open we required troops on the spot, was not Nasser winning a more famous victory

[1] 5 H 422, 7 May 1946, 849 ff.
[2] 5 H 531, 29 July 1954, 736.

at Suez than Musaddiq over the Anglo-Iranian Oil Company at Abadan? Even now the Tories did it all with a bad grace, and their spokesman Antony Head led off with the rueful remark that it was always unpalatable to national pride for a proud and great nation to take a step which looked as though she was being forced by duress to do something which she had been shouted at to do for a long time. Even now they had no policy worth speaking of. In 1954 they were doing what Labour, the anti-imperialists, the scuttlers, had refused to do in 1946, and were selling the Sudanese down the river. They still declared that the Suez Canal was a great imperial lifeline, but seemed ready — as their own 'Suez Group' back-benchers charged them — to hand it over to the fates and the furies.

Here was genuine bitterness, genuine spleen, made the sourer because both sides recognised that the security of the Middle East was a genuine British interest, and neither side had any idea how best to safeguard it. In 1946 Bevin's alternative to a Suez base was a base in Palestine: in 1954 Eden's alternative to a Suez base was a base in Cyprus. Palestine had blown up in Bevin's face, and it was confidently expected that Cyprus would do the same in Eden's. It was (surely?) pointless and dishonest for Eden to keep declaring, as he did during this rancorous debate of July 1954, that the main base for war would remain in Egypt. At once Waterhouse, die-hard leader of the Suez Group imperialists, asked him, 'What happens if these provisions are broken, as they may well be broken? Are we going to re-enter forcibly?' Obviously such a step would be out of the question: to Waterhouse it was plain that we were taking a step that was absolutely irrevocable so far as the Canal went. He believed that we were really losing our will to rule — and on this Hansard noted a cry of 'Oh!' from honourable Members.

The Radicals on the Labour benches — and there were now not so very many — pushed this point home. Crossman conceded that if this Suez agreement was the beginning of a new relationship with Egypt and the forces of nationalism in the Middle East, and not merely a scuttle out of Egypt into Cyprus, there was some hope for us in the Middle East — but there was none if the whole thing was merely a symbol of imperialism grown weaker. For eighteen months or more the Suez Group Tory rebels — aided by 'the rebel on the Front Bench', Churchill himself — had delayed meeting the inevitable, and coming to terms with President Nasser. Churchill, Crossman accused, had kept 80,000 men in the Canal Zone and had spent £100 million in order to transform what might have been a magnanimous action 'into the scuttle of imperialists who fail to keep up their imperialism.' Only the previous day, during the debate on Cyprus, the Minister of State for Colonial Affairs had declared that there were some places in the Commonwealth that could never expect to get self-government, and that Cyprus was one of them. What was Hopkinson's 'never', but an open invitation by the British House of Commons to the people of Cyprus to take whatever measures they thought they could take to make things as uncomfortable as possible for British soldiers when they established a base there? Radicals were told they were mischievous, unpatriotic, but Aneurin Bevan urged that the only way in which we could conceivably get orderly development towards self-government in the British Empire was through these people — Cypriots and others — feeling that they had their advocates in the House of Commons. If they did not have their advocates there, they would get some of their own, men who would go down into the streets with revolvers in their hands. Crossman pressed it home, and set the scene as the curtain was about to rise on four years of turbulence and rebellion in Cyprus:

> We will put the base there and then the *Enosis* (union-with-Greece) movement will get going and there will be the same dreary story as there was in Palestine. . . . One talks of being tough, and of making moderate constitutional reforms — which only have the effect of enabling the nationalist forces to exploit the situation against one. Then one sends British troops, one arrests all the nationalists, then de-arrests them and makes one of them Prime Minister a year later.[1]

Had no one in this generation ever read the history of Anglo-Irish relations? Had they not even studied what had happened in their own time in Palestine, Jordan, Egypt, and Persia? For assuredly the inhabitants of these countries had given events the most careful study, and had drawn the right conclusions. And what conclusions were these? Why, that British imperialism was something that gave them nothing — unless they took it by force or the threat of force.

It was thus useless, pointless for Lyttelton to declare that the security of the Eastern Mediterranean demanded that we maintained our power in Cyprus, and that there could be no going back on expert opinion — that is, soldiers' opinions — on this matter.

[1] ibid., 543.

The implication of that was merely that we were still as imperialist in our ideas as ever but that we were not so strong as we had been: but still strong enough, no doubt, to mete out to Cypriots what we could no longer, in the changed political climate, impose on Egyptians. The traditional attitude, the imperialist attitude, of the Conservative party — so Bevan assured it — was no longer relevant. The logical fact, one that Tories must somehow, at whatever cost, bring themselves to realise, was that in the modern world we could only govern people eventually with their own consent, and that we could not even have reasonable military relations with them unless they were prepared to accord them.

That this diagnosis might indeed be true, and that it might contain the kind of truth that must eventually prevail, thoughtful men on both Right and Left were prepared to concede. But at best it was an academic kind of concession, one which gave little help in solving the practical political issues with which statesmen were faced. Intermittently since the time of Napoleon I, and consistently since the time of Napoleon III, in whose reign the Suez Canal was opened, the relationship of the western nations with the Middle East had been a power-relationship. It would remain so. Conditions after 1945 had in no way altered the western nations' need to maintain such a relationship: indeed, their far greater dependence on Middle Eastern oil had increased the degree of necessity. Certainly it was now more difficult to establish a power-relationship than ever it had been in the nineteenth century, for on the whole the *ethos* of the western democratic world, following of necessity an American lead, condemned all imperialism as *ipso facto* wicked.

But for Great Britain circumstances altered cases: this was part of her tradition, a tradition whose pursuance had so often brought about her ears the cry of *perfide Albion*. While she found it possible to reach, even after painful hesitation, not only an understanding of but to give full political recognition to such a movement as Indian nationalism, she persisted in putting Middle Eastern nationalisms into an entirely different category. India, after all, could afford what more sensible men might describe as aberrations, for India was not threatened (or not yet, anyway) by any outside Power. This could certainly not be said of the Middle East, now not only a strategic but a great economic goal for the predatory. Russia showed signs, signs that increased as the post-war decade passed (until eventually she was supplying arms to the Arab world indiscriminately), of returning to that old sphere of influence where once the name of Tsar Nicholas I had been one to conjure with in the Holy Places. The Middle East could therefore not be allowed by the Western Powers to become a kind of no-man's-land, for plainly the area was not cut out for the role. Understanding of nationalism therein could not be carried too far, certainly not to any political abdication such as had been the outcome in India: as in Colvin's day in 1882, the presence of nationalism must be taken into account as a political factor of significance, but not of such significance that it could be allowed to tip the balance. For, if a western power-relationship were not successfully maintained, an eastern power-relationship would be successfully established.

The Middle East, then, could not be allowed to go by default. British and French opinion accused the American Government, which seemed to think in concrete terms of oil and cash readily enough, but of nothing more profound, of so letting it go — to the United States' own ultimate detriment. What was required was that the United States should cultivate a Middle East imperialism of her own — although let her by all means call it merely her Middle Eastern policy. The real problem — the one that ought to have been hammered out together by like-minded statesmen together in Washington, London, and Paris, but the one that, before 1957, never was — was how best to establish the power-relationship so that it made as many friends and as few enemies as possible. Was the task an impossible one? Very well, then, it was an impossible one: let us proceed. The Western Powers could not bring themselves to talk of client-states and satellites, but these were what they were always looking for in the Middle East. When, ultimately, it seemed that the Arabs, long the *protégé* of the one imperial Power and long the subjects of the other, were turning against all the policies that Britain and France were putting forward, Britain and France in their turn swung back again, *faute de mieux*, to look with favour on the Jews. Were the latter, beleaguered in the Levant as they were, worthy of a new, more positive patronage? It was Israelite *efficiency* in the sphere of power-politics that, as the twentieth century ended its fifth decade, seemed likely to win new friends for Zionism, of a type the movement had not previously enjoyed.

No British Government had been actively friendly to Zionism since the fall of the Lloyd George Coalition in 1922. The Colonial

z

Office had included the Jews, naturally, among the many subject-races whom it had to govern impartially and well, and successive Governments in Britain had done their best to carry out a legacy of obligation in the Levant without examining the principles on which they were trying to operate. Arabs were clients and so were Jews. This might have been very well had either client been able to recognise in Great Britain the honest broker she professed herself to be. But it was not possible that either could do so. The inroads made by the Zionist nationalist and imperialist movement into their own Arab world made Arabs aware of the political potentialities of the twentieth century's great movement, self-determination, in a way in which, outside of Egypt, they had not realised before, since the 'Arab revolt' of 1915–18 had been primarily dynastic in its impetus. The weapon which the Jews were using to such effect might prove as useful in Arab hands — and Arabs, after all, were far more numerous. The British protection of Zionism entailed a British neglect of those Arab aspirations which they had been the first to foster. The British, always (as was known) sensitive to a charge of failure in duty, could here be caught off balance. And so it proved — although it was to be the Jews who first took advantage of Britain's uneasy stance.

The presence of these two irreconcilable elements bedevilled British imperial policy in the Middle East to its ultimate point, collapse. The situation was at no time improved while for nearly thirty-five years British statesmen, bemused by the doctrine of continuity in foreign policy, continued to deny in public that there were any irreconcilables at all. Yet what, in its essence, did the policy of supporting the establishing of a Jewish 'National Home' in Palestine entail? It entailed the furthering the invasion of Palestine by immigrants, while at the same time providing for the protection of the native population against the consequences of this invasion. 'A national home,' George Antonius has remarked of this process, 'can only be established for one people in the country of another by dislodging or exterminating the people in possession.'[1] Lloyd George admitted as much in the evidence he gave to the Peel Commission investigating in 1937 the causes of the Palestine rebellion: 'the possibility of a Jewish commonwealth in which the Arab population would be in a minority was in fact contemplated.' To that, fulminated the *Round Table*, the only honourable answer was

[1] G. Antonius, *The Arab Awakening*, (London, 1938), p. 410.

that our pledges to the Arabs were never consistent with a Jewish majority in Palestine as a whole, and thus no valid promise implying this could ever have been given.[1]

The outbreak of the Palestine rebellion of 1936–39 thus differed in intensity from the other Arab rebellions against Western dominance — those in Egypt in 1919, in Iraq in 1920, in Syria in 1925 — in that the intensity of the Palestine Arabs' detestation of imperial policy was itself so much the greater. For neither Egypt nor Iraq nor Syria had undergone an actual invasion by aliens, and although there were alien governments in those countries they were not in fact so irrevocably rooted there that an aspiring nationalist might not look forward with some confidence at least to the day when his country would be free of them. But no one could hold such an opinion or dream such a dream in Mandated Palestine. Arabs, controlled by the British, were forced to suffer the entry into their midst of the Jews, whose intention (for they saw little reason to conceal it) was to establish a foreign state in their territory, either oppressing their Arab subjects or expelling them completely. British Governments continued to deny that any such thing would be allowed to come to pass, but could never answer the Arab argument that such a thing would certainly come to pass unless the British chose to stop the process which was so clearly facilitating it. The advent of Hitler to power in Germany made the whole issue more acute: Jews began to pour in, and as a result 20,000 British troops spent from 1936 through 1939 in Palestine endeavouring to keep order among people who had no wish that order should be kept. A Royal Commission (Peel's) came to the bold conclusion that the Balfour Declaration was in fact unrealisable, and that the only solution was to partition Palestine. The Arabs thought this anathema: for if the Jews were given a legalised base in the area they would assuredly use it as a military base, and make off, in no very long run, with the whole of Palestine, and doubtless with whatever other surrounding districts they claimed were owing to them through two thousand years of history.

Two years later the British Government tried to meet the Arab point, and issued the celebrated White Paper of 1939, which abandoned partition and caused a certain lull. The British announced their intention of setting up, within ten years (1949), an independent state of Palestine in which Arabs and Jews should share in the

[1] *RT*, June 1939, No. 115, p. 461.

government in a manner that would guarantee the interests of both communities.

Although they entered their formal objections, the Arabs were not too displeased about this statement of British intention. Partition had been abandoned, and with it the wicked Balfour Declaration. Independence, of a kind, would be along in ten years' time. So long, then, as the British Government stuck to these guns, all might yet be well. But Zionism had no intention of letting this or any subsequent British Government stick to any such guns. The White Paper of 1939 served notice on the Jews that Great Britain had now definitely refused to carve out any 'national home', or Zionist state, by force of British arms. The desired end, therefore, could now only be attained by force of Zionist arms. These would first have to be turned against the British, upholders of the obstructing Mandate, and then against the Arabs — not an enemy that was hated, but an inevitable enemy none the less. The Arabs made an error, in that they did not grasp that such was the Zionist outlook, and such the Zionist blueprint for the future. That the Jews could grow strong enough and confident enough to displace the British, the 'country power' in the Middle East, and seize Palestine for themselves seemed, in 1939, an impossibility, an Arabian nightmare. But by 1945 it was not an impossibility at all.

The errors already made by the British were to prove even more ruinous to British policy than to Arab aspiration. Since both Zionism and Arab nationalism, originally promoted by distinct and differing groups of British imperialists, had inevitably become imperialisms on their own account, British imperial policy had been left trying to impose a third imperialism on both, while still denying that anything of the kind was taking place. The policy survived the war. In Britain Right-wing Zionists still envisaged Jewish stability in Palestine as a constant and thus a refreshing factor amid the tangled complexities of the Levant. (It was to this original idea that Eden, deserting at long last his Arab *protégés*, returned in the sad autumn of 1956.) British Labour Party Zionists considered their plans for Palestine as a species of idealism far beyond the mundane notions of buffer-minded imperialists. From the time when a Labour Government issued a White Paper of its own, in October 1930, roundly declaring that British obligations towards both Arabs and Jews were of equal weight and in no sense irreconcilable, the Labour movement continued to assert this, even when

it became harder and harder to go on doing so and still remain anywhere within the area of commonsense. As late in the day as their
annual party conference in December 1944, Labour was loudly declaring its irrevocable support for the Jewish National Home,
Attlee making the point that there was neither object nor meaning
in this concept 'unless we are prepared to let Jews if they wish
enter . . . in such numbers as to become a majority, the Arabs being
encouraged to move out as the Jews move in'.

But it was notorious that it was the Mandate itself, which did not
permit mixed schools or allow any common system of education in
Palestine, that had become the principal stumbling-block to all
ideas of good governance. It bound a posterity that did not know,
or had forgotten it ever knew, the fact that Palestine was originally
a trophy of war at the disposal of Great Britain. By the mid-1930's
it was thought improper and immoral to make any further disposi-
tion — for that would have been sheer imperialism; and thus it was
that Palestine remained constricted within a regime, operated by the
British Colonial Office, that became less and less suited to it. It was
not merely that the Jewish population was increasing. So also was
the Arab, whose numbers had increased since 1922 from 600,000 to
to 990,000. Malcolm MacDonald, the National Government's
Colonial Secretary, wondered plaintively in public in 1938 whether
'all the authors of this great creative act' — the Balfour Declaration
— had been fully informed of the situation as regards population
even in 1917–19.[1] (Nine years later, Ernest Bevin, taking over
Palestine as a responsibility of the Foreign Office, was less plaintive.
He remarked grimly that he was sorry he could not give a definition
of the Jewish National Home, 'and Balfour is dead.')[2] MacDonald
had gone on to assert, stoutly, that although the problem was a
knotty one, of course there was a solution!

Was there? Where? Churchill at least did not suppose, either in
1938 or later, that there was any such thing. Certainly he did not
suppose that the National Government of that day, which had a
gift for mismanaging everything it touched, would be able to find
one. For it was smitten, in Palestine as elsewhere, with the vice of
infirmity of purpose, and an impotence of positive decision. These
were hard words, the harder to listen to in that it had been Churchill
who had been chiefly responsible for blocking the Government's

[1] 5 H 341, 24 November 1938, 1991 ff.
[2] 5 H 433, 18 February 1947, 1903 ff.

acceptance of the recommendations of the Peel Commission in 1937. For this Commission, discovering in Palestine an 'irrepressible conflict', quite accurately, and going on to declare that the only possible policy was to get rid of the Mandate and partition the country, shocked the conscience of both Right and Left. Its further recommendation that Britain should continue to 'mandate' both the Holy Places and the airfields was not calculated to win it friends on either side. How, Churchill demanded, are you going to defend the two bits? How, asked the Arab Committee, is the area allotted to the Arab State ever going to become solvent, unless it depends on Jewish subsidies, subsidies which would mean in fact that the Jews would be in control of the allegedly independent Arabs?

The Labour Opposition continued doggedly to declare that it was not the Mandate, but its maladministration, that was the cause of the trouble. The Liberals struck an independent line, by objecting to what it called pandering further to Arab nationalism. Had we not carved out five Arab kingdoms, emirates, and sultanates in the Middle East already? Was it not high time that the Arabs realised that their present position in the world was largely due to the 'great sacrifices' made by the Allied and Associated Powers during the 1914–18 war? Feisal's generation had understood this, or had at least realised the political necessity of seeming to understand it: the heirs of that generation must be compelled to understand it. The Liberal leader, Sinclair, paused to make a remarkable forecast. If Palestine were partitioned, there would spring up two racially totalitarian states. The Jews would be established along an indefensible coastal strip, 'congested and opulent', with behind them the pressure of impoverished and persecuted world-Jewry, and in front of them, Mount Zion. Partition, there was no doubt, 'would prove a very dangerous experiment in political chemistry.'[1]

An Anglo-Arab inquest conducted into the now notorious Husein-MacMahon correspondence of 1915 — laid on the table in Parliament for the first time in 1939 — had already delivered the verdict that His Majesty's Government had not been free to dispose of Palestine without regard for the wishes and interests of the inhabitants of Palestine. But, free or not, they had so disposed; and their posterity now began to reap the whirlwind that Balfour's bland disregard for Arabs 'who would never say they wanted'

[1] 5 H 326, 21 July 1937, 2266 ff.

Zionism had sown. Herbert Samuel (once Balfour's colleague) railed against the 1939 White Paper. By making Jewish immigration after five years dependent on Arab assent and Arab government after ten years dependent on Jewish assent, each side was given a veto on the aspirations of the other in order to induce both to become friends. Both sides would of course exercise their veto. The British Government was presumably proceeding on the principle that, 'since two negatives make a positive,' this was the way to effect a general settlement. They would be sorely disappointed. Alas, added Amery (once Balfour's aide), we have lost the situation in Palestine, as we lost it in Ireland, through a lack of whole-hearted faith in ourselves.

Nor could the impact of war on the Middle East restore a situation that was already too far gone. Churchill remained a convinced Zionist, but the armed Services he controlled as Prime Minister, as he very soon found out, remained strongly pro-Arab.[1] As early as 5 May 1940, a few days before the German deluge in Western Europe, Churchill had suggested that a Jewish Division might be raised in Palestine, so that eleven British Regular battalions might be relieved. But it was not until September 1944 that any Jewish force was raised in the Allied service, and then it was only a brigade.

From the outset, the regard of 'the Middle East club' for the Arabs had been consistent. Consistency in this was looked on as an especial virtue, for at least the members of the club, descendants alike of the old Levant Consular Service and the Arab Bureau, had not committed the politicians' blunder of setting out two divergent policies at one and the same time. Weizmann had done his work of advocacy somewhat too well during the first world war for Cairo strategists in the second to wish to make unguarded promises to Ben-Gurion. Arabs were of course devious and untrustworthy; but strategically they would always be more important and of more value than Jews, for the simple reason that in the Middle East there were more of them. They were therefore Arabs who must be won and wooed and marshalled and mobilised, if the Germans and the Italians were to be stopped from making their inroads into the Levant. It was necessary to bring Farouk in Egypt to order by an armoured *posse*, but that could always be done. The Mufti in Jerusalem was too inclined to play the role that Sherif Husein of

[1] Churchill, *Second World War*, III, 687: 'General Wavell, like most British military officers, is strongly pro-Arab.'

Mecca had played with the British in 1915, but this time with Germans. Germany now had her own 'Arab Bureau', and indeed recognised in January 1941 the 'full independence', whatever that meant to a Nazi mind, of the Arabs, a pledge also given by Italy that December. The revolt in Iraq planned by Rashid Ali in 1941 was timed to coincide with the German invasion of the Balkans and Crete, but Rashid was put down (rather to General Wavell's surprise) without great difficulty by troops of the Indian Army aided not only by the Arab Legion from Transjordan but by the Jewish Irgun. But by 1943 the measure of all these Arab dissidents had been successfully taken, the reliable Nuri es-Said was back in power in Iraq and would be kept there, and British power spanned the Middle East as extensively as before.

Arab unity, therefore, was something to be encouraged, so that a regional security might be established. The formation of an 'Arab League', long a project in the mind of Nuri, received Eden's warm support. It was a sop to Arab nationalism which seemed to hold no danger, for it had not yet been perceived that there was any political menace in Arab nationalism — at a period when it was a British axiom that Ibn Saud in Arabia detested both the Egyptians and the Hashimite kinsmen in Transjordan and Iraq with almost equal venom. Moreover, any arms which members of this Arab League possessed could only come to them from British sources, sources which it was always possible to stem completely if that should come to be necessary. The Arab States, bound in this paper League, accordingly declared war on the Axis Powers during a single week in February 1945, thus becoming just in time members of the United Nations. It was not supposed in Whitehall, as the war ended, that any new assessment needed to be made.

The change in complexion of the British Government after the general election of July 1945 made no difference to this attitude. Pro-Arab policies were still the order of the day in Bevin's Foreign Office, and these could always expect to receive a more cordial support from Eden on the Front Opposition Bench than was forthcoming from Bevin's own back-benchers, who had not forgotten that outright support of Zionism had been a consistent plank of Labour policy (as expressed at Labour party conferences) for as long as most of them could remember. What Attlee and Bevin and other Labour ministers, who had served in Churchill's wartime Coalition Cabinet, seemed more inclined to recall was the fact that they were Jewish guerillas, or Freedom Fighters as they called themselves, who had assassinated their colleague Lord Moyne, then Minister Resident in the Middle East, in November 1944. The Attlee Government decided that all of its decisions in regard to the Middle East must be based on keeping Arab friendship where the British already had it, and on getting that friendship where they did not already have it. Clearly if this was going to be done according to the principles long expressed by the Left, Arab States must be treated on a basis of free and equal partnership. The main objection to this was that such an attitude did not take into account the feeling among Arab states that they did not want to be partners with Great Britain at all, and their suspicion that 'partnership', like 'independence', was just another of those euphemisms for a state of cliency.

And of course these suspicions were quite justified. Attlee's offer to withdraw British forces from Egypt was still conditional upon Egyptian consent to negotiate a new treaty of alliance which would make Great Britain jointly responsible in time of war or emergency for the defence of Egypt and the Suez Canal. Egypt must of course grant to the British Government the facilities that would enable it, or a successor, to do these things. In the background still stood the 1936 Treaty, according preferential status to Great Britain, and still with ten years to run. Events within the decade 1946–56 clearly proved that neither a Government of the Left nor of the Right in Britain knew how to deal with an Egypt which did not *want* to be defended at all.

But more than ever, with this plan of defence in mind, the Foreign Office in 1946–47 considered Palestine as the strategic buffer to Egypt. Churchill angrily condemned this attitude, although indeed it was not one he was a stranger to. We should not have cut away the ground beneath us in Egypt in advance: 'by this unwisdom we can now be accused of having a national strategic motive for retaining our hold on Palestine'. (How paradoxical were the effects of Zionism could hardly be better exemplified: for here was a Left-wing Government being accused of strategic imperialism by the most doughty imperialist of the day.) Palestine's neighbour, Transjordan — in Jewish eyes part of Palestine anyway — now changed its name and status, becoming the sovereign state of Jordan from March 1946. Here of course was another case where status might very easily be distinguished from function, for Britain preserved the same military rights in Jordan as she had held over mandated Transjordan, and the new state still operated exclusively on the British Treasury's money. In Palestine itself the Mufti was not prosecuted as a war criminal, despite angry pressure on the Government to do so from its own benches. When British engineers began to construct not only military camps but a pipeline from the Mosul and Kirkuk oilfields in Iraq to Haifa on the Mediterranean coast, these activities were taken as a plain indication that the British intended to create a new *place d'armes*, and were determined to stay in Palestine. But Palestine proved to be not a barracks, but a battlefield. British military measures had to be undertaken against the Jewish 'Agency' from the summer of 1946, and by the end of that year it had been found necessary to quarter one-tenth of the entire British Army in the country. By the New Year of 1947 the High Commissioner had been empowered at his discretion to enforce martial law in any part of Palestine. Thus amid terror, atrocity and passion the Mandate came to a dead stop, amid a continuing chorus from the Arabs that it was anyway and had always been illegal, from the Jews that the White Paper of 1939 was illegal in that it restricted Jewish immigration in a manner on which the League of Nations Council had never pronounced, and from world opinion that it was a scandal that Cyprus should be used as a concentration camp into which 'illegal' Jewish immigrants were shepherded by the British armed forces.

British authority had broken down, and it was first to the Palestine Arabs that the British Government sought to turn to rescue it from the impasse: Bevin despaired of the Jews, who were talking 'in terms of millions'. But the Arabs were disorganised, and could do nothing either for the Foreign Office or for themselves. It was in February 1947 that Bevin first referred the Palestine issue to the United Nations. A board comprising eleven nations, among them Canada, India, and Australia, investigated the tangle, and based their conclusions broadly on the evidence that had already been compiled in the Report of the Peel Commission issued in 1937. They recommended that the Mandate should be ended, that Palestine should, after all, be partitioned, and that both a Jewish state and an Arab state, later to be confederated, should be formed. The British Government, stormed at from all sides, jeered at by Churchill still for their 'manifest incapacity', undermined by President Truman's open support for the machinations of the

Zionist lobby in Washington, accepted this recommendation, and thus returned to the position that Sir Edward Grey had once idly sketched out — that there should be some kind of international authority in Palestine. On 15 May 1948 the Mandate ended its sad life. War broke out in Palestine at once, for the Arabs were resolved to prevent the carrying-out of the United Nations' resolutions. At the United Nations Assembly at Lake Success the British at once opposed the placing of any sanctions on the attacking Arabs.

This was a gesture of despair, unlikely to win friends. It won none. Throwing up the cards in Palestine, whatever else there was to be said for it, was hardly the way to win Arab friendship. In the only place where Arabs were prepared to concede that Great Britain had indeed some imperial duties — namely, to keep the Jews at bay in Palestine — she had failed to carry them out. Shortly afterwards, during 1951 and 1952, in a state not Arab at all, it seemed also to be proved that Britain lacked the nerve and the power to defend her own legitimate oil interests in Persia. The Arab world cohered: Ibn Saud, and his son after him, made his peace with the Hashimites, and with the pleasant consciousness of American friendship behind him, prepared to wait on the sidelines while the Egyptians sought to play the dominant role in the drama of Middle East nationalism. Egypt did not play the part with any particular skill, but she could hardly fail to score the necessary points.

For the *débâcle* that the Arab League had suffered in its war with the new state of Israel in 1948 had increased to boiling-point the Arab bitterness against the British. Anglo-Egyptian relations in particular, which had been lurching downhill since the Bevin-Sidky agreement of 1946 had been abandoned, now sped vertically downwards at a spectacular pace, despite all the conciliatory actions that were taken by the British Government: the re-equipment of the Egyptian forces by modern arms, the supply of jet planes, the release of sterling balances, the suggestion that the old imperial relationship should be buried in a new — namely, in a Middle East Defence Organisation based on the pattern of the North Atlantic Treaty Organisation. In October 1951 the Egyptian Government unilaterally abrogated the Anglo-Egyptian Treaty of 1936, and bottom was reached during the murderous hours of Black Saturday in Cairo on 26 January 1952. The revolutionary junta government which deposed Farouk that summer was enabled, while the British policy of conciliation continued, to pull off two remarkable feats at British expense: the agreement of 12 February 1953, largely negotiated by Neguib, which provided for a type of self-government in the Sudan which (at any rate at the outset) was free from both British and Egyptian pressures; and the agreement of 19 October 1954 — Nasser's doing — whereby the British promised to leave the Suez Canal base in Egyptian hands, while retaining the right to return in emergency. The British evacuated the base as promised by June 1956.

But emergency occurred, for the next month Nasser commandeered the Suez Canal as an Egyptian waterway. By 5 November the British were parachuting back again, in an attempt to re-establish a naked power-relationship, since all else seemed to have failed. In this venture the Jews found themselves promoted, once more, as agents of western imperialism: for it was an Israeli punitive raid in force into the Sinai peninsula, 100 miles from the Canal, that was used as a screen for their own activities and intentions by the British and the French. It was a venture that failed as it was bound to, as its British instigators had entirely miscalculated the number of enemies that imperial ideas of this particular kind now mustered. One cannot comment on the object of the policy, as it is not yet known. What Britain intended to do with a subjugated Egypt, deserted by a Nasser as discredited as once Arabi had been, is anyone's guess. Certainly another Cromer would have been as hard to find in the mid-twentieth century as another docile Egyptian Prime Minister.

Much has already been said about the 'Suez adventure', and more will be. Its interest here is its emotional symbolism. Eden as Premier was true to the sentiments he had expressed when a young back-bencher in 1929: the Suez Canal was too vital an artery of the British Empire to be left to the mercy of the goodwill of the Egyptians. The imperialist is a single-minded man, and despite Eden's long career in European politics as a dexterous diplomat, balancing, compromising, squaring off conflicting interests, he never saw any reason to change his mind on this point. The emotional support that his action engendered in the country stood on much the same basis: if our entire history in the Middle East since 1882 was not to be made ridiculous, how could we allow ourselves to be 'pushed around' by Egyptians? A Balfour Declaration about Jews might be jettisoned without many tears being shed by the British democracy: but the Suez Canal? Did we not build it? (No.) Did Disraeli not buy it? (No.) Had we not fulfilled our duty to the world in our guardianship of it by keeping it always open to the world's commerce, even in time of war? (No.) Were not the Egyptians grateful for all that we had done for them, particularly during the second World War? (No.) Was not Nasser as sinister a figure, in his rather cardboard Egyptian way, as Hitler? (No.) And anyway, did not a Tory Government, headed by so patently sincere a figure as Eden, really have a better grasp of British interests in the Middle East than all its captious critics?

I have not much love for wooden guns, Balfour had said. It was with wooden guns, however, that British imperialism sought to equate itself with the new factors of power in the world. At once aware of this after the Suez débâcle of 1956, a new British Government set about revolutionising the entire defence structure. But it could not be overlooked in the world at large that it had been with wooden guns that Eden mounted his celebrated 'police action' in the Canal Zone, and it was equally plain that the attitude of the Conservative party on the Enosis movement in Cyprus between 1954 and 1957 was guided by the strategical opinions of the soldiers, who, it appeared, were having more influence on the conduct of foreign policy than their profession had enjoyed since 1915. In token of this a new geographical concept, one which was related entirely to other people's power politics, appeared on the map of the Middle East in these same years. This was the 'Northern Tier': a defence area against the power of Russia, consisting of Turkey, Iraq, Persia, and Pakistan. This would not in itself have been suspect had not Great Britain joined this pact, and made of it, as numbers of her own spokesmen assured the world, the majestic cornerstone of Middle East policy. What right, Arab nationalism asked, had a foreign country to assume it had a Middle East policy anyway? What was the Baghdad Pact but yet another facade for western imperialism? Russia was the excuse: but what the West wanted was bases, and Nuri's Iraq, notorious in the past as pro-British, seemed over-inclined to allow the West what it wanted at a fair price. Where there was a northern tier there was presumably a southern tier, and Egypt after the Suez expedition had no doubt who was designed to be the corner-stone of that.

Eden in one of his best speeches as Premier (in March 1956) had declared his resentment against all the talk then current that Britain must be prepared to abdicate her position as a Great Power, to become some kind of Scandinavia, unworthy of her great tradition. His last public act was to prove how sincerely he meant what he said. The support that this act gained proved also how many of his countrymen felt as he did, and by no means all of these were members of his own party. Public opinion still warmed to the idea that conservatism, Toryism, was the natural basis of any Anglo-Levantine relationship. Prestige and influence were still the essential things. Support for Eden's policy, like the policy itself, was almost entirely emotional, and because this was so it was not at all surprising (although it surprised Americans) that the angriest undercurrent of feeling ran in an anti-American direction.

For if, since the war, Great Britain had been prepared to admit, with as good a grace as could be mustered, that the United States was a greater Power than herself, then the corollary to this was that the least the United States could do was to use that power as Great Britain would have done so, confronted with the problem set by the nationalisation by the Egyptians of a canal that they had not built, did not own, and did not extensively use. It had long been clear that at Washington no one was prepared to pick up the imperialist reins in the Levant: it was therefore not only risky, but downright wrong, for the British to drop them. It was her own especial area of responsibility. To let it go was to betray the world cause of freedom for which Britain no less than America professed to stand. But Americans could not be expected to forget that they were liberals and democrats, longest-standing, indeed, of all the enemies of imperialism; and Eisenhower, who saw himself as much a moral leader as did Nehru, could not be brought to approve a militarist policy just because it was a policy produced by an ally of the United States. Both Powers now entered an area of blank incomprehension, and on the Right in Great Britain views about America of a type that had not been heard since the Washington Treaty of 1922 were, as 1956 came to its uneasy close, freely being thrown about, and the 'oil lobby' was promoted to as sinister a political stardom as ever the Zionist lobby had enjoyed. The doctrine that the realists, the imperialists, had always promulgated — that friendship by itself was no basis for an effective power-alliance — won more converts than ever before among those who hoped, with increasing desperation, that Eden held a trump card in his hand. Imperialism indeed for a time conscripted more Conservatives than wished to be reminded of it later, and Bevan, declaring afterwards (on a visit to India) that at the time of the Suez Crisis the Left found itself faced in the House of Commons not with the Conservative party as such, but with a pathological condition, put his finger on a part of the truth.

For 'Suez 1956' contained all the emotional elements the imperial idea had ever had, the admirable and the unworthy alike. The long-felt dislike of having to deal with 'a board of guardians' was expressed at Lake Success by the official British delegate to the United Nations Assembly with a vehemence far more shocking than any mild Genevan objection in the past. A large part of the British press lapsed back into an anti-foreign jargon of a kind that would have been painfully familiar to Bryce and Morley. Average Members of Parliament, tired of mouthing platitudes about foreign affairs, broke loose with fire-eating remarks about Prestige which recalled Joseph Chamberlain before the blow fell. Nationalism was very well in its way: but so much nationalism, so recently, had gained so many victories at British expense, that British patriots felt that it was time to make a stand against it — felt this sincerely, and indeed in some cases with reluctance. Gilbert Murray himself had already expressed the rising distaste. Had any Empire known to human history, he had asked in 1948, ever behaved, and continued under great provocation to behave, with such un-selfseeking liberality? And what had been its reward? A stream of abuse, 'based partly on ignorance and ingrained prejudice, but partly on deliberately hostile propaganda.'[1] That propaganda had in no way diminished in the eight years that had since passed. It was time, then, to make a stand — and where better make it than along the line of the Suez Canal?

But it was not there, after all, that the stand could be made. Power could not be established by methods of power alone, in the teeth of a hostile world opinion, its conscience angrily uneasy just then because of a callous Russian onslaught on Hungarian objectors to the Communist regime. Diplomacy had long edged its way under fire through all the entanglements of the Middle East, and had suffered many painful wounds: but at least its operations had nowhere led to so entire a fiasco as these new methods of power had to endure, for the British forces had to be withdrawn from their area of deployment less than a fortnight after they had

[1] Murray, *From the League to U.N.*, p. 169.

gone into it. The presence of wooden guns in the imperial armoury was now made plain for all to see. Eden had railed against the idea that Britain should abdicate power. Was the bleak alternative this — that if she did not she would be deposed?

No one could risk coming forward to say so. The attitude of the British public and politicians alike, after Suez 1956, was much the same as that which had been so famously illustrated after the evacuation from Dunkirk in 1940. Something had certainly occurred, and clearly something of importance: but outsiders and foreigners were quite wrong in thinking that it was as important as all that.

It was necessary, after Suez 1956, for British statesmen cautiously to feel their way forward. But in what direction, was the problem. It has already been noted in this text that although power may indeed tend to corrupt, this is a risk that nations who wish to sway the events of the world are forced to run. Status, after all, does in the eyes of men depend on function, as the erstwhile Dominions well know. The Republic of India has a status that depends on function — not the function, in her case, of power, but of her well-publicised non-commitment, neutralism and Asianhood amid the imperialist power-*blocs*. Furthermore, the long reluctance expressed in Great Britain to follow Smuts' prescription and to tie British destinies more closely and firmly to those of the democracies of Europe, has often bewildered Europeans more than it has dismayed them, since British statesmen of whatever party have displayed a tendency, when under pressure 'to do something about Europe', to fall back on tropes about our links with and commitments to the countries of the Commonwealth — links and commitments which, when closely scrutinised by critical Europeans, do not appear to be so inescapable and exclusive as the British make out. Here these critical Europeans, as so often before, go astray. For the British statesmen have here a point — although, to be sure, it is not a point they wish nowadays to be caught making. It is an imperial point. Britain, as a merely European Power, 'a part of the main', might have a function — but assuredly she would have no status. On the other hand, as progenitor of the British Commonwealth, although she may no longer under modern conditions have a function, at least she has a status. How long for? is the perplexing question. How long can status remain to her unless she finds a function to equate with it?

It is perhaps a possibility that one of the original imperial ideas has not lost its power, and that this awaits a resuscitation. This is the idea that visualises Great Britain as a moral leader, and it is one that did not fail to win support from even the most anti-imperialist of the Victorian Radicals in the highest heyday of jingoism itself. The imperial connexion, John Stuart Mill was prepared to concede in his *Representative Government*, added to the moral influence and weight in the councils of the world of the Power which, 'of all in existence, best understands liberty'. Liberty in the twentieth century has had to endure as fierce an attack as imperialism itself, but, like imperialism itself, it has managed to survive, even if it has to make its way without the confident step of its nineteenth-century youth. That moral suasion is itself a power of considerable magnitude was a point borne in on British imperialists themselves when the Commonwealth outcry against Suez 1956 reached its impressive height. British pragmatism, if no higher motive, may therefore see to it that moral suasion is used in the future as a genuine weapon in its armoury.

The Commonwealth is not a political institution. It has no key. Its only strength is in the likemindedness of its member-nations, and if a member-nation becomes no longer like-minded and desires to leave, then its departure is more a gain than a loss to the Commonwealth itself. It has survived in the teeth of much alien disbelief, and things that survive, and continue to exist, plainly fulfil a need. Not all imperialism is power-imperialism — religions and ideologies are but part of an imperialist process. The existence of a Commonwealth of Nations in itself bears witness to the force of moral, legal, and conventional bonds: and these are bonds — however surprising their existence may be — which must be assessed as political factors. If Great Britain herself can no longer 'go it alone' a fraternity of democracies may still be able to pull as much weight in the affairs of the world as John Stuart Mill would have wished.

'Many' — said Sir Winston Churchill in the India debate of 1947 —

'many have defended Britain against her foes. None can defend her against herself.'[1]

It is a powerful and a moving comment on the long history of anti-imperialism. In all the movements of liberal reform in Great

[1] 5 H 434, 6 March 1947, 676.

Britain the same process can be found: members of a privileged class working to have their privileges abolished or extended to others.

> It was people who had the vote who worked to have the franchise given to the voteless; Christians who worked for the emancipation of the Jews; Protestants for the emancipation of the Catholics; members of the Church of England who abolished the Test Acts. The same with the legalisation of trade unions, the abolition of slavery, the protection of native races — always a privileged class giving up its privileges on grounds of conscience or humane principle.[1]

It was the same, Gilbert Murray might have added, with the history of the British Empire as a whole. But no group of men that has yet governed Great Britain has come to the decision that political and international power are also privileges which may be given away on grounds of conscience or humane principle: the name of Munich still stands as a warning signpost to those who are coming too perilously close to such a decision. The liberal tradition is itself a product of power, and of power successfully asserted. In the twentieth century men have twice fought to assert it. Imperialists would say that it must always be fought for, the price of liberty not having changed its currency. They would say, too, that most men know this in their hearts, no enemy of imperial ideas having yet convinced them to the contrary. In British history, imperialism and liberalism, imperialism and socialism, were (as Milner saw) natural allies rather than natural foes. Often the clash between them was bitter, but neither side ever carried or wished to carry the war to the knife; both sides remained true, at the last, to the liberal tradition. This notable victory is not publicised, as no one contestant can take all the credit for it: but it stands all the same. The process it represents is likely to continue while the British people retain their vitality. Imperial ideas bred in the liberal tradition will always find their enemies, but it is still the imperialist who has the advantage, as to him falls the initiative. He must make his statement, throw down his gauntlet to his own generation, before his enemy can appear.

In every generation there is such an initiative, to be taken. To discover what kind of imperial idea should inform that initiative, and how it should be applied, is the cruel test that lies in wait for all British statesmanship in the second half of the twentieth century.

[1] Murray, op. cit., p. 99.

APPENDIX I

GLADSTONE ON BRITISH INTERESTS: MAY 1877
(3 H 234, 7 May 1877, 414–15, 437–8)

'. . . Now, what are British interests? and for what purpose is that phrase brought into incessant use?

'Consider the position of this Empire. Consider how from this little Island we have stretched out our arms into every portion of the world. Consider how we have conquered, planted, annexed, and appropriated at all the points of the compass, so that at few points on the surface of the earth is there not some region or some spot of British dominion near at hand. Nor even from those few points are we absent. Consider how our commerce finds its way into every port which a ship can enter. And then I ask you, what quarrel can ever arise between any two countries, or what war, in which you may not, if you be so minded, set up British interests as a ground of interference?

'That is the case of India in particular. We go to the other end of the world as a company of merchants; we develop the arts and arms of conquerors; we rule over a vast space of territory containing 200,000,000 people, and what do we say next? We lay a virtual claim to a veto upon all the political arrangements of all the countries and seas which can possibly constitute any one of the routes between England and the East, between two extremities, or nearly such, of the world. We say to one State — You must do nothing in the Black Sea at Batoum, because Batoum and Erzeroum may one day become a route to the East. We say — You must do nothing in Syria or Bagdad, because we may finally discover the Valley of the Euphrates to be the best route to the East. The Suez Canal was made for the benefit of the world; but it is thought by some of these pretenders that we, who almost furiously opposed the digging of it, have rights there which are quite distinct in kind from those of the rest of the world, and that we are entitled to assert our mastery without regard to the interests of other portions of mankind.

'. . . And then you know, Mr. Speaker, that any additions to our territory are always perfectly innocent. Sometimes they may be made not without bloodshed; sometimes they are made not without a threat of bloodshed. But that is not our fault; it is only due to the stupidity of those people who cannot perceive the wisdom of coming under our sceptre. We are endowed with a superiority of character, a noble unselfishness, an inflexible integrity which the other nations of the world are too slow to recognise; and they are stupid enough to think that we — superior beings that we are — are to be bound by the same vulgar rules that might be justly applicable to the other sons of Adam.

'. . . Sir, there were other days, when England was the hope of freedom. Wherever in the world a high aspiration was entertained, or a noble blow was struck, it was to England that the eyes of the oppressed were always turned — to this favourite, this darling home of so much privilege and so much happiness, where the people that had built up a noble edifice for themselves would, it was well known, be ready to do what in them lay to secure the benefit of the same inestimable boon for others. You talk to me of the established policy and tradition in regard to Turkey. I appeal to an established tradition, older, wider, nobler far — a tradition not which disregards British interests, but which teaches you to seek the promotion of those interests in obeying the dictates of honour and of justice.'

APPENDIX II

BALFOUR ON THE IMPERIAL IDEA: JUNE 1910
(5 H 17, 13 June 1910, 1140–46)

'... You cannot treat the problems with which we have to deal in Egypt or elsewhere as if they were problems affecting the Isle of Wight or the West Riding of Yorkshire. They belong to a wholly different category. And when the hon. Member [for Tyneside, J. M. Robertson] says, speaking to us, "What right have you to take up these airs of superiority with regard to people whom you choose to call Oriental," I take up no attitude of superiority. But I ask those two hon. Members, and everybody else who has even the most superficial knowledge of history, if they will really try to look in the face the facts with which a British statesman has to deal when he is put in a position of supremacy over great races like the inhabitants of Egypt and countries in the East. We know the civilisation of Egypt better than we know the civilisation of any other country. We know it further back; we know it more intimately; we know more about it. It goes far beyond the petty span of the history of our race, which is lost in the prehistoric period at a time when the Egyptian civilisation had already passed its prime. Look at all the Oriental countries. Do not talk about superiority or inferiority.

'Look at the facts of the case. Western nations as soon as they emerge into history show the beginnings of those capacities for self-government, not always associated, I grant, with all the virtues or all the merits, but still having merits of their own. Nations of the West have shown those virtues from their beginning, from the very tribal origin of which we have first knowledge. You may look through the whole history of the Orientals in what is called, broadly speaking, the East, and you never find traces of self-government. All their great centuries — and they have been very great — have been passed under despotisms, under absolute government. All their great contributions to civilisation — and they have been great — have been made under that form of government. Conqueror has succeeded conqueror; one domination has followed another; but never in all the revolutions of fate and fortune have you seen one of those nations of its own motion establish what we, from a Western point of view, call self-government. That is the fact. It is not a question of superiority or inferiority. I suppose a true Eastern sage would say that the working government which we have taken upon ourselves in Egypt and elsewhere is not a work worthy of a philosopher — that it is the dirty work, the inferior work, of carrying on the neces-

359

sary labour. Do let us put this question of superiority and inferiority out of our minds.

'. . . The point I am trying to press on the House is this. We have got, as I think, to deal with nations who, as far as our knowledge goes, have always been governed in the manner we call absolute, and have never had what we are accustomed to call free institutions of self-government. They have never had it; they have never, apparently, desired it. There is no evidence that until we indoctrinated them with the political philosophy, not always very profound, which has been in fashion in this country, they ever had the desire or the ambition which the hon. Member opposite very naturally and properly wishes that they should have. The time may come when they will adopt, not merely our superficial philosophy, but our genuine practice. But after 3,000, 4,000, or 5,000 years of known history, and unlimited centuries of unknown history have been passed by these nations under a different system, it is not thirty years of British rule which is going to alter the character bred into them by this immemorial tradition.

'If that be true, is it or is it not a good thing for these great nations — I admit their greatness — that this absolute government should be exercised by us? I think it is a good thing. I think that experience shows that they have got under it a far better government than in the whole history of the world they ever had before, and which not only is a benefit to them, but is undoubtedly a benefit to the whole of the civilised West. That has been pointed out by my hon. Friend and has not been denied by the Foreign Secretary [Sir Edward Grey]. We are in Egypt not merely for the sake of the Egyptians, though we are there for their sake; we are there also for the sake of Europe at large.

'If this be the task which, as it has been thrown upon us we ought to take up, as it is a task which, at all events to the best of our knowledge and belief, is of infinite benefit to the races with whom we deal, what are the special difficulties attaching to it? The difficulties are very great and inevitable. There are those who talk as if the test of the excellence of our government were the gratitude which it elicited. A great reform in these countries, probably a great reform in any country, does elicit usually — not always — gratitude at the moment of its inception. Certainly if you had consulted the fellaheen immediately following the period when we relieved them from the abominable treatment to which they were subjected before we went into Egypt, I have no doubt they would have expressed great and genuine gratitude. Generations pass. New men arise. Old memories vanish. Under a policy which casts pain and inconvenience on some members of the community ancient wrongs are forgotten, ancient benefits are forgotten likewise. All that remains are those complaints, sometimes just, most commonly, I believe, unjust, on which the agitator can work when he wishes to raise difficulties in his own interest or in the interests of some, as I think, impossible ideal.

'But if I am right, and if it is our business to govern, with or without gratitude, with or without the real and genuine memory of all the loss of which we have relieved the population, and no vivid imagination of all the benefits which we have given to them; if that is our duty, how is it to be performed, and how only can it be performed? We send out our very best to these countries. They work and strive, not for very great remuneration, not under very easy or very luxurious circumstances, to carry out what they conceive to be their duty both to the country to which they belong and the populations which they serve. They carry out that work under difficulties which we sitting here quietly in Parliament can have no conception of. You place a single British official amidst tens of thousands of persons belonging to a different creed, a different race, a different discipline, different conditions of life. These officials can do that work, I believe, better than anybody, if they merely have the sense that they are being supported. If they lose that sense for a moment, rightly or wrongly — sometimes it is wrong — their whole position is undermined. The base of their supplies, as it were, is cut off. They face a task which might well make anyone's courage fail under the happiest circumstances. They face it under circumstances which are most unhappy. Directly the native populations have that instinctive feeling that those with whom they have got to deal have not behind them the might, the authority, the sympathy, the full and ungrudging support of the country which sent them there, those populations lose all that sense of order which is the very basis of their civilisation, just as our officers lose all that sense of power and authority, which is the very basis of everything they can do for the benefit of those among whom they have been sent.

'I agree that we must not look at this thing — that we cannot look at this question — entirely from the point of view of the British officials on the spot. They may make mistakes. They may even make serious mistakes. It is perfectly impossible for this House to lay down the proposition, or to accept the principle, that, however gross the mistakes may be, that they, in these circumstances, may be condoned because mistakes made by ruling officials must never be admitted by those on whose support the ruling officials depend. What we ought to do is to sympathetically remember the difficulties under which these people work.

'The right hon. Gentleman who will follow me will explain exactly the attitude which his Government has taken up in Egypt, and he will no doubt deal in detail with the special criticisms passed. I do not mean to touch these special criticisms. I have not the knowledge. I have not the authority. But one thing is certain. Every person, with an intimate knowledge of Egypt, to whom I have spoken, whether he be a recent traveller, a man with a long official experience, or whether he be a man whose business has taken him to Egypt year by year for decade after decade — all these people have agreed with one voice that the position in Egypt is now eminently unsatisfactory. They also agree that it is eminently unsatisfactory because the authority of what they frankly say is the dominant race — and as I think ought to remain the dominant race — has been undermined.

'Whether that is the fault of the Egyptian administration, whether it is the fault of His Majesty's Government, or whether it is due to somewhat unfortunate concatenation of circumstances over which neither the Government at home nor the Government in Egypt have made adequate control, I do not know, and I do not say. What I do know, what I will say is that the situation, if I read it rightly, calls for prompt and decisive action! Two hon. Gentlemen who have spoken from the other side have derided the idea that prestige is of any value. Certainly, it is possible that prestige may be presented under the vulgarest guise as representing the crudest insolence of power, and in that shape it neither deserves, nor will it receive, respect from any party or any Member of this House. There is a meaning of the word "prestige" which I beg hon. Gentlemen to consider and to carefully weigh, for without that prestige it is vain for a handful of British officials — endow them how you like, give them all the qualities of character and genius that you can imagine — it is impossible for them to carry out the great task which in Egypt, not we only, but the civilised world have imposed upon them.

'That is the difficulty which has to be met. I am sure I am not misled by party feeling in this matter. I am quite confident at this moment a feeling has got abroad in Egypt amongst those who are, and who must remain her rulers, that the full magnitude and full character of their task is not thoroughly appreciated by those for whom they work, and that they cannot count with absolute assurance upon that support without which their task would become absolutely impossible. It is in the power, I am sure, and I feel confident, of the Government to put that right. That it is their desire to do so I cannot for a moment doubt. I know well the general view of the right hon. Gentlemen opposite, and I do earnestly beg of them, so far as I can and so far as I may, to use without any tincture of party spirit or desire to secure party advantage, to address themselves to the greatest task that can fall to their lot — the task of seeing that our civilising work in Egypt, carried on as it is by a mere handful of our countrymen, shall not suffer even in the smallest degree by a feeling, well or ill-deserved, that they are not to have from home that support without which they are helpless indeed.'

INDEX

Abbas II, Khedive of Egypt, 70
Abdullah (son of Sherif Husein), hostile to Turks, 161; talks with Storrs, 161, 163
Aborigines Committee, report of (1835), 37-8
Aborigines Protection Society, 39
Abyssinia, 97, 293, 295, 313
Acre, 165
Acton, Lord, on power, 47
Aden, 182
Adowa (Adua) (1896), 216
Afghanistan, forward policy in, 27, 32, 77, 95, 115; Russian influence in, 43; war in (1878), 44, 97; Gladstone's policy towards, 55-6; British policy in (1919), 179, 244
Africa Conference, Berlin (1884), 62-3
Aleppo, 163, 165
Alexandretta, 156, 159, 161, 165
Alfred, King, 208
Allenby, General, 154, 243, 245-6, 248
American Revolution (1776), 8-9
Amery, L. S., 81, 105, 120, 127, 129, 203; *My Political Life*, 165; on British policy in Middle East, 165-166; secretary to Curzon, 167; drafts Balfour Declaration (1917), 167; Cabinet secretarial activities of, 167; and Tanganyika mandate, 174; on imperial economic policy, 190; on Singapore base, 194; on League of Nations, 288, 293, 328, 345
Amman, 182
Amritsar, 226, 238, 306
Anderson, Sir Percy, 83, 86
Angell, Norman, 206, 232, 282, 300
'Anglo-Indians', influence and views of, 40, 42, 57, 67, 97, 145, 156
Anglo-Japanese Alliance (1902, 1905), 191 ff.
Antonius, George, *Arab Awakening*, 340
Arab Bureau (Cairo), 151, 154, 160, 164, 242, 345
Arab League (1945), 334, 346, 349
Arab Legion, 182, 334, 346
Arab Revolt (1915-18), 157, 168-9, 180

Arabi Bey, revolt led by (1882), 57-9, 211, 350
Argyll, Duke of, 40, 218
Armenia, xii, 43, 59, 72, 150
Arthur, King, 208
Asquith, H. H., a Liberal Imperialist, 88, 115; on Ulster, 133; on Union of South Africa Bill (1909), 138; deposition of, 148-9; on Palestine, 156; on Mesopotamia, 182; on foreign policy, 189
Attlee, C. R., 225, 229; on India, 234; on 'mess of centuries', 269; on Union of Democratic Control (1919), 283; on Iraq, 303; winds up *Raj*, 327-8; on Egypt (1946, 1954), 334-6; on 'scuttle', 335; on Zionism (1944), 343; policy in Egypt (1946), 347
Australia, views of 'home', 14; Home Rule in, 45; confederation movement in, 100, 138; her naval squadron, 143-4; her imperial policy, 145-6; her lack of it, 186; on Anglo-Japanese alliance, 192; scraps her battle-cruiser, 193; approves of Singapore base, 195; disapproves of Statute of Westminster (1931), 201; under strategic umbrella, 202; pact with New Zealand and United States (1950), 331
Avitabile, Italian adventurer in Punjab, 220

Baghdad, 117, 165, 175, 177, 181
Baldwin, Stanley, 193, 225, 301-2, 307; trusts the people, 267
Balfour, A. J., xii, 86, 89, 110, 112, 129, 132, 149, 160, 216; on Union of South Africa Bill (1909), 139; on British Empire, 140; on Egypt, 153, 360; his Declaration on Zionism (1917), 154, 158, 167; on power in Middle East, 168; on mandates, 174; at Washington Conference (1922), 188; on sea-power, 193; on Dominion Status, 197 ff.; on the East, 215, 217

363